Lecture Notes in Economics and Mathematical Systems

For information about Vols. 1–49, please contact your bookseller or Springer-Verlag

Vol. 50: Unternehmensforschung Heute – Übersichtsvorträge der Züricher Tagung von SVOR und DGU, September 1970. Herausgegeben von M. Beckmann. IV, 133 Seiten. 1971.

Vol. 51: Digitale Simulation. Herausgegeben von K. Bauknecht und W. Nef. IV, 207 Seiten. 1971.

Vol. 52: Invariant Imbedding. Proceedings 1970. Edited by R. E. Bellman and E. D. Denman. IV, 148 pages. 1971.

Vol. 53: J. Rosenmüller, Kooperative Spiele und Märkte. III, 152 Seiten. 1971.

Vol. 54: C. C. von Weizsäcker, Steady State Capital Theory. III, 102 pages. 1971.

Vol. 55: P. A. V. B. Swamy, Statistical Inference in Random Coefficient Regression Models. VIII, 209 pages. 1971.

Vol. 56: Mohamed A. El-Hodiri, Constrained Extrema. Introduction to the Differentiable Case with Economic Applications. III, 130 pages. 1971.

Vol. 57: E. Freund, Zeitvariable Mehrgrößensysteme. VIII,160 Seiten. 1971.

Vol. 58: P. B. Hagelschuer, Theorie der linearen Dekomposition. VII, 191 Seiten. 1971.

Vol. 59: J. A. Hanson, Growth in Open Economies. V, 128 pages. 1971.

Vol. 60: H. Hauptmann, Schätz- und Kontrolltheorie in stetigen dynamischen Wirtschaftsmodellen. V, 104 Seiten. 1971.

Vol. 61: K. H. F. Meyer, Wartesysteme mit variabler Bearbeitungsrate. VII, 314 Seiten. 1971.

Vol. 62: W. Krelle u. G. Gabisch unter Mitarbeit von J. Burgermeister, Wachstumstheorie. VII, 223 Seiten. 1972.

Vol. 63: J. Kohlas, Monte Carlo Simulation im Operations Research. VI, 162 Seiten. 1972.

Vol. 64: P. Gessner u. K. Spremann, Optimierung in Funktionenräumen. IV, 120 Seiten. 1972.

Vol. 65: W. Everling, Exercises in Computer Systems Analysis. VIII, 184 pages. 1972.

Vol. 66: F. Bauer, P. Garabedian and D. Korn, Supercritical Wing Sections. V, 211 pages. 1972.

Vol. 67: I. V. Girsanov, Lectures on Mathematical Theory of Extremum Problems. V, 136 pages. 1972.

Vol. 68: J. Loeckx, Computability and Decidability. An Introduction for Students of Computer Science. VI, 76 pages. 1972.

Vol. 69: S. Ashour, Sequencing Theory. V, 133 pages. 1972.

Vol. 70: J. P. Brown, The Economic Effects of Floods. Investigations of a Stochastic Model of Rational Investment. Behavior in the Face of Floods. V, 87 pages. 1972.

Vol. 71: R. Henn und O. Opitz, Konsum- und Produktionstheorie II. V, 134 Seiten. 1972.

Vol. 72: T. P. Bagchi and J. G. C. Templeton, Numerical Methods in Markov Chains and Bulk Queues. XI, 89 pages. 1972.

Vol. 73: H. Kiendl, Suboptimale Regler mit abschnittweise linearer Struktur. VI, 146 Seiten. 1972.

Vol. 74: F. Pokropp, Aggregation von Produktionsfunktionen. VI, 107 Seiten. 1972.

Vol. 75: GI-Gesellschaft für Informatik e.V. Bericht Nr. 3. 1. Fachtagung über Programmiersprachen · München, 9.–11. März 1971. Herausgegeben im Auftrag der Gesellschaft für Informatik von H. Langmaack und M. Paul. VII, 280 Seiten. 1972.

Vol. 76: G. Fandel, Optimale Entscheidung bei mehrfacher Zielsetzung. II, 121 Seiten. 1972.

Vol. 77: A. Auslender, Problèmes de Minimax via l'Analyse Convexe et les Inégalités Variationelles: Théorie et Algorithmes. VII, 132 pages. 1972.

Vol. 78: GI-Gesellschaft für Informatik e.V. 2. Jahrestagung, Karlsruhe, 2.–4. Oktober 1972. Herausgegeben im Auftrag der Gesellschaft für Informatik von P. Deussen. XI, 576 Seiten. 1973.

Vol. 79: A. Berman, Cones, Matrices and Mathematical Programming. V, 96 pages. 1973.

Vol. 80: International Seminar on Trends in Mathematical Modelling, Venice, 13–18 December 1971. Edited by N. Hawkes. VI, 288 pages. 1973.

Vol. 81: Advanced Course on Software Engineering. Edited by F. L. Bauer. XII, 545 pages. 1973.

Vol. 82: R. Saeks, Resolution Space, Operators and Systems. X, 267 pages. 1973.

Vol. 83: NTG/GI-Gesellschaft für Informatik, Nachrichtentechnische Gesellschaft. Fachtagung „Cognitive Verfahren und Systeme", Hamburg, 11.–13. April 1973. Herausgegeben im Auftrag der NTG/GI von Th. Einsele, W. Giloi und H.-H. Nagel. VIII, 373 Seiten. 1973.

Vol. 84: A. V. Balakrishnan, Stochastic Differential Systems I. Filtering and Control. A Function Space Approach. V, 252 pages. 1973.

Vol. 85: T. Page, Economics of Involuntary Transfers: A Unified Approach to Pollution and Congestion Externalities. XI, 159 pages. 1973.

Vol. 86: Symposium on the Theory of Scheduling and its Applications. Edited by S. E. Elmaghraby. VIII, 437 pages. 1973.

Vol. 87: G. F. Newell, Approximate Stochastic Behavior of n-Server Service Systems with Large n. VII, 118 pages. 1973.

Vol. 88: H. Steckhan, Güterströme in Netzen. VII, 134 Seiten. 1973.

Vol. 89: J. P. Wallace and A. Sherret, Estimation of Product. Attributes and Their Importances. V, 94 pages. 1973.

Vol. 90: J.-F. Richard, Posterior and Predictive Densities for Simultaneous Equation Models. VI, 226 pages. 1973.

Vol. 91: Th. Marschak and R. Selten, General Equilibrium with Price-Making Firms. XI, 246 pages. 1974.

Vol. 92: E. Dierker, Topological Methods in Walrasian Economics. IV, 130 pages. 1974.

Vol. 93: 4th IFAC/IFIP International Conference on Digital Computer Applications to Process Control, Part I. Zürich/Switzerland, March 19–22, 1974. Edited by M. Mansour and W. Schaufelberger. XVIII, 544 pages. 1974.

Vol. 94: 4th IFAC/IFIP International Conference on Digital Computer Applications to Process Control, Part II. Zürich/Switzerland, March 19–22, 1974. Edited by M. Mansour and W. Schaufelberger. XVIII, 546 pages. 1974.

Vol. 95: M. Zeleny, Linear Multiobjective Programming. X, 220 pages. 1974.

Vol. 96: O. Moeschlin, Zur Theorie von Neumannscher Wachstumsmodelle. XI, 115 Seiten. 1974.

Vol. 97: G. Schmidt, Über die Stabilität des einfachen Bedienungskanals. VII, 147 Seiten. 1974.

Vol. 98: Mathematical Methods in Queueing Theory. Proceedings 1973. Edited by A. B. Clarke. VII, 374 pages. 1974.

Vol. 99: Production Theory. Edited by W. Eichhorn, R. Henn, O. Opitz, and R. W. Shephard. VIII, 386 pages. 1974.

Vol. 100: B. S. Duran and P. L. Odell, Cluster Analysis. A Survey. VI, 137 pages. 1974.

continuation on page 323

Lecture Notes in Economics and Mathematical Systems

215

Semi-Infinite Programming and Applications

An International Symposium
Austin, Texas, September 8–10, 1981

Edited by A. V. Fiacco and K. O. Kortanek

Springer-Verlag
Berlin Heidelberg GmbH 1983

Editors

Anthony V. Fiacco
Department of Operations Research
School of Engineering and Applied Science
The George Washington University
Washington, DC 20052, USA

Kenneth O. Kortanek
Department of Mathematics
Carnegie-Mellon University
Pittsburgh, PA 15213, USA

ISBN 978-3-540-12304-0 ISBN 978-3-642-46477-5 (eBook)
DOI 10.1007/978-3-642-46477-5

Originally published by Springer-Verlag Berlin Heidelberg New York Tokyo in 1983

PREFACE

Semi-infinite programming is a natural extension of linear programming that allows finitely many variables to appear in infinitely many constraints. As the papers in this collection will reconfirm, the theoretical and practical manifestations and applications of this problem formulation are abundant and significant.

This volume presents 20 carefully selected papers that were presented at the International Symposium on Semi-Infinite Programming and Applications, The University of Texas at Austin, September 8-10, 1981. A total of 70 papers were presented by distinguished participants from 15 countries. This was only the second international meeting on this topic, the first taking place in Bad Honnef, Federal Republic of Germany in 1978. A proceedings of that conference was organized and edited by Rainer Hettich of the University of Trier and published by Springer-Verlag in 1979.

The papers in this volume could have been published in any of several refereed journals. It is also probable that the authors of these papers would normally not have met at the same professional society meeting. Having these papers appear under one cover is thus something of a new phenomenon and provides an indication of both the unification and cross-fertilization opportunities that have emerged in this field.

These papers were solicited only through the collective efforts of an International Program Committee organized according to the following research areas.

1. Planning and Control in Management, Operations Research, and Economic Systems. [A. Charnes (USA), W. W. Cooper (USA), G. B. Dantzig (USA), L. F. Escudero (Spain), L. V. Kantorovich (USSR), S. Moriguti (Japan), and A. L. Soyster (USA).]

2. Generalized Linear and Convex Programming. [A. Ben-Tal (Israel), R. J. Duffin (USA), R. G. Jeroslow (USA), B. Korte (FRG), J. Ch. Pomerol (France), and J. Stoer (FRG).]

3. Sensitivity Analysis and Extensions. [A. V. Fiacco (USA), U. Eckhardt (FRG), Y. Smeers (Belgium), and S. Zlobec (Canada).]

4. Numerical Analysis and Computational Methods. [G. H. Golub (USA), S.-Å. Gustafson (Sweden), R. Hettich (FRG), W.W.E. Wetterling (Netherlands).]

5. Variational Inequalities and Complementarity. [A. Bensoussan (France), W. Oettli (FRG), and M. Vlach (Czechoslovakia).]

6. Approximation Theory and Analysis. [A. Ben-Israel (USA), K. Glashoff (FRG), and K. O. Kortanek (USA).]

7. Moment Problems in Probability and Statistics. [A. Prèkopa (Hungary), W. Gochet (Belgium), D. M. Titterington (Scotland), C. F. Wu (USA), and M. Yamasaki (Japan).]

8. Engineering Applications. [E. Polak (USA) and I. E. Grossmann (USA).]

The 20 papers of this Volume have been distributed according to four basic themes as follows: 6 in Duality Theory, 7 in Algorithmic Developments, 4 in Problem Analysis and Modeling, and 3 in Optimality Conditions and Variational Principles.

We call your attention to the intriguing interplay between papers, particularly in different (i) duality developments, (ii) uses of optimality conditions for algorithmic development, and (iii) mathematical modeling structures for engineering sciences, operations research and economics, and probability and statistics.

During the Symposium we attempted to identify future challenges and determine some of the open problems in semi-infinite programming, and our list of opportunities is given below. It is inevitably subjective because of our own perspectives, and incomplete because it looks to the uncertain future.

(1). Engineering Design

While design vectors are finite, design parameters (frequencies, tolerances, etc.) range over infinite sets, and semi-infinite problems arise where maximizations occur as constraints. When parameters are stochastic, then the number of control variables becomes infinite and nonlinear infinite-infinite problems arise. How can this class be treated by building up from a sequence of nonlinear semi-infinite programs? Similar structures arise in signal and filter design.

(2). Numerical Analysis of Semi-Infinite Programs

While strides have been made on obtaining good locally convergent methods, what can be said about constructing globally convergent algorithms, for example with penalty methods? Which semi-infinite problems can be solved by solving a discretized finite problem? A new generation of computer software is needed which combines methods of discretization with solutions to systems of nonlinear equations. More work is required on classes of nonlinear semi-infinite programs.

(3). Saddle Value Problems and Variational Inequalities

Diverse problems in continuum mechanics and economics are biextremal, and an open problem is to construct a general uniextremal duality which uses finite element numerical methods. What kinds of bounding principles exist for Hamiltonian and Lagrangian systems? What is the connection between the theory of linear inequalities and minimax (biextremal) problems?

(4). Parametric and Sensitivity Analysis of Semi-Infinite Programs

Starting with a semi-infinite program in parametrized form establish conditions for various kinds of continuity and stability of the set of minimal solution points, e.g., consider decompositions of the parameter space. Determine the behavior of the marginal function (minimum program value) and its derivatives. How can one use second derivative information in numerical work, e.g. for decomposition algorithms?

(5). Approximation Theory and Inequalities

Standard approximation problems are semi-infinite programs, but more work is needed on how to solve extensions having more than one objective functional. Classical works of Müntz (and Erdös) characterize conditions on polynomials in order to generate continuous functions, and these results are related to semi-infinite programming (completeness questions). In some instances Markov's Inequality on the bounds of the derivative of a polynomial can be reduced to checking only a finite number of points [Duffin-Shaffer, 1938]. How can this reduction procedure be extended to other classes of functions and related functions, e.g., their derivatives?

(6). Optimal Experimental Design and Moment Problems

Develop effective numerical solution procedures for the problem of the optimal location of measuring devices so that best estimates of unknown parameters can be made. This is an optimization over probability measures on some space. The theory is related to the excessive function approach [Dynkin, Cornell] for optimal stopping problems, where finding a solution procedure is still an open question.

(7). Nonlinear Parabolic and Bang-Bang Control

Certain control problems have their controls performed by time and/or by boundary input. In the time-optimal controllability (e.g., heating processes) case, an infinite dimensional moment problem arises, while under boundary control, infinite inequalities arise because of the maximum norm. Various regularity conditions need to be ascertained, in particular their effects on convergence properties of certain algorithms. Open questions involve the role of semi-infinite quadratic programming as a tool for solving these difficult problems.

(8). Continuous Linear Programming

Can an effective continuous-time simplex method (or equivalently, an algorithm of Remez exchange type) be developed, building on the classical simplex method, for finite linear programs? The theory of semi-infinite programming is rich in extreme point structure (much like ordinary linear programming). Is there an analogy between the use of extreme points in the finite case and the infinite case? Applications to specially structured energy-economic modeling, particularly at Stanford University, are anticipated.

(9). Fuzzy Set Theory and Semi-Infinite Programming

Inexact programming involves constraints which are set-inclusive, i.e., find x_1, x_2 non-negative so that $x_1K_1 + x_2K_2 \subseteq K_3$, where K_1, K_2, K_3 are non-empty sets. Certain kinds of fuzzy set problems [Bellman, Zadeh, Zimmermann, Negoita] are inexact programs and in some cases semi-infinite programs. How broad a class is this? One conjectures that those fuzzy set problems for which one can actually compute solutions numerically are the semi-infinite programming ones. When can the infinite system be reduced to an appropriate finite one, a question also arising in other areas above?

We are especially pleased to acknowledge financial support from the Office of Naval Research (Mathematical and Information Sciences

Division), the National Science Foundation (Systems Theory and Operations Research Program, together with the Mathematics Section), and The University of Texas at Austin (Office of the President and The College of Business Administration Foundation). The symposium was a centennial event of the College of Business Administration, corresponding to the celebration of the 100th Anniversary of the founding of The University of Texas at Austin. We are indebted for the use of their excellent conference facilities and wish to express our gratitude to President Peter T. Flawn, Dr. Gerhard J. Fonken, Vice President for Academic Affairs and Research, Dean George Kozmetsky, Professor James Vick, Arrangements Chairman, and Caryn Cluiss, Symposium Secretary.

The list of Symposium participants, together with their affiliations appear at the end of the Volume. Their support of the Symposium and this Volume was indispensable. In addition, we have listed the referees of the papers of this Volume, whose assistance was invaluable to us, and to whom we are indeed most grateful. We have also included the table of contents of the book of abstracts, giving an abstract of each paper presented to the Symposium, prepared by the Program Chairman, Sanjo Zlobec, of McGill University.

Our appreciation must also be directed to our publisher, Springer-Verlag, who has continued to be extremely encouraging and helpful in every phase of manuscript preparation. Our special thanks are to Dr. Walter Kaufmann-Bühler, Mathematics Editor of Springer-Verlag New York for his efforts on our behalf.

We also wish to express our gratitude to Nancy Colmer Schaub, Carnegie-Mellon University, for her ready and unerring typing assistance in the final preparation of this Volume. A final word of gratitude is reserved for our many illustrious colleagues who took the time to prepare and present Symposium papers, and to those authors represented herein who have patiently borne with us through the review process to the final preparation of this manuscript.

A. V. Fiacco K. O. Kortanek

TABLE OF CONTENTS

PART I

DUALITY THEORY

ASCENT RAY THEOREMS AND SOME APPLICATIONS

Charles E. Blair

Abstract. We give applications of a consistency result for semi-infinite systems.

1. Introduction

In Spring 1973 I took a course on Convex Analysis taught by Bob Jeroslow. One of the exercises assigned was "prove the best result you can about when a semi-infinite system of linear inequalities $a_i x \geq b_i$ has a solution." The natural conjecture was

Theorem 1.1: Let $a_i \in R^n$, $b_i \in R$ for all $i \in I$. If there is no x such that $a_i x \geq b_i$, $i \in I$ then there is a $w \in R^n$ such that, for every N, there is a finite $F \subset I$ such that $a_i x \geq b_i$, $i \in F$ implies $wx \geq N$.

After a week or so I found a proof. Bob's reaction was "you should write that up". With his unselfish assistance I did. That was my first paper [2].

The proof of Theorem 1 in [2] was based on the Kuhn-Fourier theorem [12], which deals with the case in which I is finite. I also made use of the fact, that, given a fixed basis for a vector space, there is a bound on the size of coefficients used to represent any vector of unit length in terms of the basis. Today, I would not dismiss this result as "...a trivial exercise in linear algebra...."* Otherwise, I would use the same proof.

I regard Theorem 1.1 as the foundation of semi-infinite programming, possibly for sentimental reasons. In this paper, I wish to show how other results may be derived from it.

The vector w in Theorem 1.1 was described as an "ascent ray" by Ken Kortanek. Shortly after I showed him the result, he found the strengthening

Corollary 1.2: If there are no x such that $a_i x \geq b_i$, then the conclusion of Theorem 1.1 holds for any w in the relative interior of the cone generated by a_i.

---

*It is essentially the result that any two norms are equivalent for a finite dimensional space.

Proof: Let w be the ascent ray given by Theorem 1.1*, and w' be in the relative interior of $C(a_i)$. Then for some finite $G \subset I$, $\beta > 0$, $\alpha_i \geq 0$, $w' = \beta w + \sum_{i \in G} \alpha_i a_i$. For any N, there is a finite $F \subset I$ such that $a_i x \geq b_i$, $i \in F$ implies $wx \geq \frac{1}{\beta}(N - \sum_{i \in G} \alpha_i b_i)$. Then if $a_i x \geq b_i$, $i \in F \cup G$, $w'x = \beta(wx) + \sum_{i \in G} \alpha_i (a_i x) \geq N$.

Q.E.D.

Kortanek also found a proof of Theorem 1.1 based on a theorem involving systems of inequalities with infinite elements [7,10]. I returned the compliment by extending the infinite element theorem to cases involving strict inequalities [3]. That was my second paper.

The following result (suggested by discussion with Kortanek) complements the characterization of the set of ascent rays (or ascent vectors) in [10, Theorem 2].

Corollary 1.3: Suppose $\{x | a_i x \geq b_i, i \in I\} = \emptyset$. If T is a subspace of the linear hull of the a_i let $J_T = \{a_i | a_i \in T\}$, $R_T = ri(C(J_T))$. Let H be those subspaces T for which $\{x | a_i x \geq b_i, a_i \in T\} = \emptyset$. Then the set of ascent rays is $\bigcup_{T \in H} R_T$.

Outline of Proof: One direction of the inclusion follows immediately from Corollary 1.2. To establish the opposite inclusion consider an ascent ray w which is not in the relative interior. There must be a subspace T corresponding to a supporting hyperplane which includes w and has the subsystem determined by $a_i \in T$ inconsistent. If this subsystem has ascent rays other than R_T we can repeat the analysis, arguing by induction on the dimension.

2. Application to Semi-Infinite Programming

Theorem 2.1: Suppose there are x such that $a_i x \geq b_i$, $i \in I$ and that every such x satisfies $cx \geq d$ (i.e., the semi-infinite program has value $\geq d$). Then there is a w and sequences of finite sets $F_j \subset I$ and numbers N_j, M_j such that

(i) If $a_i x \geq b_i$, $i \in F_j$ then $(w + N_j c)x \geq M_j$ for $j = 1,2,\ldots$

(ii) $\lim_{j\to\infty} N_j = \infty$

(iii) $\underline{\lim}_{j\to\infty} \frac{M_j}{N_j} \geq d$

---

*The proof of the Theorem 1.1 in [2] uses for w the sum of any set of basis vectors for a_i.

Proof: Choose w to be a fixed vector in the relative interior of $C(\{a_i\} \cup \{c\})$. For each j, there is no x such that $a_i x \geq b_i$ and $-cx \geq -d + \frac{1}{j}$. By Corollary 1.2, there is a finite $F_j \subset I$ such that $a_i x \geq b_i$, $i \in F_j$, $-cx \geq -d + \frac{1}{j}$ implies $wx \geq j$. By the duality theorem of linear programming there are $\alpha_i \geq 0$ and $N_j \geq 0$ such that $\sum_{i \in F_j} \alpha_i a_i - N_j c = w$, and $\Sigma\, \alpha_i b_i + N_j(-d + \frac{1}{j}) \geq j$. If we take $M_j = N_j(d - \frac{1}{j}) + j$ then (i) and (iii) are clearly satisfied, and (ii) follows because otherwise there would be no x satisfying $a_i x \geq b_i$, $i \in I$. Q.E.D.

The proof of Theorem 2.1 in [2, Corollary 2] was cumbersome, partly because I obtained the result from Theorem 1.1 rather than Corollary 1.2.

The following strengthening is due to Jeroslow [8].

Corollary 2.2: Under the same assumptions as Theorem 2.1, there exists $w' \in R^n$ and w_0 such that, for every $0 < \theta < 1$, there is a finite $F_\theta \subset I$ such that, if $a_i x \geq b_i$ $i \in F_\theta$, then $(\theta w + c)x \geq d - \theta w_0$.

Proof: First we apply Theorem 2.1 as above to obtain w, N_j, M_j, F_j. We will show that the conclusion of Corollary 2.2 holds if we take $w' = \frac{1}{N_1} w$, $w_0 > d - \frac{M_1}{N_1}$. Let $0 < \theta < 1$. Let α_j be such that $\alpha_j + (1 - \alpha_j)(\frac{N_1}{N_j}) = \theta$. By (ii), $\operatorname{Lim} \alpha_j = \theta$. By (i) if $a_i x \geq b_i$, $i \in F_1 \cup F_j$ then $(\alpha_j(w' + c) + (1 - \alpha_j)(\frac{N_1}{N_j} w' + c))x =$ $(\theta w' + c)x \geq \alpha_j \frac{M_1}{N_1} + (1 - \alpha_j)\frac{M_j}{N_j}$. By (ii) and (iii) we may choose j so that the right-hand side is $\geq d - \theta w_0$. Q.E.D.

3. Intersections of Convex Sets

The conditions under which an infinite family of convex sets has non-empty intersection have been studied by many people [1, 4, 9]. The case of a family of closed convex sets can be treated immediately using Theorem 1.1.

Corollary 3.1: Let K_i, $i \in I$ be closed convex sets. If $\cap K_i = \emptyset$, then there is a w such that, for every N, there is a finite $F \subset I$, and closed half spaces $H_i \supset K_i$ such that $wx \geq N$ for every $x \in \bigcap_{i \in F} H_i$.

Proof: Each K_i may be represented as the solution set of a system of linear inequalities corresponding to supporting hyperplanes. Since the intersection of the K_i is empty, the system formed by taking all the representing systems is inconsistent, and we may apply Theorem 1.1. The existence of suitable half spaces follows from the duality theorem for linear programming. Q.E.D.

To study families of open convex sets we make use of representations as solutions of systems of strict inequalities. Hence we need to extend Theorem 1.1 to systems including strict inequalities.

Lemma 3.2: If there is no x such that $a_i x \geq b_i$, $i \in I$ and $a_i x > b_i$, $i \in J$, then for some $j \in J$ every x such that $a_i x \geq b_i$, $i \in I \cup (J-j)$ satisfies $-a_j x \geq -b_j$. (Hence Theorem 2.1 and Corollary 2.2 apply).

Proof: We will show that, if, for every j, there is an x_j satisfying $a_j x_j \geq b_i$, $i \in I \cup (J-j)$ and $a_j x_j > b_j$, then there is an x with $a_i x \geq b_i$, $i \in I$ and $a_i x > b_i$ $i \in J$. Let $y_1, y_2, \ldots$ be a countable subset of the x_j such that every x_j is a limit point of a subsequence. This implies $a_j y_i \geq b_j$ for every i and $a_j y_i > b_j$ for at least one i. Choose $\alpha_i > 0$ so that $\Sigma\alpha_i = 1$ and $\Sigma\alpha_i ||y_i|| \leq 1 + \inf ||y_i||$. Then $x = \Sigma\alpha_i y_i$ is defined and satisfies the desired system. Q.E.D.

Theorem 3.3: Let $V_i \subset R^n$, $i \in I$, be open convex sets. If $\cap V_i = \emptyset$ then either (i) the closures of the V_i have empty intersection (and Corollary 3.1 applies) or (ii) there is a $j \in I$, a halfspace $\{x|cx<d\} \supset V_j$, $w \in R^n$, and $w_0 \in R$ such that, for every $0 < \theta < 1$, there is a finite $F \subset I$ and closed halfspaces $H_i \supset V_i$ such that $((\theta w+c)x \geq d-\theta w_0$ for every $x \in \bigcap_{i \in F} H_i$.

The intuitive content of Theorem 3.3 is that there are three ways in which the V_i may have empty intersection. The least interesting possibility is that some finite subfamily has empty intersection (in this case Helly's Theorem implies there are n+1 with empty intersection). The second possibility is that the V_j "march off to infinity" in the manner described in Corollary 3.1. Finally case (ii) describes a situation in which the intersection gets squashed to nothingness. A typical example illustrating case (ii) for n = 2 would be the family $\{(x,y)|y<0\}$ $\{(x,y)|\frac{1}{k}x+y>-\frac{1}{k}\}$, $k = 1,2, \ldots$

Proof of Theorem 3.3: The assertion $\cap V_i = \emptyset$ implies that a system of strict inequalities $a_j x > b_j$, $j \in J$ has no solution, where each inequality is a supporting hyperplane of some V_i. Lemma 3.2 implies that one of the inequalities is negated by all the others. If case (i) does not hold then the system consisting of the others has a solution and we may apply Corollary 2.2. As in Corollary 3.1 the appropriate halfspaces may be obtained by the duality theorem of linear programming.

Q.E.D.

4. Convex Optimization Application

In this section we use the results of Section One to analyze optimization problems involving closed convex functions.

Theorem 4.1: Let $f = \sup\{\alpha_i x + \beta_i | i \in I\}$; $g_j = \sup\{\gamma_{ij}x + \delta_{ij} | i \in I_j\}$, $j \in J$ (here α, x, $\gamma \in R^n$). Assume there is x for which $g_j(x) \leq 0$ and that $f(x) \geq L$ for all such x (i.e., the convex optimization program is feasible and has value $\geq L$). Then there is $w \in R^n$ such that for all ε, $N > 0$ there are affine functions $h_j \leq g_j$, $h \leq f$; $\theta \geq 0$; $F \subset J$ finite; $\lambda_j \geq 0$ such that

$$(4.1) \qquad h(x) + \sum_{j\in F} \lambda_j h_j(x) + \theta wx \geq L - \varepsilon + N\theta$$

for all x.

Proof: The hypothesis implies that there are no x satisfying the semi-infinite system of inequalities $\alpha_i x \leq -\beta_i + L - \varepsilon$, $\gamma_{ij}x \leq -\delta_{ij}$. Theorem 1.1 gives a w such that, for every N, there is a finite subsystem which implies $wx \geq N$. The duality theorem of linear programming implies that the inequality $wx \geq N$ may be obtained as a non-negative linear combination of the members of the finite subsystem. This means there are finite $D \subset I$, $F \subset J$, $F_j \subset I_j$ and r_i, $s_{ij} \geq 0$ such that

$$(4.2) \qquad \sum_{i\in D} r_i\alpha_i + \sum_{j\in F}\sum_{i\in F_j} s_{ij}\gamma_{ij} = -w$$

$$(4.3) \qquad \Sigma r_i(-\beta_i+L-\varepsilon) + \Sigma\,\Sigma\, s_{ij}(-\delta_{ij}) \leq -N$$

Since there is an x for which $g_j(x) \leq 0$ we may assume $\Sigma r_i = R > 0$. Let $\theta = 1/R$, $\lambda_j = \theta(\Sigma s_{ij})$, $h_j(x) = (\theta/\lambda_j)\Sigma s_{ij}(\gamma_{ij}x + \delta_{ij})$, $h(x) = \theta\Sigma r_i(\alpha_i x + \beta_i)$. Note that h_j and h are convex combinations of affine supporting functions, hence are also affine supporting functions. (4.1) may be obtained by multiplying (4.2) by $-\theta x$ and (4.3) by θ and adding. Q.E.D.

Theorem 4.1 in turn implies a "limiting Lagrangian" result of Jeroslow [8].

Corollary 4.2: Assume that, in addition to the assumptions of Theorem 4.1, there is an $\underline{x}$ with $g_j(\underline{x}) \leq 0$, $f(\underline{x})$ finite. Then for θ arbitrarily close to zero there are λ_j with

$$(4.4) \qquad h(x) + \Sigma\lambda_j h_j(x) + \theta wx \geq L - \varepsilon.$$

Proof: It suffices to show that θ approaches zero as N goes to infinity in (4.1). Clearly we have $\theta \leq (N-w\underline{x})^{-1}(f(\underline{x})-L+\varepsilon)$. Given two values of θ, λ_j suitable for any intermediate value of θ may be obtained as convex combinations of the λ_j for the extreme values. Q.E.D.

We can also obtain the Slater point theorem from Theorem 4.1.

Corollary 4.3: Suppose J is finite and there is an $\underline{x}$ with $g_j(x) < 0$, $f(\underline{x})$ finite. Then there are λ_j with

$$f(x) + \Sigma\lambda_j g_j(x) \geq L \tag{4.5}$$

for all x.

Proof: For $N > w\underline{x}$ (4.1) implies $\lambda_j \leq (-1/g_j(\underline{x}))(f(\underline{x}) - L + \varepsilon)$. As ε approaches zero, compactness implies the λ_j have a limit point which satisfies (4.5). Q.E.D.

Uzawa, and more recently, Duffin [5], have shown that in the case in which some of the constraints are affine the Slater point need only be strict for the non-affine constraints. We establish a finite-dimensional version of this result.

Corollary 4.4:* Suppose J is finite and that $||\alpha_i||$, $|\beta_i|$, $||\gamma_{ij}||$, $|\delta_{ij}| \leq M$ for all i, j (this is equivalent to assuming the functions are continuous). If there are $\underline{x}$, β for which $g_j(\underline{x}) \leq 0$ and $\gamma_{ij}\underline{x} + \delta_{ij} \leq \beta < 0$ for all but finitely many (i,j) then there are λ_i for which (4.5) holds.

Proof: We repeat the proof of Theorem 4.1, showing that for large N and small ε the values of the λ_j stay bounded. Then a compactness argument as in Corollary 4.3 completes the proof.

From (4.2) and (4.3) we obtain

$$(L-\varepsilon)-h(x) + \theta\Sigma\Sigma-s_{ij}(\gamma_{ij}x+\delta_{ij}) \leq \theta(wx-N) \tag{4.6}$$

for all x. When $N > w\underline{x}$ this implies $\theta s_{ij} \leq \frac{1}{\beta}(L-f(\underline{x})-\varepsilon)$ for all but finitely many s_{ij}. To deal with the remaining θs_{ij} we consider (4.2) and (4.3) as a system of linear inequalities involving these variables. For large N and small ε this can be considered as a system with fixed left-hand-side and right-hand-side in a bounded region. Hence the solution may be assumed to be in a bounded region. Q.E.D.

---

*The referee suggests [13, Theorem 28.2] as also relevant.

5. What About Systems With Infinitely Many Variables?

I consider semi-infinite programming a nearly complete theory, but there are interesting questions lurking on the boundary between semi-infinite programming and infinite systems.

One way to consider such problems is via functional analysis. A representative result is a corollary of a theorem of Hahn [6, p. 86].

Theorem 5.1: If X is a reflexive Banach space and a_i are continuous linear functionals, the system of inequalities $a_i x \geq b_i$, $i \in I$ has no solution if and only if, for every N, there is a finite $F \in I$ and a functional w_N with $||w_N|| \leq 1$ such that $w_N x \geq N$ for all x such that $a_i x \geq b_i$, $i \in F$.

When X is ℓ^2, Theorem 5.1 gives a condition under which a system with countably many variables has a solution with the sum of squares converging. Early work of this type is reported in Chapter 3 of the still interesting [11].

It is easy to see that Theorem 1.1 does not generalize to the context of Theorem 5.1. We cannot have w_N the same for all N. A simple example is to take a_i an orthonormal basis for ℓ^2 and let b_i go to infinity.

If one is interested in solutions to infinite systems which are not in ℓ^2 some restriction is necessary on the type of inequalities allowed. A natural restriction is that each of the inequalities involve only finitely many variables. Morley [14] has announced a result of this type. It claims that, if a system is inconsistent, then the system is equivalent to a canonical inconsistent system, in the sense that each inequality of the canonical system is implied by finitely many inequalities of the original system. In Morley's result the canonical system has uncountably many inequalities.

We outline a possible analysis based on countable systems. Let (S) be an inconsistent system. An FV subsystem is a subsystem of (S) involving only finitely many variables. Define an ordinal-valued rank for (S) as follows: (S) has rank zero iff (S) contains an inconsistent FV subsystem (Theorem 1.1 characterizes such subsystems). (S) has rank α if (S) has no smaller rank and there is a sequence of inequalities $a_i x \geq b_i$ of rank zero such that for any i and any $\varepsilon > 0$ the system (S) $\cup \{-a_i x \geq -b_i + \varepsilon\}$ is an inconsistent system of rank $< \alpha$.

I conjecture that for every countable ordinal α, there are systems of rank α and (less confidently) that every inconsistent (S) has a countable ordinal rank.

Finally, we wish to give an example indicating the difficulties that confront any attempt to allow infinitely many variables in each inequality. Consider a system involving the variables x_S for every $S \subset [0,1]$ as follows: each variable is between zero and one, $x_{[0,1]} = 1$, $x_{\{r\}} = 0$ for all r, and if the sets S_i are disjoint and $T = \cup S_i$ then $-x_T + \Sigma x_{S_i} = 0$. This system has a solution if and only if there is a countably additive measure defined on all subsets of the reals. Banach and Kuratowski proved this system is inconsistent assuming the continuum hypothesis. Later work indicates that some special set theory axiom is needed to prove this system has no solutions.

References

(1) BEN-TAL, A., E. ROSINGER AND A. BEN-ISRAEL — A Helly-Type Theorem and Semi-infinite Programming. In Constructive Approaches to Mathematical Models, edited by Coffman and Fix. Academic Press, 1979.

(2) BLAIR, C. — A Note on Infinite Systems of Linear Inequalities in R^n. Journal of Mathematical Analysis and its Applications 48 (1974), 150-154.

(3) BLAIR, C. — An Extension of a Theorem of Jeroslow and Kortanek. Israel Journal of Mathematics 17 (1974), 111-115.

(4) BORWEIN, J. — Direct Theorems in Semi-Infinite Convex Programming. Mathematical Programming 21 (1981), 301-318.

(5) DUFFIN, R. — Convex Programs Having Some Linear Constraints. Proceedings National Academy of Science 74, (1977), 26-28.

(6) DUNFORD, N. AND J. SCHWARTZ — Linear Operators, Vol. I. Interscience, 1958.

(7) JEROSLOW, R. AND K. KORTANEK — On Semi-Infinite Systems of Linear Inequalities. Israel Journal of Mathematics 10 (1971), 252-258.

(8) JEROSLOW, R. — A Limiting Lagrangian for Infinitely Constrained Convex Optimization in R^n. Journal of Optimization Theory and Applications 33, (1981), 479-495.

(9) KLEE, V. — The Critical Set of a Convex Body. American Journal of Mathematics 75 (1953), 178-188.

(10) KORTANEK, K. — Constructing a Perfect Duality in Infinite Programming. Applied Mathematics and Optimization 3 (1977), 357-372.

(11) RIESZ, F. — Les Systemes d'Equations Lineaires à une Infitè d'Inconnues. Gauthier-Villars, 1913.

(12) STOER, J. AND C. WITZGALL — Convexity and Optimization in Finite Dimensions I. Springer-Verlag, 1970.

(13) ROCKAFELLAR, R. — Convex Analysis. Princeton University Press, 1969.

(14) MORLEY, T. — "A Farkas Lemma for Certain Infinite Programs," presented at the International Symposium on Semi-Infinite Programming and Applications, Austin, Texas, September 8-10, 1981.

SEMI-INFINITE PROGRAMMING DUALITY: HOW SPECIAL IS IT?

Jonathan M. Borwein[1]

Abstract. In this article we describe and compare some frameworks within which semi-infinite programming duality theory can be studied. The emphasis is on abstract duality and reduction theorems for infinite systems.

1. Introduction.

Our goal in this paper is to outline various methodologies: specifically, for establishing semi-infinite duality results; and, more generally, for analyzing semi-infinite programs. Two primary reasons come to mind for this project. Firstly, we wish to use semi-infinite programming as a "litmus test" for more general formulations. If a duality theory is proposed or established for a class of programs including semi-infinite programming, then it should be possible to re-derive known results about semi-infinite programming in a relatively straightforward way.

Secondly, we wish to isolate those properties of semi-infinite programs which are relevant to a given formulation. Again, this will have the effect of putting semi-infinite programming in a broader context, and of answering the partly facetious question in the title. Ideally, we also discover extensions or insights along the way and gain insight into the underlying structure.

To these ends, we consider the three main techniques for studying semi-infinite structures. (i) Direct reduction methods, wherein the system is replaced by a finite subsystem. These methods divide naturally into primal and dual types. (ii) Abstract formulations, in which the semi-infinite program is viewed as an abstract program of the same class (linear, convex, n-times differentiable, etc.). (iii) Non-smooth analysis may be performed, essentially by aggregating the constraints as one real valued maximum. One then applies convex or non-smooth characterizations of optimality.

An extremely pleasant history and survey of basic semi-infinite duality results may be found in [29]. The entire volume merits attention.

The outline of the paper is as follows. Sections Two and Three discuss Primal and Dual direct methods respectively. Section Four outlines abstract linear duality theory. Section Five considers three different specializations of this theory to semi-infinite linear programming. Section Six briefly discusses abstract convex duality and then turns to semi-infinite differentiable programming. Section Seven consists of some few remarks on non-smooth techniques. We have tried to construct the sections so that they can be read somewhat independently.

---

[1] Research partially supported by NSERC Grant A5116.

2. Direct Techniques: (I) Primal reduction theorems.

Throughout this section we consider the program

$$(2.1) \qquad v(P) := \inf f(x) \text{ subject to } \begin{array}{l} g(x,t) \le 0 \ , \ \forall t \in T \ , \\ x \in C \end{array}$$

where X is a finite dimensional vector space of dimension n, and T is an, as yet unspecified, index set. We suppose that $f : X \to]-\infty,\infty]$ and $g : X \times T \to]-\infty,\infty]$. In the semi-infinite problem T is infinite. A primal reduction theorem gives conditions under which T may be replaced by a finite subset in (2.1) without changing the infimal value $v(P)$. Such theorems were given first in [2] and then by the author in [8]. A related result may be found in [28]. The theorem in [8] goes as follows. We suppose that T is compact, that f is quasi-convex and upper semi-continuous, that C is closed and convex and that (A1) g is quasi-convex in x and (separately) upper semi-continuous in x and t. It is shown in [8] that this is equivalent to joint upper semi-continuity.

Theorem 2.1. ([8]) With (P) as above, suppose 'Slater's condition' is satisfied in the following sense:

Given any $n+1$ points $t_0, t_1, \ldots, t_n$ in T, there exists

$$(2.3) \qquad x \in C \text{ with } g(x,t_i) < 0 \quad (0 \le i \le n) \ .$$

Then

(a) There exist n points $t_1, t_2, \ldots, t_n$ in T with no solution to

$$(2.4) \qquad f(x) < v(P) \ , \ g(x,t_i) < 0 \quad (1 \le i \le n) \ , \ x \in C \ .$$

(b) If, in addition, each $g(\cdot,t_i)$ is strictly quasi-convex then

$$(2.5) \qquad v(P) = \inf\{f(x) \mid g(x,t_i) \le 0 \quad (1 \le i \le n) \ , \ x \in C\} \ .$$

(c) Suppose now that $v(P)$ is finite and each $g(\cdot,t_i)$ and f is convex and finite on C. Then there exist non-negative numbers λ_i $(1 \le i \le n)$ with

$$(2.6) \qquad v(P) = \inf\{f(x) + \sum_{i=1}^{n} \lambda_i g(x,t_i) \mid x \in C\} \ .$$

Thus the primal reduction (a) relies on quasi-convexity. If the functions are actually convex, one may dualize and produce a Lagrange multiplier theorem as in (c). Of course, once one has (b) one may proceed, in anyway one wishes, to study this standard finitely constrained non-linear program [8].

The proof applies a Helly-type theorem for open convex sets in n-dimensions [8], [42]. From (2.1) we know that

$$C \cap \{x|f(x) < v(P)\} \cap \bigcap_{t\in T} \{x|g(x,t) < 0\} = \emptyset .$$

With the exception of C each of these sets is open and convex. Our Helly theorem guarantees (under assumption (A1) on g) that some subfamily containing at most $n+1$ of these sets fails to meet in C. Slater's condition (2.3) shows that

$$\{x|f(x) < v(P)\}$$

must be among these sets. We now have (2.4), from which (2.5) and (2.6) follow in standard ways. Even if (2.3) fails one may formulate a Fritz John result [8].

As will be apparent, the theorem relies intrinsically on the finite dimensionality of the space X. This given, the remaining hypotheses for parts (a) and (b) (the primal reduction) are really as weak as can be expected.

In [8] it is shown that the case in which (P) is a non-smooth or differentiable semi-infinite program may be satisfactorily treated in similar fashion. In this case the reduction theorem is applied to the appropriate directional derivatives. These techniques may also be used to produce higher order duality results related to those in ([3], [34], [50] and Section 6).

Before turning to other results, we observe that the classical linear semi-infinite program of Charnes, Cooper, Kortanek, [14] meets the conditions of Theorem 2.1 if one imposes the standard canonical closure conditions, ([22] and Sections 3 and 4 below. This is discussed in [8]). Observe also that the closed convex set C may itself admit a semi-infinite description.

We now turn to primal reduction results which rely on Helly's theorem for closed convex sets rather than for open ones. Consider the program

$$\text{(2.8)} \qquad \text{(Q)} \qquad v(Q) := \min\{f(x)|x \in C\} ,$$

where $f : X \to]-\infty,\infty]$ is quasi-convex and lower semi-continuous while C is convex non-empty and closed, and admits a description as

$$\text{(2.9)} \qquad C := \cap \{C_i|i \in I\} ,$$

for a family non-empty closed convex sets $\{C_i|i \in I\}$. Thanks to the Hahn-Banach Separation Theorem [61], every closed convex set has such a description in terms of half spaces. For any $\theta > 0$ we know that

$$\text{(2.10)} \qquad \{x|f(x) \le v(Q) - \theta\} \cap \cap\{C_i|i \in I\} = \emptyset .$$

Now (2.10) expresses the fact that a family of closed convex subsets of a finite dimensional vector space has empty intersection. Under the appropriate _recession conditions_ we know that there will exist some subfamily of at most $n+1$ subsets with empty intersection. Since C is non-empty, $\{x|f(x) \le v(Q) - \theta\}$ is one of these sets while the remaining n lie in $\{C_i | i \in I\}$. The appropriate recession condition is ([12], [61]) that

$$(2.11) \qquad L(\theta) := \text{rec}\{x|f(x) \le v(Q) - \theta\} \cap \text{rec } C$$

should be linear. Here

$$(2.12) \qquad \text{rec } C := \{d \in X | C + td \subset C \ , \ \forall t \ge 0\} \ .$$

When f is convex (2.11) simplifies since all the non-empty level sets of a convex function share the same recession cone. We have now derived the following reduction theorem which is implicit in [13] and whose cognates may be found in [41], [60] and elsewhere.

Theorem 2.2. With (Q) as above, suppose that, for all $\theta > 0, L(\theta)$ _in_ (2.11) _is linear. Then_

$$(2.13) \qquad v(Q) = \sup_{I(n)} \inf_{X}\{f(x)|x \in C_i \ , \ i \in I(n)\}$$

where $I(n)$ _ranges over all subsets of_ I _with at most_ n _elements. In addition_ $v(Q)$ _is attained._

We may view this result as duality theorem in which the right hand side of (2.13) is a dual program.

Suppose now that f is quasi-convex and finite on C and that

$$C_i := \{x|f_i(x) \le 0\} = \bigcap_{\varepsilon>0} \{x|f_i(x) \le \varepsilon\} \ ,$$

for quasi-convex lower semi-continuous functions f_i. Then Theorem 2.2 ensures us that, for each $\theta > 0$, one can find a subset $I(\theta)$ of I, with cardinality n, and positive numbers $\varepsilon_i (i \in I(\theta))$ such that

$$(2.14) \qquad v(Q) - \theta \le \inf\{f(x)|f_i(x) \le \varepsilon_i \ , \ i \in I(\theta)\} \ .$$

Since this last program satisfies Slater's condition as C is non-empty, Lagrange multipliers exist assuming the functions involved are convex. We may thus derive that non-negative numbers $\lambda_i (i \in I(\theta))$ exist with

$$(2.15)\qquad v(Q) - \theta < \inf_X f(x) + \sum_{i\in I(\theta)} \lambda_i f_i(x) .$$

Alternatively we may replace f and each f_i by some affine minorant [10] and apply linear programming duality. In either case the requirement (2.11) becomes that all common recession conditions of f and the $f_i (1 \in I)$ be lineality directions [61].

Suppose that L is not linear. The approach in [13] is to perturb f linearly so that (2.11) does hold for the perturbed function. For these purposes it is convenient to replace f by a linear minorant c . This may be achieved either by adding a dummy variable as in [37], or by separation as in [13]. Thus we start with some linear c and consider

$$(2.16)\qquad (\hat{Q})\qquad v(Q) := \inf\{\langle c,x\rangle \mid x \in C\} .$$

We now look for a linear functional w and a constant $\bar{w}$ such that

$$(2.17)\qquad L(\theta) := \text{rec}\{x \mid \langle c + \theta w,x\rangle \le 0\} \cap \text{rec}\ C$$

is linear for all $\theta > 0$, and such that

$$(2.18)\qquad v(Q) - \theta\bar{w} < \inf\{\langle c + \theta w,x\rangle \mid x \in C\}.$$

That this is always possible is shown in [13] and [24] and below in Section 3. Our previous result concerned the case $w = 0$, $\bar{w} = 1$. Similarly, we now discover that (2.13) holds with f replaced by $c + \theta w$. In the convex case we also may now derive (2.15) with f replaced by $f + \theta w$ and θ replaced by $\bar{w}\theta$.

If we finally let θ tend to zero in (2.15), we see that

$$(2.19)\qquad v(Q) = \lim_{\theta\to 0^+} \sup_{\Lambda_n} \inf_X\{f(x) + \theta\langle w,x\rangle + \sum_{i\in I} \lambda_i f_i(x)\} = \lim_{\theta\to 0^+} \inf_C\{f(x) + \theta\langle w,x\rangle\}$$

where Λ_n denotes all non-negative functions on I whose supports have finite cardinality (of at most n). This is the basic limiting Lagrangian result as derived in [13] and studied originally in [37] and elsewhere, [4], [20], [21].

It is clearly possible to combine (2.6) and (2.19) to derive reduction results for mixed semi-infinite constraint structures. One merely applies (2.19) to the result in (2.6) after picking an appropriate representation for C .

We complete this section by observing that (2.19) may be used to derive the Lagrange multiplier theorem. Suppose that I is finite and that Slater's condition holds for $f_i (i \in I)$. Thus there is some $\varepsilon > 0$ with $f_i(\hat{x}) \le -\varepsilon (i \in I)$, $f(\hat{x}) < \infty$. Then also (2.19) shows that for $\theta > 0$ there exists $\lambda(\theta) \in \Lambda_n$ with

(2.20) $$v(Q) \le \liminf_{\theta \to 0^+} \{f(x) + \theta\langle w,x\rangle + \sum_{i \in I} \lambda_i(\theta) f_i(x)\} ,$$

for all x in X.

Substituting $\hat{x}$ in (2.20), we discover that

(2.21) $$\varepsilon \limsup_{\theta \to 0^+} \sum_{i \in I} \lambda_i(\theta) \le f(\hat{x}) - v(Q) .$$

Since I is finite, and (2.21) shows that $\lambda(\theta)$ remains bounded, $\lambda(\theta)$ has a cluster point $\bar{\lambda}$ and (2.20) now shows that $\bar{\lambda}$ is the appropriate Lagrange multiplier.

3. Direct Techniques: (II) Dual reduction theorems.

The original linear semi-infinite programming duality [14], [15], [22], the limiting Lagrangian of Jeroslow [37], [38], and the ascent ray theorems of Blair [4], [5] are all essentially dual reduction results for linear semi-infinite programs. In this section we explicate certain of these theorems and relate them to our primal recession results.

Let C be a closed (non-empty) convex set and suppose that

(3.1) $$C = \bigcap_{i \in I} \{x \mid \langle a_i, x\rangle \le b_i\}$$

for some family (a_i) of linear functionals and real numbers (b_i). We define the moment cone associated with (a_i, b_i) by

(3.2) $$M := \text{coco}\{(-a_i, b_i) \mid i \in I\} + (0, \mathbb{R}_+)$$

This moment cone has been central to analysis of semi-infinite duality ([17], [29], [43], [44], [62], and elsewhere). We begin by relating M to (2.17) and (2.18).

Theorem 3.1. ([13]) *Let w lie in X and $\bar{w}$ in $\mathbb{R}$. Then*

(3.3) $$(w, \bar{w}) \in \text{rel int } M ,$$

if and only if

(3.4) (i) $-\bar{w} < \inf\{\langle w,x\rangle \mid x \in C\}$, and

(3.5) (ii) $x \in \text{rec } C, \langle w,x\rangle = 0 \Rightarrow x \in -\text{rec } C$.

(b) In particular, any such w and $\bar{w}$ satisfy (2.17) and (2.18). Moreover, since rel int M is non empty such points exist.

It is an easy exercise to check part (b). Part (a), which illustrates a general duality between "recession" (compactness) and "relative interior", [51], [61], is established via separation arguments. Theorem 3.1 shows that, while M depends on the representation of C , relint M and cl M depend only on C .

Vectors satisfying (3.3) are the central examples of ascent directions [4], [5]. The theorem thus illustrates the fact that the perturbations of Section Two correspond closely to ascent rays and provide a primal rather than dual reduction process.

Example 3.2. Consider the semi-infinite linear program

(3.6) $$(SIP) \quad v(P) := \inf\{\langle c,x\rangle \mid \langle a_i,x\rangle \le b_i \ , \ \forall i \in I\} ,$$

and its dual

(3.7) $$(SID) \quad v(D) := \sup\{-\sum_{i\in I} \lambda_i b_i \mid \sum_{i\in I} \lambda_i a_i = -c, \ \lambda \in \Lambda\} .$$

Then $v(P) \ge v(D)$ is an immediate weak duality inequality. Now (2.15) shows that (with $\theta > 0$, $w,\bar{w}$ as above)

(3.8) $$v(P) - \theta\bar{w} \le \inf_x \langle c + \theta w, x\rangle + \sum_{i\in I(\theta)} \lambda_i(\langle a_i,x\rangle - b_i)$$

for $\lambda \in \Lambda_n$. This implies that for $\theta > 0$,

(3.9) $$(c + \theta w, -v(P) + \theta\bar{w}) \in M ,$$

or, in Blair's terms, $(w,\bar{w})$ is an ascent vector. From (3.9) it follows that $(c,-v(P)) \in \text{cl } M$. If one assumes that M is closed this implies that, for some λ in Λ

(3.10) $$-c = \sum_{i\in I} \lambda_i a_i \ , \ v(P) \le -\sum_{i\in I} \lambda_i b_i \ ,$$

and so $v(P) = v(D)$ and $v(D)$ is attained. Thus we have shown, as a consequence of the primal reduction results, why the closedness of M is sufficient for dual perfect duality. (See [7], [43] and Section Four below).

Extensions of this kind of analysis can be made to handle the convex semi-infinite programming case by looking at affine minorants [38], [40]. Recall that the representation of C is said to be canonically closed, [15], [22] if

(3.11)

(i) $A := \{(-a_i, b_i) \mid i \in I\}$ is compact,

(ii) $\langle a_i, x \rangle < b_i,\ \forall i \in I$ has simultaneous solution.

We already know from Theorem 2.1 that this implies that $v(P) = v(D)$ and $v(D)$ is attained when $v(P)$ is finite. Let us finish this section by giving a very geometric proof that canonical closure yields a closed moment cone; and so Example 3.2 applies.

Proposition 3.3. A canonically closed representation of C yields a closed moment cone.

Proof: Observe that

(3.12) $M = \text{cone}\ (\text{co}A_0)$ where $A_0 := A \cup \{(0,1)\}$.

Since A is compact (by (3.11)(i)) and finite dimensional, conv A_0 is also closed and bounded by Carathéodory's Theorem [63]. Now (3.11)(ii) implies that $0 \notin \text{co}A_0$. It is easy to verify that the cone generated by a closed bounded convex set which misses the origin is closed. Since (3.12) shows M is of this form, M is closed. □

This analysis can be extended to allow a finite number of exceptional constraints which fail to satisfy (3.11)(ii) strictly [7], [23]. Observe also that finite dimensionality is only used to ensure that conv A is closed and bounded. If this hypothesis is substituted for (3.11) (i), the proposition has content in an arbitrary topological vector space.

We conclude this section by observing that multicriteria semi-infinite programs may be analysed similarly [8]. Without further restriction, however, Pareto semi-infinite convex programs do not admit finite equivalent subprograms. This is discussed in [8]. An interesting application of these notions to minimax results is given in [6].

4. Abstract Linear Duality

Throughout this section we consider the following abstract linear program

$$(4.1) \qquad (LP) \qquad v(P) := \inf\{\langle c,x\rangle \mid Ax - b \in -S,\ x \in K\} ,$$

and its dual program

$$(4.2) \qquad (LD) \qquad v(D) := \sup\{\langle -b,y'\rangle \mid A^T y' + c \in K^+,\ y' \in S^+\} .$$

Here $A : X \to Y$ is a continuous linear mapping between locally convex topological vector spaces; $S \subset Y$ and $K \subset X$ are closed convex cones. The form $\langle \cdot,\cdot \rangle$ represents both the natural pairing between X and its (continuous real) dual space X^*, and that between Y and Y^*. The dual spaces are endowed with topologies in which their duals are the original spaces. Finally, K^+ and S^+ are the dual or polar cones of K and S ($S^+ := \{y' \in Y^* \mid \langle s,y'\rangle \geq 0,\ \forall s \in S\}$), while $b \in Y$ and $c \in X^*$ and A^T is the adjoint of A. We always have $v(P) \geq v(D)$ as a weak duality estimate. We now outline an abstract duality theory for (LP) and (LD). We then show in Section Five how by judiciously choosing X and Y, S, and K, one may view (SIP) of (3.6) in various different settings; and we contrast these various approaches.

In keeping with terminology in the literature, let us say that (LP) and (LD) are in primal (dual) perfect duality if either (i) $v(P) = \infty$, $v(D) = -\infty$ or (ii) $v(P) = v(D)$ and $v(P)(v(D))$ is attained when finite. The relevant results specialized from [7], which are also treated to some degree in [26], [44], [45], [53], [65], and elsewhere, are collected in the following theorem. In analogy with the semi-infinite case, we begin by defining two moment cones

$$(4.3) \qquad M(P) := [A,c](K) + (S, \mathbb{R}_+) ,$$

and

$$(4.4) \qquad M(D) := [-A^T,b](S^+) + (K^+, \mathbb{R}_+) .$$

Theorem 4.1. ([7]) (a) With (LP) and (LD) as above, suppose that $M(P)$ is closed. Then (LP) and (LD) are in primal perfect duality for all b in Y. Dually, if $M(D)$ is closed, then (LP) and (LD) are in dual perfect duality for all c in X^*.
(b) Conversely, suppose that (LD) is feasible and that (LP) and (LD) are in primal perfect duality for all b in Y. Then $M(P)$ is closed. Dually, if (LP) is feasible and (LP) and (LD) are in dual perfect duality for all c in X^*, then $M(D)$ is closed.

Paraphrasing this result, in the interesting case in which (LP) is feasible, M(D) is closed if and only if dual perfect duality occurs for every dual right hand side vector. In the semi-infinite setting, Jeroslow calls this uniform duality [38], [23]. The proof may be viewed as a fairly straightforward exercise in the analysis of marginal functions [7]. The next theorem gives the most accessible conditions involving (LP) for closure of the moment cones.

Theorem 4.2. ([7]) *Suppose that* (LP) *and* (LD) *are as above.*
(a) *Suppose that* K *is locally compact and that*

(4.5) $$L := \{x \in X | Ax \in -S,\ x \in K, \langle c,x\rangle \le 0\} ,$$

is linear. Then M(P) *is closed.*

(b) *Suppose either that*

(4.6) (i) $$[A(K)-b] \cap -\text{int } S \neq \emptyset ,$$

or that X *and* Y *are Banach spaces and*

(4.7) (ii) $$b \in \text{int } [A(K) + S] .$$

Then M(D) *is closed and, in addition,* (LD) *has a non-empty equicontinuous solution set whenever* v(P) *is finite.*

Part (a) is an abstract recession direction result ([26], [32], [53], [61], [65]), while b(i) is an abstract Slater condition ([17], [32], [49]). Part b(ii) gives an open mapping condition which is applicable in many setting in which int S is empty ([7], [10], [12], [59]). In infinite dimensions there is a considerable, but not complete, duality between recession and interiority conditions ([36], [51], [59], [61]). The theorem has an obvious dual version for (LD); with the proviso that all topologies must be compatible so that in b(ii) X and Y are reflexive. Finally, we observe that any constraint qualification for (LP) must yield uniform duality since the qualification is independent of the objective function.

5. Specializations.

Example 5.1. (Product spaces) Consider $Y := \prod_I \mathbb{R}, S := \prod_I \mathbb{R}_+$. Thus Y is the direct product of I copies of the real line in the product topology and S is the set of all elements of Y with non-negative coordinates. Now Y is a locally convex space which is not metrizable unless I is countable and is not normable unless I is finite. Also S has no interior when I is infinite. The dual space Y^* becomes

$\prod_I \mathbb{R}$ the direct sum of $\mathbb{R}$ over I , or a generalized finite sequence space [9], [43]. The dual cone S^+ is Λ of (2.19) and sequel. Necessarily A is given by $(Ax)_i = \langle a_i,x\rangle$ for a_i in X^* ; and (LP) coincides with (SIP) of (3.6) if we also assume that $X = K$ is finite dimensional.

Case (i). $X = K$ is finite dimensional. We are now studying (SIP) and (SID) of Example 3.7. The condition (4.5) for primal perfect duality is that K be locally compact (which it is) and that L be linear, where L is given by

(5.1) $$L := \{x \in X | \langle a_i,x\rangle \le 0 \ (\forall i \in I), \langle c,x\rangle \le 0\} .$$

Notice that L coincides with $L(\theta)$ of (2.11) because $f := c$ is linear and C is given by (3.1). Thus we recover Theorem 2.2 and (2.15) in the linear case. The condition for dual perfect duality is that $M(D)$ be closed in the finite dimensional space X^* . In this case, however, $M(D)$ coincides with M as defined by (3.2). Moreover, Proposition 3.3 gives a standard condition (canonical closure) for $M(D)$ to be closed.

Case (ii). X is finite dimensional and K is polyhedral. The primal duality condition is entirely analogous. The dual condition requires that

$$M(D) = M + (K^+,0) ,$$

be closed. Presuming that M is closed this will hold by the recession theory if $M \cap (-K^+,0)$ is linear [61]. This is certainly true if

(5.2) $$0 = \{y' \in Y^* | \langle b,y'\rangle \le 0, A^T y' \in K^+\} .$$

This is guaranteed by the existence of a point $\hat{x}$ with

(5.3) $$\langle a_i,\hat{x}\rangle < b_i \ (\forall i \in I), \ \hat{x} \in K .$$

Thus (5.3) in conjunction with compactness of $\{(a_i,b_i) | i \in I\}$ ensures that $M(D)$ is closed. This allows for the treatment of finitely many extra linear inequalities. Suppose finally that $X := \mathbb{R}^n$ and $K := \mathbb{R}^n_+$. We may now impose a Slater condition on (LD). This condition, the dual of (4.6)(i), is that one can solve

(5.4) $$\lambda \in \Lambda , \ \sum_{i \in I} \lambda_i a_i + c > 0 .$$

This is Karlin and Studden's condition [18], [39] and ensures primal perfect duality. It has an obvious extension to any pointed cone K in X finite dimensional. In fact, it is an equivalent way of ensuring that L in (4.5) is zero.

Case (iii). The analysis may be applied when X is infinite dimensional. As long as K is locally compact, primal perfect duality follows analogously from (4.5). Closure of $M(D)$ may still be established in many cases, as was discussed after Proposition 3.3. One can also consider the case where Y is a much more general product space.

We next consider the most frequent formulation of (SIP) which is - either explicitly or implicitly - to set the problem in a continuous function space.

Example 5.2. (Continuous function spaces) Suppose that $Y := C(T)$, the space of continuous functions on some compact Hausdorff space T endowed with the supremum norm. For the moment X is arbitrary as is K. Now any continuous linear $A : X \to C(T)$ may be written as $(Ax)(t) = \langle a(t),x\rangle$ for some family $(a(t))$ in X^* with a weakly continuous A^*. Thus the problem becomes

$$(5.5) \qquad \text{(LCP)} \qquad v(P) := \inf\{\langle c,x\rangle \mid \langle a(t),x\rangle \le b(t)\ (\forall t \in T),\ x \in K\}\ .$$

Since $Y^* = M(T)$, the regular Borel measures on T, the dual problem becomes

$$(5.6) \qquad \text{(LCD)} \qquad v(D) := \sup\{-\int_T b(t)d\mu \mid \int_T a(t)d\mu \in -c + K^+,\ \mu \ge 0\}\ .$$

Here the integral of a is a weak or Pettis integral [63]. This is to say that $\int_T \langle a(t),x\rangle d\mu + \langle c,x\rangle \ge 0$ for all x in K. Thus the dual variables range over $M^+(T)$, the cone of non-negative Borel measures. Conditions for duality may be read off from Theorem 4.2. The primal condition (4.5) applies when X is finite dimensional or K is locally compact. The dual Slater condition (4.6) is now applicable. In particular, the canonical closure conditions ensure that the problem may be posed in this setting and that $M(D)$ is closed. More generally, we need to know that

(5.7) (i) a is weakly continuous, b is continuous,

and

(ii) $\langle a(t),\hat{x}\rangle < b(t),\ \forall t \in T$, for some $\hat{x} \in K$.

This does not require X to be finite dimensional. Of course, one wants to replace $M^+(T)$ in (5.6) by Λ. The following extension of a well-known result ([29], [62], [64]) indicates how one proceeds. Let

(5.8) $C(\mu) := \mathrm{co}\{(a(t),b(t)) \mid t \in \mathrm{supp}\ \mu\}$,

where supp μ is the support of μ .

Theorem 5.3. Suppose that a is weakly continuous, b is continuous and that X is a Banach space. Then

(5.9) (a) $\iota := \int_T (-a(t),b(t))d\mu \in \mu(T)\mathrm{cl}\ C(\mu)$.

(b) Thus

(5.10) $M(D) \subset \mathbb{R}_+ \mathrm{clco}\{(-a(t),b(t)) \mid t \in T\} + (K^+,\mathbb{R}_+)$.

(c) If X is finite dimensional "cl" may be removed in (5.9) and (5.10). This implies that

(5.11) $M(D) = M + (K^+,0)$,

and that (LCD) and (SID) are equivalent.

Proof. (a) Let $c(t) := (-a(t),b(t))$. Then $c(T)$ is weak-star compact in $X^* \times \mathbb{R}$. As X is a Banach space $\mathrm{clco}\ c(T)$ is also compact. It follows that ι exists as a point of $X^* \times \mathbb{R}$ [63, 75] and must lie in $\mu(T)\mathrm{cl}\ C(\mu)$. If not one may separate ι from $\mu(T)\mathrm{cl}\ C(\mu)$ in the weak-star topology. Thus we obtain $\bar{y} \in X \times \mathbb{R}$ and $\varepsilon > 0$ with

(5.12) $\langle\iota,\bar{y}\rangle + \varepsilon \le \mu(T)\ \langle c(t),\bar{y}\rangle$ for all $t \in \mathrm{supp}\ \mu$.

Integration yields, after dividing both sides by $\mu(T) = \mu(\mathrm{supp}\ \mu)$,

(5.13) $\langle\iota,\bar{y}\rangle + \varepsilon \le \int_{\mathrm{supp}\ \mu} \langle c(t),\bar{y}\rangle d\mu = \langle\iota,\bar{y}\rangle$

which is impossible.

(b) Each y in $M(D)$ may be expressed as $\iota + (k^+,r)$ for some ι as in (5.9) and $k^+ \in K^+$, $r \ge 0$. Since $C(\mu) \subset \mathrm{clco}\ c(T)$ and $\mu(T) \ge 0$, (5.10) follows.

(c) Both T and supp μ are compact. As X is finite dimensional both $\mathrm{co}\ c(T)$ and $\mathrm{co}\ c(\mathrm{supp}\ \mu)$ are compact in $X^* \times \mathbb{R}$. Finally, (5.11) holds. Indeed (5.10) now shows that

$$M(D) \subset M + (K^+,0) ,$$

and the other containment follows since any member of Λ lies in S^+. Thus any feasible value for (LCD) is also taken on in (SID) and the programs are equivalent. □

Corollary 5.4. Suppose either that (a) $C(\mu)$ is closed or that (b) $C(\mu)$ has non-empty relative interior (in its weak-star closed affine span) then

$$(5.14) \qquad \int_T (-a(t),b(t))d\mu \in \mu(T)C(\mu) .$$

Proof. The first alternative was covered in the previous theorem. The second alternative follows from a proper separation argument [64] and is similar to that in the previous theorem. Note that $C(\mu)$ need only have relative interior in some topology whose dual is $X \times \mathbb{R}$. □

Theorem 5.3(c) is a reduction theorem for continuous programs. It shows that any condition ensuring duality for (SIP) and (LCD) ensures duality for (SIP) and (SID). We also observe that Corollary 5.4(b) holds for general measures and functions when X is finite dimensional [29], [62], [64].

Example 5.5. (Bounded sequence spaces) We may also model the semi-infinite program in an ℓ_∞ space. Let X be a Banach space and $Y := \ell_\infty(I)$, the space of bounded functions on I in the supremum norm. We let S be the cone of non-negative bounded functions on I.

Case (i). Y is endowed with the weak topology $\sigma(\ell_\infty,\ell_1)$ induced by ℓ_1. Now we require that A be continuous from X to (ℓ_∞,σ). The simplest way to ensure this is for X to be the dual of a Banach space Z endowed with the weak topology $\sigma(X,Z)$ and for A to be given by $(Ax)_i = \langle a_i,x\rangle$ for $a_i \in Z$ with $\sup_I \|a_i\| < \infty$. This guarantees that A^T maps ℓ_1 into Z and A has the requisite continuity properties. We also require that $a \in Z$ and that $b \in \ell_\infty$. Primal and dual conditions may now be derived from Theorem 4.1 and Theorem 4.2(a). Note that while S has norm interior it has no weak-star interior and (4.6) is not relevant. Condition (4.5) is as before. The dual condition is that $M(D)$ should be closed (norm or weakly) in Z. As

$$M(D) = [-A^T,b](\ell_1^+) + (K^+,\mathbb{R}_+) ,$$

one may proceed as in Example 5.1. Supposing that K^+ is locally compact, it suffices that

$$(5.15) \qquad \langle a_i,\bar{x}\rangle < b_i , \ (\forall i \in I) , \ x \in K ,$$

has solution, and that

$$(5.16) \qquad (ii) \qquad \theta := \{ \sum_{i \in I} \lambda_i(-a_i,b_i) \mid \sum_{i \in I} \lambda_i = 1,\ \lambda_i \geq 0\} ,$$

is closed. This ensures that the argument of Proposition 3.3 can be mimicked. The set θ is the ideally convex hull of $\{(-a_i,b_i) | i \in I\}$ and in finite dimensions coincides with the convex hull ([32] and below). In particular, the canonical closure conditions again imply dual perfect duality. More generally, the multiplier lies in ℓ_1^+ and again we seek a reduction theorem to allow us to replace ℓ_1^+ by Λ . Such a theorem is given at the end of this section.

Case (ii). Y is endowed with the norm topology, S is as before and $(Ax)_i = \langle a_i,x\rangle$ for a_i in X^* with $\sup_I ||a_i|| < \infty$. The dual problem now lies in ℓ_∞^* which is an unpleasant space. Nonetheless, as ℓ_∞^+ has non-empty norm-interior we may use Slater's condition to guarantee dual perfect duality in ℓ_∞^* . The condition becomes: there exists $\varepsilon > 0$ such that

$$(5.17) \qquad \langle a_i,\bar{x}\rangle \leq b_i - \varepsilon \ (\forall i \in I)\bar{x} \in K$$

has solution. The primal condition is unchanged. In either case we are faced with a non-negative multiplier $\mu \in \ell_\infty^*$ and a Lagrangian inequality of the form

$$(5.18) \qquad \langle c,x\rangle + \mu(Ax-b) \geq v \quad \text{for all} \quad x \in K ,$$

for some real number v . The process of replacing μ by some $\lambda \in \ell_1^+$ is, in general, highly delicate and reliant on the structure of X , [46], [56], [57]. The only easily formulated general condition appears to be

$$(5.19) \qquad A(K) - b \subset c_0 - \ell_\infty^+ .$$

This says that every $Ax-b$ occurring in (5.18) is majorized by some c_0 sequence. Here $c_0(I)$ is the generalized sequence space of sequences converging to zero, [19]. Condition (5.19) may be read as saying that only finitely many of the constraints are badly non-feasible. It is a condition highly plausible in economic models [46], [56]. In the case in which X is a sequence space, a similar condition has been studied by Ponstein [56]. Given (5.19), one argues as follows. There is a positive projection P of ℓ_∞^* onto ℓ_1 such that $I-P$ is positive and annihilates c_0 [19]. Then (5.18) shows that

$$\langle c,x\rangle + \langle P\mu,Ax-b\rangle - b \geq \langle P\mu-\mu,Ax-b\rangle$$

and, for x in K , $\langle P\mu-\mu, Ax-b\rangle \geq \langle P\mu-\mu, p\rangle$ for some p in c_0 . Thus $\langle P\mu-\mu, Ax-b\rangle \geq 0$ and

(5.20) $\quad \langle c,x\rangle + \langle P\mu, Ax-b\rangle \geq v$ for all $x \in K$.

Thus $P\mu \in \ell_1^+$ is the desired ℓ_1 multiplier. We have established the following Theorem.

Theorem 5.6. Under condition (5.19), $(\ell_\infty^+)^+$ may be replaced by ℓ_1^+ in (LD).

Notice that even when X is finite dimensional and Slater's condition holds (5.19) and canonical closure are distinct and non-comparable conditions. We conclude this section with the following simple result ([32], [64]) which allows ℓ_1^+ to be replaced by Λ in (LD).

Proposition 5.7. Suppose that X is finite dimensional and that d_i lie in X^* for i in I . Suppose that

(5.21) $\quad x^* := \sum_{i\in I} \mu_i d_i \in X^*$

for some $\mu \in \ell_1^+$. Then

(5.22) $\quad x^* = \sum_{i\in I} \lambda_i d_i$

for some λ in Λ .

Proof. The result could be deduced from a more general version of Corollary 5.4 in [64]. Suppose $x^* \notin C := \text{cone}\{d_i | i \in \text{supp } \mu\}$. Then x^* may be properly separated from C [32] since $\dim X < \infty$. This ensures the existence of $x \in X$ with

(i) $\quad \langle x^*, x\rangle \leq 0 \leq \inf\{\langle d_i, x\rangle | i \in \text{supp } \mu\}$,

and

(ii) $\quad \langle x^*, x\rangle < \sup\{\langle d_i, x\rangle | i \in \text{supp } \mu\}$.

But (i) and (ii) contradict (5.22). □ The result holds with the same proof if μ has arbitrary positive components.

One may now use Carathéodory's Theorem [1] to replace Λ by Λ_n .

It is also possible to consider $\ell_\infty(I)$ as $C(\beta(I))$ where $\beta(I)$ is the Stone-Čech compactification of I , [19]. This enables one to read results for $\ell_\infty(I)$ out of Example 5.2. Unfortunately, the final results involve $\beta(I)$ not only I !

Example 5.8. Consider the one variable linear program

(5.23) $v(P) := \inf\{\langle c,x\rangle \mid \frac{1}{i} x \le 1 , \forall i \ge 1\}$,

for some $c \in \mathbb{R}$. It is easily verified that conditions of Example 5.5(ii) hold. These are recapitulated, for convex programs, as (6.2). With these conditions it is immediate from our analysis that dual perfect duality holds and thus that the moment cone M is closed. It is equally clear, however, that the constraints are not canonically closed. Thus when X is finite dimensional the linear version of (6.2) gives verifiable conditions for the moment cone to be closed which are distinct from canonical closure.

We close this section by observing that Cybenko's result in [18], which may be considered as an exact penalty method for continuous (SIP), has extensions to abstract linear programs of the types discussed above. We also note that continuous time linear programs as in [48], [7] are extremely rich examplars of the importance of correctly choosing the spaces in which one sets a given problem.

6. Abstract convex and differentiable programming.

Most of what has been described about linear programming carries over to convex or differentiable semi-infinite programming. In the non-homogeneous convex case one loses the symmetry of the results in section 4, but sufficient analogues exist ([9], [47], [59]). The outline remains the same. One models the problem in an abstract setting and wishes to establish first abstract duality and second semi-infinite duality. As was exemplified in Section 5, if the one step is easy the other tends to be hard and conversely.

Alternatively, one may model the problem via convex perturbational duality methods [25], [59]. This has been outlined for limiting Lagrangians and perfect duality in [9]. The only additional result we give here is a reduction theorem for convex programs. The hypotheses can be somewhat relaxed. We first give an example.

Example 6.1. Consider the convex program

(6.1) $v := \inf\{f_0(x) \mid f_i(x) \le 0 \ (\forall i \in I),\ x \in C\}$

where $f_i\colon X \to \mathbb{R}$ for all $i \in \{0\} \cup I$ and C are convex. Let us suppose that v is finite and

(6.2) (i) $\sup_{i \in I} |f_i(x)| < \infty$, for all $x \in C$,

(6.2)

(ii) $f_i(\hat{x}) \le -\varepsilon$, $\forall i \in I$, <u>for some</u> $\varepsilon > 0$, $\hat{x} \in C$,

(iii) $(f_i(x)) \in \ell_\infty^- + c_0$, <u>for all</u> $x \in C$.

Condition (i) ensures that $F(x) := (f_i(x))$ defines an abstract convex function between X and $\ell_\infty(I)$. Condition (ii) is Slater's condition [49] in this setting. The abstract Lagrange multiplier theorem [10], [49] yields some $\mu \in (\ell_\infty^+)^+$ with

$$(6.3)\qquad v := \inf\{f_0(x) + (\mu F)(x) \mid x \in C\} .$$

Condition (iii) now guarantees that the analogous argument to that of Theorem 5.6 applies and that one may assume μ lies in ℓ_1^+ . Note that (iii) may be expressed as

$$\limsup_{i \in I} f_i(x) \le 0 \ , \ \forall x \in C .$$

Thus one has

$$(6.4)\qquad v = \inf\{f_0(x) + \sum_{i \in I} \mu_i f_i(x) \mid x \in C\} .$$

Again one wishes to replace μ by $\lambda \in \Lambda$. The following reduction theorem shows when one can do this.

<u>Theorem 6.2. Let</u> $f_i : X \to \mathbb{R}$ <u>be convex for</u> $i \in I \cup \{0\}$. <u>Suppose that</u> X <u>is finite dimensional and that</u> g , <u>defined by</u>

$$(6.5)\qquad g(x) := f_0(x) + \sum_{i \in I} \mu_i f_i(x) \ , \ \mu \in \ell_1^+ ,$$

<u>is a finite convex function and satisfies</u>

$$(6.6)\qquad g(x) \ge v$$

<u>for all</u> $x \in C$. <u>Then there exists</u> $\lambda \in \Lambda$ <u>such that for</u> $x \in C$

$$(6.7)\qquad f_0(x) + \sum_{i \in I} \lambda_i f_i(x) \ge v .$$

<u>Proof</u>. Since $\operatorname{supp} \mu$ is countable we assume that $\mu_i > 0$ and that $\{0\} \cup I = \mathbb{N}$. Since each f_i is continuous Fenchel's Theorem or the Sandwich Theorem [10], [25], [66] guarantees that there exist affine functions m_i such that

(6.8)
(i) $m_i \le f_i$

(ii) $m_0(x) + \sum_{i=1}^{n} \mu_i m_i(x) + \sum_{i=n+1}^{\infty} \mu_i f_i(x) \ge v$, for all $\forall x \in C$.

Let $r_n := \sum_{i=n+1}^{\infty} \mu_i f_i$ and let $S := co\{s_j | j \in J\}$ be a simplex in X with $0 \in \text{int } S$. Since (6.5) implies r_n converges pointwise to zero and as J is finite, one observes from (6.8) that

(6.9) $$z_n := (m_0(s_j) + \sum_{i=1}^{n} \mu_i m_i(s_j) | j \in J)$$

defines a bounded finite dimensional sequence, and so has a convergent subsequence $(z_{n(k)} | k \in \mathbb{N})$. Define $n(0) = 0$ and

(6.10) $$M_k := \sum_{i=n(k)+1}^{n(k+1)} \mu_i m_i / \rho_k ,$$

where

(6.11) $$\rho_k := \sum_{i=n(k)+1}^{n(k+1)} \mu_i .$$

Then $\sum_{k \in \mathbb{N}} \rho_k = \sum_{i \in \mathbb{N}} \mu_i < \infty$ and (6.9) shows that

$$v \le m_0(s_j) + \sum_{k=0}^{\infty} \rho_k M_k(s_j) ,$$

which sum exists for each $j \in J$. Since each M_k is affine this shows that

(6.12) $$m_0(x) + \sum_{k=0}^{\infty} \rho_k M_k(x) \ge v , \forall x \in X .$$

It is now relatively simple to deduce from Proposition 5.7 (or otherwise) that, for all x in X ,

(6.13) $$m_0(x) + \Sigma \lambda_k M_k(x) \ge v ,$$

for some $\lambda \in \Lambda$. Since $\rho_k M_k \le \sum_{i=m(k)+1}^{m(k+1)} \mu_i f_i$, (6.7) follows. □

Observe that Theorem 6.2 does apply to the functions in (6.4), and that semi-infinite duality is guaranteed by (6.2). This completes our example.

A similar development may be given for continuous convex programs. The corresponding reduction theorem follows from Theorem 2.1.

The differentiable semi-infinite problem is treated as follows. Firstly, one produces an associated linear or convex program involving derivatives. This usually requires some constraint qualification. Secondly, the associated program is handled by the results of one or more of the previous sections. The duality results of these sections become Kuhn-Tucker and Fritz John results for the differentiable program. Alternatively, the abstract duality theory may be developed directly as in [11], [30], [49] and then reduction theorems may be used to replace the abstract multipliers by members of Λ. As mentioned previously, higher order problems may be treated this way.

For many purposes it is most desirable to model a differentiable program in the setting of Example 5.2. There are at least two good reasons for this. Firstly, the value function of a semi-infinite program is not continuous in the product topology, while it is in the supremum topology when Slater's condition holds. Secondly, the corresponding reduction theorem (Theorem 5.3) is more generally applicable than is its ℓ_∞ counterpart. We conclude this section with a derivation of simple second order conditions for semi-infinite programming.

Example 6.3. Consider the program

$$(6.14) \qquad (DP) \qquad v(P) := \min\{f(x) \mid g(x,t) \le 0 \ (\forall t \in T)\} .$$

Let x_0 be a given feasible point with $f(x_0) = v(P)$. We suppose that X is finite dimensional and that T is compact. We suppose that f is twice continuously differentiable and that the functions $g(\cdot,t)$ are twice continuously differentiable, uniformly in $t \in T$. We also presume that g is jointly continuous. It follows from the uniformity assumptions that both the gradient $\nabla g(x_0,t)$ and the Hessian $\nabla^2 g(x_0,t)$ are continuous in t. Let us define the critical set [3], [33] by

$$(6.15) \qquad K(x_0) := \{h \in X \mid \langle\nabla f(x_0),h\rangle \le 0,\ \langle\nabla g(x_0,t),h\rangle + g(x_0,t) \le 0,\ \forall t \in T\} .$$

Theorem 6.4. Suppose that (DP) is as above and that there exists $\hat{h} \in X$ such that

$$(6.16) \qquad (CQ) \qquad \langle\nabla g(x_0,t),\hat{h}\rangle + g(x_0,t) < 0 \ , \ \forall t \in T .$$

Let $d \in \operatorname{cone} K(x_0)$. Then there exists $\lambda \in \Lambda$ with

$$(6.17) \qquad (i) \qquad \nabla f(x_0) + \sum_{t\in T} \lambda(t)\nabla g(x_0,t) = 0 ,$$

(6.18) (ii) $\nabla^2 f(x_0)(d,d) + \sum_{t\in T} \lambda(t)\nabla^2 g(x_0,t)(d,d) \geq 0$.

and

(6.19) (iii) (a) $\lambda(t)g(x_0,t) = 0$,

(b) $\lambda(t)\langle\nabla g(x_0,t),d\rangle = 0$.

Proof. There is no loss in assuming d lies in $K(x_0)$; this we do. Let $h \in X$, $x \in \mathbb{R}$ and define α on $\mathbb{R}_+$ by $\alpha(s) := x_0 + sd + s^2 h$. Let us set $G((h,r),t) := rg(x_0,t) + \langle\nabla g(x_0,t),h\rangle + \frac{1}{2}\nabla^2 g(x_0,t)(d,d)$. Then G is linear in (h,r) and continuous in t . Now a Taylor series expansion shows that (for fixed (h,r))

(6.20) $$g(\alpha(s),t) = (1-s-rs^2)g(x_0,t) + s(g(x_0,t) + \langle\nabla g(x_0,t),d\rangle) + s^2(rg(x_0,t) + \langle\nabla g(x_0,t),h\rangle + \frac{1}{2}\nabla^2 g(x_0,t)(d,d)) + o(s^2) ,$$

uniformly in t . For small $s, 1-s-rs^2$ is positive. Since $d \in K(x_0)$ and x_0 is feasible it follows that

(6.21) $$g(\alpha(s),t)+o(s^2) \leq 0, \ \forall t \in T \ \underline{\text{if}} \ G((h,r),t) \leq 0 , \ \forall t \in T .$$

Now (CQ) implies that g is regular at x_0 ([12], [35]) and so that

(6.22) $$g(\beta(s),t) \leq 0 , \ \forall t \in T ,$$

where $\alpha(s)-\beta(s) = o(s^2)$. This is also easy to establish directly. Now a similar expansion to (6.20) shows that

(6.23) $$f(\beta(s))-f(x_0) = s\langle\nabla f(x_0),d\rangle + s^2(\langle\nabla f(x_0),h\rangle + \frac{1}{2}\nabla^2 f(x_0)(d,d)) + o(s^2) .$$

Since $\beta(s)$ is feasible and $d \in K(x_0)$ it follows that

(6.24) $$F(h) := \langle\nabla f(x_0),h\rangle + \frac{1}{2}\nabla^2 f(x_0)(d,d) \geq 0 .$$

Thus we have shown that in the following continuous linear program

(6.25) (LP) $$0 = \min\{F(h) \mid G((h,r),t) \leq 0 , \ \forall t \in T\} .$$

The constraint qualification shows that $(n\hat{h},n)$ satisfies Slater's condition, for $n \in \mathbb{N}$ sufficiently large. By construction $G((h,r),\cdot)$ is continuous. It follows, either from Theorem 2.1 or from Example 5.2, that

$$(6.26)\qquad F(h) + \sum_{t\in T} \lambda(t)G((h,r),t) \geq 0 \quad \text{for all} \quad h \in X, r \in \mathbb{R} ,$$

for some $\lambda \in \Lambda$. Letting h and r range over X and $\mathbb{R}$ respectively shows that (6.17) and (6.19)(a) hold. Setting $h = 0$, $r = 0$ shows that (6.18) holds. Finally, as d lies in $K(x_0)$ and (6.17) and (6.19)(a) hold while λ is non-negative, one must have

$$(6.27)\qquad \sum_{t\in T} \lambda(t)(\langle\nabla g(x_0,t),d\rangle + g(x_0,t)) = 0 .$$

Because d lies in $K(x_0)$ and λ is non-negative this shows that

$$(6.28)\qquad \lambda(t)(\langle\nabla g(x_0,t),d\rangle + g(x_0,t)) = 0 .$$

In conjunction with (6.19(a), (6.28) gives (6.19)(b). □

Even if (6.16) fails, one may derive a Fritz John condition of the type in [49]. These results coincide with the differentiable inequality case of Ioffe's in [34] and extend the differentiable case in [3]. Our proof technique is somewhat simpler and can be extended to cover many second order non-smooth cases and more general constraints. Under the additional hypothesis that one may solve

$$(6.29)\qquad \langle\nabla g(x_0,t),z\rangle = \nabla^2 g(x_0,t)(d,d) , \ \forall t \in T ,$$

for each $d \in X$, it follows, as in [3], that the same $\lambda \in \Lambda$ will work for each $d \in K(x_0)$. Condition (6.29) is a generalization of McCormick's condition [52]. It certainly holds if $\nabla g(x_0,\cdot)$ is surjective, as does (6.16).

If X is infinite dimensional our development produces the same result with λ replaced by $\mu \in M^+(T)$.

7. Non smooth techniques.

These techniques are well exemplified in [3], [34], [55] amongst other places. We thus restrict ourselves to a very few observations on the process involved. The basic idea used is to study g given by

$$(7.1)\qquad g(x) := \sup_T g(x,t)$$

instead of the parametrized $g(\cdot,t)$. It is possible to give adequate or better descriptions of generalized gradients [16], [54], [55] and higher derivatives of g [3], [34] in terms of those for $g(\cdot,t)$ and thus to recover results for the semi-infinite program from those for

(7.2) $\quad v := \min\{f(x) \mid g(x) \le 0\}$.

This approach is not appropriate for convex or linear semi-infinite programming since it demands that the minimum in (7.2) be attained - to allow one to compute generalized gradients. Most, if not all, of the results obtainable this way can also be obtained by abstract techniques, but the real strength of the method lies in the growing development of a calculus for such non-smooth functions [16], [58]; and in the framework that this provides for the study of sensitivity theory, [33], [58].

Another advantage of the "max function" formulation is that it often allows one to study convergence theory for semi-infinite programming in terms of that for more general programming classes. For example, the cutting place methods of Gustafson and Kortanek [31] may be viewed as specializations of the convex cutting plane method of Kelley [1] applied to g given by (7.1).

8. Conclusion.

We have described two general techniques for the study of semi-infinite programs and indicated a third method. While the direct methods are in many ways more appealing, it is the author's feeling that most duality results about semi-infinite programming are best observed as exemplars of more general optimization schemes. This redounds to the advantage of both the semi-infinite example and the general model. From the viewpoint of application, however, the most appropriate framework is often that with the greatest intuitive content for the individual investigator. This, of course, depends both on the problem and the practitioner.

The results discussed in this paper by no means exhaust the field nor are the references comprehensive. The flavour I hope is authentic if somewhat idiosyncratic. Finally, I am indebted to Charles Blair, Dick Duffin, Bob Jeroslow and especially Ken Kortanek for many stimulating and provocative interchanges on this topic. The views and misviews of the subject expressed herein are my own; much of my understanding of the subject I owe to them.

References

(1) BAZARAA, M.S., AND C.M. SHETTY: Nonlinear Programming. New York: John Wiley, 1979.

(2) BEN-TAL, A., A. BEN-ISRAEL, AND E. ROSINGER: A Helly-type theorem and semi-infinite programming. Constructive Approaches to Mathematical Models. New York: Academic Press (1979), 127-135.

(3) BEN-TAL, A., M. TEBOULLE, AND J. ZOWE: Second order necessary optimality conditions for semi-infinite programming problems. Semi-Infinite Programming (edited by R. Hettich). Springer-Verlag, 1979.

(4) BLAIR, C.E.: A note on infinite systems of linear inequalities in R^n. J. Math. Anal. and Appl. 48(1) (1974), 150-154.

(5) BLAIR, C.E.: A survey of ascent ray results and their applications. This Proceedings.

(6) BLAIR, C.E., R.J. DUFFIN, AND R.G. JEROSLOW: A limiting infisup theorem. To appear in JOTA.

(7) BORWEIN, J.M.: Adjoint process duality. To appear in Math of Operations Research.

(8) BORWEIN, J.M.: Direct theorems in semi-infinite convex programming. Math. Programming 21 (1981), 301-318.

(9) BORWEIN, J.M.: A note on perfect duality and limiting Lagrangeans. Math. Programming 18 (1980), 330-337.

(10) BORWEIN, J.M.: A Lagrange multiplier theorem and a sandwich theorem for convex relations. Math. Scand 48 (1981), 189-204.

(11) BORWEIN, J.M.: Weak tangent cones and optimization in Banach spaces. SIAM J. Control Optimization 16 (3)(1978), 512-522.

(12) BORWEIN, J.M.: Convex relations in analysis and optimization. Generalized Concavity in Optimization and Economics. New York: Academic Press (1981), 335-377.

(13) BORWEIN, J.M.: The limiting Lagrangian as a consequence of Helly's Theorem. J.O.T.A. 33 (4)(1981), 497-513.

(14) CHARNES, A., W.W. COOPER, AND K.O. KORTANEK: Duality in semi-infinite programs and some works of Haar and Caratheodory. Management Science 9 (1963), 209-229.

(15) CHARNES, A., W.W. COOPER, AND K.O. KORTANEK: On representations of semi-infinite programs which have no duality gaps. Management Science 12 (1965), 113-121.

(16) CLARKE, F.H.: Generalized gradients and applications. Trans. Amer. Math. Soc. 205 (1975), 245-262.

(17) CRAVEN, B.D.: Mathematical Programming and Control Theory. London: Chapman and Hall, 1978.

(18) CYBENKO, G.: Affine minimax problems and semi-infinite programming. To appear.

(19) DAY, M.M.: Normed linear spaces, 3rd edition. Springer-Verlag, 1973.

(20) DUFFIN, R.J.: Convex analysis treated by linear programming. Mathematical Programming 4 (1973), 125-143.

(21) DUFFIN, R.J. AND R.G. JEROSLOW: Lagrangean functions and affine minorants. Mathematical Programming Study 14 (1981), 48-60.

(22) DUFFIN, R.J. AND L.A. KARLOVITZ: An infinite linear program with a duality gap. Management Science 12 (1965), 122-134.

(23) DUFFIN, R.J., L.A. KARLOVITZ AND R.G. JEROSLOW: Uniform duality in semi-infinite linear programming. To appear.

(24) ECKHARDT, U.: Theorems on the dimension of convex sets. Linear Algebra and its Applications 12 (1975), 63-76.

(25) EKELAND, I. AND R. TEMAM: Convex Analysis and Variational Problems. Amsterdam: North-Holland, 1976.

(26) FAN, KY: Asymptotic cones and duality of linear relations. J. Appr. Theory 2 (1969), 152-159.

(27) FIACCO, A.V. AND G.P. MCCORMICK: Nonlinear Programming: Sequential Unconstrained Minimization Techniques. New York: John Wiley, 1968.

(28) FLACHS, J.: Saddle-point theorems for rational approximation. CSIR Technical Report, TWISK 219 (1981).

(29) GLASHOFF, K.: Duality theory of semi-infinite programming. Semi-Infinite Programming (edited by R. Hettich). Springer-Verlag, 1979.

(30) GUIGNARD, M.: Generalized Kuhn-Tucker conditions for mathematical programming in a Banach space. SIAM J. Control 7 (1969), 232-241.

(31) GUSTAFSON, S.-A. AND K. KORTANEK: Numerical Solution of a class of semi-infinite programming problems. NRLQ 20 (1973), 477-504.

(32) HOLMES, R.B.: Geometric Functional Analysis. New York: Springer-Verlag, 1975.

(33) IOFFE, A.D.: Necessary and sufficient conditions for a local minimimum. SIAM J. Control Optimization 17 (1979), 245-288.

(34) IOFFE, A.D.: Second-order conditions in nonlinear nonsmooth problems of semi-infinite programming. This proceedings.

(35) IOFFE, A.D.: Regular points of Lipschitz functions. Trans. A.M.S. 251 (1979), 61-69.

(36) JAMESON, G.J.: Ordered Linear Spaces. Lecture Notes in Math 141. New York: Springer-Verlag, 1970.

(37) JEROSLOW, R.G.: A limiting Lagrangian for infinitely-constrained convex optimization in R^n. J.O.T.A. 33 (1981), 479-495.

(38) JEROSLOW, R.G.: Uniform duality in convex semi-infinite problems. To appear.

(39) KARLIN, S.J. AND W.J. STUDDEN: Tchebycheff Systems: with Applications in Analysis and Statistics. New York: John Wiley, 1966.

(40) KARNEY, D.F.: Asymptotic convex duality. To appear.

(41) KARNEY, D.F.: Duality gaps in semi-infinite linear programming - an approximation problem. Math. Programming 20 (1981), 129-143.

(42) KLEE, V.: The critical set of a convex body. American Journal of Mathematics 75 (1953), 178-188.

(43) KORTANEK, K.O.: Constructing a perfect duality in infinite programming. Applied Mathematics and Optimization 3 (1977), 357-372.

(44) KRABS, W.: Optimization and Approximation. New York: John Wiley, 1979.

(45) KRETSCHMER, K.S.: Programming in paired spaces. Canadian J. Math. 16 (1961), 221-238.

(46) LUCAS, R.E. AND E.C. PRESCOTT: A note on price systems in infinite dimensional space. International Economic Review 13 (1972), 416-422.

(47) LEVINE, P. AND J.-Ch. POMEROL: Sufficient conditions for Kuhn-Tucker vectors in convex programming. SIAM J. Control Optimization 17 (1979), 689-699.

(48) LEVINSON, N.: A class of continuous linear programming problems. J. Math. Anal. Appl. 16 (1966), 73-83.

(49) LUENBERGER, D.G.: Optimization by Vector Space Methods. New York: John Wiley, 1969.

(50) MAURER, H. AND J. ZOWE: Second order necessary and sufficient conditions for infinite dimensional programming problems. Math. Programming 16 (1979), 641-652.

(51) MOREAU, J.J.: Fonctionelles convexes. Equation aux dérivées partielles. Séminaire J. Leray, College de France, 1966.

(52) MCCORMICK, G.P.: Second order conditions for constrained minima. SIAM J. Applied Math. 15 (1967), 641-652.

(53) NAKAMURA, T. AND M. YAMASAKI: Sufficient conditions for duality theorems in infinite linear programming problems. Hiroshima Math. J. 9 (1979), 323-334.

(54) PENOT, J.P.: Calcul sous-differential et optimisation. J. Funct. Anal. Appl. 27 (1978), 248-276.

(55) PSHENICHNYI, B.N.: Necessary conditions for an extremum. New York: Marcel Dekker, 1971.

(56) PONSTEIN, J.: On the use of purely finitely additive multipliers in mathematical programming, J.O.T.A. 33 (1981), 37-55.

(57) ROCKAFELLAR, R.T. AND R.J.-B. WETS: The optimal recourse problem in discrete time, L^1-multipliers for inequality constraints. SIAM J. on Control and Optimization 16 (1978), 16-36.

(58) ROCKAFELLAR, R.T.: The Theory of Subgradients and its Applications to Problems of Optimization, Convex and Non-Convex Functions. Berlin: Helderman Verlag, 1981.

(59) ROCKAFELLAR, R.T.: Conjugate Duality and Optimization, Philadelphia: SIAM Publications, 1974.

(60) ROCKAFELLAR, R.T.: Helly's theorem and minima of convex functions. Duke Mathematical Journal 32 (1965), 381-397.

(61) ROCKAFELLAR, R.T.: Convex Analysis. Princeton: Princeton Univ. Press, 1970.

(62) ROGOSINSKI, W.W.: Moments of non-negative mass. Proc. Roy. Soc. (London), Series A 245 (1958), 1-27.

(63) RUDIN, W.: Functional Analysis. New York: McGraw-Hill, 1973.

(64) TIJS, S.H. AND J.M. BORWEIN: Some generalizations of Caratheodory's theorem via baycentres, with application to mathematical programming. Canad. Math. Bull. 23 (1980), 339-346.

(65) YAMASAKI, M.: Duality theorems in mathematical programming and their applications. J. Sci. Hiroshima Univ. 30 (1968), 331-356.

(66) ZOWE, J.: Sandwich theorems for convex operators with values in an ordered vector space. J. Math. Anal. and Appl. 66 (1978), 292-296.

A SADDLE VALUE CHARACTERIZATION OF FAN'S EQUILIBRIUM POINTS

A. Charnes, K. O. Kortanek and V. Lovegren

Abstract. A fixed-point, equilibrium problem of Fan (1959, [6]) involves lists of convex functions $f = (f_1,...,f_n)$ and concave functions $g = (g_1,...,g_n)$, respectively, defined over the simplex S which have certain positivity properties. A real number λ^* is termed an <u>equilibrium value</u> of the system $\{f,g\}$ if and only if there exists a point z^*, termed an <u>equilibrium point</u>, satisfying $g(z^*) = \lambda^* f(z^*)$. Fan shows that λ^* exists and is positive and that z^* is unique such that $\lambda^{*-1} = \max_{\alpha \in S} \min_{z \in S} \frac{\alpha^T f(z)}{\alpha^T g(z)}$.

In this paper we consider the biextremal problem $V_M(\lambda) = \max_{\alpha \in S} \min_{z \in S} \alpha^T[\lambda f(z) - g(z)]$ for $\lambda \geq 0$ and develop a dual pair of (uniextremal) separably-infinite programs which is equivalent to the biextremization. We show that the pair is in perfect duality with attainment, and that it yields a saddle point of the saddle value problem. By establishing the (Lipschitz) continuity of $V_M(\cdot)$ and using the Fan assumptions we show that $V_M(\cdot)$ has a unique zero. In this case one of the separably-infinite programs recovers the Fan equilibrium point, also shown to be part of a saddle point of ratio game, $\frac{\alpha^T f(z)}{\alpha^T g(z)}$.

1. Introduction: A Biextremal Formulation

In 1953 A. Charnes [2] showed how directly from the data a bilinear saddle value problem with polyhedral constraints could be replaced with a pair of uniextremal dual linear programming problems. The original saddle value problem is as follows.

<u>For a given</u> $m \times n$ <u>matrix</u> A,

<u>find</u> $\max_{p \in \mathbb{R}^m} \min_{q \in \mathbb{R}^n} p^T A q$

This research was partly supported by ONR Contract N00014-75-C-0569 with the Center for Cybernetic Studies, The University of Texas at Austin, and National Science Foundation Grant ECS80-26777 at Carnegie-Mellon University.

subject to (I) (II)

$$\sum_{i=1}^{m} p_i = 1 \qquad \sum_{j=1}^{n} q_j = 1$$

$$p^T D \leq d^T \qquad Bq \geq b \tag{1}$$

$$p \geq 0 \qquad q \geq 0$$

where D is an $m \times r$ matrix, B is an $s \times n$ matrix, $d \in \mathbb{R}^r$, and $b \in \mathbb{R}^s$.

By means of a new construct "separably-infinite programming", Charnes, Gribik, and Kortanek [4] developed a uniextremal duality for a general kind of separability and functional bilinearity in the saddle function, namely find

$$\sup_{p \in P} \inf_{q \in Q} F(p,q) := \sum_{j=1}^{n'} \sum_{i=1}^{m'} g_i(p) a_{ij} h_j(q) \tag{2}$$

where each g_i is closed concave, each h_j is closed convex, and where $F(\cdot,q)$ is concave for each fixed q and $F(p,\cdot)$ is convex for each fixed p, and where P and Q are arbitrary closed convex sets in $\mathbb{R}^m$ and $\mathbb{R}^n$ respectively, and n',m' are fixed positive integers, [5]. In addition, all functions are assumed to be proper.

Building on these recent developments we investigate a class of equilibrium problems of Fan [6] which is related to ratio games and certain economic growth models of von Neumann. Our approach will be to study the Fan problem by means of a biextremal problem formulation of the type (2) above.

The Fan problem is the following one.

Let S denote the $(n-1)$ dimensional simplex: $z_i \geq 0$, $i = 1,\ldots,n$; $\Sigma_{i=1}^{n} z_i = 1$, and $S_i = \{z \in S \mid z_i = 0\}$ for $i = 1,\ldots,n$. A system of $2n$ real valued functions $f \equiv (f_1,\ldots,f_n)$, $g \equiv (g_1,\ldots,g_n)$ is specified on S having the following properties:

(a) each f_i is continuous and convex on S,

(b) each g_i is continuous and concave and positive on S,

(c) $f_i(z) \leq 0$ for $z \in S_i$, $i = 1,\ldots,n$, and

(d) for each $z \in S$, there is an index i for which $f_i(z) > 0$.

Definition. A real number λ^* will be called an equilibrium value of the system $\{f,g\}$ iff there exists a point $z^* \in S$, termed an equilibrium point which satisfies the n equations,

$$g_i(z^*) = \lambda^* f_i(z^*), \qquad i = 1,\ldots,n. \tag{3}$$

Under assumptions (a) - (d), Fan proved that (f,g) has a unique equilibrium value λ^* which is positive, and that it has a unique equilibrium point z^*, all $z_i^* > 0$ such that

$$\lambda^{*-1} = \max_{\alpha \in S} \min_{z \in S} \frac{\alpha^T f(z)}{\alpha^T g(z)} .$$

The basic biextremal problem which we employ for the Fan equilibrium problem is the following one.

$$V_M(\lambda) = \max_{\alpha \in S} \min_{z \in S} L_\lambda(\alpha, z), \tag{4}$$

where $L_\lambda(\alpha,z) = \alpha^T[\lambda f(z) - g(z)]$ and where λ is non-negative. Since the set S is compact, it is well known that $L_\lambda(\alpha,z)$ has a saddle point. However, in this paper we develop an equivalent dual pair of uniextremal separably-infinite programs for $V_M(\lambda)$ and show that the pair is in perfect duality with attainment and that it yields a saddle point for $L_\lambda(\alpha,z)$. This is an extension of the Charnes result of 1953 [2]. We straightforwardly establish Lipschitz continuity of $V_M(\cdot)$, and together with assumptions (a) - (d) we show that $V_M(\cdot)$ has a unique zero, λ^*. In this case, we use Fan's Corollaries to show that λ^* is the Fan equilibrium value and that any saddle point of $L_{\lambda^*}(\alpha,z)$ recovers the Fan equilibrium point z^*, as does one of the separably-infinite programs of the dual pair. It is then straightforward to demonstrate that λ^{*-1} is the saddle value of the ratio game $\dfrac{\alpha^T f(z)}{\alpha^T g(z)}$.

2. A Separably-Infinite, Biextremal Formulation of the Fan Equilibrium Problem

Notations for supporting hyperplane representations are introduced first for (4) above, where it shall be assumed that S is contained in the domain of each f_i and each g_i, and each function is closed and proper.

2.1. Epigraph of convex function f_i; $q_0^i \geq f_i(z)$:
$u_0^i(\beta)q_0^i + u^i(\beta)^T z \geq u_{n+1}^i(\beta)$, where $u^i(\beta) \in \mathbb{R}^n$,
$u_0^i(\beta)$, $u_{n+1}^i(\beta) \in \mathbb{R}$, $u_0^i(\beta) \geq 0$, for all $\beta \in S$.

2.2. Hypograph of concave function g_i; $p_0^i \leq g_i(z)$:
$v_0^i(\beta')p_0^i + v^i(\beta')^T z \leq v_{n+1}^i(\beta')$, where $v^i(\beta') \in \mathbb{R}^n$,
$v_0^i(\beta')$, $v_{n+1}^i(\beta') \in \mathbb{R}$, $v_0^i(\beta') \geq 0$ for all $\beta' \in S$.

Analogous to Borwein and Kortanek [1], we define

$$I_i^0 = \{\beta \in S \mid u_0^i(\beta) > 0\}$$

and write,

$$f_i(z) = \begin{cases} \sup\limits_{\beta \in I_i^0} \left\{ \dfrac{u_{n+1}^i(\beta) - u^i(\beta)^T z}{u_0^i(\beta)} \right\}, & \text{if } u^i(\beta)^T z \geq u_{n+1}^i(\beta) \\ & \text{whenever } u_0^i(\beta) = 0 \\ +\infty, & \text{otherwise.} \end{cases}$$

Similarly for g_i we set $J_i^0 = \{\beta' \in S \mid v_0^i(\beta') > 0\}$ and obtain

$$g_i(z) = \begin{cases} \inf\limits_{\beta' \in J_i^0} \left\{ \dfrac{v_{n+1}^i(\beta') - v^i(\beta')^T z}{v_0^i(\beta')} \right\}, & \text{if } v^i(\beta')^T z \leq v_{n+1}^i(\beta') \\ & \text{whenever } v_0^i(\beta') = 0 \\ -\infty, & \text{otherwise.} \end{cases}$$

Because of the properness assumption, I_i^0 and $J_i^0 \neq \emptyset$ for each i.

Now the epigraph of the convex function (λ fixed and non-negative) given by $h_{i,\lambda}(x) = \lambda f_i(x) - g_i(x)$ can be constructed in a natural way from 2.1. and 2.2. With the introduction of these supporting hyper-planes, (4) is then equivalent to:

<u>Find</u> $$V_M(\lambda) = \max_{\alpha} \min_{q_0, p_0, z} \alpha^T [\lambda I_n \mid -I_n \mid \underset{\approx}{0}] \begin{bmatrix} q_0 \\ p_0 \\ z \end{bmatrix}$$

<u>subject to</u>

$$\begin{bmatrix} e_i^T u_0^i(\beta) & \underset{\sim}{0}^T & u^i(\beta)^T \\ \underset{\sim}{0}^T & -e_i^T v_0^i(\beta') & -v^i(\beta')^T \\ \underset{\sim}{0}^T & \underset{\sim}{0}^T & e_i^T \\ \underset{\sim}{0}^T & \underset{\sim}{0}^T & e^T \end{bmatrix} \begin{bmatrix} q_0 \\ p_0 \\ z \end{bmatrix} \geq \begin{bmatrix} u_{n+1}^i(\beta) \\ -v_{n+1}^i(\beta') \\ \underset{\sim}{0} \\ 1 \end{bmatrix} \tag{5}$$

<u>for all</u> $\beta, \beta' \in S$, $i = 1,\ldots,n$

<u>and</u> $\alpha \geq 0$, $\alpha^T e = 1$ <u>where</u> $e^T = (1,\ldots,1)$, $e_i^T = (0,\ldots,1,\ldots,0)$ (6)

(with 1 in position i) are all n-vectors, where $\underset{\sim}{0}$ is the zero n-vector, and $\underset{\approx}{0}$ is the zero $n \times n$ matrix. Denote the set of $(q_0, p_0, z) \in \mathbb{R}^{3n}$ satisfying (5) by Q.

In addition, the last inequality in (5) is meant to be an equality, which will be clear by unconstraining its dual variable in sign.

One can see how (5) is a generalization of (1) where now the 3n-vector (q_0, p_0, z) replaces the n-vector q of (1) and the semi-infinite inequality system (5) replaces the finite system $Bq \geq b$ of (1). On the other hand the structure of the α-variables in (6) is simpler than the structure of the p-variables in (1).

3. Equivalent Dual Pair of Separably-Infinite Programs

The following pair of programs is a specialization respectively of the pair of Programs I and II in Section 3 of Charnes, Gribik, and Kortanek [5]. The pair is valid for any finite lists of closed and proper convex functions f_i and closed proper concave functions g_i, respectively, defined over S.

Program I

Find
$$V_I(\lambda) = \sup \sum_{i,\beta} y_i^{(1)}(\beta) u_{n+1}^i(\beta) - \sum_{i,\beta'} y_i^{(2)}(\beta') v_{n+1}^i(\beta') + \theta_0$$

where $y_i^{(1)}(\cdot)$, $y_i^{(2)}(\cdot)$ are generalized finite sequences over S; $\{\theta_\ell\}_{\ell=0}^n \in \mathbb{R}^{n+1}$, $\alpha \in \mathbb{R}^n$ subject to the inequalities (6) above and

$$\sum_{i,\beta} \begin{bmatrix} e_i u_0^i(\beta) \\ \underset{\sim}{0} \\ u^i(\beta) \end{bmatrix}^T y_i^{(1)}(\beta) - \sum_{i,\beta'} \begin{bmatrix} \underset{\sim}{0} \\ e_i v_0^i(\beta') \\ v^i(\beta') \end{bmatrix}^T y_i^{(2)}(\beta') + \sum_{i=1}^n \begin{bmatrix} \underset{\sim}{0} \\ \underset{\sim}{0} \\ e_i \end{bmatrix}^T \theta_i$$

$$+ \begin{bmatrix} \underset{\sim}{0} \\ \underset{\sim}{0} \\ e \end{bmatrix}^T \theta_0 - \alpha^T \left[\lambda I_n \,\middle|\, -I_n \,\middle|\, \underset{\approx}{0} \right] = \begin{bmatrix} \underset{\sim}{0} \\ \underset{\sim}{0} \\ \underset{\sim}{0} \end{bmatrix}^T$$

(equation among vectors in 3n-space)

and $y_i^{(1)}(\cdot) \geq 0$, $y_i^{(2)}(\cdot) \geq 0$, $\theta_i \geq 0$ for $i = 1,\ldots,n$.

Observe that θ_0 is unconstrained in sign corresponding to the intended equality of the last inequality in (5).

Program II

Find $\quad V_{II}(\lambda) = \inf x_0$

from among $\{x_i\}_{i=0}^{n} \in \mathbb{R}^{n+1}$, q_0, p_0, z each in $\mathbb{R}^n$

subject to the (semi-infinite) inequalities (5) above and

$$- [\lambda I_n \mid -I_n \mid \underset{\sim}{0}] \begin{bmatrix} q_0 \\ p_0 \\ z \end{bmatrix} + \sum_{i=1}^{n} (-e_i)x_i + ex_0 = \underset{\sim}{0} \tag{8}$$

and $x_i \geq 0$ for $i = 1,\ldots,n$.

To see the specialization of [5], let $A = [\lambda I_n \mid -I_n \mid \underset{\sim}{0}]$, appearing in (8) and observe that the maximizing variables α lie in S while the minimizing variables lie in Q. The convex cone C of coefficients of the minimizing variables is spanned by:

$$\begin{bmatrix} e_i u_0^i(\beta) \\ \underset{\sim}{0} \\ u^i(\beta) \\ -u_{n+1}^i(\beta) \end{bmatrix}, \begin{bmatrix} \underset{\sim}{0} \\ -e_i v_0^i(\beta') \\ -v^i(\beta') \\ v_{n+1}^i(\beta') \end{bmatrix}, \begin{bmatrix} \underset{\sim}{0} \\ \underset{\sim}{0} \\ e_i \\ 0 \end{bmatrix}_i, \begin{bmatrix} \underset{\sim}{0} \\ \underset{\sim}{0} \\ e \\ -1 \end{bmatrix}, \begin{bmatrix} \underset{\sim}{0} \\ \underset{\sim}{0} \\ \underset{\sim}{0} \\ 1 \end{bmatrix}_{\beta,\beta' \in S.} \tag{9}$$

Observe that in the maximizing player I's problem the α-decision variables are augmented by (i) generalized finite sequences $y_i^{(1)}(\cdot)$, $y_i^{(2)}(\cdot)$ associated with semi-infinite inequalities in (5) of Player II's constraint set and (ii) $\{\theta_\ell\}_{\ell=0}^{n}$ associated with the last $n + 1$ inequalities in (5). Analogously, the minimizing Player II's (q_0,p_0,z)-decision variables are augmented with $\{x_i\}_{i=0}^{n}$, associated with Player I's constraint set (6).

We now prove perfect duality and attainment.

Theorem 1. Assume that the convex cone spanned by (9) is closed. Then for any $\lambda \geq 0$,

$$V_I(\lambda) = V_{II}(\lambda) = V_M(\lambda),$$

with attainment in each of three programs. Moreover, this common value is the saddle value of $L_\lambda(\alpha,z)$, and any $\hat{\alpha}$ which is part of an optimal solution to $V_I(\lambda)$ and any $\hat{z}$ which is part of an optimal solution to $V_{II}(\lambda)$ together comprise a saddle point of $L_\lambda(\alpha,z)$.

Proof. The convex cone of coefficients of the α-variables is closed since it is finitely generated, while by assumption the convex cone spanned by (9) is closed.

According to Theorem 3 [5] and Proposition 3 [1], it suffices to verify the following two conditions in order to establish perfect duality between $V_I(\lambda)$ and $V_{II}(\lambda)$ and the existence of a saddle point to $L_\lambda(\alpha,z)$.

Condition 1.

$$\alpha \in 0^+S \quad \text{and} \quad \alpha^T[\lambda I_n \mid -I_n \mid \underset{\approx}{0}]\begin{pmatrix} q_0 \\ p_0 \\ z \end{pmatrix} \geq 0$$

for all $(q_0, p_0, z) \in Q$ implies

$$-\alpha \in 0^+S \quad \text{and} \quad -\alpha^T[\lambda I_n \mid -I_n \mid \underset{\approx}{0}]\begin{pmatrix} q_0 \\ p_0 \\ z \end{pmatrix} \geq 0$$

for all $(q_0, p_0, z) \in Q$.

But $0^+S = \{0\}$, so condition 1 holds trivially. Condition 1 itself implies

$$V_I(\lambda) = V_{II}(\lambda) = V_M(\lambda)$$

and that $V_I(\lambda)$ is attained.

Condition 2.

$$(q_0, p_0, z) \in 0^+Q \quad \text{and} \quad \alpha^T[\lambda I_n \mid -I_n \mid \underset{\approx}{0}]\begin{pmatrix} q_0 \\ p_0 \\ z \end{pmatrix} \leq 0 \tag{10a}$$

for all $\alpha \in S$ implies

$$-(q_0, p_0, z) \in 0^+Q \quad \text{and} \quad \alpha^T[\lambda I_n \mid -I_n \mid \underset{\approx}{0}]\begin{pmatrix} -q_0 \\ -p_0 \\ -z \end{pmatrix} \leq 0 \tag{10b}$$

for all $\alpha \in S$.

But $(q_0, p_0, z) \in 0^+Q$ implies that it satisfies the homogenization of (5), in particular, $e^T z = 0$. From this, one first observes that $z = 0$. From $z = 0$ and the non-emptiness of both I_i^0 and J_i^0 (for each i), it follows that

$$q_0^i \geq 0 \quad \text{and} \quad p_0^i \leq 0, \qquad i = 1,2,\ldots,n.$$

Now from (10a) we obtain

$$\sum_{i=1}^{n} \alpha_i(\lambda q_0^i - p_0^i) \leq 0 \quad \text{for all} \quad \alpha \in S,$$

which implies $\lambda q_0^i - p_0^i \leq 0$, $i = 1,\ldots,n$. Since $\lambda \geq 0$, it follows that

$$\lambda q_0^i = p_0^i = 0.$$

Hence $\lambda q_0 = p_0 = z = \underset{\sim}{0}$, and so (10a) implies (10b) trivially. Condition 2 itself implies that

$$V_I(\lambda) = V_{II}(\lambda) = V_M(\lambda)$$

and that $V_{II}(\lambda)$ is attained. Both conditions together imply attainment in all three programs and the required saddle value equality $\max_\alpha \min_z L_\lambda(\alpha,z) = \min_z \max_\alpha L_\lambda(\alpha,z)$. ■

Canonical closure of the linear inequality system (5) is a sufficient condition for C to be closed, see Charnes, Cooper, Kortanek [3] and Glashoff [7], and as is well known canonically closed representations always exist.

<u>Theorem 2</u>. $V_M(\lambda)$ is Lipschitz continuous in λ for $\lambda \geq 0$, i.e., there exists a positive number L such that

$$|V_M(\lambda_1) - V_M(\lambda_2)| \leq L|\lambda_1 - \lambda_2|$$

whenever $\lambda_1 \geq 0$ and $\lambda_2 \geq 0$.

<u>Proof</u>. Using $L_\lambda(\alpha,z)$ introduced in (4), we see that for $\lambda_1 \geq 0$, $\lambda_2 \geq 0$

$$L_{\lambda_1}(\alpha,z) - L_{\lambda_2}(\alpha,z) = \alpha^T f(z)(\lambda_1 - \lambda_2).$$

Hence $L_{\lambda_1}(\alpha,z) \leq L_{\lambda_2}(\alpha,z) + |\lambda_1 - \lambda_2|L$, where

$$L = (\max_{\alpha \in S} \|\alpha\|)(\max_{z \in S} \|f(z)\|).$$

Hence, for each fixed α we have

$$\min_{z \in S} L_{\lambda_1}(\alpha,z) \leq \min_{z \in S} L_{\lambda_2}(\alpha,z) + |\lambda_1 - \lambda_2|L$$

and therefore, maximizing over α yields

$$\max_{\alpha \in S} \min_{z \in S} L_{\lambda_1}(\alpha,z) \leq \max_{\alpha \in S} \min_{z \in S} L_{\lambda_2}(\alpha,z) + |\lambda_1 - \lambda_2|L$$

i.e.,

$$V_M(\lambda_1) \leq V_M(\lambda_2) + |\lambda_1 - \lambda_2|L. \tag{11}$$

Reversing the roles of λ_1 and λ_2 yields

$$V_M(\lambda_2) \leq V_M(\lambda_1) + |\lambda_1 - \lambda_2|L, \tag{12}$$

and (11) and (12) yield

$$-|\lambda_1 - \lambda_2|L \leq V_M(\lambda_1) - V_M(\lambda_2) \leq |\lambda_1 - \lambda_2|L. \quad ■$$

4. The Fan Equilibrium as the Unique Zero of $V_M(\cdot)$

We first establish the existence of a zero.

Theorem 3. There is a positive number λ_0 such that $V_M(\lambda_0) = 0$.

Proof. We use the facts that $g_0(z) := \max_i\{-g_i(z)\}$ is a negative continuous function on S, while $f_0(z) := \max_i\{f_i(z)\}$ is a positive continuous function on S. In particular, there exists $z^* \in S$ such that $\min_z f_0(z) = f_0(z^*) > 0$. We see first by Theorem 1 that

$$V_M(0) = \min_z \max_\alpha\{-\sum_{i=1}^n \alpha_i g_i(z)\} = \min_z g_0(z) < 0.$$

On the other hand,

$$V_M(\lambda) = \min_z \max_\alpha\{\sum_{i=1}^n \alpha_i[\lambda f_i(z) - g_i(z)]\} = \min_z \max_i\{\lambda f_i(z) - g_i(z)\}.$$

Since S is compact and each g_i is continuous on S, there exists a positive K such that $g_i(z) \le K$ for $i = 1,\ldots,n$.

Hence, for each $z \in S$

$$\lambda f_i(z) - g_i(z) \ge \lambda f_i(z) - K, \qquad i = 1,\ldots,n,$$

which implies that

$$\max_i\{\lambda f_i(z) - g_i(z)\} \ge \lambda \max_i f_i(z) - K \quad \text{for all } z \in S.$$

Hence, $V_M(\lambda) \ge \lambda \min_z f_0(z) - K = \lambda f_0(z^*) - K$, and for any $\bar{\lambda} > K/f_0(z^*)$ it follows that $V_M(\bar{\lambda}) > 0$. Therefore, by continuity of $V_M(\cdot)$, there exists λ_0, $0 < \lambda_0 < \bar{\lambda}$ such that $V_M(\lambda_0) = 0$. ■

We now use portions of Fan's Corollaries 1 through 3 [6], §11 to show that λ_0 is uniquely determined and that the Fan equilibrium point is the only saddle point of $V_M(\lambda_0)$.

Corollaries 1, 2, and 3; Fan [6], §11.

Let λ^* be the Fan equilibrium value and z^* the equilibrium point (3) of $\{f_1,\ldots,f_n;g_1,\ldots,g_n\}$, and let ρ be any positive number. Then the following hold.

(i) $z = z^*$ is the only solution $z \in S$ of the system of inequalities

$$\lambda^* f_i(z) \le g_i(z), \qquad i = 1,\ldots,n.$$

(ii) $\rho < \lambda^*$ if and only if there exists $\bar{z} \in S$ such that

$$\rho f_i(\bar{z}) - g_i(\bar{z}) < 0, \qquad i = 1,\ldots,n,$$

and

(iii) $\rho > \lambda^*$ if and only if there exist n positive numbers $\bar{\alpha}_i$ such that

$$\sum_{i=1}^{n} \bar{\alpha}_i [\rho f_i(z) - g_i(z)] > 0 \quad \text{for all} \quad z \in S.$$

<u>Theorem 4</u>. There is only one non-negative zero of $V_M(\cdot)$, λ_0, and it equals the Fan equilibrium value λ^*. Any saddle point of $V_M(\lambda^*)$ is of the form $(\bar{\alpha}, z^*)$, where z^* is the Fan equilibrium point and $\bar{\alpha} \in S$.

<u>Proof</u>. In Corollaries 2 and 3 above set $\rho = \lambda_0$. If $\lambda_0 > \lambda^*$, then using (iii) we write

$$V_M(\lambda_0) = \max_{\alpha} \min_{z} \sum_{i} \alpha_i [\lambda_0 f_i(z) - g_i(z)] \geq \min_{z} \sum_{i} \bar{\alpha}_i [\lambda_0 f_i(z) - g_i(z)] > 0,$$

contradicting $V_M(\lambda_0) = 0$. Hence $\lambda_0 \leq \lambda^*$.

Assume that $\lambda_0 < \lambda^*$, and let $(\bar{\alpha}, \bar{z})$ denote a saddle point of $V_M(\lambda_0)$, i.e.,

$$\sum_{i=1}^{n} \alpha_i [\lambda_0 f_i(\bar{z}) - g_i(\bar{z})] \leq V_M(\lambda_0) \leq \sum_{i=1}^{n} \bar{\alpha}_i [\lambda_0 f_i(z) - g_i(z)] \tag{13}$$

for all $\alpha \in S$ and $z \in S$.

Since each $\bar{\alpha}_i \geq 0$ and $\Sigma_{i=1}^{n} \bar{\alpha}_i = 1$, property (ii) above and the right-most inequality of (13) imply that $V_M(\lambda_0) < 0$ which is of course a contradiction. Hence, $\lambda_0 = \lambda^*$, completing the proof of the first part of the theorem.

The final part of the proof uses the left-most inequality of (13), namely (with $\lambda_0 = \lambda^*$ established):

$$\sum_{i} \alpha_i [\lambda^* f_i(\bar{z}) - g_i(\bar{z})] \leq V_M(\lambda^*) = 0, \tag{14}$$

for all $\alpha_i \geq 0$, $\sum_i \alpha_i = 1$. But setting $\alpha^k = (0,\dots,1,\dots,0)$, 1 is in the kth position, $k = 1,\dots,n$, implies from (14) that

$$\lambda^* f_i(\bar{z}) \leq g_i(\bar{z}), \qquad i = 1,\dots,n. \tag{15}$$

But by (i) above $\bar{z} = z^*$ is the only solution to the inequality system (15). Hence $\bar{z} = z^*$. ■

5. <u>The Fan Equilibrium Value as Saddle Value of a Ratio Game</u>

In Theorem 2 of §11 [6], Fan establishes

$$\lambda^{*-1} = \max_{\alpha} \min_{z} \frac{\sum_i \alpha_i f_i(z)}{\sum_i \alpha_i g_i(z)} . \tag{16}$$

Viewing the ratio in (16) as a payoff function, (16) itself is a result on the value of a ratio game. The next theorem gives more on the value of this game.

Theorem 5. Let λ^* denote the Fan equilibrium value of the system $\{f_1,\ldots,f_n;g_1,\ldots,g_n\}$. Then λ^{*-1} is the saddle value of the ratio game having payoff function,

$$K(\alpha,z) = \frac{\alpha^T f(z)}{\alpha^T g(z)} .$$

Proof. Let (α^*,z^*) be a saddle point of $V_M(\lambda)$.

Then it follows from the saddle value inequalities (13) in particular that

$$\lambda^*\alpha^T f(z^*) \leq \alpha^T g(z^*) \text{ for all } \alpha \in S,$$

where in addition the right-side is positive for each $\alpha \in S$. Hence

$$\frac{\alpha^T f(z^*)}{\alpha^T g(z^*)} \leq \lambda^{*-1} \quad \text{for all } \alpha \in S. \tag{17}$$

Now the right-side of the saddle value inequalities (13) reads,

$$\alpha^{*T} g(z) \leq \lambda^*\alpha^{*T} f(z) \quad \text{for all } z \in S$$

and so

$$\lambda^{*-1} \leq \frac{\alpha^{*T} f(z)}{\alpha^{*T} g(z)} \quad \text{for all } z \in S. \tag{18}$$

Combining (17) and (18) and using the $K(\alpha,z)$ notation we obtain,

$$K(\alpha,z^*) \leq \lambda^{*-1} \leq K(\alpha^*,z) \quad \text{for all } \alpha,z \text{ in } S. \tag{19}$$

As is standard, (19) implies

$$\lambda^{*-1} = \max_{\alpha} \min_{z} K(\alpha,z) = \min_{z} \max_{\alpha} K(\alpha,z) . \ \blacksquare$$

Remark. Under the more general assumptions on the f_i and g_i functions of Section 3, there is also a useful relationship between saddle points of $L_\lambda(\alpha,z)$ and $K(\alpha,z)$ which is the following. $K(\alpha,z)$ has a positive saddle value μ if and only if there is a positive zero, λ_0, of $V_M(\cdot)$. Moreover, in this case (α^0,z^0) is a saddle point of $L_{\lambda_0}(\alpha,z)$ if and only if (α^0,z^0) is a saddle point of $K(\alpha,z)$, and $\mu = \lambda_0^{-1}$.

The proof of Theorem 5 shows that if (α^0, z^0) is a saddle point of $L_{\lambda_0}(\alpha, z)$ where $V_M(\lambda_0) = 0$, $\lambda_0 > 0$, then (α^0, z^0) is a saddle point of $K(\alpha, z)$. Basically reversing the steps in the argument gives the other implication.

6. Conclusion

In this paper we develop a saddle value problem formulation for an equilibrium problem of Fan. Employing separably-infinite programming we give an equivalent dual pair of uniextremal problems for the purpose of making it easier to actually solve for the Fan equilibrium point. The uniextremal duality provides interpretations for the variables of each problem of the separably-infinite dual pair, even when they are not at their optimal values. As an illustration of such interpretations in a related economic context, see Kortanek and Pfouts [9].

The Fan equilibrium problem is basically a fixed point problem, and one establishes existence and uniqueness by other methods. Fixed point methods are certainly useful, perhaps even necessary for establishing existence, but it is difficult to obtain analytic information such as interpretations of the variables when they are not at their optimal values.

The basic tool employed in Fan's proof (§11 [6]) is Sperner's lemma. J. M. Borwein has pointed out that the existence of equilibrium is also a direct consequence of a standard variational inequality result whose proof itself relies on the Fan-Kakutani fixed-point theorem, see the Corollary in §21 of Holmes [8]. The existence result may be restated as follows. Let $d : S \to \mathbb{R}^n$ be continuous such that (a) $d_i \leq 0$, (b) $d_i(S_i) < 0$ and (c) $\max_I d_i = 0$. Then there exists $x \in S^0$ with $d(x) = 0$. The variational inequality result provides existence of an $x_0 \in S$ such that $d(x_0)^T(x - x_0) \geq 0$ for all $x \in S$. Uniqueness of the equilibrium point can readily be established from the strict quasi-convexity of each ratio f_i/g_i, which essentially establishes Fan's Corollaries 1, 2, and 3 of §11 [6].

REFERENCES

[1] BORWEIN, J. M. AND K. O. KORTANEK: Fenchel Duality and Separably-Infinite Programs. Accepted Optimization; Math. OP & Stat (Ilmenau). To appear 1983.

[2] CHARNES, A.: Constrained Games and Linear Programming. Proc. Nat. Acad. Sci., USA 38 (1953), 639 - 641.

[3] CHARNES, A., W. W. COOPER AND K. O. KORTANEK: Duality, Haar Programs, and Finite Sequence Spaces. Proc. Nat. Acad. Sci., USA 68 (1962), 605 - 608.

[4] CHARNES, A., P. R. GRIBIK AND K. O. KORTANEK: Separably-Infinite Programs. Zeitschrift für Operations Research 24 (1980), 33 - 45.

[5] CHARNES, A., P. R. GRIBIK AND K. O. KORTANEK: Polyextremal Principles and Separably-Infinite Programs. Zeitschrift für Operations Research 24 (1980), 211 - 234.

[6] FAN, K.: Convex Sets and Their Applications. Argonne National Laboratory, Summer 1959.

[7] GLASHOFF, K.: Duality Theory of Semi-Infinite Programming, in Semi-Infinite Programming ed. R. Hettich. Lecture Notes in Control and Information Sciences ed. A. V. Balakrishnan and M. Thomas. Berlin-Heidelberg-New York: Springer-Verlag, 1979.

[8] HOLMES, RICHARD B.: Geometric Functional Analysis and its Applications. Berlin-Heidelberg-New York: Springer-Verlag, 1975.

[9] KORTANEK, K. O. AND R. W. PFOUTS: A Biextremal Principle for a Behavioral Theory of the Firm. Math. Modelling 3 (1982), in press.

DUALITY IN SEMI-INFINITE LINEAR PROGRAMMING

R.J. Duffin[1], R.G. Jeroslow[2], and
L.A. Karlovitz

Abstract. For the case of a consistent semi-infinite linear program, we provide several hypotheses, which are both necessary as well as sufficient, that there be no duality gap between the program and its formal dual (with attainment of value in the dual), for every linear objective function. Earlier work provided sufficient conditions for no duality gap for all linear objective functions, or a necessary and sufficient condition for no duality gap for a fixed linear criterion.

1. Introduction

If we formally utilize linear programming duality, dual of the program

$$\inf cx$$

$$\text{subject to } a^i x \geq b_i, \quad \text{for } i \in I \tag{1.1}$$

(where $c, a^i, x \in R^n$ and $b_i \in R$, and $I \neq \phi$ is an index set), would be the formal program

$$\sup \sum_{i \in I} \lambda_i b_i$$

$$\text{subject to } \sum_{i \in I} \lambda_i a^i = c, \quad \lambda_i \geq 0 \text{ for } i \in I \tag{1.2}$$

The sense of the summations in (1.2), when I is an infinite index set, shall be that all sums are evaluated as finite sums. We consider solely those multiplier vectors $(\lambda_i | i \in I)$ in (1.2) such that $\{i \in I | \lambda_i \neq 0\}$ is finite.

The duality construction of (1.2) from (1.1) is of interest for I a finite index set, for then the Duality Theorem of Linear Programming (see e.g., [11], [12]) applies to the pairs of programs (1.1) and (1.2) and, e.g., if both (1.1) and (1.2) are consistent, they have the same value. However, when I is infinite, it is possible for (1.1) and (1.2)

---

[1]The first author's research has been partially supported by grant DAAG-29-80-C-0637 of the Army Research Office, Research Triangle Park, North Carolina.

[2]The second author's research has been partially supported by NSF grant ECS8001763.

to both be consistent and have different values. In [4], Duffin and Karlovitz provided a sufficient condition which avoids the cited "pathology" for I infinite, and allows the use of the kind of linear duality which one is accustomed to for I finite.

This paper continues the work of the first and third author, and extends results from their joint unpublished note [5]. The sufficient hypothesis for linear duality for I infinite, as given in [4], does not treat all cases of I finite, due to an interiority condition of the hypothesis; here we obtain a complete generalization of finite linear duality (Theorem 3.2 below). Moreover, we obtain a necessary and sufficient condition for linear duality to hold, when one allows c in (1.1) and (1.2) to vary over R^n.

Our results also extend the work by Charnes, Cooper, and Kortanek [3] on such duality results. For $c \in R^n$ held fixed in (1.1) and (1.2), the recent paper of Karney [7] is of particular interest. Alternate treatments of a closely-related topic, that of semi-infinite convex programming has been provided by Borwein [2] and Jeroslow [6]. The literature on semi-infinite programming is, by now, quite extensive and we have indicated those papers most closely related to our own.

For any set $S \subseteq R^n$, $c\ell(S)$ denotes the (topological) closure of S; and cone (S) denotes the cone generated by S, i.e.,

$$\text{cone } (S) = \{ \sum_{s \in S} \lambda_s s \mid \lambda_s \geq 0 \text{ for } s \in S\} \qquad (1.3)$$

Thus, $c\ell$ cone (S) denotes the closure of cone (S). Similarly, conv (S) will be used to denote the convex hull (span) of S.

The program (1.1) is <u>feasible</u> if it has solutions. It is <u>bounded in value</u> if it is consistent and there exists a number z^* such that all solutions $x \in R^n$ to (1.1) satisfy $cx \geq z^*$; z^* is then called a bound on that value. It is <u>unbounded in value</u> if, for each $n \in Z$, there exists a solution $x^{(n)}$ with $cx^{(n)} \leq -n$.

2. The Homogeneous Case

It is convenient for us to first treat the homogeneous case of all $b_i = 0$, $i \in I$, in (1.1).

When all $b_i = 0$, then (1.1) becomes

$$\inf cx$$

$$\text{subject to } a^i x \geq 0, \quad \text{for } i \in I \qquad (2.1)$$

and (1.2) becomes

$$\sup 0$$

$$\text{subject to } \sum_{i \in I} \lambda_i a^i = c, \ \lambda_i \geq 0 \text{ for } i \in I \tag{2.2}$$

Now (2.1) is always consistent (take $x = 0$). A remark, which we next give as a proposition, is helpful.

Proposition 2.1. The program (2.1) is unbounded in value if and only if there exists $x^* \in R^n$ satisfying:

$$a^i x^* \geq 0, \quad \text{for } i \in I \tag{2.3}$$

$$\text{and} \quad cx^* < 0 \tag{2.4}$$

If (2.1) is bounded in value, its value is zero.

Proof. If x^* exists, then $cx^* \leq -1$ without loss of generality, and for each n we have $a^i x^{(n)} \geq 0$, $i \in I$, and $cx^{(n)} < -n$ with $x^{(n)} = nx^*$, hence (2.1) is unbounded in value.

Conversely, if x^* does not exist, there can be no sequence $\{x^{(n)} \mid n=1,2,3,\ldots\}$ since $x^{(1)}$ cannot exist (i.e., we cannot have $a^i x^{(1)} \geq 0$ for $i \in I$ and $cx^{(1)} \leq -1$). Hence (2.1) is bounded in value.

Finally, if (2.1) is bounded in value, there is no solution to (2.3) and (2.4), hence the value of (2.1) is zero.

Q.E.D.

We shall say that the constraint system of (1.1) i.e., the linear inequalities

$$a^i x \geq b_i, \quad \text{for } i \in I \tag{2.5}$$

yields LP duality with respect to $c \in R^n$, if exactly one of the following conditions holds: (i) The program (1.1) is unbounded in value and (1.2) is inconsistent; (ii) The program (1.2) is unbounded in value and (1.1) is inconsistent; (iii) Both (1.1) and (1.2) are inconsistent; or (iv) Both (1.1) and (1.2) are consistent and have the same value, and that value is attained in (1.2). We say that (2.5) yields uniform LP duality if (2.5) yields LP duality for every $c \in R^n$.

It is useful to relate this property of uniform LP duality to the closure of the cone $C = \text{cone}(\{a^i \mid i \in I\})$ for the program (2.1).

Theorem 2.2. The constraint system of the homogeneous program (2.1) yields uniform LP duality, if and only if, the cone $C = \text{cone}(\{a^i \mid i \in I\})$ is closed.

Proof. Suppose (2.1) yields uniform LP duality. Let $c \in c\ell(C)$. If $c \notin C$, then (2.2) is inconsistent. Since (2.1) is consistent, the program (2.1) must be unbounded in value. By Proposition 2.1, there exists x^* satisfying (2.3) and (2.4). From (2.3), we have $vx^* \geq 0$ for all $v \in C$; by continuity, also $vx^* \geq 0$ for all $v \in c\ell(C)$. But $cx^* < 0$ by (2.4), a contradiction. Hence $c \in C$, and C is closed.

Suppose that C is closed. Let $c \in R^n$ be arbitrary. Since (2.1) is consistent, either (2.1) is unbounded in value or bounded in value. If (2.1) is unbounded in value, clause (i) in the definition of uniform LP duality must hold. If (2.1) is bounded in value, its value is zero by Proposition 2.1. We show that clause (iv) holds by showing that (2.2) is consistent.

If (2.2) is not consistent, $c \notin C = c\ell(C)$. Hence, by the Separating Hyperplane Theorem [12], there exists x^* with $cx^* < 0$ and $vx^* \geq 0$ for all $v \in c\ell(C)$. In particular, $a^i x^* \geq 0$ for $i \in I$. Thus x^* solves (2.3) and (2.4). By Proposition 1.1, (2.1) is unbounded in value, a contradiction. Hence, (2.2) must be consistent.

Q.E.D.

We next proceed to provide a condition on an arbitrary set of vectors $\{a^i \mid i \in I\} \subseteq R^n$ (such as those in (2.1)) which is necessary and sufficient to guarantee that $C = \text{cone}\,(\{a^i \mid i \in I\})$ is closed. We first derive this condition in the case that an interiority assumption holds; specifically, the existence of a vector x^0 with this property:

$$a^i x^0 > 0 \quad \text{for } i \in I \tag{2.6}$$

Our condition for the vectors $\{a^i \mid i \in I\}$ will involve the result of taking non-negative combinations of these vectors, but it will <u>not</u> involve the limit requirements that would occur if closure conditions were stipulated.

We shall say that the sets of vectors $\{a^i \mid i \in I\}$ and $\{\alpha^j \mid j \in J\}$ are <u>positively equivalent</u> if:

$$\text{cone}\,(\{a^i \mid i \in I\}) = \text{cone}\,(\{\alpha^j \mid j \in J\}) \tag{2.7}$$

Note that (2.7) says that any a^i respectively α^j is a non-negative combination of $\{\alpha^j \mid j \in J\}$ resp. $\{a^i \mid i \in I\}$.

<u>Theorem 2.3</u>. Suppose that the set of vectors $\{a^i \mid i \in I\}$ satisfies (2.6).

For $C = \text{cone}\,(\{a^i \mid i \in I\})$ to be closed, it is both necessary and sufficient, that this set possess a positively equivalent set $\{\alpha^j \mid j \in J\}$ of non zero vectors $\alpha^j \neq 0$ which is compact.

<u>Proof</u>. We first prove "necessity".

If C is closed, the set S is compact, where

$$S = C \cap \{x \in R^n \mid \|x\| = 1\} \tag{2.8}$$

as S is the intersection of C and a compact set. Any element of S is an element of C, and also $C = \text{cone}\,(S)$. Thus S is positively equivalent to $\{a^i | i \in I\}$, and clearly S consists of nonzero vectors.

We next prove "sufficiency." Since each α^j is a nonnegative combination of $\{a^i | i \in I\}$ and $\alpha^j \neq 0$, at least one positive multiplier occurs in the combination. By (2.6), we have $\alpha^j x^0 > 0$.

Without loss of generality, we may assume that the set $\{a^i | i \in I\}$ is compact and all $a^i \neq 0$. By [12], the set $K = \text{conv}(\{a^i | i \in I\})$ is compact as well. To show that $C = \text{cone}(\{a^i | i \in I\})$ is closed, it suffices to show that $v \notin C$ implies $v \notin c\ell(C)$.

Suppose $v \notin C$. Whenever $\lambda > 0$, we must then have $\lambda v \notin K$. Also $0 \notin K$, for (2.6) implies that $wx^0 > 0$ for all $w \in K$. Therefore, the compact set K is entirely disjoint from the closed half line $M = \{\lambda v \mid \lambda \geq 0\}$, and by [8] there is a strictly separating hyperplane, i.e., a vector $\bar{x}$ with

$$\beta = \inf_{w \in K} w\bar{x} > \sup_{\lambda > 0} \lambda v \cdot \bar{x} \ (=0) \tag{2.9}$$

Now if the supremum in (2.9) were positive, by homogeneity it is $+\infty$, and this contradicts (2.9). Therefore, the supremum in (2.9) is zero, as we have written parenthetically.

We reach a contradiction to $v \in c\ell(C)$ as follows. Suppose that $c^{(n)} \to v$ with all $c^{(n)} \in C$. Write

$$c^{(n)} = \sum_{i \in I} \lambda_i^{(n)} a^i, \quad \text{all } \lambda_i^{(n)} \geq 0 \tag{2.10}$$

$$\delta_n = \sum_{i \in I} \lambda_i^{(n)} \geq 0 \tag{2.11}$$

If $\liminf \delta_n \to 0$, then $c^{(n)} \to 0$ and hence $v = 0 \in C$, a contradiction. Without loss of generality, there is a scalar $\varepsilon > 0$ with $\delta_n \geq \varepsilon$ for all n. We have by (2.9)

$$v\bar{x} = \lim_n c^{(n)}\bar{x} = \lim_n \delta_n \Big(\sum_{i \in I} \Big(\frac{\lambda_i^{(n)}}{\delta_n}\Big) a^i \Big) \bar{x}$$

$$\geq \varepsilon \liminf_n \Big(\sum_{i \in I} \Big(\frac{\lambda_i^{(n)}}{\delta_n}\Big) a^i \Big) \bar{x} \geq \varepsilon \beta > 0 \tag{2.12}$$

since $\sum_{i \in I} \Big(\frac{\lambda_i^{(n)}}{\delta_n}\Big) a^i \in K$. But, also by (2.9), $v\bar{x} \leq 0$. This is the desired contradiction. Q.E.D.

Regarding Theorem 2.3, two remarks are in order.

First, the equivalent positive set $\{\alpha^j \mid j \in J\}$ guaranteed by the theorem may necessarily have redundancies, i.e., vectors α^{j0} which are in the cone generated by the remaining vectors. This occurs essentially because a set of extreme points need not be closed.

Second, the "sufficiency" part of the theorem fails without the hypothesis (2.6). In fact, let C be the cone generated by the vectors (0,1,1), (0,0,1), (0,0,-1) and $(\frac{1}{n}, \frac{1}{n^2}, 1)$. This set of points T is compact (as it is closed and bounded) and does not contain zero. One easily shows that (1,0,0) is a limit point of C (as $n(\frac{1}{n}, \frac{1}{n^2}, 1) + n(0,0,-1) = (1,\frac{1}{n},0)$) but $(1,0,0) \notin C$.

As the hypothesis (2.6) was among those given by Duffin and Karlovitz in [4] as sufficient for the closure of C, Theorem 2.3 establishes the necessity of the other hypothesis (i.e., compactness), at least up to the choice of a positive equivalent set. The proof of "sufficiency" in Theorem 2.3 is an alternate proof to the original one [4], and we gave it here for purposes of being self-contained.

We next use Theorem 2.3 to obtain necessary and sufficient conditions for $C = \text{cone}(\{a^i \mid i \in I\})$ to be closed, independent of the interiority hypothesis (2.6). Our proof is based on the (quite standard) technique of writing a cone as a direct sum of its linearity space and a pointed cone (see e.g., [12]).

Theorem 2.4. The following are equivalent:

(i) $C = \text{cone}(\{a^i \mid i \in I\})$ is closed.

(ii) The set $\{a^i \mid i \in I\}$ has positive equivalent set $S \cup T$ where S is finite and cone (S) is a linear space which is also contained in C, T is compact, and there exists a vector x^0 such that:

$$sx^0 = 0 \quad \text{for } s \in S \tag{2.13}$$

$$tx^0 > 0 \quad \text{for } t \in T \tag{2.14}$$

In addition,

$$st = 0 \text{ for } s \in S \text{ and } t \in T \tag{2.15}$$

(iii) The set $\{a^i \mid i \in I\}$ has a positive equivalent set $S \cup T$, where S is finite, T is compact and there exists a vector x^0 such that (2.13) and (2.14) hold.

(iv) The set $\{a^i \mid i \in I\}$ has a positive equivalent set $S \cup T$, where cone (S) is closed, T is compact, and there exists a vector x^0 such that (2.13) and (2.14) hold.

Proof. i) → ii) As C is closed, so is the linear space $L = C \cap (-C)$. Let $L^\perp$ denote the perpendicular space of L, i.e., $L^\perp = \{v \in R^n \mid vw = 0 \text{ for all } w \in L\}$. One easily verifies that

$$C = L + (C \cap L^\perp) \tag{2.16}$$

Indeed, since $C \supseteq L$ and $C \supseteq C \cap L^\perp$ and C is a cone, $C \supseteq L + (C \cap L^\perp)$.

Moreover, if $c \in C$, let pr(c) denote its projection on $L^{\perp}$, i.e.,

pr(c) = c′ where c′ = c-ℓ is chosen so that

$$c = \ell + c' \text{ with } \ell \in L \text{ and } c' \in L^{\perp} \qquad (2.17)$$

(As $R^n = L \oplus L^{\perp}$, the choice of ℓ and c′ are unique in (2.17)). Then $c = \ell + c'$, $\ell \in L$, and $c' \in C \cap L^{\perp}$ as $c' = c + (-\ell) \in C + C = C$. Hence $C \subseteq L + (C \cap L^{\perp})$, and (2.16) holds.

Since the closed cone $C' = C \cap L^{\perp}$ is pointed in $L^{\perp}$ (i.e., $C' \cap (-C') = \{0\}$), there exists $x^0 \in L^{\perp}$ with

$$tx^0 > 0 \quad \text{for } t \in C',\ t \neq 0 \qquad (2.18)$$

By (2.17), for each $c \in C$, pr(c) is a non-negative combination of elements of $\{a^i \mid i \in I\}$, since $C = \text{cone}\,\{a^i \mid i \in I\}$, $c' = \text{pr}(c) = c + (-\ell)$, and both c and (-ℓ) are such nonnegative combinations.

Now assume that C′ is not {0}. Then

$$C' = \text{cone}\,(\{\text{pr}(c) \mid c \in C \text{ and } \text{pr}(c) \neq 0\}) \qquad (2.19)$$

and we note that

$$\text{pr}(c)\, x^0 > 0 \quad \text{for all } c \in C \text{ with } \text{pr}(c) \neq 0 \qquad (2.20)$$

so that (2.6) holds with $\{\text{pr}(c) \mid c \in C \text{ and } \text{pr}(c) \neq 0\}$ replacing $\{a^i \mid i \in I\}$.

By Theorem 2.3, there exists a compact set T, not containing the zero vector, such that T is a positive equivalent of $\{\text{pr}(c) \mid c \in C \text{ and } \text{pr}(c) \neq 0\}$, and such that C′ = cone (T). Therefore (2.14) holds, and each $t \in T$ is a nonnegative combination of $\{a^i \mid i \in I\}$. Moreover, since $C' \subseteq L^{\perp}$, $t \cdot \ell = 0$ for all $\ell \in L$.

The linear space L has a linear basis $v^{(1)}, \ldots, v^{(t)}$ (say). Let us put $S = \{\pm v^{(1)}, \ldots, \pm v^{(t)}\}$. Then cone (S) = L is a linear space, S is finite, and (2.13) holds since $S \subseteq L$ and $x^0 \in L^{\perp}$. Moreover, since $S \subseteq L \subseteq C$, each $s \in S$ is a nonnegative combination of $\{a^i \mid i \in I\}$. Also cone (S) = L is contained in C. As $S \subseteq L$, (2.15) is immediate.

Thus, each element of $S \cup T$ is in cone $(\{a^i \mid i \in I\})$, but also

$$\begin{aligned} \text{cone}\,(S \cup T) &= \text{cone}\,(S) + \text{cone}\,(T) \\ &= L + C' \\ &= C \end{aligned} \qquad (2.21)$$

by (2.16). Hence, $S \cup T$ is a positive equivalent of $\{a^i \mid i \in I\}$.

If C′ = {0}, we take T=∅ and (ii) easily follows. In fact, C=L and we can take $x^0 = 0$ in this case.

ii) → iii) This is immediate.

iii) → iv) This follows from the fact that cone (S) is closed when

S is finite [11].

iv) → i) Let $c^{(n)} \in C$ and suppose $c^{(n)} \to c^0$. We wish to prove $c^0 \in C$.

If $T = \emptyset$, we have $C = \text{cone}\,(S) = \text{cone}\,(\{a^i \mid i \in I\})$, and C is closed by hypothesis. In what follows, we assume $T \neq \emptyset$.

Now $C = \text{cone}\,(\{a^i \mid i \in I\}) = \text{cone}\,(S \cup T) = \text{cone}\,(S) + \text{cone}\,(T)$, hence $c^{(n)} = s^{(n)} + t^{(n)}$ where each $s^{(n)} \in \text{cone}\,(S)$ and each $t^{(n)} \in \text{cone}\,(T)$. We have $c^0x^0 = \lim c^{(n)}x^0 = \lim_n (s^{(n)}x^0 + t^{(n)}x^0) = \lim_n t^{(n)}x^0$ using (2.13). Write

$$t^{(n)} = \sum_{t\in T} \lambda_t^{(n)} t, \text{ all } \lambda_t^{(n)} \geq 0 \tag{2.22}$$

$$\alpha_n = \sum_{t\in T} \lambda_t^{(n)} \geq 0 \tag{2.23}$$

$$\text{and} \quad \alpha = \inf_{t\in T} tx^0 = \min_{t\in T} tx^0 > 0 \tag{2.24}$$

where (2.24) holds by the compactness of T. If the sequence of α_n were not bounded, then by

$$t^{(n)}x^0 = \sum_{t\in T} \lambda_t^{(n)} tx^0 \geq \alpha_n\alpha \tag{2.25}$$

the sequence $t^{(n)}x^0$ is also not bounded. This contradicts $c^0x^0 = \lim_n t^{(n)}x^0$. Hence the sequence α_n is bounded, and by (2.22) so is the sequence of vectors $t^{(n)}$. Without loss of generality, $t^{(n)} \to t^0$ for some vector t^0.

By Theorem 2.3 cone (T) is closed. As each $t^{(n)} \in \text{cone}\,(T)$, we have $t^0 \in \text{cone}\,(T)$. Since $s^{(n)} = c^{(n)} - t^{(n)}$ and $c^{(n)} \to c^0$ and $t^{(n)} \to t^{(0)}$, we have $s^{(n)} \to c^0 - t^0$. Since cone (S) is closed and each $s^{(n)} \in \text{cone}\,(S)$, $c^0 - t^0 \in \text{cone}\,(S)$. Thus $c^0 \in \text{cone}\,(T) + \text{cone}\,(S) = C$.

Q.E.D.

The first and third author had earlier established hypothesis (iii) of Theorem 2.4 as a sufficient condition for (i), in their unpublished note [5].

3. The Inhomogeneous Case and Duality Results

We reduce the inhomogeneous case to the homogeneous one by standard techniques. We give details so that the reader may verify for himself that the role played by uniform LP duality is as claimed below, since this uniformity is new.

Lemma 3.1. Suppose that (1.1) is consistent.

The constraints (2.5) of (1.1) yield LP duality with respect to $c \in R^n$, if and only if, for every $d \in R$, the constraints

$$a^i x - b_i x_{n+1} \geq 0 \quad \text{for } i \in I \tag{3.1}$$

$$x_{n+1} \geq 0$$

yield LP duality with respect to $(c,-d) \in R^{n+1}$.

Proof. Suppose that the constraints (2.5) yield LP duality with respect to $c \in R^n$ and let $d \in R$. We show that (3.1) yields LP duality for objective function $(c,-d)$.

Since (3.1) is a homogeneous system, we need only show that if its dual is inconsistent, (3.1) has a value of $-\infty$ for the objective function $(c,-d)$. The dual is:

$$\sup 0$$

$$\text{subject to } \theta(0,1) + \sum_{i \in I} \lambda_i (a^i, -b_i) = (c,-d) \tag{3.2}$$

$$\theta \geq 0, \ \lambda_i \geq 0 \quad \text{for } i \in I$$

which is equivalent to:

$$\sum_{i \in I} \lambda_i a^i = c, \ \lambda_i \geq 0 \quad \text{for } i \in I \tag{3.3}$$

$$\sum_{i \in I} \lambda_i b_i \geq d \tag{3.4}$$

Assume (3.3) and (3.4) are inconsistent. Note that (3.3) is the dual constraints to (2.5), which by hypothesis has LP duality. As the value in a dual is attained when LP duality holds and the dual is consistent, it follows that at least one of these two conditions obtains: (α) The system (3.3) alone is inconsistent; or (β) The system (3.3) alone is consistent, and also (1.1) is consistent, but $d > \inf \{cx | a^i x \geq b_i \text{ for } i \in I\} = z_0$ (say).

If (α) holds, by our hypothesis, the primal (1.1) is unbounded in value. Thus, for any number n however large, there exists $x^{(n)}$ such that $(a^i, -b_i)\ (x^{(n)}, 1) \geq 0$ for $i \in I$, yet $cx^{(n)} < d - n$, i.e., $(c,-d)\ (x^{(n)}, 1) < -n$. Therefore (3.1) has value $-\infty$.

When (β) holds, there exists a point $\bar{x}$ with $(a^i, -b_i)\ (\bar{x}, 1) \geq 0$ for $i \in I$ and $c\bar{x} < d$, i.e., $(c,-d)\ (\bar{x}, 1) < 0$. By Proposition 2.1, (3.1) again has value $-\infty$.

To prove the "if" part of the Lemma, we suppose that (3.1) yields LP duality with respect to $(c,-d) \in R^{n+1}$ for all $d \in R$. We must prove that we have LP duality between (1.1) and (1.2).

As (1.1) is consistent, there are two cases: first, that (1.1) is unbounded in value, in which case there is nothing to prove; or second, that (1.1) is bounded in value.

In the second case, let $z_0 = \inf\{cx \mid a^i x \geq b_i \text{ for } i \in I\}$. We first show that (3.1) for $d = z_0$ cannot be unbounded in value, by contradiction.

If (3.1) were unbounded in value, by Proposition 2.1 there is a solution to

$$x^*_{n+1} \geq 0,\ a^i x^* - b_i x^*_{n+1} \geq 0 \quad \text{for } i \in I \tag{3.5}$$
$$cx^* - z_0 x^*_{n+1} < 0$$

If $x^*_{n+1} > 0$, we may assume $x^*_{n+1} = 1$ by homogeneity, and we have a contradiction to the definition of z_0. If $x^*_{n+1} = 0$, let $\bar{x}$ be any feasible solution to (1.1). Then for all $\lambda \geq 0$, $\bar{x} + \lambda x^*$ is a solution to (1.1) as one easily verifies (i.e., $a^i(\bar{x} + \lambda x^*) \geq a^i\bar{x} + \lambda a^i x^* \geq b_i + 0 = b_i$ for $i \in I$), yet since $cx^* < 0$, we have $c(\bar{x} + \lambda x^*) < z_0$ for large $\lambda \geq 0$. This also contradicts the definition of z^0.

Since (3.1) is bounded in value for $d = z_0$ and LP duality holds, there is a solution to (3.3) and (3.4) for $d = z_0$. Thus, the value of (1.2) is that of (1.1), and (1.2) attains its value; so LP duality holds for (1.1).

Q.E.D.

We now state the main result of our paper.

<u>Theorem 3.2</u>. Suppose that (1.1) is consistent, and let $G = \{(a^i, -b_i) \mid i \in I\} \cup \{(0,1)\}$, $C = \text{cone}(G)$. Then the following are equivalent:

(i) The program (1.1) yields uniform LP duality.

(ii) The constraint system (3.1) yields uniform LP duality.

(iii) C is closed.

(iv) The set G has a positive equivalent set $S \cup T$, where S is finite and cone (S) is a linear space which is also contained in C, T is compact, and there exists a vector $\bar{x}$ with

$$s\bar{x} = s_{n+1} \quad \text{for every } (s, -s_{n+1}) \in S,\ s_{n+1} \in R \tag{3.6}$$

$$t\bar{x} > t_{n+1} \quad \text{for every } (t, -t_{n+1}) \in T,\ t_{n+1} \in R \tag{3.7}$$

Moreover, whenever $(s, -s_{n+1}) \in S$ the equality $sx = s_{n+1}$ is implied by (1.1) and the equality $sx = 0$ is implied by (2.1). Furthermore,

$$st + s_{n+1}t_{n+1} = 0 \text{ if } (s, -s_{n+1}) \in S \text{ and } (t, -t_{n+1}) \in T \tag{3.8}$$

(v) The set G has a positive equivalent set $S \cup T$, where S is finite, T is compact, and there exists a vector $\bar{x}$ such that (3.6) and (3.7) hold.

(vi) The set G has a positive equivalent set $S \cup T$, where cone (S) is closed, T is compact, and there exists a vector $\bar{x}$ such that (3.6) and (3.7) hold.

Proof. (i) ⇔ (ii) This follows easily from Lemma 3.1.

(ii) ⇔ (iii) By Theorem 2.2.

(iii) → (iv) By the fact that Theorem 2.4(i) implies Theorem 2.4(ii) for C = cone (G), the set G has a positive equivalent $S \cup T$, with S and T as described, and there exists (x^0, x^0_{n+1}) such that (2.13) and (2.14) hold, i.e.,

$$sx^0 = s_{n+1}x^0_{n+1} \quad \text{for every } (s,-s_{n+1}) \in S,\ s_{n+1} \in R \tag{3.9}$$

$$tx^0 > t_{n+1}x^0_{n+1} \quad \text{for every } (t,-t_{n+1}) \in T,\ t_{n+1} \in R \tag{3.10}$$

If $x^0_{n+1} > 0$ in (3.9) and (3.10), we may assume $x^0_{n+1} = 1$ and by putting $\bar{x} = x^0$, we are done. Suppose that $x^0_{n+1} = 0$.

Since (1.1) is consistent, there exists a vector x^* with

$$sx^* \geq s_{n+1} \quad \text{for every } (s,-s_{n+1}) \in S,\ s_{n+1} \in R \tag{3.11}$$

$$tx^* \geq t_{n+1} \quad \text{for every } (t,-t_{n+1}) \in T,\ t_{n+1} \in R \tag{3.12}$$

Indeed, (3.11) and (3.12) follow since every element of $S \cup T$ is a non-negative linear combination of G, and we may chose x^* to satisfy

$$a^i x^* \geq b_i \quad \text{for } i \in I \tag{3.13}$$

Since cone (S) is actually a linear space, if $(s,-s_{n+1}) \in S$ we have $(-s,s_{n+1}) \in \text{cone}(S) \subseteq C$, hence also $-sx^* \geq -s_{n+1}$. Combining this with (3.11), we see that

$$sx^* = s_{n+1} \quad \text{for every } (s,-s_{n+1}) \in S,\ s_{n+1} \in R \tag{3.14}$$

The same deduction shows that $sx = s_{n+1}$ whenever x solves (1.1) and that $sx = 0$ whenever x solves (2.1) (for then $(x,0)$ solves $a^i x - b_i x_{n+1} \geq 0$ for $i \in I$, $x_{n+1} \geq 0$).

Put $\bar{x} = x^* + x^0$. By adding (3.9) and (3.14) and recalling that $x^0_{n+1} = 0$, we obtain (3.6). Similarly, by adding (3.10) and (3.12), we obtain (3.7). Also (3.8) follows from (2.15).

(iv) → (v) This is immediate.

(v) → (vi) Immediate.

(vi) → (iii) We rewrite (3.6) and (3.7) as

$$(s,-s_{n+1})(\bar{x},1) = 0 \quad \text{for every } (s,-s_{n+1}) \in S \tag{3.15}$$

$$(t,-t_{n+1})(\bar{x},1) > 0 \quad \text{for every } (t,-t_{n+1}) \in T. \tag{3.16}$$

Taking $x^0 = (\bar{x},1)$, the result follows since Theorem 2.4(iv) implies Theorem 2.4(i).

Q.E.D.

Theorem 3.3. Suppose that the strict inequality system

$$a^i x > b_i,\ i \in I \tag{3.17}$$

has a solution. With G and C as in Theorem 3.2, the following are equivalent:

(i) The program (1.1) yields uniform LP duality.

(ii) The constraint system (3.1) yields uniform LP duality.

(iii) C is closed.

(iv) The set G has a positive equivalent set of non-zero vectors which is compact.

Proof. The equivalences (i) $\Leftrightarrow$ (ii) $\Leftrightarrow$ (iii) are from Theorem 3.2. Put $x^0 = (\bar{x},1)$, where $\bar{x}$ solves (3.17). Then for $i \in I, (a^i,-b_i)x^0 > 0$. Also $(0,1)x^0 > 0$. Hence condition (2.6) holds with respect to the set G. By Theorem 2.3, (iii) and (iv) are equivalent.

Q.E.D.

Acknowledgement. We wish to thank the referee and Professor Charles E. Blair for pointing out an error in the statement of Theorem 2.3 in an earlier draft. The referee also provided a shorter proof of the "necessity" part of that result, which we have adapted and used here with our revision of Theorem 2.3.

References

[1] BLAIR, C.E.: A Note on Infinite Systems of Linear Inequalities in R^n. Journal of Mathematical Analysis and Applications 48 (1974), 150-154.

[2] BORWEIN, J.: Direct Theorems in Semi-Infinite Convex Programming, Mathematical Programming 21 (1981), 301-318.

[3] CHARNES, A., COOPER, W.W., and KORTANEK, K.O.: On Representations of Semi-Infinite Programs Which Have No Duality Gaps. Management Science 12 (1965), 113-121.

[4] DUFFIN, R.J. and KARLOVITZ, L.A.: An Infinite Linear Program with a Duality Gap. Management Science, 12 (1965), 122-134.

[5] DUFFIN, R.J. and KARLOVITZ, L.A.: Unpublished note, 1971.

[6] JEROSLOW, R.G.: Uniform Duality in Semi-Infinite Convex Optimization, April 1981.

[7] KARNEY, D.F.: Duality Gaps in Semi-Infinite Linear Programming: An Approximation Problem. Mathematical Programming 20 (1981), 129-143.

[8] KELLEY, J.L. and NAMIOKA, I.: Linear Topological Spaces, Springer-Verlag, New York, 1963. 247+ pp.

[9] KORTANEK, K.O.: Perfect Duality in Generalized Convex Programming in Finite Dimensions, Department of Mathematics, Carnegie-Mellon University, Tech Rep. no. 26, November, 1975.

[10] KRETSCHMER, K.S.: Programmes in Paired Spaces. Canadian Journal of Mathematics 13 (1961), 221-238.

[11] ROCKAFELLAR, R.T.: Convex Analysis, Princeton University Press, Princeton, New Jersey, 1970. 432+ pp.

[12] STOER, J. and WITZGALL, C.: Convexity and Optimization in Finite Dimensions: I, Springer-Verlag, New York, 1970. 268+ pp.

ON THE ROLE OF DUALITY IN THE THEORY OF MOMENTS [1)]

J. H. B. Kemperman

ABSTRACT

New and old results in the theory of moments with special stress on duality methods and their relation to the theory of semi-infinite programming.

1. Introduction

As is well known, there is a close resemblance between the theory of moments on the one hand and the theory of finite and semi-infinite linear programming on the other. There is no essential difference between the two areas as is also clear from the works of L. Kantorovich, H. Kellerer and many others and the seminal paper by Charnes, Cooper and Kortanek (1963).

One could say that a main characteristic of the latter area is the much greater stress on good numerical procedures. The theory of moments has moved on a more theoretical plane though good use of the theory has been made by statisticians and numerical analysts, scientists and engineers.

Both areas are concerned with a real-valued linear function $f(.)$ on a real linear space E, which is subject to linear inequalities of the form

$$f(h_j) \le \eta_j \quad \text{for all} \quad j \in J.$$

Usually, f is assumed to be nonnegative on a given convex cone C in E, and one is interested in minimizing or maximizing the value $f(g)$ which f has at a given point g of E.

In the theory of moments, the elements $x \in E$ usually represent real-valued measurable functions $x(.)$ on a fixed measurable space S, while $f(x)$ can be represented as a integral

$$f(x) = \int x(s)\ \mu(ds) = \mu(x)$$

of $x(.)$ relative to an (unknown) measure μ on S. We will only consider the case where μ is an ordinary finite and nonnegative measure.

---

1) This research was supported in part by the National Science Foundation.

Then C will often contain many nonnegative measurable functions $x(.)$ on S.

Duality has always played a central role, in both areas and in about the same way. The present paper surveys a number of duality methods which have been very useful in the theory of moments, and also presents many new results, sometimes without proof. Excellent surveys of a different nature are the works of Krein (1951), Karlin and Studden (1966), Krein and Nudel'man (1977).

In Sections 2 and 4 there are some very general results for the case that S is a completely regular topological space (a very weak assumption). They enable us to handle a large variety of moment problems. Some proofs are in the appendix, (Section 8).

In Section 3 we consider the usual case of semi-infinite linear programming where J is finite and S is a measurable space (no topology). In the remaining sections, μ is an arbitrary probability measure on the product of two completely regular spaces possessing preassigned marginal distributions (projections). The basic theory is in Section 5. Certain applications are presented in Section 6, including new proofs of results due to Kantorovich, Rubinstein, Nachbin and Strassen.

The problem of minimizing $\mu(h) = \int h(s,t)\ \mu(ds,dt)$, where μ has given marginals, is nothing but a generalized transportation problem. In Section 7, we discuss its relation to the so-called transshipment problem.

2. A general moment problem

Let S be a fixed measurable space such that each 1-point set $\{s\}$ is measurable. Further $M_o(S)$ denotes a fixed non-empty set of finite (nonnegative) measures on S. For $f: S \to R$ as a measurable function, we shall be interested in the bounds

$$(2.1)\qquad \begin{aligned} L_o(f) &= L(f, M_o(S)) = \inf\{\mu(f): \mu \in M_o(S)\}; \\ U_o(f) &= -L_o(-f) \quad\quad\;\; = \sup\{\mu(f): \mu \in M_o(S)\}, \end{aligned}$$

where

$$\mu(f) = \int f(s)\ \mu(ds).$$

We take $L_o(f) = -\infty$ when $\mu(f^-) = +\infty$ for some $\mu \in M_o(S)$, where $f^- = \max(-f, 0)$. Similarly, $U_o(f) = +\infty$ if $\mu(f^+) = +\infty$ for some $\mu \in M_o(S)$.

If $M_o(S)$ consists of all finite measures on S then $L_o(f) = 0$ when $f \geq 0$, (that is, $f(s) \geq 0$ for all $s \in S$), and $L_o(f) = -\infty$, otherwise. If $M_o(s)$ consists of all probability measures on S then $L_o(f) = \inf f = \inf\{f(s): s \in S\}$ and $U_o(f) = \sup f$. Other examples can be found in Kemperman (1972) p. 110.

Often S is a product space $S = S_1 \times S_2 \times \ldots \times S_n \times \ldots$ with points $s = (s_1, s_2, \ldots)$ such that $s_n \in S_n$. In this case, each probability measure μ on S determines a stochastic process with components $X_n = X_n(s_n) = s_n$ taking values in S_n $(n = 1, 2, \ldots)$. Thus, a set $M_o(S)$ of probability measures on S may describe a collection of stochastic processes, such as the set of all martingales satisfying certain linear inequalities.

Let J be an arbitrary fixed index set. For each $j \in J$, let $h_j: S \to R$ be a given measurable function and η_j a given real constant. By $M_1(S)$ we will denote the possibly empty collection consisting of all $\mu \in M_o(s)$ which satisfy

(2.2) $\quad \mu(h_j^+) < +\infty$ and $\mu(h_j) \le \eta_j$, for each $j \in J$;

(if h_j is bounded below this would imply that h_j is μ-integrable). In order that $M_1(S)$ be non-empty, it is clearly necessary that

(2.3) $\quad L_o(\sum_{j\in J} \beta_j h_j) \le \sum_{j\in J} \beta_j \eta_j$ whenever $\beta_j \ge 0$ for all $j \in J$.

Here, we will only allow nonnegative functions β_j on J such that $\beta_j = 0$ for all but finitely many indices j.

Let $g: S \to R$ be a fixed measurable function. We shall also be interested in the moment problem of determining the lower bound

(2.4) $\quad L_1(g) = L(g, M_1(S)) = \inf\{\mu(g): \mu \in M_1(S)\}$

and the upper bound

(2.5) $\quad U_1(g) = -L_1(-g) \qquad = \sup\{\mu(g): \mu \in M_1(S)\}$.

We take $U_1(g) = +\infty$ if $\mu(g^+) = \infty$ for some $\mu \in M_1(S)$ and similarly for $L_1(g)$. Writing $g = \sum\beta_j h_j + (g - \sum\beta_j h_j)$, it is clear that

$$U_1(g) \le U_1^*(g), \tag{2.6}$$

where

(2.7) $\quad U_1^*(g) = \inf\{\sum_J \beta_j\eta_j + U_o(g - \sum_J \beta_j h_j): \ \beta_j \ge 0 \ (j \in J)\}$,

with all but finitely many β_j equal to zero.

In the case where $M_o(S)$ consists of all probability measures on S, formula (2.7) reduces to

(2.8) $\quad U_1^*(g) = \inf\{\alpha + \sum_J \beta_j\eta_j: \beta_j \ge 0 \ \ (j \in J);\ g \le \alpha + \sum_J \beta_j h_j\}$;

($U_1^*(g) = \infty$ if the latter infimum is over the empty set). If $M_o(S)$ consists of all finite measures on S then

(2.9) $U_1^*(g) = \inf\{\sum_J \beta_j\eta_j : \beta_j \geq 0 \ (j \in J);\ g(s) \leq \sum_J \beta_j h_j(s) \ (s \in S)\}.$

EXAMPLE 1. Let $M_o(S)$ consist of all finite measures on S and suppose further that J is finite. Then the problem of calculating $U_1^*(g)$ as in (2.9) is usually called the primal problem of semi-infinite programming.

EXAMPLE 2. Suppose in addition that S is finite. One may as well take $J = \{1, \ldots, m\}$ and $S = \{1, \ldots, n\}$ with m and n as positive integers. Putting $a_{jk} = h_j(k)$, $c_k = g(k)$ and $x_k = \mu(\{k\})$, the problem of determining $U_1(g)$ as in (2.5) is precisely the standard linear programming problem to determine the maximum $U_1(g)$ of $c_1x_1 + \ldots + c_nx_n$ subject to $\sum_k a_{jk}x_k \leq \eta_j$ $(j = 1, \ldots, m)$ and $x_k \geq 0$ $(k = 1, \ldots, n)$. And $U_1^*(g)$ in (2.9) is precisely the value of the associated dual problem. As is well-known, (2.6) holds with the equality sign as soon as both the primal problem and the dual problem are feasible. Equivalently, as soon as $M_1(S)$ is non-empty and, moreover, g is bounded above by some linear combination $\sum_J \beta_j h_j$ with nonnegative coefficients.

Except for Section 3, we will always take S as a topological Hausdorff space, made into a measurable space by the σ-field of all Borel subsets (that is, the smallest σ-field containing all open subsets of S). In particular, every finite subset of S is (Borel) measurable. Let $C_b(S)$ denote the set of all bounded and continuous functions $f: S \to R$. Each finite (Borel) measure μ on S determines the nonnegative (linear) functional $\mu(f) = \int f(s)\,\mu(ds)$ on $C_b(S)$. The space of finite measures on S will be supplied with the usual weak topology. It is the coarsest topology such that the function $\mu \to \mu(f)$ is continuous for each $f \in C_b(S)$. Thus, a sequence or net $\{\mu_r\}$ of finite measures on S converges to the finite measure μ if and only if $\lim_r \mu_r(f) = \mu(f)$ for each $f \in C_b(S)$.

In order that this topology be Hausdorff it is necessary and sufficient that the finite measure μ be completely determined by the corresponding function $\mu(f)$ on $C_b(S)$. It would be sufficient that for each open subset U of S one has

(2.10) $\mu(U) = \sup\{\mu(f): f \in C_b(S);\ f \leq I_U\},$

with I_U as the characteristic function of U. This property does hold when S is metrizable. For, let $d(s, t)$ be a metric for S and apply the monotone convergence theorem to the increasing sequence in $C_b(S)$ defined by $f_k(s) = \min(1, kd(s, U^c))$, with U^c as the complement of U in S.

We usually also like our finite measure μ to be <u>tight</u> in the sense that, for each $\varepsilon > 0$, there exists a compact subset K of S such that $\mu(K^c) < \varepsilon$. This implies that the corresponding functional $\mu(f)$ on $C_b(S)$ is <u>tight</u>. That is, for each $\varepsilon > 0$, there exists a compact subset K of S such that $\mu(f) \leq \varepsilon$ whenever $f: S \to [0, 1]$ is continuous and further $f(s) = 0$ for $s \in K$.

For technical reasons, we will from now on assume that the space S is <u>completely regular</u>. This means that, for each $s_o \in S$, and each open neighborhood U of s_o, there exists a continuous function $\phi: S \to [0,1]$ satisfying $\phi(s_o) = 0$ and $\phi(s) = 1$ for $s \notin U$. Complete regularity is a rather weak assumption. It would be sufficient that S be either compact or metrizable.

For such spaces we have the following important converse. Namely, to each tight nonnegative functional $L(f)$ on $C_b(S)$ there corresponds a unique inner regular finite measure μ on S such that $L(f) = \mu(f)$ for all $f \in C_b(S)$, (see Schwartz (1973) p. 61 and Fremlin (1974) p. 214). One way of proving this is to use the Stone Cech compactification of the completely regular space S. The uniqueness follows from Lemma 3 in Section 8.

A finite measure μ on S is said to be <u>inner regular</u> when

(2.11) $$\mu(B) = \sup\{\mu(K): K \subset B;\ K \text{ compact}\}$$

holds for each Borel subset B of S. This implies condition (2.10) with U open (see Lemma 3) and also that μ is tight.

There exist examples (Schwartz (1973) p. 31, 120) of a separable metric space as well as a non-metrizable compact space carrying finite Borel measures which are not inner regular. Fortunately, in most applications the space S has the property that <u>each</u> finite Borel measure on S is inner regular (in the strong sense (2.11)). Such spaces are called Radon spaces, see Schwartz (1973) for an extensive treatment. Any universally measurable subset of a Radon space is again a Radon space. Every Polish space is a Radon space as well as each continuous image of a Polish space (a so-called Suslin space). A space S is said to be Polish if it is separable and metrizable and admits a metric making S into a complete metric space. Every second countable locally compact space is Polish and thus a Radon space.

In Theorem 1 and 2 below, we take $M_o(S)$ as a <u>convex</u> set of finite measures on S. It is assumed that <u>either</u> S is metrizable <u>or</u> each $\mu \in M_o(S)$ is inner regular. The topology on $M_o(S)$ is the usual weak topology induced by $C_b(S)$.

We will further assume that each function $h_j: S \to R$ $(j \in J)$ is lower semi-continuous (l.s.c.) and that it belongs to the following convex cone of functions H_o which is associated to the given collection $\{h_k, k \in J\}$. Namely, $h \in H_o$ if and only if one can find nonnegative numbers ρ_k $(k \in J)$, all but finitely many equal to zero, such that the function $\emptyset = \sum_{k \in J} \rho_k h_k$ on S is nonnegative and that, moreover, $h + \varepsilon\emptyset$ is bounded below for each number $\varepsilon > 0$. Obviously, $h_j \in H_o$ as soon as h_j is bounded below. Since h_j is l.s.c. this is always true when S is compact.

Theorem 1. Suppose, in addition, that $M_o(S)$ is compact. Then $M_1(S)$ is compact. Moreover, condition (2.3) is not only necessary but also sufficient for $M_1(S)$ to be non-empty.

Theorem 2. Suppose $M_o(S)$ is compact and further that $M_1(S)$ is non-empty. Also assume that the function $g: S \to R$ is upper semi-continuous such that $-g \in H_o$. Then (2.6) holds with the equality sign. Moreover, the supremum in (2.5) is assumed provided $U_1(g)$ is finite.

The proof of the above theorems is given in the appendix (Section 8). For the case where S is compact and $M_o(S)$ is the (convex and compact) set of all inner regular probability measures on S, the above theorems are due to Ky Fan (1959), see also Kemperman (1972) p. 108, 112.

An important application is that where $S = S_1 \times S_2 \times \ldots$ is a finite or countable product of completely regular spaces S_i, while $M_o(S)$ consists of all inner regular probability measures μ on S such that the S_i-marginal $\pi_i\mu$ coincides with a preassigned inner regular probability measure P_i on S_i $(i = 1, 2, \ldots)$. It is obvious that $M_o(S)$ is convex. One can show that $M_o(S)$ is compact as well, (see Section 5).

Here, the S_i-marginal $\nu_i = \pi_i\mu$ of the finite measure μ on the product space S is the measure on S_i defined by

$$(2.12) \quad \nu_i(B) = \mu(S_1 \times S_2 \times S_{i-1} \times B \times S_{i+1} \times \ldots),$$

with B as an arbitrary Borel subset of S_i. If μ is inner regular then ν_i is inner regular. One may also define ν_i by means of

$$(2.13) \qquad \int f \, d\nu_i = \int f(s_i) \, \mu(ds) \quad \text{for all } f \in C_b(S_i),$$

where $s_i \in S_i$ denotes the i-th coordinate of $s = (s_1, s_2, \ldots) \in S$.

3. The finite case

In the present Section, S carries no special topology and is merely a measurable space. Let $a_i: S \to R$ $(i = 1, \ldots, n)$ and $b: S \to R$ be given measurable functions. Consider further the associated function $a: S \to R^n$ defined by $a = (a_1, \ldots, a_n)$ and let $A_n = \text{convc}(a(S))$ denote the convex cone generated by the points $a(s)$ $(s \in S)$. In other words, a point $y = (y_1, \ldots, y_n)$ in R^n belongs to A_n if and only if

(3.1) $y_i = \mu(a_i) = \int a_i(s)\, \mu(ds)$ for $i = 1, \ldots, n$

is true for some (nonnegative) measure μ on S of finite support; (using a "basic" solution, or applying Caratheodory's theorem, one may even assume that the support contains at most n points). The following result is due to Richter (1957) and Rogosinsky (1958). The proof that (i) implies (ii) proceeds by an induction with respect to n.

Lemma 1. Let $y = (y_1, \ldots, y_n) \in R^n$ be given. Then the following are equivalent.

(i) There exists a finite or infinite measure μ on S which satisfies the moment conditions (3.1), with each a_i being μ-integrable.

(ii) There exists a measure μ on S having a finite support of at most n points and satisfying (3.1).

(iii) $y \in A_n$ where $A_n = \text{convc}(a(S))$.

Therefore, it is natural to call A_n a moment space. Given $y \in A_n$, let $M[y]$ denote the set of all measures μ on S (finite or infinite) which satisfy the moment conditions (3.1); this includes the assumption that a_i be μ-integrable $(i = 1, \ldots, n)$. Let $M_f[y]$ denote the (non-empty) set of all $\mu \in M[y]$ which have a finite support consisting of no more than n+1 points. We shall be interested in determining

(3.2) $U(y) = \sup\{\mu(b): \mu \in M[y];\ \mu(|b|) < \infty\}$.

One can show that the right hand side remains unchanged if the supremum is relaxed by allowing that $\mu \in M[y]$ satisfies $\mu(b^+) = \infty$. The above equivalence of (i) and (ii) relative to the $n + 1$ functions $a_1, \ldots, a_n, b$ implies that

(3.3) $U(y) = \sup\{\mu(b): \mu \in M_f[y]\}$;

(since $M_f[y]$ is non-empty we have $U(y) > -\infty$ for all $y \in A_n$). Similarly,

(3.4) $U(y) = \sup\{y_{n+1}: (y, y_{n+1}) \in A_{n+1}\}$,

$(y \in y_n \subset R^n$ and $y_{n+1} \in R)$. Here, A_{n+1} denotes the convex cone $A_{n+1} = \text{convc}(f(S))$ spanned by the range of the function $f: S \to R^{n+1}$ defined by $f(s) = (a_1(s), \ldots, a_n(s), b(s))$ $(s \in S)$. Observe that $(y, U(y))$ is a boundary point of A_{n+1} as soon as $U(y)$ is finite, (still assuming that y belongs to the projection A_n of A_{n+1} onto

R^n).

Suppose that the functions $a_1, \ldots, a_n$ on S were linearly dependent. Thus, there exist scalars $\lambda_1, \ldots, \lambda_n$ not all zero such that $\lambda_1 a_1(s) + \ldots + \lambda_n a_n(s) = 0$ for all $s \in S$. But then each $y \in A_n$ satisfies $\lambda_1 y_1 + \ldots + \lambda_n y_n = 0$, to the effect that some of the moment conditions (3.1) would be redundant. Without loss of generality, we may restrict ourselves to the non-redundant case where $a_1, \ldots, a_n$ are linearly independent. Equivalently, $\mathrm{int}(A_n)$ is non-empty.

Let C denote the set of all n-tuples $c = (c_1, \ldots, c_n)$ of real numbers such that

(3.5) $$b(s) \leq c_1 a_1(s) + \ldots + c_n a_n(s) \quad \text{for all} \quad s \in S.$$

Each $\mu \in M_f[y]$ satisfies (3.1). Integrating (3.5) relative to μ, we see from (3.3) that, for each $y \in A_n$,

(3.6) $$U(y) \leq \inf_{c \in C}(c_1 y_1 + \ldots + c_n y_n).$$

In particular, $U(y)$ is finite as soon as C is non-empty. If C is empty then the right hand side of (3.6) will be interpreted as $+\infty$. Note that the problem of calculating the right hand side of (3.6) is a typical problem in semi-infinite programming.

<u>Theorem</u> 3. Let $y \in R^n$ be fixed such that

(3.7) $$y \in \mathrm{int}(A_n).$$

Then (3.6) holds with the equality sign. In particular, $U(y) = +\infty$ (for all $y \in \mathrm{int}(A_n)$) when C is empty. Moreover, if C is non-empty (so that $U(y)$ is finite) the infimum in (3.6) is assumed by some $c \in C$.

<u>Proof</u>. If $U(y) = +\infty$ then C must be empty and (3.6) trivially holds with the equality sign. Hence, suppose that $U(y)$ is finite. Then through the boundary point $(y, U(y))$ of the convex cone A_{n+1} there passes a supporting hyperplane. More precisely, there exist numbers $c_1, \ldots, c_n, c_{n+1}$ not all zero such that $c_1 y_1 + \ldots + c_n y_n + c_{n+1} U(y) = 0$ while $c_1 z_1 + \ldots + c_n z_n + c_{n+1} z_{n+1} \geq 0$ for all $z \in A_{n+1}$. If $c_{n+1} = 0$ then $c_1 y_1 + \ldots + c_n y_n = 0$ and $c_1 z_1 + \ldots + c_n z_n$ for all $(z_1, \ldots, z_n) \in A_n$; but this contradicts (3.7). Hence $c_{n+1} \neq 0$ and one may as well assume that $c_{n+1} = -1$. We now have

$$U(y) = c_1 y_1 + \ldots + c_n y_n$$

and

$$z_{n+1} \leq c_1 z_1 + \ldots + c_n z_n \quad \text{for all} \quad z \in A_{n+1}.$$

But A_{n+1} contains each points $f(s) = (a_1(s), \ldots, a_n(s), b(s))$ $(s \in S)$, consequently (3.5) holds, that is, $c = (c_1, \ldots, c_n)$ belongs to C. This completes the proof of Theorem 3.

In many applications one is only interested in probability measures μ on S. This amounts to taking $a_1(s) = 1$ for all $s \in S$ and further $y_1 = 1$. Hence, in this case condition (3.7) says precisely that $(y_2, \ldots, y_n)$ is in the interior of the convex hull of the set of points $(a_2(s), \ldots, a_n(s))$ in R^{n-1} $(s \in S)$.

Theorem 3 is due to Richter (1957). It was also discovered in 1960 by Isii (1960) and by Karlin, see Karlin and Studden (1966) p. 472. Related results can be found in Kemperman (1965), (1968), Glashoff (1979) and Gustafson (1979a), (1979b). For the convenience of the reader, we have selected the present notations quite close to those in the latter three papers.

Theorem 3 has many interesting consequences. Let us introduce the function

$$V(y) = \inf_{c \in C}(c_1y_1 + \ldots + c_ny_n), \qquad (y \in R^n). \tag{3.8}$$

It is clearly concave and upper semi-continuous (u.s.c.). From (3.6),

$$-\infty < U(y) \le V(y) \quad \text{for all} \quad y \in A_n. \tag{3.9}$$

Theorem 3 tells us that $U(y) = V(y)$ on $\mathrm{int}(A_n)$. It follows that

$$U(y) = V(y) \quad \text{for all} \quad y \in A_n, \tag{3.10}$$

provided also $U(y)$ is u.s.c. on A_n; (as a concave function, $U(y)$ is always u.s.c. on $\mathrm{int}(A_n)$). In view of (3.4), it would be sufficient that the set A_{n+1} be closed. The result (3.10) for this case is due to Haar (1924), see Glashoff (1979).

<u>Theorem</u> 4. Suppose that S is compact, that $a_j: S \to R$ is continuous $(j = 1, \ldots, n)$ and that $b: S \to R$ is upper semi-continous. Assume further that there exist real constants $d_1, \ldots, d_n$ and $q \ge 0$ such that

$$d_1a_1(s) + \ldots + d_na_n(s) > qb(s) \quad \text{for all} \quad s \in S. \tag{3.11}$$

Then C is non-empty, hence, $U(y)$ and $V(y)$ are finite on A_n. Moreover, $U(y)$ is u.s.c. on all of A_n and, in fact, (3.10) holds.

We also assert that, for each $y \in A_n$, the supremum in (3.3) is assumed.

REMARK. Since a l.s.c. function on a compact set assumes its smallest value, condition (3.11) is equivalent to the existence of real numbers $d_1, \ldots, d_n$ and $q \ge 0$ such that

$$1 \le d_1a_1(s) + \ldots + d_na_n(s) - qb(s) \quad \text{for all} \quad s \in S. \tag{3.12}$$

If $q > 0$ then (3.12) clearly implies that C is non-empty. But also when $q = 0$ since the u.s.c. function $b(s)$ on the compact set S is bounded above. For the same reason, (3.12) with $q = 0$ implies the analogous condition with $q > 0$. If C is known to be non-empty then even condition (3.12) with $q < 0$ implies the analogous condition with $q = 0$ and thus also with $q > 0$.

Condition (3.11) or (3.12) with $q > 0$ is usually called the Krein condition or Slater condition, see Duffin and Karlowitz (1965). Theorem 4, for the special case that $b(s)$ is continuous, was proved by Glashoff and Gustafson (1978); they even showed that A_{n+1} is closed in this case. A far generalization (without proof) of Theorem 4 is given as Theorem 6 in Section 4.

Proof of Theorem 4. Let y_o be a fixed point in the closure $cl(A_n)$ of A_n. Put

(3.13) $$U^o = \overline{\lim_{y \to y_o}}\, U(y),$$

where y is restricted to A_n. It must be shown that

(3.14) $$U(y_o) \geq U_o,$$

each time that $y_o \in A_n$; (upper semi-continuity of $U(.)$ at y_o). Since (3.14) is obvious when $U^o = -\infty$, one may assume that $U^o > -\infty$. By (3.8), (3.9) (where C is known to be empty), this means that U^o is finite.

We will prove a little more. Namely, only assuming that $y_o \in cl(A_n)$ and that U^o is finite, it will be shown that $y_o \in A_n$ in such a way that (3.14) holds.

Let $y_r = (y_{r1}, \ldots, y_{rn})$ be a sequence in A_n converging to $y_o = (y_{o1}, \ldots, y_{on})$, in such a way that $U(y_r)$ converges to U^o as defined by (3.13), where U^o is assumed to be finite. By (3.3), there exist measures μ_r on S of the form

$$\mu_r(g) = p_{r1}g(s_{r1}) + \ldots + p_{rn}g(s_{rn}),$$

with $p_{ri} \geq 0$, $s_{ri} \in S$, such that

$$\mu_r(a_j) = \sum_{i=1}^{n} p_{ri}a_j(s_{ri}) = y_{rj} \quad (j=1,\ldots,n); \quad \sum_{i=1}^{n} p_{ri}b(s_{ri}) = U_o + \varepsilon_r,$$

where $\{\varepsilon_r\}$ converges to zero. Using (3.12), it follows that

$$\sum_{i=1}^{n} p_{ri} \leq \sum_{i=1}^{n} p_{ri}\left[\sum_{j=1}^{n} d_j a_j(s_{ri}) - qb(s_{ri})\right] = \sum_{j=1}^{n} d_j y_{rj} - q(U_o + \varepsilon_r).$$

Here, the right hand side is a bounded function of r, (it has the finite limit $\sum_{j=1}^{n} d_j y_{ro} - qU_o)$, consequently, the numbers $p_{ri} \geq 0$ are uniformly bounded.

Drawing a subnet, one may assume that p_{ri} converges to a number $p_{oi} \geq 0$ $(i = 1, \ldots, n)$ and that s_{ri} converges to a point $s_{ro} \in S$ $(i = 1, \ldots, n)$. Thus the net $\{\mu_r\}$ converges (weakly) to the measure μ_o defined by $\mu_o(g) = p_{o1}g(s_{o1}) + \ldots + p_{on}g(s_{on})$. In particular, since $a_j(.)$ is continuous, $\mu_o(a_j) = \lim_r \mu_r(a_j) = \lim_r y_{rj} = y_{oj}$ $(j = 1, \ldots, n)$, showing that $y_o \in A_n$. Moreover, since $b(.)$ is u.s.c. we have $\mu_o(b) \geq \overline{\lim_r}\, \mu_r(b) = U_o$, showing that $U(y_o) \geq U_o$.

Starting with $y_o \in A_n$, the last assertion of the theorem follows in the same way by choosing the μ_r such that $\mu_r(a_j) = y_{oj}$ $(j = 1, \ldots, n)$ and $\mu_r(b) \uparrow U(y_o)$, where $U(y_o)$ is known to be finite. Selecting an appropriate subnet, one arrives at a measure μ_o such that $\mu_o(a_j) = y_{oj}$ $(j = 1, \ldots, n)$ and $\mu_o(b) \geq U(y_o)$. Obviously, the latter inequality must hold with the equality sign. This completes the proof of Theorem 4.

Let us go back to the general case. Let $y \in A_n$ be given and assume that the supremum $U(y)$ in (3.3) is assumed by a measure μ, (depending on y); sufficient conditions for this are given by Theorem 4. Suppose further that C is non-empty, that $U(y) = V(y)$ and that the infimum $V(y)$ as in (3.8) is assumed by some $(c_1, \ldots, c_n) \in C$, depending on y; (by Theorem 3, the latter two assumptions hold as soon as $y \in \text{int}(A_n)$). Integrating the inequality (3.5) relative to the measure on hand, we see that μ must be supported by the contact set

(3.15) $\quad B(c) = \{s \in S: b(s) = c_1a_1(s) + \ldots + c_na_n(s)\}.$

Conversely, for any $c \in C$ and any measure μ supported by a finite subset of the corresponding contact set $B(c)$ (a so-called critical measure), one obviously has that

(3.16) $\quad U(y) = \int b(s)\, \mu(ds), \quad \text{where} \quad y = \int a(s)\, \mu(ds).$

In particular, (3.16) yields a "parametric" representation of the function $U(.)$ restricted to those $y \in \text{int}(A_n)$ for which the supremum in (3.3) is assumed. Here, μ is an arbitrary critical measure (which acts as the parameter).

This approach invites a closer study of the possible contact sets $B(c)$ as in (3.15) where $c = (c_1, \ldots, c_n)$ satisfies (3.5). Often the set $B(c)$ is a relatively small finite set of points. Suppose for instance that $S = R$ and $a_j(s) = s^{j-1}$ $(j = 1, \ldots, n)$. Then (3.5) leads to a polynomial of degree at most $n - 1$ which supports $b(.)$ from above. If $b(s) = s^N$ ($N \geq n$ an integer) then $N = 2M$ must be even and $B(c)$ consists of at most $(n + 1)/2$ points, (since all real zeros of $c_1 + c_2 s + \dots + c_n s^{n-1} - s^{2M}$ have multiplicity ≥ 2).

4. A general result

Let us return to the situation of Section 2, where S is a completely regular space. We shall only be interested in inner regular finite measures and these may be identified with the tight nonnegative (linear) functionals on $C_b(S)$.

A major drawback of the Theorems 1 and 2 is that the associated formulae (2.3) and (2.7) leave open the problem of determining the quantity $L_o(f)$ defined by (2.1), except in some very simple cases. Therefore, we now state a very general theorem which will often take care of that problem.

Let $a_i(s)$ $(i \in I)$ be an arbitrary collection of l.s.c. functions on S and let α_i $(i \in I)$ be an associated set of real constants. We will take $M_o(S)$ as the set of all finite inner regular (see (2.11)) measures μ on S which satisfy the moment conditions

(4.1) $\quad \mu(a_i) = \int a_i(s)\, \mu(ds) \leq \alpha_i \quad$ for all $i \in I$.

Here, we also require that each function a_i is at least improperly integrable in the sense that $\mu(a_i^+) < \infty$.

Let A_o denote the convex cone consisting of all functions $a: S \to R$ to which there corresponds a nonnegative function $\emptyset$ of the form $\emptyset = \sum_{k \in I} \rho_k a_k$ with $\rho_k \geq 0$, all but finitely many ρ_k equal to zero, such that $a + \varepsilon\emptyset$ is bounded below for each $\varepsilon > 0$. It suffices that $a(s)$ itself is bounded below. As our first condition, we require that

(4.2) $\quad a_i \in A_o \quad$ for each $i \in I$.

In the presence of this condition, we have that a_i is μ-integrable for each $\mu \in M_o(S)$ and each $i \in I$, (compare the analogous situation in the footnote to Section 8). If S is compact then each function $a_i(s)$ is bounded below so that (4.2) is trivially true.

As our next condition, we require the existence of nonnegative numbers d_i $(i \in I)$, all but finitely many equal to zero, such that

(4.3) $\quad 1 \leq \sum_{i \in I} d_i a_i(s) \quad$ for all $s \in S$.

Clearly, this condition is of the same type as the Slater condition (3.12), (where $-b$ is l.s.c. while the f_i are continuous).

Next, we impose a "tightness" condition on the given collection of pairs (a_i, α_i) $(i \in I)$; it holds trivially when S is compact. Namely, assume that, for each number $\varepsilon > 0$, there exists a compact subset K_ε of S such that the following is true. Let f be a continuous function $f: S \to [0, 1]$ such that $f(s) = 0$ for all $s \in K_\varepsilon$. Then one can find nonnegative numbers γ_i $(i \in I)$, all but finitely many equal to zero, such that

$$(4.4) \qquad f(s) \le \sum_{i \in I} \gamma_i a_i(s) \quad \text{for all} \quad s \in S; \quad \sum_{i \in I} \gamma_i \alpha_i \le \varepsilon.$$

<u>Theorem</u> 5. Assume that the above conditions hold. Then in order that $M_o(S)$ be non-empty, it is necessary and sufficient that

$$(4.5) \qquad \sum_{i \in I} \beta_i \alpha_i \ge 0$$

whenever the constants β_i $(i \in I)$ are nonnegative, all but finitely many equal to zero, in such a way that

$$(4.6) \qquad \sum_{i \in I} \beta_i a_i(s) \ge 0 \quad \text{for all} \quad s \in S.$$

Moreover, $M_o(S)$ is compact.

The proof of Theorem 5 will appear elsewhere. It employs a standard Hahn Banach type argument (see Kemperman (1965)).

Suppose that $I' \subset I$ is such that all the functions $a_i(s)$ $(i \in I')$ are nonnegative. Then one may relax the conditions of the theorem by allowing countably many non-zero coefficients d_i with $i \in I'$ in (4.3), and similarly in (4.4) and the definition of A_o, provided that one simultaneously strengthens the main condition (4.5) by allowing countably many non-zero β_i $(i \in I')$.

In the following theorem, $b: S \to R$ is a given upper semi-continuous function such that $-b \in A_o$ (as is always true when S is compact), we maintain the assumptions preceding Theorem 5, except that condition (4.3) is relaxed as follows. Namely, we assume that there exist numbers $d_i \ge 0$ $(i \in I)$, all but finitely many equal to zero, and further a number $q \ge 0$ such that

$$(4.7) \qquad 1 \le \sum_{i \in I} d_i a_i(s) - qb(s) \quad \text{for all} \quad s \in S.$$

We further assume that $M_o(S)$ is non-empty and we shall be interested in the best bound

$$(4.8) \qquad U_o(b) = \sup\{\mu(b): \mu \in M_o(S)\}.$$

<u>Theorem</u> 6. Under the above assumptions, we have that

(4.9) $U_o(b) = \inf\{\sum_{i\varepsilon I} c_i\alpha_i : c_i \geq 0;\ b(s) \leq \sum_{i\varepsilon I} c_i a_i(s)$ for all $s \varepsilon S\}$,

(all but finitely many c_i $(i \varepsilon I)$ equal to zero). Moreover, $U_o(b)$ is finite and the supremum in (4.8) is assumed.

Theorem 6 is an easy consequence of Theorem 5, namely, by adjoining to the set of pairs (a_i, α_i) $(i \varepsilon I)$ the new pair $(-b, \alpha_o)$ with $-\alpha_o$ equal to the right hand side of (4.9). Also note that Theorem 4 is contained in the special case of Theorem 6 where S is compact and I is finite.

5. A general transportation problem

From now on we take S of the form $S = S_1 \times S_2$ with S_1 and S_2 as given measurable spaces. Let further P_1 and P_2 be given probability measures on S_1 and S_2, respectively. Finally, $M_o(s) = M_o(S_1 \times S_2)$ will denote the set of all probability measures μ on S such that the S_i-marginal (see (2.12) for the definition) of μ equals P_i $(i = 1, 2)$; (in the topological case below we will also assume that μ is inner regular). We shall be interested in the quantities

(5.1) $L_o(h) = \inf\{\int h(s, t)\ \mu(ds, dt) : \mu \varepsilon M_o(S_1 \times S_2)\}$

and

(5.2) $U_o(h) = \sup\{\int h(s, t)\ \mu(ds, dt) : \mu \varepsilon M_o(S_1 \times S_2)\}$,

where h is a given measurable function on $S_1 \times S_2$.

Let A and B be measurable subsets of S_1 and S_2, respectively. One may interpret $P_1(A)$ as the total available supply of a certain commodity from sources within the set A and $P_2(B)$ as the total demand from customers within B. In this context, $\mu(A \times B)$ can be interpreted as the total amount of commodity shipped from point $s \varepsilon A$ to some point $t \varepsilon B$. Interpreting $h(s, t)$ as the unit shipping cost, for a direct shipment from s to t, the problem (5.1) on hand is to satisfy all demands and simultaneously to minimize the total transportation cost. But note that we do not require that h is nonnegative or that $h(s, s) = 0$.

From now on we assume that S_1, S_2 are completely regular topological spaces (e.g., metrizable spaces), that the given measures P_1 and P_2 are inner regular and that $M_o(S_1 \times S_2)$ is taken as the class of all inner regular probability measures on $S_1 \times S_2$ having P_i as its S_i-marginal $(i = 1, 2)$.

We supply $M_o(S) = M_o(S_1 \times S_2)$ with the usual weak topology induced by $C_b(S)$. We claim that $M_o(S)$ is <u>compact</u>.

Proof. For, let $\{\mu_r\}$ be an arbitrary subnet in $M_o(S)$. Each probability measure μ_r on $S = S_1 \times S_2$ has the given measures P_1 and P_2 as marginals. Here, P_i is inner regular and thus tight (see the comments following (2.10)). Hence, for each $\varepsilon > 0$, there exists a compact subset $K_{i,\varepsilon}$ of S_i such that $P_i(K^c_{i,\varepsilon}) \le \varepsilon$ (where the complement is relative to S_i); $i = 1, 2$. Then $K_\varepsilon = K_{1,\varepsilon} \times K_{2,\varepsilon}$ is a compact subset of $S = S_1 \times S_2$ such that

$$\mu_r(K^c_\varepsilon) \le P_1(K^c_{1,\varepsilon}) + P_2(K^c_{2,\varepsilon}) \le 2\varepsilon.$$

Therefore, each μ_r belongs to the set M_* of all inner regular probability measures μ on S such that $\mu(K^c_\varepsilon) \le 2\varepsilon$ for each $\varepsilon > 0$. Since M_* is compact (see below), the net $\{\mu_r\}$ admits a convergent subnet with limit $\mu_o \in M_*$. Using the definition (2.13) of marginal, it is easily seen that $\mu_o \in M_o(S)$.

That M_* is compact is well-known in the special case where S is metrizable, see Billingsley (1968) p. 37. For the more general case that S is completely regular, one may argue as follows.

One may identify the finite inner regular measures on S with the set of tight nonnegative (linear) functionals $\mu(f)$ on $C_b(S)$ supplied with the topology of pointwise convergence. Therefore, M_* may be identified with the set of functions $f \to \mu(f)$ on $C_b(S)$ such that $\mu(1) = 1$; $\mu(f) \ge 0$ if $f \ge 0$; $\mu(\alpha f + \beta g) = \alpha\mu(f) + \beta\mu(g)$; $\mu(f) \le 2\varepsilon$ when $\varepsilon > 0$, $0 \le f \le 1$ and $f(s) = 0$ on K_ε, again with the topology of pointwise convergence; (implicitly, we also used (8.1); also note that each such functional is tight). Consequently M_* may be identified with a closed subset of the product space $\prod_f [\inf f, \sup f]$ with the product topology, (one component for each $f \in C_b(S)$). It follows from Tychonoff's theorem that M_* is compact.

As an application, suppose $h = h(s, t)$ is a l.s.c. function on $S = S_1 \times S_2$ which is bounded below. It follows from (8.1) that the function $\mu \to \mu(h)$ on the compact set $M_o(S)$ is also l.s.c., therefore, it assumes its smallest value. In other words, the infimum (5.1) is assumed. Similarly, the supremum in (5.2) is assumed when $h\colon S \to R$ is u.s.c. and bounded above.

Consider the special case where S_1 and S_2 are copies of the same metrizable space T having $d(s, t) \ge 0$ as a matric. The corresponding infimum $L_o(d)$ in (5.1) is then called the Wasserstein distance $W_d(P_1, P_2)$ between the inner regular probability measures P_1 and P_2 on T (relative to the metric d). The fact that the infimum $L_o(d) = W_d(P_1, P_2)$ is assumed can be expressed by saying that there exists a pair of random variables X and Y taking values in T, having the distributions P_1 and P_2, respectively, and such that $Ed(X, Y) = W_d(P_1, P_2)$. See Dudley (1976), chapter 20, for a proof in the case of a separable metric space. Major (1978) p. 504 found a simple explicit formula for $W_d(P_1, P_2)$ when $T = R$ while the metric is of the form $d(s, t) = \phi(s - t)$ with ϕ convex.

Often the measure $\mu \in M_o(S_1 \times S_2)$ is subject to further conditions of the form

(5.3) $\quad \mu(h_j) = \int h_j(s, t)\, \mu(ds, dt) \le \eta_j$ for each $j \in J$,

with $h_j(s, t)$ as a l.s.c. function. Since presently $M_o(S_1 \times S_2)$ is compact, we are in a good position to apply Theorems 1 and 2. However, this leaves open the problem of determining $L_o(h)$ as in (2.1) or (5.1). Therefore, we prefer to apply Theorem 5.

For $i = 1, 2$, let F_i be a given convex cone of P_i-integrable bounded below l.s.c. functions $\phi_i: S_i \to R$, containing all bounded l.s.c. functions on S_i. Suppose further that, for each $j \in J$, one can find $\phi_{j,i} \in F_i$ $(i = 1, 2)$, such that the l.s.c. function

$$h_j'(s, t) = h_j(s, t) + \phi_{j,1}(s) + \phi_{j,2}(t)$$

is bounded below.

<u>Theorem</u> 7. In order that there exists $\mu \in M_o(S_1 \times S_2)$ satisfying (5.3), it is necessary and sufficient that

(5.4) $\quad \phi_1(s) + \phi_2(t) + \sum_{j \in J} \beta_j h_j(s, t) \ge 0$ for all $s \in S_1$, $t \in S_2$

implies that

(5.5) $\quad P_1(\phi_1) + P_2(\phi_2) + \sum_{j \in J} \beta_j \eta_j \ge 0.$

Here, the β_j $(j \in J)$ are nonnegative constants, all but finitely many equal to zero. Further ϕ_i is an arbitrary member of F_i $(i = 1, 2)$.

<u>Proof</u>. The necessity of (5.5) is obvious from an integration of (5.4). For $j \in J$, let $\eta_j' = \eta_j + P_1(\phi_{j,1}) + P_2(\phi_{j,2})$. If $\mu \in M_o(S_1 \times S_2)$ satisfies $\mu(h_j') \le \eta_j'$ then it also satisfies $\mu(h_j) \le \eta_j$ (and conversely), since $\phi_{j,1}(s) + \phi_{j,2}(t)$ integrates out to exactly $P_1(\phi_{j,1}) + P_2(\phi_{j,2})$. Therefore, replacing the pairs (h_j, η_j) by (h_j', η_j'), we may assume that all functions h_j $(j \in J)$ are bounded below.

Let μ be a finite inner regular measure on $S = S_1 \times S_2$. It belongs to $M_o(S)$ if and only if

(5.6) $\quad \int \phi_1(s)\, \mu(ds, dt) \le P_1(\phi_1)$; $\int \phi_2(t)\, \mu(ds, dt) \le P_2(\phi_2)$

holds for all $\phi_1 \in F_1$, $\phi_2 \in F_2$. After all, both $f_i \in F_i$ and $-f_i \in F_i$

when $f_i \varepsilon C_b(S_i)$, $(i = 1, 2)$.

Hence, it suffices to prove that μ can be found so as to satisfy both (5.3) and (5.6), assuming condition (5.5). This we do by applying Theorem 5 with the collection of pairs (a_i, α_i) $(i \varepsilon I)$ replaced by the set of pairs $(h_j(s, t), \eta_j)$ $(j \varepsilon J)$ together with the pairs $(\phi_1(s), P_1(\phi_1))$ with $\phi_1 \varepsilon F_1$ and the pairs $(\phi_2(t), P_2(\phi_2))$ with $\phi_2 \varepsilon F_2$. Since the main condition (4.5) of Theorem 5 is then exactly the main condition (5.5) of Theorem 7, it suffices to verify the three side conditions in Theorem 5. Condition (4.2) is trivially satisfied since the l.s.c. functions $h_j(s, t)$, $\phi_1(s)$ and $\phi_2(t)$ $(j \varepsilon J;\ \phi_1 \varepsilon F_i)$ are all bounded below. Also condition (4.3) holds since the function $\phi_i \equiv 1$ belongs to F_i.

As to condition (4.4), let $\varepsilon > 0$ be given. For $i = 1, 2$, choose K_i as a compact subset of S_i such that $P_i(K_i^c) \leq \varepsilon/2$ and define, for $s \varepsilon S_i$, $\phi_i(s) = 0$ for $s \varepsilon K_i$ and $\phi_i(s) = 1$, otherwise. Then any $f\colon S \to [0, 1]$, such that $f(s, t) = 0$ for $(s, t) \varepsilon K_1 \times K_2$, will satisfy

$$f(s, t) \leq \phi_1(s) + \phi_2(t) \quad \text{where} \quad P_1(\phi_1) + P_2(\phi_2) \leq \varepsilon.$$

Since $\phi_i \varepsilon F_i$ $(i = 1, 2)$ and $K_1 \times K_2$ is compact, this establishes the last condition (4.4).

The following is an immediate corollary. Here, $L_b(S_i)$ is the class of all functions $\phi_i\colon S_i \to R$ which are l.s.c. and bounded.

<u>Theorem</u> 8. Let h be a l.s.c. and bounded below function on $S_1 \times S_2$ and let $L_o(h)$ be defined by (5.1). Then

$$(5.6) \qquad L_o(h) = \sup[P_2(\phi_2) - P_1(\phi_1)],$$

where ϕ_1, ϕ_2 are subject to $\phi_1 \varepsilon L_b(S_1)$, $-\phi_2 \varepsilon L_b(S_2)$ and the inequalities

$$(5.7) \qquad \phi_2(t) - \phi_1(s) \leq h(s, t) \quad \text{for all} \quad s \varepsilon S_1,\ t \varepsilon S_2.$$

Moreover, the infimum in (5.1) is assumed.

<u>Proof</u>. From Theorem 7, there exists $\mu \varepsilon M_o(S_1 \times S_2)$ satisfying $\mu(h) \leq \eta$ if and only if $\phi_i \varepsilon L_b(S_i)$ $(i = 1, 2)$ and $\phi_1(s) + \phi_2(t) + \beta h(s, t) \geq 0$ (all $s \varepsilon S_1$, $t \varepsilon S_2$) imply $P_1(\phi_1) + P_2(\phi_2) + \beta\eta \geq 0$. Here, $\beta \geq 0$. Since this is trivially true when $\beta = 0$, one may assume $\beta = 1$. Replacing ϕ_2 by $-\phi_2$, we see that the smallest possible value η is given by the right hand side of (5.6). This proves Theorem 8. Another proof of the last assertion was given earlier in this Section.

REMARK. Note that in terms of the transportation problem having $h(s, t)$

as a transportation cost function, the quantities $\phi_1(s)$ and $\phi_2(t)$ admit the usual interpretation (see Gale (1960) p. 15) as commodity prices at the source point $s \in S_1$ and the destination point $t \in S_2$, respectively. The functions ϕ_1^* and ϕ_2^* which assume the supremum in (5.6), if they exist, indicate how sensitive the minimum transportation cost $L_o(h)$ is under small changes of P_1 and P_2. And the measure μ which attains the infimum in (5.1) (which always exists) must be carried by the set

$$\{(s,t): h(s,t) = \phi_2^*(t) - \phi_1^*(s)\},$$

for each such optimal pair (ϕ_1^*, ϕ_2^*).

6. Theorems of Kantorovich, Rubinstein, Nachbin, and Strassen

From now on we take $S_1 = S_2 = T$ as the same completely regular space. Further $h(s, t)$ is a bounded below lower semi-continuous function on $T \times T$. Since conditions (5.4) or (5.7) are often difficult to verify, one wonders whether it suffices to verify only the case $\phi_1 = \phi_2$. This leads us to introduce the class L_h of all bounded universally measurable functions $\phi: T \to R$ which satisfy

(6.1) $\quad \phi(t) - \phi(s) \le h(s, t)$ for all $s, t \in T$;

(the "L" stands for Lipschitz). One must have $h(t, t) \ge 0$ $(t \in T)$ in order that L_h be non-empty. The inequalities (6.1) are equivalent to

(6.2) $\quad \phi(t) - \phi(s) \le h_*(s, t)$ for all $s, t \in T$,

hence, $L_h = L_{h_*}$. Here, h_* will denote the function on $T \times T$ associated to h which is defined by

(6.3) $\quad h_*(s, t) = \inf[h(t_1, t_2) + h(t_2, t_3) + \dots + h(t_{n-1}, t_n)].$

Here, $t_1 = s$; $t_n = t$ and $n \ge 1$. The case $n = 1$ of an empty sum is allowed only when $s = t$ and leads to $h_*(t, t) \le 0$. Note that $h_* \le h$ and

(6.4) $\quad h_*(s, t) \le h_*(s, u) + h_*(u, t)$,

for all $s, t, u \in T$. If $h_*(u, u) < 0$ for a single $u \in T$ then (from (6.4) with $t = u$ or $s = u$) one has $h(s, u) = -\infty$ and $h(u, t) = -\infty$, thus, $h(s, t) = -\infty$ for all $s, t \in T$. From (6.2), if L_h is non-empty then h_* is bounded below and $h_*(t, t) = 0$ for all $t \in T$.

REMARK. If $h(s, t)$ is interpreted as a transportation cost, along a direct route from s to t, then $h_*(s, t)$ represents the minimal cost of shipping a unit amount from s to t under so-called transshipment, where it is allowed to ship the commodity indirectly along any path $(t_1 = s, t_2, \ldots, t_{n-1}, t_n = t)$ in T leading from s to t. In most applications one would have $h(t, t) = 0$ for all $t \in T$.

From now on we assume that the completely regular space T is also a Suslin space, hence, T is second countable and metrizable. Any Borel subset T of any Polish space X has these properties, see Schwartz (1973); in the latter case, T is only Polish when it happens to be a G_δ subset of X. Recall that a finite Borel measure on a Suslin space is always inner regular.

DEFINITION. By $H(S) = H(T \times T)$ we shall denote the class of all functions $h(s, t)$ on $T \times T$ which are bounded below, lower semi-continuous and satisfy both

$$(6.5) \qquad h(s, t) \le h(s, u) + h(u, t) \quad \text{for all} \quad s, t, u \in T$$

and

$$(6.6) \qquad h(t, t) = 0 \quad \text{for all} \quad t \in T.$$

The class $H(T \times T)$ was already employed by Levin and Milyutin (1978) for the special case that T is compact. If $h \in H(S)$ then the function $\phi(t) = \inf_u h(u, t)$ clearly satisfies (6.1) and $\inf h \le \phi \le 0$, thus, ϕ is bounded. Since T is a Suslin space, the function ϕ is also universally measurable so that $\phi \in L_h$, showing that L_h is non-empty.

<u>Theorem</u> 9. We have for each $h \in H(T \times T)$ that

$$(6.7) \qquad L_o(h) = \sup\{(P_2 - P_1)(\phi) : \phi \in L_h\},$$

where $L_o(h)$ was defined in (5.1).

<u>Sketch of a proof</u>. Let the suprema in (5.6) and (6.7) be denoted by U and U', respectively. Integrating (6.1) relative to a measure $\mu \in M_o(T \times T)$, we see that $U' \le L_o(h) = U$. To prove that $U \le U'$, let ϕ_1 and ϕ_2 be as in Theorem 8 and define

$$\phi(t) = \inf_u [\phi_1(u) + h(u, t)].$$

Here, $\phi_1(u)$ and $h(u, t)$ are l.s.c. and it follows (using that T is Suslin) that ϕ is universally measurable. It is obvious that $\phi_2 \le \phi \le \phi_1$, thus, ϕ is bounded. Moreover, using (6.5),

$$\phi(t) = \inf_u [\phi_1(u)+h(u,t)] \le \inf_u [\phi_1(u)+h(u,s)]+h(s,t) = \phi(s) + h(s,t),$$

showing that $\phi \in L_h$. Hence,

$$U' \geq P_2(\phi) - P_1(\phi) \geq P_2(\phi_2) - P_1(\phi_1),$$

which establishes that $U' \geq U$.

EXAMPLE 1. Choose $d(s, t)$ as any fixed metric for T. Obviously, $d \in H(T \times T)$. In addition, we have $d(s, t) = d(t, s)$ and $d(s, t) > 0$ for $s \neq t$ (and $d(s, t)$ is continuous). It follows from Theorem 9 that the Wasserstein distance $W_d(P_1, P_2) = L_o(d)$ between the probability measures P_1, P_2 on T satisfies

(6.8) $$W_d(P_1, P_2) = \sup[P_2(\phi) - P_1(\phi)],$$

where ϕ ranges through the bounded functions on T which satisfy the Lipschitz condition $\phi(t) - \phi(s) \leq d(s, t)$, $(s, t \in T)$. Obviously, each such function ϕ is continuous and therefore in the present case the space T need not be Suslin, but only metrizable. A somewhat weaker result was obtained by Dudley (1976), chapter 20; (he assumes that $d(., t)$ is P_1-integrable and $d(s, .)$ is P_2-integrable, and allows unbounded functions ϕ in (6.8)). For the case of a compact metric space, the result (6.8) represents a classical result due to Kantorovich and Rubinstein (1958).

EXAMPLE 2. That condition (6.5) for $h \in H(T \times T)$ cannot be omitted in Theorem 9 can be seen from the situation $T = R^k$ with $h(s, t) = |s - t|^p$ and $p > 1$, (where $|s - t|$ is the Euclidean distance between s and t). Taking very small steps, one sees from (6.3) that $h_* = 0$ in this case. It follows from (6.1) with h replaced by h_* that $L_h = L_{h_*}$ consists of the constant functions only. Hence, (6.7) is false whenever $P_1 \neq P_2$.

EXAMPLE 3. Let the space T be endowed with a closed quasi (or pseudo) partial ordering $\leq$, (also called partial ordering). The set $G = \{(s, t): s \leq t\}$ is called the graph of the partial ordering. It can be any closed subset of $T \times T$ such that $(t, t) \in G$ while $(s, u) \in G$ and $(u, t) \in G$ together imply $(s, t) \in G$, (any $s, t, u \in T$). Now choose

(6.9) $$\begin{aligned} h(s, t) &= 0 \quad \text{if} \quad (s, t) \in G; \\ &= 1 \quad \text{if} \quad (s, t) \notin G. \end{aligned}$$

It is obvious that $h \in H(T \times T)$.

Let I_G consist of all universally measurable functions $\phi: T \to R$ which are increasing (= non-decreasing relative to the given partial ordering) and satisfy $0 \leq \phi \leq 1$. If $\phi \in L_h$ then, from (6.1), $\sup \phi \leq 1 + \inf \phi$. In fact, one easily verifies that in the present case the class L_h consists of all functions $c - \phi$ with c as a constant function and $\phi \in I_G$. It follows immediately from (6.7) that

(6.10) $\quad L_o(h) = \sup\{P_1(\phi) - P_2(\phi): \phi \in I_G\}.$

Since the infimum (5.1) is assumed, the result (6.10) is largely equivalent to the following result due to Strassen (1965). The analogous result where $\varepsilon = 0$ and T is compact (not necessarily metrizable) is due to Nachbin (1951), (1965). Many related results can be found in the work of Kamae, Krengel and O'Brien (1977) and Kamae and Krengel (1978).

Theorem 10. Let T be a metrizable Suslin space (e.g., a Polish space) endowed with a closed partial ordering. Put $G = \{(s,t): s \leq t\}$ and let ε be a given number, $0 \leq \varepsilon \leq 1$. Then the following are equivalent.

(i) One has $P_1(\phi) \leq P_2(\phi) + \varepsilon$, for all $\phi \in I_G$.

(ii) There exists a probability measure μ on $T \times T$ having marginals P_1 and P_2, respectively, such that $\mu(G) \geq 1 - \varepsilon$.

(iii) There exist random variables X and Y taking values in T with distributions P_1 and P_2, respectively, such that $P(X \leq Y) \geq 1 - \varepsilon$.

REMARK. One can show that (i) is equivalent to $P_1(B) \leq P_2(B) + \varepsilon$ for each "upper" set B of the form

$$B = \{t: s \leq t \text{ for some } s \in K\},$$

with K as a compact subset of T.

Theorem 9 can be generalized as follows. Let H_* be an arbitrary subset of $H(T \times T)$ and let $\varepsilon(h)$ be a given real-valued function on H_*. Question: does there exist $\mu \in M_o(T \times T)$ such that

(6.11) $\quad \int h(s, t)\, \mu(ds, dt) \leq \varepsilon(h)$ for each $h \in H_*$?

Using Theorem 1, one easily shows that this is true if and only if

(6.12) $\quad P_2(\phi) - P_1(\phi) \leq \varepsilon'(h)$ for each $h \in H_*'$ and each $\phi \in L_h$.

Here, H_*' denotes the convex hull of H_*. Moreover,

(6.13) $\quad \varepsilon'(h) = \inf\{\sum_j \beta_j \varepsilon(f_j): f = \sum_j \beta_j f_j;\ \beta_j \geq 0;\ f_j \in H_*\},$

(finite sums only). As one application, one has the following curious result. Here, T is supplied with a closed partial ordering. It is further assumed that P_2 is stochastically larger than P_1 in the sense that there exist random variables X and Y taking values in T having distributions P_1 and P_2, respectively, and such that $X \leq Y$. Let further $h \in H(T \times T)$ and the real number α be fixed. For instance, h might derive from another closed partial ordering as in (6.9).

Theorem 11. In order that there exist random variables X, Y with values in T and distributions P_1, P_2, respectively, satisfying both $X \le Y$ and $Eh(X, Y) \le \alpha$, it is necessary and sufficient that

$$P_1(\phi) \le P_2(\phi) + \alpha$$

for each bounded universally measurable function $\phi: T \to R$ such that

(6.14) $\phi(s) \le \phi(t) + h(s, t)$ whenever $s \le t$.

REMARK. If h derives as in (6.9) from another closed partial ordering $\le_1$ then $Eh(X, Y) \le 0$ means that $P(X \le_1 Y) = 1$. One easily constructs an example of pairs P_1, P_2 of probability measures on a 4-point space $T = \{1, 2, 3, 4\}$ and further two partial orderings $\le$ and $\le_1$ on T such that the conditions $P(X \le Y) = 1$ and $P(X \le_1 Y) = 1$ can be realized separately but not simultaneously, (where each time X, Y have distributions P_1, P_2, respectively). This also shows that the convex hull H_*' in condition (6.12) cannot be replaced by H_*.

7. Transshipment

Here, we will elaborate on the interpretation of $L_o(h)$ defined by (5.1) in terms of a transportation problem and especially the associated transshipment problem, see the remarks following (5.2) and (6.4). The subsequent discussion is partly heuristic.

It will be convenient to regard a path $(t_1, t_2, \dots, t_n)$ in T as an element of the n-fold Cartesian product T^n. Mass (commodity) at t not moved at all will be regarded as having been shipped along the path (t, t). An actual transshipment procedure, leading from an initial mass distribution P_1 (of the commodity on hand) to the final mass distribution P_2, can be described as a sequence $\{\gamma_n\}_{n=2}^{\infty}$ of measures with γ_n as a measure on T^n. Then $\gamma_n(A_1 \times A_2 \times \dots \times A_n)$ would represent the amount of mass which is shipped along some path $(t_1, \dots, t_n)$ for which $t_j \in A_j$ $(j = 1, \dots, n)$. Here, we think of t_1 as the initial position and t_n as the final position. The total transshipment cost would be

$$(7.1) \qquad \sum_{n=2}^{\infty} \int \sum_{i=1}^{n-1} h(t_i, t_{i-1})\, d\gamma_n = \int h(s, t)\, \sigma(ds, dt),$$

where

$$(7.2) \qquad \sigma(A \times B) = \sum_{n=2}^{\infty} \sum_{i=1}^{n-1} \gamma_n(T^{i-1} \times A \times B \times T^{n-i-1}).$$

Here, $\sigma(A, B)$ represents the total mass which at some stage of the transshipment is directly moved from a point in A to a point in B, (counting each stage; thus, the same mass might be counted several times in $\sigma(A, B)$).

To make sure that both sides of (7.1) are well-defined, we will assume that the measure σ is finite. In order that the starting distribution be P_1 and the final distribution be P_2, one must have

$$(7.3) \qquad P_1(A) = \sum_{n=2}^{\infty} \gamma_n(A \times T^{n-1}); \; P_2(A) = \sum_{n=2}^{\infty} \gamma_n(T^{n-1} \times A).$$

The marginals Q_1 and Q_2 of σ are given by

$$(7.4) \qquad \begin{aligned} Q_1(A) &= \sum_{n=2}^{\infty} \sum_{i=1}^{n-1} \gamma_n(T^{i-1} \times A \times T^{n-i}); \\ Q_2(A) &= \sum_{n=2}^{\infty} \sum_{i=1}^{n-1} \gamma_n(T^{i} \times A \times T^{n-1-i}). \end{aligned}$$

These represent the total mass which leaves A or arrives in A, respectively, (usually while in transit; again, the same mass element might be counted several times, namely, each time it leaves A or arrives in A, respectively). It follows from (7.3) and (7.4) that

$$(7.5) \qquad Q_1(A) - P_1(A) = Q_2(A) - P_2(A) = \sum_{n=3}^{\infty} \sum_{i=1}^{n-2} \gamma_n(T^{i} \times A \times T^{n-1-i}).$$

The latter sum represents the amount of mass which passes through A counting each time that the mass element is in A, but not counting the starting time or final arrival time.

In the special case that the cost function $h(s, t)$ satisfies (6.5), the sum in (7.1) is no smaller than $h(t_1, t_n)$, hence,

$$\mu(A \times B) = \sum_{n=2}^{\infty} \gamma_n(A \times T^{n-2} \times B) \quad \text{satisfies} \quad \int h \, d\mu \le \int h \, d\sigma.$$

From (7.3), this measure μ has marginals P_1 and P_2. Hence, as is intuitive, there is no improvement in cost by allowing transshipment. But, if (6.5) fails to hold for a single triplet s, t, and u, then transshipment does improve the shipping cost (as compared to direct shipping), for instance when P_1 is carried by $\{s\}$ and P_2 by $\{t\}$.

The result (7.5) suggests the problem of determining

$$(7.6) \qquad A(h) = \inf\{\int h(s, t) \, \sigma(ds, dt): \pi_2\sigma - \pi_1\sigma = P_2 - P_1\},$$

where $\pi_1\sigma$ and $\pi_2\sigma$ denote the marginals of the (variable) finite measure σ on $T \times T$. If ever $h(t, t) < 0$ then clearly $A(h) = -\infty$, thus, one may as well assume that $h(t, t) \ge 0$ for all $t \in T$. Since there is no need for σ to have any mass on the diagonal (for, one is only interested in the difference $\pi_2\sigma - \pi_1\sigma$ which is not effected by the mass of σ on the diagonal), one may as well assume that $h(t,t) = 0$ for all $t \in T$. From the definition of L_h and an integration of (6.1), we have

(7.7) $\qquad A(h) \geq B(h)$, where $B(h) = \sup\{(P_2 - P_1)(\phi) : \phi \in L_h\}$.

Now suppose that h_* defined by (6.3) is bounded below and lower semi-continuous. Then $h_* \in H(T \times T)$ (see (6.5)) and Theorem 9 yields that $L_o(h_*) = B(h_*)$. Since in (5.1) the infimum is assumed, there exists a measure μ on $T \times T$ having the marginals P_1 and P_2, such that $\mu(h_*) = L_o(h_*) = B(h_*) = B(h)$, (the latter since $L_h = L_{h_*}$).

The definition (6.3) of h_* suggests that the cost $\mu(h_*)$ can be realized as the cost of a suitable transshipment with P_1 as the starting distribution and P_2 as the finish distribution. But then the previous discussion, in particular (7.5), would imply that $A(h) \geq \mu(h_*) = B(h)$, therefore,

(7.8) $\qquad A(h) = B(h)$.

For the case that T is compact (under a mild side condition which is satisfied when h is bounded), the result (7.8) was proved by Levin and Milyutin (1978). They obtained many other important results for the compact case.

By the way, infimum (7.6) is sometimes not assumed. For instance, in Example 2 with $h(s, t) = |s - t|^p$ and $p > 1$, one has $h_* = 0$ and $A(h) = 0$. But it $P_1 \neq P_2$ there does not exist any measure σ on $T \times T$ with $\sigma(h) = 0$ and marginals Q_1 and Q_2 such that $Q_2 - Q_1 = P_2 - P_1$.

8. Appendix

Here, we prove Theorems 1 and 2.

Lemma 3. Suppose $h: S \to R$ is lower semi-continuous and bounded below and let μ be a finite measure on S. Unless S is metrizable, we also assume that S is completely regular and that μ is inner regular. Then

(8.1) $\qquad \mu(h) = \sup\{\mu(f) : f \in C_b(S);\ f \leq h\}$.

REMARK. If S is a metric space then in (8.1) one may restrict f to the class $C_u(S)$ of all bounded uniformly continuous functions on S.

Proof. One may assume that $h \geq 0$. Suppose first that S is a metrizable space with metric $d(s, t)$. Consider the increasing sequence

$$f_k(s) = \inf_t (h(t) + kd(s, t)),$$

$(k = 1, 2, \ldots)$ of functions on S. Obviously $0 \le f_k(s) \le h(s)$. It is easy to see that $|f_k(s') - f_k(s)| \le kd(s, s')$, thus f_k is uniformly continuous.

Let $s \in S$ and $\varepsilon > 0$ be given. Since h is l.s.c. there exists a number $\delta > 0$ such that $h(t) > h(s) - \varepsilon$ whenever $d(s, t) < \delta$. It follows that $f_k(s) \ge \min(h(s) - \varepsilon, k\delta)$, hence, $\{f_k(s)\}$ converges increasingly to $h(s)$. Consequently, $f_k' = \min(k, f_k(s))$ is a sequence in $C_b(S)$ which converges increasingly to h. Using the monotone convergence theorem, one obtains (8.1).

Next, suppose that S is completely regular and that μ is inner regular. Consider first the situation that $h = I_U$ is the characteristic function of an open subset U of S. Let $\varepsilon > 0$. By inner regularity, see (2.11), there exists a compact subset K of U such that $\mu(U \cap K^c) < \varepsilon$. To each $x \in K$ there corresponds a continuous function $\phi_x: S \to [0, 1]$ satisfying $\phi_x(x) = 1$ and $\phi_x(s) = 0$ for $s \in U^c$. One has $\phi_x(s) > 1 - \varepsilon$ on an open neighborhood V_x of x. Finitely many $V_{x_1}, \ldots, V_{x_n}$ will cover K. Then $f = \max(\phi_{x_1}, \ldots, \phi_{x_n})$ satisfies $f \le I_U$ and $f \ge (1 - \varepsilon)I_K$, hence, $\mu(f) \ge (1 - \varepsilon)(\mu(U) - \varepsilon)$. Letting $\varepsilon \downarrow 0$, one obtains (8.1) with $h = I_U$. For arbitrary h, (8.1) easily follows by introducing the open sets $U_{n,j} = \{s \in S: h(s) > j2^{-n}\}$ and noting that $h_n = 2^{-n} \sum_{j=1}^{\infty} I_{U_{n,j}}$ converges increasingly to h.

<u>Proof of Theorem</u> 1. It is given that $M_o(S)$ is a convex and compact set of finite measures on S. Unless S is metrizable, it is also assumed that S is completely regular and that each $\mu \in M_o(S)$ is inner regular. Suppose $h: S \to R$ is lower semi-continuous and bounded below. Then (8.1) holds for each $\mu \in M_o(S)$. Thus the set $M = \{\mu \in M_o(S): \mu(h) \le \eta\}$ (with η a real constant) is the intersection of $M_o(S)$ with the collection of sets $M^f = \{\mu: \mu(f) \le \eta\}$, one for each $f \in C_b(S)$ with $f \le h$. Since each set M^f is closed (by the definition of the weak topology), it follows that M is a closed and thus compact subset of $M_o(S)$.

Let us first consider the case that, for each $j \in J$, the l.s.c. function $h_j: S \to R$ is bounded below. It follows from the above remarks that the set $M_j = \{\mu \in M_o(S): \mu(h_j) \le \eta\}$ is compact. Moreover, $M_1(S)$ is precisely the intersection of all sets M_j $(j \in J)$.

We must show that this intersection is non-empty. By compactness, it suffices to show that each finite intersection $M_{j_1} \cap M_{j_2} \cap .. \cap M_{j_m}$ is non-empty. One may as well assume that $J = \{1, \ldots, m\}$ is finite. It must be shown that $\mu(h_j) \leq \eta_j$ $(j = 1, \ldots, m)$ holds for at least one $\mu \in M_o(S)$.

Let W denote the set of points $w = (w_1, \ldots, w_m)$ in R^m such that $\mu(h_j) \leq w_j$ $(j = 1, \ldots, m)$ holds for some $\mu \in M_o(S)$. It must be shown that $(\eta_1, \ldots, \eta_m) \in W$. Since $M_o(S)$ is convex, the set W is a convex subset of R^m with the additional property that $w \in W$ and $w \leq w'$ imply $w' \in w$.

We further claim that W is closed. Let $w_r = (w_{r1}, \ldots, w_{rm})$ be a sequence in W converging to $w_o = (w_{o1}, \ldots, w_{om})$. Let $\mu_r \in M_o(S)$ be such that $\mu_r(h_j) \leq w_{rj}$ $(j = 1, \ldots, m)$. Since $M_o(S)$ is compact, we can draw a convergent subnet $\{\mu_r\}$ with limit $\mu_o \in M_o(S)$. Since h_j is a l.s.c. function on $M_o(S)$ (because of (9.1)), it follows that

$$\mu_o(h_j) \leq \underline{\lim_r}\, \mu_r(h_j) \leq \underline{\lim_r}\, w_{rj} = w_{oj},$$

$(j = 1, \ldots, m)$, implying that $w_o \in W$.

We conclude that W is an intersection of closed half spaces

$$V = \{w \in R^m\colon \beta_1 w_1 + \ldots + \beta_m w_m \geq \gamma\}$$

with $\beta_j \geq 0$ $(j = 1, \ldots, m)$. It suffices to show that $(\eta_1, \ldots, \eta_m) \in V$. If $\mu \in M_o(S)$ then $w_j = \mu(h_j)$ $(j = 1, \ldots, m)$ defines a point $w \in W$ V, thus, $\beta_1\mu(h_1) + \ldots + \beta_m\mu(h_m) \geq \gamma$. It follows from (2.1) that $L_o(\beta_1 h_1 + \ldots + \beta_m h_m) \geq \gamma$. Applying (2.3) we conclude that $\beta_1\eta_1 + \ldots + \beta_m\eta_m \geq \gamma$, that is, $(\eta_1, \ldots, \eta_m) \in V$.

This establishes the special case where each function h_j on S is bounded below. As to the general case, it is given that for each $j \in J$ there exists a <u>nonnegative</u> function of the form $\emptyset_j = \sum_{k\in J} \rho_{jk} h_k$ with $\rho_{jk} \geq 0$ (all but finitely many equal to zero) such that $h_{j,\varepsilon} = h_j + \varepsilon\emptyset_j$ is bounded below for each $\varepsilon > 0$. Define

$$\zeta_j = \sum_{k\in J} \rho_{jk}\eta_k; \qquad \eta_{j,\varepsilon} = \eta_j + \varepsilon\zeta_j, \qquad (j \in J;\ \varepsilon > 0).$$

Using that $\mu(h_j) \leq \mu(h_j + \varepsilon\emptyset_j) = \mu(h_{j,\varepsilon})$, one easily sees that the condition that $\mu(h_j) \leq \eta_j$ (all $j \in J$) is equivalent to the condition that $\mu(h_{j,\varepsilon}) \leq \eta_{j,\varepsilon}$ (all $j \in J$; $\varepsilon > 0$).*)

---

*) If true then all functions $h_j + \varepsilon\emptyset_j$ $(j \in J;\ \varepsilon > 0)$ would be μ-integrable, equivalently, all functions h_j $(j \in J)$ are μ-integrable.

Thus, $M_1(S)$ can also be defined as the set of all $\mu \in M_o(S)$ satisfying $\mu(h) \leq \eta$ for all pairs $(h_{j,\varepsilon}, \eta_{j,\varepsilon})$ $(j \in J;\ \varepsilon > 0)$. Moreover, the given condition (2.3) for the system of pairs (h_j, η_j) $(j \in J)$ implies the analogous condition for the system of pairs $(h_{j,\varepsilon}, \eta_{j,\varepsilon})$ $(j \in J;\ \varepsilon > 0)$, where each function $h_{j,\varepsilon}$ is l.s.c. and bounded below. From what has been proved already, it follows that $M_1(S)$ is non-empty and compact.

Proof of Theorem 2. It suffices to show that for each finite number $\gamma \leq U_1^*(g)$ there exists $\mu \in M_1(S)$ such that $\mu(g) \geq \gamma$. In other words, it suffices to show that $M_2(S)$ is non-empty, where $M_2(S)$ is defined as the set of all $\mu \in M_1(S)$ such that $\mu(g) \leq \gamma$. In other words, $M_2(S)$ consists of all $\mu \in M_o(S)$ such that $\mu(h_j) \leq \eta_j$, for each $j \in J$, and further $\mu(-g) \leq -\gamma$. Here, $h_o = -g$ is l.s.c. and belongs to H_o.

To prove that $M_2(S)$ is non-empty, we simply apply Theorem 1 with $M_1(S)$ replaced by $M_2(S)$, that is, with J replaced by $J \cup \{0\}$, provided we put $h_o = -g$ and $\eta_o = -\gamma$. It suffices to verify condition (2.3) for the system of pairs (h_j, η_j) with $j \in J \cup \{0\}$. Since $M_1(S)$ is given to be non-empty, that condition is satisfied for the special case $\beta_o = 0$. Thus, one may as well take $\beta_o = 1$ and it remains to show that

$$-\gamma + \sum_{j \in J} \beta_j \eta_j \geq L_o(-g + \sum_{j \in J} \beta_j h_j) = -U_o(g - \sum_{j \in J} \beta_j h_j),$$

(the latter by the definitions of L_o and U_o). Here, $\beta_j \geq 0$ for all $j \in J$ with all but finitely many β_j equal to zero. And this inequality follows directly from $\gamma \leq U_1^*(g)$ and the definition (2.7) of $U_1^*(g)$.

References

(1) BILLINGSLEY, P.: Convergence of Probability Measures. New York: John Wiley and Sons, 1968.

(2) CHARNES, A. and COOPER, W.W. and KORTANEK, K.O.: Duality in semi-infinite programs and some work of Haar and Caratheodory. Management Science 9 (1963), 209-228.

(3) DUDLEY, R.M.: Probabilities and Metrics. Lecture Notes No. 45. Aarhus Universitet, 1976.

(4) DUFFIN, R.J. and KARLOVITZ, L.A.: An infinite linear program with a duality gap. Management Science 12 (1965), 122-134.

(5) FREMLIN, D.H.: Topological Riesz Spaces and Measure Theory. Cambridge: At the University Press, 1974.

(6) GALE, D.: Theory of Linear Economic Models. New York: McGraw-Hill, 1960.

(7) GLASHOFF, D.: Duality theory of semi-infinite programming. pp. 1-16 in Hettich (1979).

(8) GUSTAFSON, S-A.: On numerical analysis in semi-infinite programming. pp. 51-65 in Hettich (1979).

(9) GUSTAFSON, S-A.: On semi-infinite programming in numerical analysis. pp. 137-153 in Hettich (1979).

(10) HAAR, A.: Über lineare Ungleichungen. Acta Math. (Szeged) 2 (1924-26), 1-14.

(11) HETTICH, R. (Ed.): Semi-infinite Programming. Lecture Notes in Control and Information Sciences No. 15. Berlin: Springer Verlag, 1979.

(12) HOFFMAN-JØRGENSEN, J.: Probability in Banach Spaces. pp. 2-186 in: Lecture Notes in Mathematics No. 598, (P. L. Hennequin, Ed.). Berlin: Springer Verlag, 1977.

(13) ISII, K.: The extrema of probability determined by generalized moments (I): Bounded random variables. Annals of the Institute of Mathematical Statistics 12 (1960), 119-133.

(14) KAMAE, T. and KRENGEL, U. and O'BRIEN, G.L.: Stochastic inequalities on partially ordered spaces. Annals of Probability 6 (1978), 899-912.

(15) KAMAE, T. and KRENGEL, U.: Stochastic partial ordering. Annals of Probability 6 (1978), 1044-1049.

(16) KANTOROVICH, L. and RUBINSTEIN, G.: On a space of completely additive functions (Russian). Vestnik Leningrad Univ., Ser. Mat. Astronom. 13 (1958), 52-59.

(17) KARLIN, S. and STUDDEN, W.: Tchebycheff Systems: with Applications in Analysis and Statistics. New York: Wiley, 1966.

(18) KEMPERMAN, J.H.B.: On the sharpness of Tchebycheff type inequalities. Indagationes Mathematicae 27 (1965), 554-601.

(19) KEMPERMAN, J.H.B.: The general moment problem, a geometric approach. Annals of Mathematical Statistics 39 (1968), 93-122.

(20) KEMPERMAN, J.H.B.: On a class of moment problems. Proceedings Sixth Berkeley Symposium on Mathematical Statistics and Probability 2 (1972), 101-126.

(21) KREIN, M.G.: The ideas of P. L. Cebysev and A. A. Markov in the theory of limiting values of integrals and their further development. Uspehi Mat. Nauk 6 (1951), 3-130 (Russian). English translation: American Mathematical Society Translations, Series 2, 12 (1959), 1-121.

(22) KREIN, M.G. and NUDEL'MAN, A.A.: The Markov Moment Problem and Extremal Problems. Providence: American Mathematical Society, 1977.

(23) KY FAN: Convex Sets and their Applications. Argonne: Argonne National Laboratory, 1959.

(24) LEVIN, V.V. and MILYUTIN, A.A.: The problem of mass transfer with a discontinuous cost function and a mass statement of the duality problem for convex problems. Russian Math. Surveys 34 (1978), 1-78.

(25) MAJOR, P.: On the invariance principle for sums of independent identically distributed random variables. Journal of Multivariate Analysis 8 (1978) 487-517.

(26) NACHBIN, L.: Linear continuous functionals positive on the increasing continuous functions. Summa Brasil. Math. 2 (1951), 135-150.

(27) NACHBIN, L.: Topology and Order. New York: Van Nostrand, 1965.

(28) PARTHASARATHY, K.R.: Probability Measures on Metric Spaces. New York: Academic Press, 1967.

(29) RICHTER, H.: Parameterfreie Abschätzung und Realisierung von Erwartungswerten. Blätter Deutscher Gesellschaft Versicherungsmathematik 3 (1957), 147-161.

(30) ROGOSINSKY, W.W.: Moments of non-negative mass. Proceedings Royal Society London, Ser. A, 245 (1958), 1-27.

(31) RUBINSHTEIN, G.S.: Duality in mathematical programming and some problems of convex analysis. Russian Math. Surveys 25 (1970), 171-200.

(32) SCHWARTZ, L.: Radon Measures on arbitrary Topological Spaces and Cylindrical Measures. Oxford: University Press, 1973.

(33) STRASSEN, V.: The existence of probability measures with given marginals. Annals of Mathematical Statistics 36 (1965), 423-439.

(34) TOPSØE, F.: Topology and Measure. Lecture Notes in Mathematics No. 133. Berlin: Springer Verlag, 1970.

(35) VARADARAJAN, V.V.: Measures on topological spaces. Mat. Sbornik (N. S.) 55 (97) (1961), 35-100. (Russian). English translation: American Mathematical Society Translations, Series 2, 48 (1965), 161-228.

EXISTENCE THEOREMS IN SEMI-INFINITE PROGRAMS

Maretsugu Yamasaki

Abstract.

Existence of multipliers for semi-infinite nonlinear programs is established by means of an independence condition of the constraints which stemmed from the study of the conditional Gauss variational problem in potential theory. In the case where the objective function is a quadratic form, our results are generalizations of those for the conditional Gauss variational problem.

1. Introduction with problem setting.

The conditional Gauss variational problem (= CGVP) is one of the important examples in the theory of semi-infinite programs. In the study of CGVP, Ohtsuka [3] introduced an independence condition. This notion was generalized by the author [5; 6] and applied to semi-infinite linear programs and CGVP. The regularity condition (R) due to Voigt [4] for the dual problem of a semi-infinite linear program may be regarded as a variation of our independence condition. In this paper, we shall show that our independence condition is also effective in the study of a larger class of semi-infinite programs.

More precisely, let X and Y be real linear spaces which are in duality with respect to the bilinear functional ((,)) and P be a convex cone in X. Denote by w(X, Y) the weak topology on X which is compatible with the duality. Let f_i ($i = 1,\cdots, n$) be a real valued function on P which is positively homogeneous and additive and let A be the transformation from P into the n-dimensional Euclidean space R^n defined by $Ax = (f_1(x), \cdots, f_n(x))$. Given a subset D of P, $z_0 = (c_1, \cdots, c_n) \in R^n$ and an extended real valued function F on X, let us consider the following nonlinear semi-infinite program:

(NSIP) Minimize $F(x)$ subject to $x \in D$ and $Ax = z_0$.

Denote by S (resp. S_0) the set of all feasible (resp. optimal) solutions of NSIP and by V the value of NSIP, i.e.,

$$V = \inf\{F(x);\ x \in S\},$$

$$S = \{x \in D;\ Ax = z_0\},$$

$$S_0 = \{x \in S;\ V = F(x)\}.$$

Here we use the convention that $V = \infty$ in case S is empty. One of our aims is to establish the existence of multipliers for NSIP. As an application of our results, we give an estimation of the directional derivative of the marginal function of NSIP. In our study, we need the independence condition of the constraints. In the case where F is a quadratic form, NSIP is called a semi-infinite quadratic program (= SIQP) in Section 3. For SIQP, we do not need the Gâteaux-differentiability of F and we can improve the results in Section 2.

As for the existence of an optimal solution of NSIP or SIQP, we have some results which are analogous to those for CGVP. Most of them are essentially covered by the general existence theorem [1; Proposition 1.2 in Chapter II], so we omit them.

2. Existence theorems for NSIP.

Let $x \in P$. We say that $\{f_i\} = \{f_i;\ i = 1, \cdots, n\}$ is x-independent if there exists a set $\{x_j\} = \{x_j;\ j = 1, \cdots, n\}$ in P called a system of components of x such that $x - x_j \in P$ for each j and the determinant of the matrix $[f_i(x_j)]$ does not vanish. It should be noted that the condition $\det[f_i(x_j)] \neq 0$ in this definition is equivalent to that $\{Ax_j;\ j = 1, \cdots, n\}$ is linearly independent. A system of components $\{x_j\}$

of x is called to be full if $x = \sum_{j=1}^{n} x_j$.

We proved in [5; Theorems 4 and 5] that $\{f_i\}$ is x-independent for some $x \in P$ such that $Ax = z_0$ if and only if z_0 is an interior point of A(P).

In case F is finite at x, we call the limit as $t \to +0$, if it exists, of $[F(x + tu) - F(x)]/t$ the directional derivative of F at x in the direction u and denote it by $F'(x; u)$. If there exists $y \in Y$ such that $F'(x; u) = ((u, y))$ for all $u \in X$, we say that F is Gâteaux-differentiable at x, call y the Gâteaux-differential at x of F, and denote it by $F'(x)$.

In order to obtain an existence theorem, we assume that the set D satisfies the following conditions:

(2. 1) D is a cone.

(2. 2) If $x \in D$, then D contains the set $C[x] = \{u \in P;\ x - u \in P\}$.

We prepare

Lemma 2.1. For each $x \in D$, the set $P_D(x) = \{u \in P;\ x + u \in D\}$ is a cone.

Proof. Let $u \in P_D(x)$ and t be a positive number. Then $tu \in P$ and $x + u \in D$. If $0 < t \leq 1$, then

$$x + u - (x + tu) = (1 - t)u \in P,$$

so that $x + tu \in D$ by (2. 2). If $t > 1$, then

$$t(x + u) - (x + tu) = (t - 1)x \in P,$$

so that $x + tu \in D$ by (2. 1) and (2. 2).

First we consider the case where D is not necessarily convex. As an extension of [5; Proposition 9], we have

Theorem 2.1. Let $z_0 \neq 0$ and $\bar{x} \in S_0$ and assume that F is Gâteaux-differentiable at $\bar{x}$ and that $\{f_i\}$ is $\bar{x}$-independent. Then there exists a unique point $w = (r_1, \cdots, r_n) \in R^n$ such that

(2. 3) $$((u, F'(\bar{x}))) \geq \sum_{i=1}^{n} r_i f_i(u) \quad \text{for all } u \in P_D(\bar{x}),$$

(2. 4) $$((\bar{x}, F'(\bar{x}))) = \sum_{i=1}^{n} r_i f_i(\bar{x}).$$

For a system of components $\{x_j\}$ of $\bar{x}$, $\{r_i\}$ is the solution of the equations

(2. 5) $$\sum_{i=1}^{n} r_i f_i(x_j) = ((x_j, F'(\bar{x}))).$$

Proof. Since $z_0 \neq 0$, there exists a full system of components $\{\bar{x}_j\}$ of $\bar{x}$ by [6; Theorem 4]. For $u \in P_D(\bar{x})$, let $\{t_j\}$ be the solution of the equations

(2. 6) $$\sum_{i=1}^{n} f_i(\bar{x}_j)t_j = f_i(u)$$

and let t_0 be a positive number such that $\sum_{j=1}^{n} |t_j| < 1/t_0$. With a parameter t such that $0 < t < t_0$, we set

$$x(t) = \bar{x} - t\sum_{j=1}^{n} t_j\bar{x}_j + tu.$$

By the relation

$$\bar{x} - t\sum_{j=1}^{n} t_j\bar{x}_j - (1 - t\sum_{j=1}^{n} |t_j|)\bar{x} = t\sum_{j=1}^{n} (|t_j|\bar{x} - t_j\bar{x}_j) \in P,$$

we see that $x(t) \in P$. We have

$$2\bar{x} + tu - x(t) = \bar{x} + t\sum_{j=1}^{n} t_j\bar{x}_j$$

$$= (1 - t\sum_{j=1}^{n} |t_j|)\bar{x} + t\sum_{j=1}^{n} (|t_j|\bar{x} + t_j\bar{x}_j) \in P,$$

so that $x(t) \in C[2\bar{x} + tu]$. Since $P_D(\bar{x})$ is a cone by Lemma 2.1, $\bar{x} + (t/2)u \in D$, so that $2\bar{x} + tu \in D$ by (2. 1). Thus $x(t) \in D$ by (2. 2). Since A is additive and positively homogeneous, we have $A(|t_j|\bar{x} - t_j\bar{x}_j) = |t_j|A\bar{x} - t_jA\bar{x}_j$, so that

$$Ax(t) = A\bar{x} - t\sum_{j=1}^{n} t_jA\bar{x}_j + tAu = z_0$$

by (2. 6). Therefore $x(t) \in S$ for all t, $0 < t < t_0$. We have

$$F(\bar{x}) = V \leq F(x(t)) = F(\bar{x} + tv) \quad \text{with } v = u - \sum_{j=1}^{n} t_j\bar{x}_j.$$

Since F is Gâteaux-differentiable at $\bar{x}$, we have

$$(2.\ 7)\qquad 0 \le F'(\bar{x}; v) = ((v, F'(\bar{x}))) = ((u, F'(\bar{x}))) - \sum_{j=1}^{n} t_j((\bar{x}_j, F'(\bar{x}))).$$

Let $\{r_i\}$ be the solution of the equations

$$(2.\ 8)\qquad \sum_{i=1}^{n} r_i f_i(\bar{x}_j) = ((\bar{x}_j, F'(\bar{x}))).$$

Since $\{\bar{x}_j\}$ is a full system of components of $\bar{x}$ and each f_i is additive, we have (2. 4) by (2. 8). It follows from (2. 6), (2. 7) and (2. 8) that

$$((u, F'(\bar{x}))) \ge \sum_{j=1}^{n} t_j((\bar{x}_j, F'(\bar{x}))) = \sum_{j=1}^{n} t_j \sum_{i=1}^{n} r_i f_i(\bar{x}_j) = \sum_{i=1}^{n} r_i f_i(u),$$

which shows (2. 3). Let $\{x_j\}$ be any system of components of $\bar{x}$. Since x_j and $\bar{x} - x_j$ belong to $P_D(\bar{x})$, we have by (2. 3) and (2. 4)

$$((x_j, F'(\bar{x}))) \ge \sum_{i=1}^{n} r_i f_i(x_j),$$

$$((\bar{x} - x_j, F'(x))) \ge \sum_{i=1}^{n} r_i f_i(\bar{x} - x_j) = \sum_{i=1}^{n} r_i f_i(\bar{x}) - \sum_{i=1}^{n} r_i f_i(x_j) = ((\bar{x}, F'(\bar{x}))) - \sum_{i=1}^{n} r_i f_i(x_j),$$

so that

$$\sum_{i=1}^{n} r_i f_i(x_j) = ((x_j, F'(\bar{x}))).$$

Namely $\{r_i\}$ satisfies (2. 5). To prove the uniqueness of w, it suffices to note that the solution of the equations (2. 5) is unique by the condition $\det[f_i(x_j)] \neq 0$.

Remark 2.1. In the case where $f_i(x) = ((x, y_i))$ $(y_i \in Y)$ for each i, A is a linear transformation from X into R^n and its adjoint A* is given by

$$A^*w = A^*(r_1, \cdots, r_n) = \sum_{i=1}^{n} r_i y_i.$$

Thus (2. 3) and (2. 4) can be written in the following form:

(2. 9) $F'(\bar{x}) - A^*w \in P_D(\bar{x})^+$ (the dual cone of $P_D(\bar{x})$),

(2. 10) $((\bar{x}, F'(\bar{x}) - A^*w)) = 0.$

Remark 2. In the case where D is convex and w(X, Y)-closed, $P_D(x) = D$ for each $x \in D$ and the above existence theorem is a disguised standard Lagrange multiplier result. As for the standard known results relating multiplier rules, we refer to [2]. The author is indebted to the referee for this reference.

Hereafter in this section we assume that F is Gâteaux-differentiable at each point of D. For each $\bar{x} \in S_0$, denote by $S_0^*(\bar{x})$ the set of all points $w = (r_1, \cdots, r_n) \in R^n$ which satisfy (2. 4) and

(2. 11) $((u, F'(\bar{x}))) \geq \sum_{i=1}^{n} r_i f_i(u)$ for all $u \in D$.

In case D is convex, the existence of multipliers for NSIP can be stated in the following form:

Theorem 2.2. Let D be convex and $\bar{x} \in S_0$. If $\{f_i\}$ is x-independent for some $x \in S$, then $S_0^*(\bar{x})$ is nonempty.

Proof. Since S is convex, we have $F(\bar{x}) \leq F(\bar{x} + t(u - \bar{x}))$ for all $u \in S$ and t, $0 < t \leq 1$. Thus $0 \leq ((u - \bar{x}, F'(\bar{x})))$ for all $u \in S$, and hence

$$((\bar{x}, F'(\bar{x}))) = \min\{((u, F'(\bar{x}))); u \in S\}.$$

If $\{f_i\}$ is x-independent for some $x \in S$, then z_0 is an interior point of A(D). We see by [5; Theorem 3] that there exists $w \in R^n$ such that $((\bar{x}, F'(\bar{x}))) = ((z_0, w))_2$ and $((Au, w))_2 \leq ((u, F'(\bar{x})))$ for all $u \in D$, where $((\ ,\ ))_2$ denotes the usual inner product in R^n. It is clear that $w \in S_0^*(\bar{x})$.

We say that the Gâteaux-differential F' of F is of positive type on D if the following conditions are fulfilled:

(2. 12) $((x - u, F'(x) - F'(u))) \geq 0$ for all $x, u \in D$.

(2. 13) $((x - u, F'(x) - F'(u))) = 0$ implies $F'(x) = F'(u)$ whenever x and u belong to D.

We have

Theorem 2.3. Let D be convex and assume that the Gâteaux-differential F' of F is of positive type on D. Then $S_0^*(\bar{x}) = S_0^*(\hat{x})$ for all $\bar{x}, \hat{x} \in S_0$.

Proof. By the convexity of D and (2. 12), we see that F is convex on D (cf. [1; Proposition 5.5]). Since $F(\bar{x}) = F(\hat{x}) = V$ and $\bar{x} + t(\hat{x} - \bar{x}) \in S$ for all t, $0 < t < 1$, we have

$$V = F(\bar{x}) \leq F(\bar{x} + t(\hat{x} - \bar{x})) \leq tF(\hat{x}) + (1 - t)F(\bar{x}) = V,$$

so that $((\hat{x} - \bar{x}, F'(\bar{x}))) = 0$. Similarly $((\bar{x} - \hat{x}, F'(\hat{x}))) = 0$, and hence $((\bar{x} - \hat{x}, F'(\bar{x}) - F'(\hat{x}))) = 0$. We have $F'(\bar{x}) = F'(\hat{x})$ by (2. 13). If $w = (r_1, \cdots, r_n) \in S_0^*(\bar{x})$, then

$$((u, F'(\hat{x}))) = ((u, F'(\bar{x}))) \geq \sum_{i=1}^{n} r_i f_i(u)$$

for all $u \in D$ and

$$\begin{aligned} ((\hat{x}, F'(\hat{x}))) = ((\bar{x}, F'(\hat{x}))) &= ((\bar{x}, F'(\bar{x}))) \\ &= ((A\bar{x}, w))_2 = ((z_0, w))_2 \\ &= ((A\hat{x}, w))_2 \end{aligned}$$

by (2. 4). Thus $w \in S_0^*(\hat{x})$ and $S_0^*(\bar{x}) \subset S_0^*(\hat{x})$. Since the discussion is symmetric, we have $S_0^*(\hat{x}) \subset S_0^*(\bar{x})$ and hence $S_0^*(\bar{x}) = S_0^*(\hat{x})$.

We show that our existence theorems are effective in the study of some properties of the marginal function of NSIP. For $z \in R^n$, let us put

$$V(z) = \inf\{F(x);\ x \in S(z)\},$$

$$S(z) = \{x \in D;\ Ax = z\},$$

$$S_0(z) = \{x \in S(z);\ V(z) = f(x)\}$$

and call $V(z)$ the marginal function of NSIP. By [6; Theorem 6], we see that $V(z)$ is upper semicontinuous in the interior of $A(D)$ if D is convex.

We say that F is continuously Gâteaux-differentiable at $\bar{x}$ if it is Gâteaux-differentiable at $\bar{x}$ and if

$$[F(\bar{x} + tu) - F(\bar{x})]/t \to ((x, F'(\bar{x})))$$

as $t \to +0$ and $u \to x$ with respect to $w(X, Y)$.

We have

Theorem 2.4. Let $z_0 \neq 0$ and $\bar{x} \in S_0(z_0)$ and assume that F is continuously Gâteaux-differentiable at $\bar{x}$ and that $\{f_i\}$ is $\bar{x}$-independent. Then

$$\limsup_{h\to+0}[V(z_0 + hv) - V(z_0)]/h \le ((v, w(\bar{x}, z_0)))_2$$

for every $v \in R^n$, where $w(\bar{x}, z_0)$ is the unique point determined by (2. 3) and (2. 4).

Proof. Let $\{\bar{x}_j\}$ be a full system of components of $\bar{x}$. By [6; Lemma 4], there exists h_0 such that

$$z_0 + hv = \sum_{j=1}^{n} t_j^{(h)} A\bar{x}_j, \quad t_j^{(h)} \ge 0$$

for all h, $0 < h < h_0$. Writing $x^{(h)} = \sum_{j=1}^{n} t_j^{(h)}\bar{x}_j$, we see that $x^{(h)} \in S(z_0 + hv)$, so that

$$V(z_0 + hv) - V(z_0) \le F(x^{(h)}) - F(\bar{x}).$$

By the relation

$$hv = \sum_{j=1}^{n} (t_j^{(h)} - 1)A\bar{x}_j,$$

we have

$$\lim_{h\to+0} t_j^{(h)} = 1 \quad \text{and} \quad \lim_{h\to+0} [t_j^{(h)} - 1]/h = s_j$$

for each j, where $\{s_j\}$ is defined by

$$\sum_{j=1}^{n} s_j A x_j = v.$$

Let us put

$$u^{(h)} = \sum_{j=1}^{n} [(t_j^{(h)} - 1)/h]\bar{x}_j.$$

Then $x^{(h)} = \bar{x} + hu^{(h)}$ and $u^{(h)}$ tends to $u = \sum_{j=1}^{n} s_j\bar{x}_j$ as $h \to +0$ with respect to $w(X, Y)$. Since F is continuously Gâteaux-differentiable at $\bar{x}$, we have

$$\limsup_{h\to+0}[V(z_0 + hv) - V(z_0)]/h \le \limsup_{h\to+0}[F(\bar{x} + hu^{(h)}) - F(\bar{x})]/h$$
$$= ((u, F'(\bar{x}))) = \sum_{j=1}^{n} s_j((\bar{x}_j, F'(\bar{x}))).$$

By Theorem 2.1, there exists a unique $w(\bar{x}, z_0) = (r_1,\cdots, r_n)$ which satisfies (2. 3) and (2. 4). Then we have by (2. 5)

$$\sum_{j=1}^{n} s_j((\bar{x}_j, F'(x))) = \sum_{j=1}^{n} s_j \sum_{i=1}^{n} r_i f_i(\bar{x}_j)$$
$$= \sum_{i=1}^{n} r_i \sum_{j=1}^{n} s_j f_i(\bar{x}_j) = ((v, w(\bar{x}, z_0)))_2.$$

This completes the proof.

This is a generalization of [5; Theorem 20].

3. Semi-infinite quadratic program

Let $G(x, u)$ be an extended real valued function defined on $P \times P$ which satisfies the following conditions:

(G. 1) $0 \le G(x, u) = G(u, x)$ for all $x, u \in P$.

(G. 2) For each $u \in P$, $G(x, u)$ is additive and positively homogeneous with respect to x.

For a fixed $y_0 \in Y$, let us consider NSIP in the case where $F(x) = G(x, x) - 2((x, y_0))$ and $D = \{x \in P;\ G(x, x) < \infty\}$ and call it a semi-infinite quadratic program (= SIQP).

It is easily seen that D satisfies conditions (2. 1) and (2. 2). For $x, u \in D$, we have $u \in P_D(x)$ if and only if $G(x, u) < \infty$. If $x \in D$ and $u \in P_D(x)$, then $F'(x; u) = 2[G(x, u) - ((u, y_0))]$. Note that F is not Gâteaux-differentiable in general.

For SIQP, we have the following existence theorem:

Theorem 3.1. Let $z_0 \neq 0$ and $\bar{x} \in S_0$ and assume that $\{f_i\}$ is $\bar{x}$-independent. Then there exists a unique point $w = (r_1, \cdots, r_n) \in R^n$ such that

$$(3.\ 1) \quad G(\bar{x}, u) - ((u, y_0)) \geq \sum_{i=1}^{n} r_i f_i(u) \quad \text{for all } u \in D,$$

$$(3.\ 2) \quad G(\bar{x}, \bar{x}) - ((\bar{x}, y_0)) = \sum_{i=1}^{n} r_i f_i(\bar{x}).$$

For a system of components $\{x_j\}$ of $\bar{x}$, $\{r_i\}$ is the solution of the equations

$$(3.\ 3) \quad \sum_{i=1}^{n} r_i f_i(x_j) = G(\bar{x}, x_j) - ((x_j, y_0)).$$

Proof. Let $u \in P_D(\bar{x})$ and let $\{\bar{x}_j\}$ and $x(t)$ be the same as in the proof of Theorem 2.1. Writing

$$v_j = |t_j|\bar{x} - t_j\bar{x}_j, \quad \bar{v} = \sum_{j=1}^{n} v_j \quad \text{and} \quad c = \sum_{j=1}^{n} |t_j|,$$

we have v_j, $\bar{v} \in D$, $\bar{v} \in P_D(\bar{x})$ and $x(t) = (1 - ct)\bar{x} + t\bar{v} + tu$. By (G. 1) and (G. 2), we have

$$G(x(t), x(t)) = (1 - ct)^2 G(\bar{x}, \bar{x}) + t^2 G(\bar{v} + u, \bar{v} + u)$$
$$+ 2t(1 - ct)G(\bar{x}, \bar{v} + u),$$
$$G(\bar{x}, \bar{v}) = \sum_{j=1}^{n} G(\bar{x}, v_j) = cG(\bar{x}, \bar{x}) - \sum_{j=1}^{n} t_j G(\bar{x}, \bar{x}_j).$$

Since $F(\bar{x}) \leq F(x(t))$ for all t, $0 < t < t_0$, we have

$$0 \leq \frac{d}{dt} F(x(t))\Big|_{t=0} = -2cG(\bar{x}, \bar{x}) + 2G(\bar{x}, \bar{v} + u)$$
$$- 2((u + \bar{v} - c\bar{x}, y_0))$$
$$= -2\sum_{j=1}^{n} t_j G(\bar{x}, \bar{x}_j) + 2G(\bar{x}, u) - 2((u - \sum_{j=1}^{n} t_j\bar{x}_j, y_0)),$$

so that

$$(3.\ 4) \quad G(\bar{x}, u) - ((u, y_0)) \geq \sum_{j=1}^{n} t_j[G(\bar{x}, \bar{x}_j) - ((\bar{x}_j, y_0))].$$

Let $\{r_i\}$ be the solution of the equations

(3. 5) $\sum_{i=1}^{n} r_i f_i(\bar{x}_j) = G(\bar{x}, \bar{x}_j) - ((\bar{x}_j, y_0))$.

Then we have

$$\sum_{j=1}^{n} t_j[G(\bar{x}, \bar{x}_j) - ((\bar{x}_j, y_0))] = \sum_{i=1}^{n} r_i f_i(u),$$

and hence

(3. 6) $G(\bar{x}, u) - ((u, y_0)) \geq \sum_{i=1}^{n} r_i f_i(u)$

for $u \in P_D(\bar{x})$. This inequality is obvious in case $G(\bar{x}, u) = \infty$, so that (3. 6) holds for all $u \in D$. The rest of the proof is carried out by the same argument as in the proof of Theorem 2.1.

We say that G is of positive type if

(G. 3) $2G(x, u) \leq G(x, x) + G(u, u)$

for all $x, u \in D$. If G is of positive type, then D is a convex set and F is a convex function on D.

For $\bar{x} \in S_0$, denote by $S_0^*(\bar{x})$ the set of all points $w = (r_1, \cdots, r_n) \in R^n$ which satisfy (3. 1) and (3. 2).

We have

Theorem 3.2. Assume that G is of positive type. Then $S_0^*(\bar{x}) = S_0^*(\hat{x})$ for all $\bar{x}, \hat{x} \in S_0$.

Proof. Let $\bar{x}, \hat{x} \in S_0$. Then $(\bar{x} + \hat{x})/2 \in S_0$ and

$$F((\bar{x} + \hat{x})/2) = [F(\bar{x}) + F(\hat{x})]/2 - [G(\bar{x}, \bar{x}) - 2G(\bar{x}, \hat{x}) + G(\hat{x}, \hat{x})]/4,$$

so that $G(\bar{x}, \bar{x}) + G(\hat{x}, \hat{x}) = 2G(\bar{x}, \hat{x})$. We show that $G(\bar{x}, u) = G(\hat{x}, u)$ for all $u \in D$. Supposing the contrary, we can find $u_0 \in D$ such that $G(\bar{x}, u_0) > G(\hat{x}, u_0)$. Then

$$2G(\bar{x}, \hat{x} + tu_0) \leq G(\bar{x}, \bar{x}) + G(\hat{x} + tu_0, \hat{x} + tu_0)$$

for all $t > 0$ by (G. 3), so that

$$tG(u_0, u_0) + 2[G(\hat{x}, u_0) - G(\bar{x}, u_0)] \geq 0.$$

This is a contradiction. Thus $G(\bar{x}, u) = G(\hat{x}, u)$ for all $u \in D$. The rest of the proof is carried out by the same reasoning as in the proof of Theorem 2.3.

For SIQP, we can prove an analogy of Theorem 2.4 without the assumption that F is continuously Gâteaux-differentiable at $\bar{x}$. In fact, using the same notation as in the proof of Theorem 2.4, we have

$$F(x^{(h)}) - F(\bar{x}) = \sum_{j=1}^{n} \sum_{k=1}^{n} (t_j^{(h)} - 1)(t_k^{(h)} - 1)G(\bar{x}_j, \bar{x}_k) - 2\sum_{k=1}^{n} (t_k^{(h)} - 1)((\bar{x}_k, y_0)),$$

so that

$$\limsup_{h\to+0}[V(z_0 + hv) - V(z_0)]/h$$

$$\leq \sum_{j=1}^{n} \sum_{k=1}^{n} (s_j + s_k)G(\bar{x}_j, \bar{x}_k) - 2\sum_{k=1}^{n} s_k((\bar{x}_k, y_0))$$

$$= 2\sum_{k=1}^{n} s_k[G(\bar{x}, \bar{x}_k) - ((\bar{x}_k, y_0))].$$

The rest of the proof is the same as in the proof of Theorem 2.4. Thus we have

Theorem 3.3. Let $z_0 \neq 0$ and $\bar{x} \in S_0(z_0)$. If $\{f_i\}$ is $\bar{x}$-independent, then

$$\limsup_{h\to+0}[V(z_0 + hv) - V(z_0)]/h \leq 2((v, w(\bar{x}, z_0)))_2$$

for all $v \in R^n$, where $w(\bar{x}, z_0)$ is the unique point determined by (3. 1) and (3. 2).

Finally we show that SIQP contains CGVP. In order to define CGVP, let K be a compact Hausdorff space. Denote by C(K) the set of all real valued continuous functions on K, by M(K) the set of all real Radon measures on K of any sign and by $M^+(K)$ the subset of M(K) which consists of non-negative measures. Let g be a lower semicontinuous function on K × K such that $0 \leq g(s, t) = g(t, s) \leq \infty$ for all $s, t \in K$. This g is called a positive symmetric kernel in potential theory. For $\nu, \mu \in M^+(K)$, the g-potential $G\nu$ of ν and the mutual energy

$G(\mu, \nu)$ of μ and ν are defined by

$$G\nu(s) = \int g(s, t)d\nu(t),$$

$$G(\mu, \nu) = \int G\nu(s)d\mu(s).$$

The quantity $G(\nu, \nu)$ is called the potential energy of ν.

Given a set $\{f, f_1, \cdots, f_n\}$ of real valued continuous functions on K and a set $\{c_1, \cdots, c_n\}$ of real numbers, CGVP is the problem to minimize the Gauss integral

$$I(\nu) = G(\nu, \nu) - 2\int f(s)d\nu(s)$$

subject to $\nu \in M^+(K)$ and $\int f_i(s)d\nu(s) = c_i$ for each i.

By choosing

$$X = M(K),\ Y = C(K),\ P = M^+(K),$$
$$D = \{\nu \in M^+(K);\ G(\nu, \nu) < \infty\},$$
$$F(\nu) = I(\nu),\ z_0 = (c_1, \cdots, c_n),$$
$$((\sigma, p)) = \int p(s)d\sigma(s) \quad \text{for } \sigma \in M(K) \text{ and } p \in C(K),$$
$$A\nu = \left(\int f_1(s)d\nu(s), \cdots, \int f_n(s)d\nu(s)\right),$$

we see that CGVP is a semi-infinite quadratic program. Note that the set D is not convex in general (cf. [5]).

References

[1] EKELAND, I, AND TEMAN, R: Convex analysis and variational problems. North-Holland, Amsterdam, 1976.

[2] POURCIAU, B, H: Modern multiplier rules. Amer. Math. Monthly 87(1980), 433 - 452.

[3] OHTSUKA, M: On potentials in locally compact spaces. J.

Sci. Hiroshima Univ. Ser. A-I Math. 25(1961), 135 - 352.

[4] VOIGT, H: Ein Dualitätsatz der semi-infiniten linearen Optimierung. Math. Operationsforsch. Statist. Ser. Optim. 12(1981), 27 - 30.

[5] YAMASAKI, M: Semi-infinite programs and conditional Gauss variational problems. Hiroshima Math. J. 1 (1971), 177 - 226.

[6] YAMASAKI, M: An independence condition in semi-infinite programs. Ibid. 3(1973), 15 - 24.

PART II

ALGORITHMIC DEVELOPMENTS

An Algorithm for a Continuous Version of the Assignment Problem

E. J. Anderson and A. B. Philpott

Abstract

In this paper continuous forms of the transportation problem and the assignment problem are formulated and discussed. An algorithm for the solution of the continuous assignment problem is described. This algorithm is a continuous analogue of the usual transportation algorithm.

1. The continuous transportation problem

This paper has grown out of an interest in linear programming over infinite dimensional spaces; such problems are called continuous linear programs. A large number of papers have appeared in the literature on this subject. They have mostly been concerned with the duality structure of such linear programs. This paper follows a rather different approach and is primarily concerned with an algorithm for the solution of a certain class of continuous linear programs. In fact the formulation of implementable algorithms for continuous linear programs is surprisingly straightforward in some cases.

When looking at continuous versions of linear programming algorithms it is sensible to start with the simplest of LP problems. For this reason we consider the Transportation Problem (TP).

$$\text{TP:minimize} \sum_{i=1}^{m} \sum_{j=1}^{n} c_{ij}x_{ij}$$

with

$$(1.1) \qquad \sum_{j=1}^{n} x_{ij} = a_i, \qquad i=1,2,...m,$$

(1.2) $\sum_{i=1}^{m} x_{ij} = b_j, \qquad j=1,2,\ldots n,$

$x_{ij} \geq 0.$

The continuous version of this problem will be called the Continuous Transportation Problem (CTP). To formulate CTP we require the following definitions. For continuous functions f_1 on X and f_2 on Y define $\hat{f}_1$ and $\hat{f}_2$ on X×Y by

$$\hat{f}_1(x,y) = f_1(x),$$

$$\hat{f}_2(x,y) = f_2(y).$$

We may now formulate CTP as

$$\text{CTP:minimize} \int_{X\times Y} c(x,y)d\rho(x,y)$$

with

(1.3) $\int_{X\times Y} \hat{f}_1(x,y)d\rho(x,y) = \int_X f_1(x)d\mu_1(x),$

for all continuous functions f_1 on X,

(1.4) $\int_{X\times Y} \hat{f}_2(x,y)d\rho(x,y) = \int_Y f_2(y)d\mu_2(y),$

for all continuous functions f_2 on Y,

$\rho \geq 0.$

Here ρ, μ_1 and μ_2 are non-negative Radon measures and c is a continuous function. X and Y are compact spaces with $\mu_1(X)=\mu_2(Y)$. The constraints (1.3) and (1.4) are the continuous versions of (1.1) and (1.2); they amount to asking that the projections of ρ onto the two coordinate axes are equal to the given measures μ_1 and μ_2. The choice of space within which ρ must lie is a delicate matter and effects the duality structure of this problem. However these difficulties will not be dealt with here.

The problem CTP has a long history. It was first posed as long ago as 1781 by Monge[6], and has been considered since then by Appell[2], by Kantorovitch[3] and by Levin and Milyutin[5]. If we take X as a region in the plane, then we obtain a version of the "cutting and filling" problem.

This is the problem of levelling a patch of ground at least cost when there is some function giving the cost of moving unit mass of material between any two points.

It is natural to begin by writing down the dual problem for CTP (DCTP) which has the following form.

$$\text{DCTP: maximize} \quad \int_X r(x)\,d\mu_1(x) + \int_Y s(y)\,d\mu_2(y)$$

with

$$r(x) + s(y) \leq c(x,y), \text{ for all } x \in X,\ y \in Y, \tag{1.5}$$

where r and s are continuous functions defined on X and Y.

We can now write down what is often called a weak duality result.

<u>Lemma 1.</u>

If ρ is feasible for CTP and r, s are feasible for DCTP then

$$\int_{X\times Y} c(x,y)\,d\rho(x,y) \geq \int_X r(x)\,d\mu_1(x) + \int_Y s(y)\,d\mu_2(y). \tag{1.6}$$

Moreover if there is equality in (1.6) then ρ is optimal for CTP and r, s are optimal for DCTP.

<u>Proof</u>: As μ_1 and μ_2 are the projections of ρ

$$\int_{X\times Y} \{r(x) + s(y)\}\,d\rho(x,y) = \int_X r(x)\,d\mu_1(x) + \int_Y s(y)\,d\mu_2(y).$$

So the required inequality follows from (1.5). Now if r^*, s^* and ρ^* achieve equality in (1.6) then for any ρ feasible for CTP we have

$$\int_{X\times Y} c(x,y)\,d\rho(x,y) \geq \int_X r^*(x)\,d\mu_1(x) + \int_Y s^*(y)\,d\mu_2(y)$$
$$= \int_{X\times Y} c(x,y)\,d\rho^*(x,y).$$

Hence ρ^* is optimal for CTP. Similarly r^*, s^* are optimal for DCTP.

Kretschmer[4] has proved a strong duality result for CTP and DCTP. Essentially this states that the values of the primal problem and the dual problem coincide. We shall make some brief comments about strong duality at the end of the paper.

2. Basic solutions and assignments

One aspect of ordinary linear programming problems which is central to algorithms for their solution is the existence of a special set of solutions called basic, amongst which there is an optimal solution. Basic solutions are just the extreme points of the set of feasible solutions. It can be shown that the set of feasible solutions for CTP is weak* compact, and thus there exists an extreme point optimal solution. But what are the extreme points?

In the ordinary transportation problem, one implication of being able to choose an extreme point optimal solution is that, when m=n and all the a's and b's are equal to 1, an optimal solution can be found which is an assignment. The equivalent property for CTP does not hold, as we shall see.

For simplicity we shall take X and Y to be the closed line interval [0,1]. From now on we let μ_1 and μ_2 both equal the Lebesgue measure on the line, which is just the equivalent of the a's and b's being 1. Later we shall also assume that c has continuous first partial derivatives.

A non-negative measure ρ satisfying (1.3) and (1.4) is called an assignment if the support of ρ is within the closure of the graph of a 1-1 function. This amounts to saying that the pattern of mass transfer between the two line segments is given by a 1-1 measure preserving function $f:[0,1]\to[0,1]$, with mass from point x being transferred only to f(x). For convenience we also refer to the function f as an assignment. More generally, if a function $f:[0,1]\to[0,1]$ exists such that the support of ρ is within the closure of G(f) where $G(f)=\{(x,f(x)):x\in[0,1]\}$, then we say that f is a defining function for ρ.

We might expect that under the condition that μ_1 and μ_2 are Lebesgue measure, the optimal solution to CTP could be chosen to be an assignment. That this is not the case is shown by the example in Figure 1. Here the cost function is given by

$$c(x,y) = 4x^2y - xy^2$$

whose contours are shown. The optimal solution has a defining function

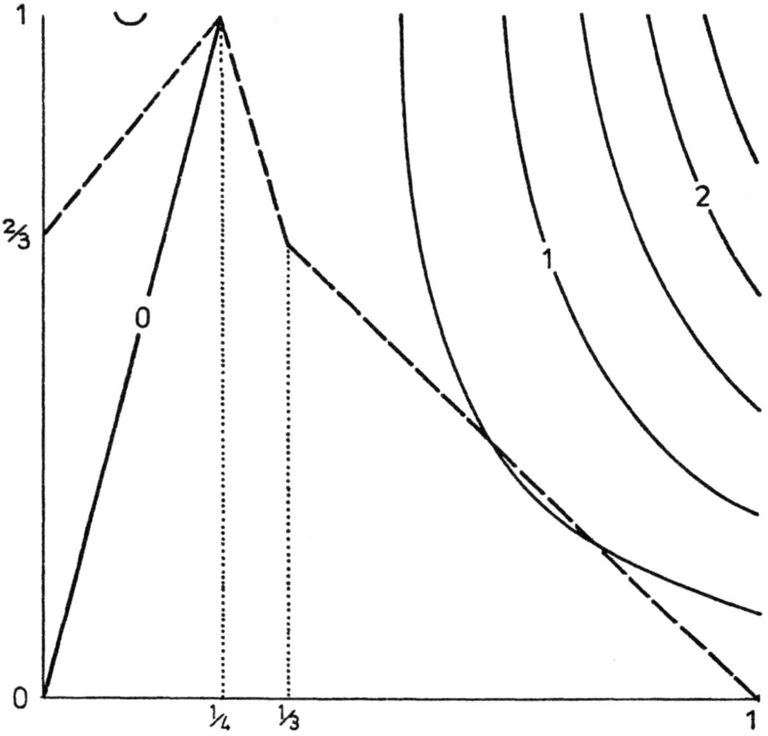

Figure 1. An Optimal Solution Which Is Not An Assignment.

given by

$$
\begin{aligned}
f(x) &= (2/3) + (4x/3), & x &\in [0,1/4),\\
&= 2 - 4x, & x &\in [1/4,1/3),\\
&= 1 - x, & x &\in [1/3,1].
\end{aligned}
$$

This is shown by the dashed line in the figure and can be shown to be optimal by considering the following solution to the dual problem.

$$
\begin{aligned}
r(x) &= (80/27)x^3 + (16/9)x^2 - (4/9)x, & x &\in [0,1/4),\\
&= -16x^3 + 16x^2 - 4x + (8/27), & x &\in [1/4,1/3),\\
&= -3x^3 + 5x^2 - x + (1/27), & x &\in [1/3,1],
\end{aligned}
$$

$$
\begin{aligned}
s(y) &= 2y^3 - 5y^2 + 4y - (28/27), & y &\in [0,2/3),\\
&= (1/4)y^3 - y^2 + y - (8/27), & y &\in [2/3,1].
\end{aligned}
$$

If a solution has a defining function then it is clear that the solution is an extreme point of the feasible set. Moreover it is not difficult to show that if ρ is an extreme point then there cannot be any rectangle $[a,b]\times[c,d]$ on all of which ρ is positive (in the sense that $\rho(S)>0$ for any set S of positive measure within the rectangle). Otherwise we can find a signed measure which can be added and subtracted from ρ without causing it to become infeasible. It seems to be difficult to be any more specific about the nature of the extreme points of the feasible set. However we conjecture that, if c is well enough behaved, the optimal ρ will have its support within the closure of the graphs of one or more functions.

3. The continuous assignment problem and its algorithm

Because of the difficulties of finding conditions under which CTP has well behaved solutions we shall restrict attention to the Continuous Assignment Problem (CAP). This has the following form

$$\text{CAP:minimize} \int_0^1 c(x,f(x))dx$$

with $\mu(f(S)) = \mu(S)$ for all measurable sets S in $[0,1]$,

and f a 1-1 mapping from $[0,1]$ to $[0,1]$.

This problem is equivalent to CTP with the extra condition that the solution be an assignment. In this case we can derive a similar result to Lemma 1.

Lemma 2.

If f is an assignment such that there exist measurable functions r and s with

(3.1) $\qquad r(x) + s(y) \leq c(x,y), \quad x,y \in [0,1],$

(3.2) $\qquad r(x) + s(f(x)) = c(x,f(x)), \quad x \in [0,1],$

then f is optimal for CAP.

Proof: For any assignment f', we have, using (3.1) and (3.2),

$$\int_0^1 c(x,f(x))dx = \int_0^1 \{r(x) + s(f(x))\}dx$$
$$= \int_0^1 r(x)dx + \int_0^1 s(f'(x))dx$$
$$\leq \int_0^1 c(x,f'(x))dx.$$

In many circumstances the solution to CAP will have a defining function which is piecewise continuous. Then it will consist of a finite number of line segments, which will be at 45 degrees to the horizontal. We will describe an algorithm which, given such a solution, will find an improved solution whenever it is not optimal. The algorithm is a continuous version of the well known form of the simplex algorithm for the transportation problem.

The first step is to specify functions r and s. Just as in the discrete version of the transportation algorithm, these are used to test for optimality, and in the event that the current solution is not optimal, they indicate how to improve it. Considered as a solution to the transportation problem, an assignment is highly degenerate. In the discrete case we would break the degeneracy by introducing infinitesimal transfers (ε-transfers) where in fact there are none. Just where these ε-transfers are put will determine the exact form of r and s and the resulting pivot operation. The choice of r and s which we shall make in the continuous problem corresponds to putting these ε-transfers just to the right or left of the existing transfers.

In fact we specify r as follows. Put $r(0)=0$, and when f is continuous at x with $f(x)=y$, set

$$\frac{d}{dx}r(x) = \frac{\partial}{\partial x}c(x,y).$$

At discontinuities of f, r is determined by specifying that it be continuous.

Then define s by

$$s(f(x)) = c(x,f(x)) - r(x), \quad x \in [0,1].$$

From Lemma 2 we see that if $r(x)+s(y) \leq c(x,y)$ everywhere then this solution is optimal. On the other hand if $r(x^*)+s(y^*) > c(x^*,y^*)$ for some x^* and y* then we shall show that there is an improvement that can be made.

Let $z=f^{-1}(y^*)$ and suppose first that $z>x^*$. As c is continuous and r, s and f are piecewise continuous, we can (by perturbing x* if necessary) choose x* so that f is continuous at x* and z. Define f' from f as follows.

$$
\begin{aligned}
f'(x) &= f(x), & x &\in [0,x^*), \\
&= f(z + x^* - x), & x &\in [x^*,x^*+\varepsilon), \\
&= f(x - \varepsilon), & x &\in [x^*+\varepsilon,z], \\
&= f(x), & x &\in (z,1].
\end{aligned}
$$

Then f' is also a 1-1 measure preserving function and defines a new feasible solution for CAP. An example of the change that this produces is shown in Figure 2.

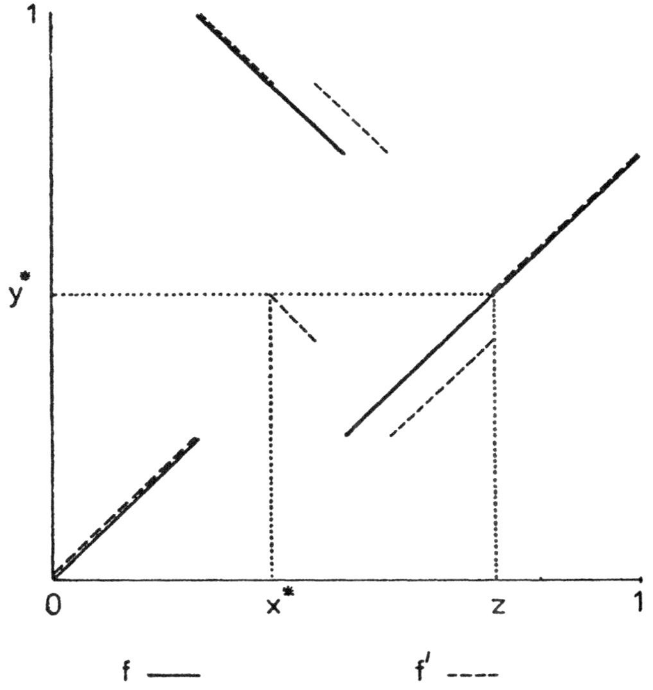

Figure 2. An Example of One Step in the Algorithm

When ε is small enough so that f is continuous on (z−ε,z), the objective function value for f' is given by

$$\int_0^1 c(x,f'(x))dx = \int_0^1 c(x,f(x))dx + \varepsilon c(x^*,y^*) - \varepsilon c(z,y^*)$$

$$+ \varepsilon \int_{x^*}^{z} \frac{\partial}{\partial x} c(x,y)\Big|_{y=f(x)} dx + O(\varepsilon^2)$$

$$= \int_0^1 c(x,f(x))dx + \varepsilon c(x^*,y^*) - \varepsilon(r(z) + s(y^*))$$

$$+ \varepsilon(r(z) - r(x^*)) + O(\varepsilon^2)$$

$$< \int_0^1 c(x,f(x))dx,$$

for ε chosen small enough. Thus f' is an improvement on f for small ε. A similar argument can be used when $z<x^*$.

We remark that the line we introduce in the pivot step above can have either of two slopes (+1 or -1). We may as well choose the one which gives the largest improvement and this depends on the sign of the mixed second partial derivative of c at (x^*,y^*). It is also sensible to make as large a change as possible in order to obtain the maximum improvement. This means deciding at what point the order ε^2 term starts to dominate. With these additions the algorithm has been succesfully implemented on a minicomputer at Cambridge for cost functions which are quartics.

We remark that what we have said so far goes some way towards showing strong duality for CTP and CAP. First note that the finite assignments which we consider are dense in the solution space for both CAP and CTP. If there is an optimal solution which is a finite assignment, then there can be no improvement on it and so the r and s which we define must satisfy (1.5). It can be shown that these r and s are continuous, and hence from Lemma 1 they are dual optimal and there is no duality gap. We shall consider these questions further in [1].

Acknowledgement

The authors would like to acknowledge the contribution of Dr. P. Nash to this paper.

References

(1) ANDERSON, E.J., AND A.B.PHILPOTT: Duality and an algorithm for a class of continuous transportation problems, in preparation.

(2) APPELL, P.: Le problème géométrique des déblais et remblais, Memorial des Sciènces Mathématiques, 1928.

(3) KANTOROVITCH, L.V.: On the translocation of masses, Doklady Akad. Nauk.SSSR, 37 (1942), 199-201.

(4) KRETSCHMER, K.S.: Programmes in paired spaces, Canadian J. Math., 13 (1961), 323-334.

(5) LEVIN, V.L. AND A.A.MILYUTIN: The problem of mass transfer with a discontinuous cost function, Russian Math. Surveys, 34 (1978), 1-78.

(6) MONGE, G.: Mémoires de l'Académie des Sciènces, 1781.

NUMERICAL ESTIMATION OF OPTIMA BY USE OF DUALITY INEQUALITIES*

R. J. Duffin

Abstract. In order to use a duality inequality to estimate the minimum value of a convex program, no nonlinear equality constraints should appear in the program or the dual program. The reason for this is that it is impractical to find feasible solutions to nonlinear equations. Unfortunately the usual Lagrange type dual program has equality constraints. To avoid this difficulty a modified dual program is developed by using suitable support planes. Only inequality constraints then arise.

1. Introduction

If a feasible solution to a nonlinear minimization program is known, then an upper bound to the minimum value f^* is given by the value f of the objective function for the feasible solution. Suppose a dual program is known and a feasible solution is obtainable with ψ being the value of the dual objective function. Then an estimate of f^* is $(f + \psi)/2$, and the error cannot exceed $(f - \psi)/2$.

In order to apply this estimation technique in practical calculations, there are three essential requirements:

(a) A dual program must be found.

(b) All functions should be given explicitly.

(c) All equality constraints should appear linearly.

If any of these properties are absent, the technique would have very little value for numerical work. For example if there were nonlinear equality constraints of an irreducible nature there would be great difficulty in finding feasible solutions to such nonlinear equations.

Obviously a linear program satisfies properties (abc). A geometric program is also seen to satisfy (abc). Another example is a DC network of nonlinear resistors. The primal variables are the node voltages. The dual variables are the resistor currents [2,3,4].

Wolfe and others developed a Lagrange dual program [1]. However property (c) would usually not hold. A previous note [5] pointed out that a certain class of Wolfe programs were easily transformed to (abc) type.

Rockafellar and others developed dual programs by use of conjugate

---

*Study supported by ARO Grant DAAG-29-80-C-0037, Army Research Office, Research Triangle Park, North Carolina.

functions. However, property (b) would usually not hold because conjugate functions are defined implicitly.

The first problem treated here is termed Program A. It is to seek the minimum value f^* of a convex function $f(r)$ for $r \in R^n$. A dual program is formulated by introducing a cone made up of $n + 1$ planes tangent to f. A dual objective function is then determined by the apex of the cone. These developments are easy to generalize when convex inequality constraints are adjoined to Program A. Properties (abc) hold for these programs.

The convex functions introduced here are assumed to have continuous first derivatives given by explicit formulae.

2. Minima of Functions of One Variable

Let $f(x)$ be a convex function for real x and let $p(x)$ be its derivative, df/dx.

Suppose f has a minimum value f^* at a point x^* as shown in Figure 1. Let x_1 be a point where $p < 0$ and let x_2 be a point where $p > 0$. Tangent lines are shown at the points x_1 and x_2.

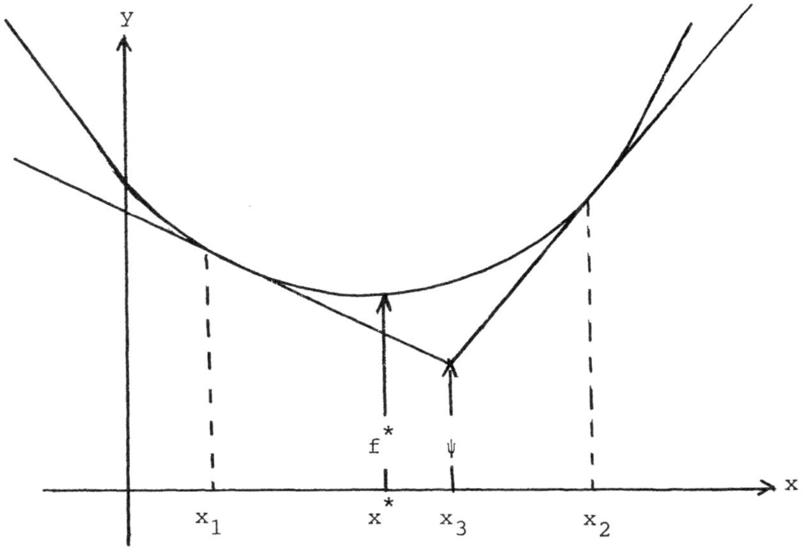

Figure 1. A Convex Curve with a Support Cone

They form a support cone with apex at $x = x_3$, $y = \psi$. It is geometrically evident that $\psi \leq f^*$. Then solving the tangent line equations for the point of intersection gives

$$\psi = (p_2\varphi_1 - p_1\varphi_2)/(p_2 - p_1),$$

where

$$p_1 = p(x_1), \qquad \varphi_1 = f(x_1) - x_1 p(x_1), \qquad \text{etc.}$$

Thus a dual to the minimization program is

<u>Program X. Seek the supremum of</u> $\psi(x_1,x_2)$ <u>subject to the constraints</u>

$$p(x_1) < 0, \qquad p(x_2) > 0.$$

This dual program satisfies the conditions (a,b,c) and gives a practical estimation algorithm for f^*.

It is also important to estimate the point x^* where f takes on its minimum value. Obviously x^* is in the interval (x_1,x_2).

3. Minima of Functions of Two Variables

The above algorithms for functions of one variable are to be generalized for functions of several variables. Actually attention will be restricted to the case of two variables because the extension to more variables will then be apparent.

Consider a convex function $f(x,y)$ of two variables which has a minimum value f^* at a finite point of the plane. Such a function is plotted as a surface in Figure 2. Also shown there are three tangent

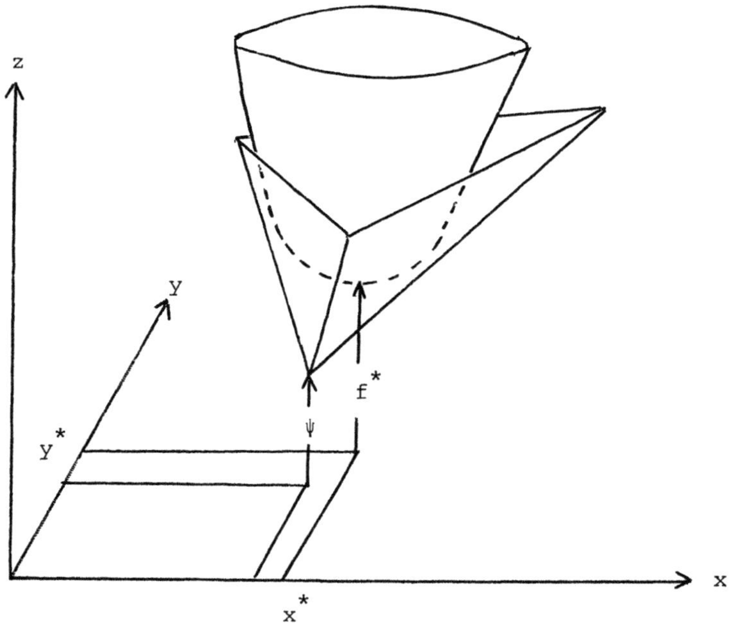

Figure 2. A Convex Surface with a Support Cone

planes to the convex surfaces. The equation of such a plane is

$$z = xp_1 + yq_1 + \varphi_1$$

where p_1, q_1, and φ_1 denote the functions

$$p = \partial f/\partial x, \qquad q = \partial f/\partial y,$$
$$\varphi = f - x\,\partial f/\partial x - y\,\partial f/\partial y$$

all evaluated at a fixed point (x_1,y_1). The <u>Legendre function</u> φ is the z intercept of the tangent plane.

If $r = (x,y)$ and $r_1 = (x_1,y_1)$ are any two points of the (x,y) plane, a fundamental inequality for differentiable convex functions may be stated in the form

$$z = xp_1 + yq_1 + \varphi_1 \leq f(x,y) \equiv f(r).$$

Thus the tangent plane is always below the surface $z = f(x,y)$.

The three tangent planes form a support cone with apex at the point (x,y,ψ). The apex function ψ, so defined, is to serve as a dual objective function.

4. The Apex Program

We are now prepared to formulate a dual to the following primal program,

<u>Program A. Seek the minimum value</u> f^* <u>of a convex function</u> $f(r)$.

To form a dual program the apex function ψ is expressed in terms of the Legendre function $\varphi(r) = f(r) - xp(r) - yq(r)$.

<u>Program X. Seek the supremum of the weighted mean of the Legendre function</u>

$$\psi(r_1,r_2,r_3) = [w_1\varphi(r_1) + w_2\varphi(r_2) + w_3\varphi(r_3)]/(w_1 + w_2 + w_3).$$

<u>Here the weights</u> w_1,w_2,w_3 <u>are cofactors of the first row of the matrix</u>

$$\Delta = \begin{vmatrix} 1 & 1 & 1 \\ p_1 & p_2 & p_3 \\ q_1 & q_2 & q_3 \end{vmatrix}$$

<u>where</u> $p_1 = \partial f(r_1)/\partial x$, $q_1 = \partial f(r_1)/\partial y$ <u>etc. The constraints are the inequalities on the cofactors</u>

$$w_1 = p_2q_3 - p_3q_2 > 0, \quad w_2 = p_3q_1 - p_1q_3 > 0, \quad w_3 = p_1q_2 - p_2q_1 > 0$$

<u>obtained by a suitable choice of the points</u> r_1,r_2,r_3.

To justify that Programs A and X are actually dual, we prove the following duality inequality.

<u>Theorem 1</u>. <u>If the points</u> r_1, r_2, r_3 <u>satisfy the constraints of the Apex Program</u> X <u>then</u>

$$\psi(r_1,r_2,r_3) \leq f^* \leq f(r)$$

<u>for an arbitrary point</u> r.

<u>Proof</u>. Because f is convex, the following basic inequalities hold for points r_1, r_2, r_3 and r:

$$\begin{aligned} xp_1 + yq_1 + \varphi_1 &\leq f(r) \\ xp_2 + yq_2 + \varphi_2 &\leq f(r) \qquad (4.1) \\ xp_3 + yq_3 + \varphi_3 &\leq f(r). \end{aligned}$$

The weights are positive, so we may multiply the inequalities by the weights and then add. Thus

$$x\Sigma w_i p_i + y\Sigma w_i q_i + \Sigma w_i \varphi_i \leq f(r)\Sigma w_i.$$

The cofactors of a row are orthogonal to any other row, so

$$\Sigma w_i p_i = 0, \qquad \Sigma w_i q_i = 0.$$

Dividing by Σw_i proves the duality inequality.

An equivalent expression for the apex objective function is

$$\psi = \bar{w}_1\varphi_1 + \bar{w}_2\varphi_2 + \bar{w}_3\varphi_3.$$

Here $\bar{w}_1, \bar{w}_2, \bar{w}_3$ are normalized weights, any all positive solution of the equation system:

$$\begin{vmatrix} 1 & 1 & 1 \\ p_1 & p_2 & p_3 \\ q_1 & q_2 & q_3 \end{vmatrix} \begin{vmatrix} \bar{w}_1 \\ \bar{w}_2 \\ \bar{w}_3 \end{vmatrix} = \begin{vmatrix} 1 \\ 0 \\ 0 \end{vmatrix}.$$

5. <u>The Question of a Duality Gap</u>

Suppose that the set of minimum points of a convex function is a bounded set H. Let f^* be the minimum value of f. The set H is a convex set such as shown shaded in Figure 3. Let H^+ be the set where $f(r) \leq f^* + \delta$ for some $\delta > 0$. Clearly H^+ is a bounded convex set containing H in its interior.

There are points r_1, r_2 where an exterior normal to H^+ has the direction of the x axis, y axis and point r_3 where an interior normal makes an angle of 45° with the x axis. The gradients at r_1, r_2, r_3 do not vanish because r_1, r_2, r_3 are not in the set H. Thus the gradient vector is in the direction of the exterior normal, so

$$(p_1 = \alpha,\ q_1 = 0), \qquad (p_2 = 0,\ q_2 = \beta), \qquad (p_3 = -\gamma,\ q_3 = -\gamma)$$

where α, β and γ are positive. Thus the Δ matrix becomes

$$\Delta = \begin{vmatrix} 1 & 1 & 1 \\ \alpha & 0 & -\gamma \\ 0 & \beta & -\gamma \end{vmatrix} .$$

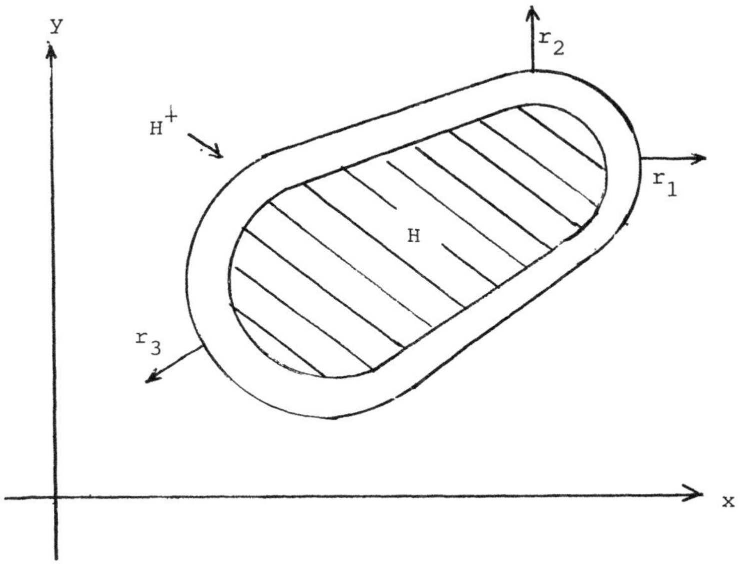

Figure 3. The Set of Minimum Points

The corresponding cofactors are $w_1 = \beta\gamma$, $w_2 = \gamma\alpha$, $w_3 = \alpha\beta$. These are all positive, so the constraints of Program X are satisfied for every $\delta > 0$.

Now let $\delta \to 0$ through a sequence. This sequence can be chosen so that $r_1 \to r_1^*$, a point of H. Of course

$$f(r_1^*) = f^*, \quad p(r_1^*) = 0, \quad q(r_1^*) = 0.$$

Since f and its derivatives are continuous functions, we get

$$\varphi_1 = f(r_1) - x_1 p(r_1) - y_1 q(r_1) \to f^*.$$

Likewise $\varphi_2 \to f^*$ and $\varphi_3 \to f^*$. Since ψ is a mean of the φ we find

$$\psi(r_1, r_2, r_3) \to f^* \quad \text{as} \quad \delta \to 0.$$

Thus there is no duality gap.

The above analysis proves the first part of the following theorem.

Theorem 2. If the minimum points of a convex function form a bounded set, then the dual program X is feasible. Moreover the supremum value of the dual is equal to the minimum value of the convex function.

Conversely if the dual program is feasible, then the convex function has a finite minimum value, and the minimum points form a bounded set.

Proof. For the second part, suppose, on the contrary, that $f(r_i) = f^*$ for an unbounded sequence of points $\{r_i\}$. Then the system of inequalities (4.1) now becomes:

$$\begin{aligned} x_i p_1 + y_i q_1 + \varphi_1 &\le f^* \\ x_i p_2 + y_i q_2 + \varphi_2 &\le f^* \\ x_i p_3 + y_i q_3 + \varphi_3 &\le f^* \end{aligned} \quad . \tag{5.1}$$

Divide these inequalities by $|x_i| + |y_i|$. Then there will be a subsequence such that as $i \to \infty$

$$x_i/(|x_i| + |y_i|) \to x_0, \qquad y_i/(|x_i| + |y_i|) \to y_o.$$

Then $|x_0| + |y_0| = 1$ and the limit of (5.1) is

$$\begin{aligned} x_0 p_1 + y_0 q_1 + t_1 &= 0 \\ x_0 p_2 + y_0 q_2 + t_2 &= 0. \\ x_0 p_3 + y_0 q_3 + t_3 &= 0 \end{aligned} \tag{5.2}$$

Here $t_1 \ge 0$, $t_2 \ge 0$, $t_3 \ge 0$. But t_1 and t_2 are not both zero because

$$\begin{vmatrix} p_1 & q_1 \\ p_2 & q_2 \end{vmatrix} = \begin{vmatrix} p_1 & p_2 \\ q_1 & q_2 \end{vmatrix} = w_3 > 0.$$

Next multiply the equations (5.2) by w_1, w_2, w_3 and add. By orthogonality this gives

$$w_1 t_1 + w_2 t_2 + w_3 t_3 = 0.$$

This is a contradiction because $w_1 > 0$ and $w_2 > 0$. This completes the proof of the theorem.

6. Estimating the Coordinates of an Optimum Point

Again we illustrate a general method by treating the case of a function of two variables.

Theorem 3. Suppose that the points r_1, r_2, r_3 satisfy the constraints of Program X, and let r_0 be an arbitrary point. Then the system of inequalities

$$x p_1 + y q_1 + \varphi_1 \le f(r_0) \tag{6.1}$$

$$x p_2 + y q_2 + \varphi_2 \le f(r_0) \tag{6.2}$$

$$x p_3 + y q_3 + \varphi_3 \le f(r_0) \tag{6.3}$$

determines a triangle T which contains the optimum points of Program A.

Proof. Since Program X is feasible, we know by virtue of Theorem 2 that f has minima. We have seen before that the above system of inequalities has a solution by taking $x = x_0$ and $y = y_0$.

The same argument used for the second part of Theorem 2 shows that the system of inequalities has a bounded feasible region. It then follows that the feasible region is a triangle T because there are three constraints.

Let r^* be an optimum point. Thus $f(r^*) = f^*$ and

$$x^* p_1 + y^* q_1 + \varphi_1 \leq f(r^*) \leq f(r_0), \text{ etc.}$$

Thus r^* satisifes the system of inequalities, and so is in T.

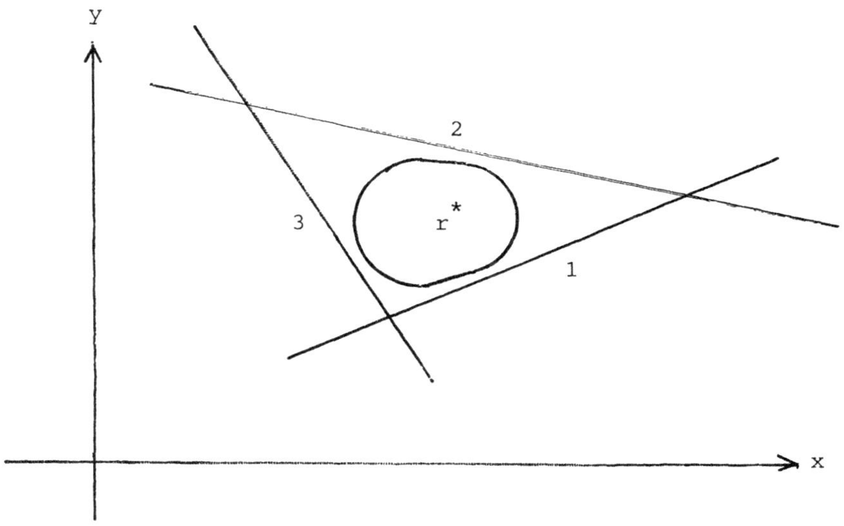

Figure 4. Contour Lines of Cone and Surface

Figure 4 shows an optimum point located in a triangle with sides 1, 2, and 3. The side 1 is the line determined by relation (6.1) of Theorem 3 interpreted as an equation, etc.

7. Estimating Constrained Minima

The extension of the above algorithms when the primal program has constraints is quite direct. For example the following is a typical constrained minimization program.

<u>Program A'. Seek the minimum value</u> f^* <u>of</u> $f(r)$ <u>subject to the constraint</u>

$$g(r) \leq 0$$

<u>where</u> f <u>and</u> g <u>are both assumed to be differentiable convex functions.</u>

A dual program is often formulated in terms of the Lagrangian function

$$F(r,\lambda) = f(r) + \lambda g(r), \qquad \lambda \geq 0.$$

We now let

$$P = \partial F/\partial x, \qquad Q = \partial F/\partial y,$$
$$\Phi = F - xP - yQ.$$

The functions F, P, Q and Φ will now play a role in direct analogy to the functions f, p, q and φ in the unconstrained case. In particular we note that F is a convex function of r. This leads to the following dual program.

<u>Program X'. Seek the supremum of the apex function</u>

$$\Psi(r_1,r_2,r_3,\lambda) = \frac{w_1\Phi(r_1,\lambda) + w_2\Phi(r_2,\lambda) + w_3\Phi(r_3,\lambda)}{w_1 + w_2 + w_3}.$$

<u>Here</u> w_1,w_2,w_3 <u>are cofactors of the first row of the</u> Δ <u>matrix. The constraints are</u> $\lambda \geq 0$ <u>and</u>

$$w_1 > 0, \qquad w_2 > 0, \qquad w_3 > 0.$$

Then the following duality inequality holds

<u>Theorem 4. If</u> r_1,r_2,r_3,λ <u>satisfy the constraints of Program</u> X', <u>then</u>

(7.1) $$\Psi(r_1,r_2,r_3,\lambda) \leq f^* \leq f(r)$$

<u>whenever</u> r <u>satisfies the constraint of Program</u> A'.

<u>Proof</u>. It follows from Theorem 2 that for this value of λ the function F has a minimum value, say when $r = r^\lambda$. Then, as is clear, the following duality inequality holds.

(7.2) $$F(r^\lambda,\lambda) \leq F(r,\lambda) = f(r) + \lambda g(r) \leq f(r)$$

whenever r satisfies the constraint of Program A'. For this value of λ the constraints of Program X' hold. Then Theorem 1 applies, giving

(7.3) $$\Psi(r_1,r_2,r_3,\lambda) \leq F(r^\lambda,\lambda).$$

But (7.2) and (7.3) together imply (7.1), and the proof is complete.

Can there be a duality gap in (7.2), and hence in (7.1)? As is well known, the duality gap can be avoided if the Slater constraint qualification $g(r') < 0$ holds for some point r' [6].

8. Discussion

The above analysis gives a general strategy for estimating optima. However, no discussion has been given of search procedures. Such tactics are left to the skill of the numerical analyst.

Note that the apex function Ψ is expressed as a mean of Φ_1, Φ_2, Φ_3. Instead one could use as a dual objective function

$$\Psi' = \min(\Phi_1, \Phi_2, \Phi_3).$$

This would give a simpler algorithm, but it would not be as accurate.

The function Φ may be termed a Legendre-Lagrangian. In a previous note [5] it was used as a dual objective function. In that note it was observed that if the minimum point is known to be in a given polyhedral cone, then a simple transformation converts all constraints into inequality form.

References

[1] WOLFE, P.: A Duality Theory for Nonlinear Programming. Quart. J. Appl. Math 19 (1961), 237 - 244.

[2] DUFFIN, R. J.: Dual Programs and Minimum Cost. SIAM Jour. 10 (1962), 117 - 123.

[3] DUFFIN, R. J.: Duality Inequalities of Mathematics and Science, in Nonlinear Programming. eds. Rosen, J. B., Mangasarian, O. L. and Ritter, K. New York: Academic Press, 1970, 401 - 423.

[4] DUFFIN, R. J.: Electrical Network Models, in Studies in Graph Theory. ed. Fulkerson, D. R. Mathematical Association of America, Studies in Mathematics 11 (1975), 94 - 138.

[5] DUFFIN, R. J.: Transformations that Aid Numerical Solution of Nonlinear Programs. Opsearch 18 (1981), 158 - 166.

[6] DUFFIN, R. J.: An Elementary Treatment of Lagrange Multipliers, in Extremal Methods and Systems Analysis. eds. Fiacco, A. V. and Kortanek, K. O. New York: Springer-Verlag, 1980, 357-373.

GLOBALIZATION OF LOCALLY CONVERGENT ALGORITHMS FOR NONLINEAR OPTIMIZATION PROBLEMS WITH CONSTRAINTS

H. Gfrerer

J. Guddat

Hj. Wacker

W. Zulehner

Abstract

The continuation method known for the numerical solution of nonlinear equations is applied to nonlinear optimization problems with constraints. Moving along the homotopy path, only the active constraints are considered. We assume that there exists only a finite number of critical points, i.e. points where the index set of the active constraints changes. Then a theoretic concept of a globally convergent algorithm consists of the following three phases:

1. Inside a stability set the solution is computed by help of classical continuation.

2. At the boundary of a stability set a critical point $\bar{t}$ has to be determined.

3. Passing $\bar{t}$, the new active index set must be identified.

For the case of convex problems a concrete imbedding is proposed which is based on the theory of parametric optimization.

1. Introduction

In the following we want to report on some results concerning the globalization of locally convergent optimization. Globalization here is meant in the sense of continuation methods. Proofs are omitted. We refer to [3], [4]. We discuss problems of the following kind:

(P) $$\min\{f_0(x) \mid f_j(x) \leq 0,\ j = 1,2,\ldots,m\}.$$

This problem is imbedded via a homotopy

P(t) $$\min\{h_0(x,t) \mid h_j(x,t) \leq 0,\ j = 1,\ldots,m\} \qquad t \in T := [0,1].$$

To dispense with difficulties touching existence and uniqueness problems we assume:

Parts of the work were supported by the Fonds zur Förderung der Österreichischen Forschung (Projekt 3472).

(E1) There exists a continuous function $x : T \to \mathbb{R}^n$ such that for each $t \in T$, $x(t)$ is an isolated local minimizer for $P(t)$.

(E2) $x(0)$ is explicitly known.

(E3) $P(1) = P$.

(E3), which gives a connection between (P) and $P(t)$, can always be easily realized. (E2) needs some care and is more difficult than for nonlinear equations. (E1) is rather crucial to verify. Up to now, only for special classes are there sufficient conditions from which (E1) can be guaranteed a priori. See part 4 for instance.

Besides imbedding, the second feature of our concept is that only equation constraints are involved. This can be done without loss of generality by working only with active constraints

$$I(t) := \{j \in \{1,\dots,m\} \mid h_j(x(t),t) = 0\}.$$

Therefore, instead of $P(t)$ we solve

$$P^I(t) := \min\{h_0(x,t) \mid h_j(x,t) = 0,\ j \in I\}, \qquad t \in T.$$

We give some notations and assumptions.

(V1) There exists a neighbourhood C of $\{(x(t),t) \mid t \in T\} \subset \mathbb{R}^n \times T$ such that for all $(x,t) \in C$, $h_i(x,t)$, $i = 0,\dots,m$ are twice continuously differentiable with respect to x ($\nabla_x h_i$ denotes the gradient, $\nabla_{xx} h_i$ denotes the Hessian) and continuously differentiable with respect to t ($\nabla_t h_i$ denotes the partial derivative) and $\nabla_{xt} h_i$ exists and is continuous.

(V2) The gradients of the active constraints

$$\{\nabla_x h_i(x(t),t)\}_{i \in I(t)}$$

are linearly independent for each $t \in T$.

(V1),(V2) imply that there exists $u : T \to \mathbb{R}^m$, $u(t) = (u_1(t),\dots,u_m(t))$, uniquely defined such that $(x(t),u(t))$ satisfies the first order Kuhn-Tucker conditions:

$$\left.\begin{aligned} \nabla_x l(x,u,t) &= 0 \\ h_j(x(t),t) &\le 0 \\ u_j(t) &\ge 0 \\ u_j(t)h_j(x(t),t) &= 0 \end{aligned}\right. \qquad j = 1,\dots,m$$

with

$$l(x,u,t) := h_0(x(t),t) + \sum_{j=1}^{m} u_j(t)h_j(x(t),t).$$

Additionally we need some kind of second order conditions. We first define:

$$I^+(t) := \{j \in I(t) \mid u_j(t) > 0\}, \quad I^0(t) := \{j \in I(t) \mid u_j(t) = 0\}.$$

(V3) For each non-zero y with $\nabla_x h_j(x(t),t)^T y = 0$, $j \in I^+(t)$, $t \in T$, we have

$$y^T \nabla_{xx} l^{I(t)}(x,u,t) y > 0$$

where

$$l^{I(t)}(x,u,t) := h(x(t),t) + \sum_{j \in I(t)} u_j(t) h_j(x(t),t).$$

2.1. Local Stability Sets, Critical Points

We first introduce the concept of a local stability set.

Definition 1: Let $t_0 \in T$, $I_0 := I(t_0)$. The maximal connected subset of $\{t \in T \mid x(t)$ is a local minimizer of $P^{I_0}(t)\}$ to which t_0 belongs is called the local stability set with respect to t_0, denoted by $S(t_0)$.

This definition does not necessarily mean that while working with the fixed index set I_0 there is no other index $j \notin I_0$ allowed to become active. Any index may join the index set I_0 -- which of course remains active -- as long as $x(t)$ remains a local minimizer of $P^{I_0}(t)$.

We give a first characterization of $S(t_0)$.

Theorem 1: Assume (E1), (V1), (V2), and (V3). Then $S(t_0)$ is the maximally connected subset of $\{t \in T \mid I^+(t) \subset I(t_0) \subset I(t)\}$ to which t_0 belongs.

Proof: (See [3].)

The next lemma gives some important properties of $S(t_0)$ and the solution $(x^{I_0}(t), u^{I_0}(t))$ of $P(t)$ in a set $D(t_0)$ containing $S(t_0)$.

Lemma 1: Assume (E1), (V1), (V2), (V3), and $t_0 \in T$. Then:

1. $S(t_0)$ is closed for each $t_0 \in T$.
2. Let $S(t_0) = [\underline{t}, \overline{t}]$, $I_0 := I(t_0)$. Then there exists a maximally connected relatively open subset $D(t_0)$ of T with $S(t_0) \subset D(t_0)$ and continuous functions $x^{I_0} : D(t_0) \to \mathbb{R}^n$, $u^{I_0}(t) : D(t_0) \to \mathbb{R}^{m_0}$, ($m_0 = |I_0|$ where $u_j^{I_0}$, $j \in I_0$ denotes the components of u^{I_0}) with

(i) $x^{I_0}(t) = x(t)$, $u_j^{I_0}(t) = u_j(t)$, $j \in I_0$, $t \in S(t_0)$.

(ii) $\nabla_x h_j(x^{I_0}(t),t)$, $j \in I_0$ are linearly independent for each $t \in D(t_0)$.

(iii) $(x^{I_0}(t), u^{I_0}(t))$ satisfies the first order Kuhn-Tucker conditions for $P^{I_0}(t)$, $t \in D(t_0)$.

(iv) $(x^{I_0}(t), u^{I_0}(t))$ satisfies the second order Kuhn-Tucker conditions for $P^{I_0}(t)$, $t \in D(t_0)$.

(v) $x^{I_0}(t)$ is an isolated local minimizer for $P^{I_0}(t)$, $t \in D(t_0)$.

3. $(x^{I_0}(t), u^{I_0}(t))$ are continuously differentiable on $D(t_0)$.

Proof:

1. See [4].
2. See [4].
3. We apply the Implicit Function Theorem to the following system (first order Kuhn-Tucker conditions for $P^{I_0}(t)$):

$$F(z^{I_0}(t),t) := \begin{bmatrix} \nabla_x h_0(x(t),t) + \sum_{j\in I_0} u_j(t)\nabla_x h_j(x(t),t) = 0 \\ h_j(x(t),t) = 0, \quad j \in I_0 \end{bmatrix} = 0 \qquad (*)$$

Because of (V1), h_j, $\nabla_x h_j$ are continuously differentiable with respect to both x and t. The Jacobian of (*): $A := F'_z(z(t),t)$ is regular by (V2), (V3).

Therefore the assumptions to apply the Implicit Function Theorem to $F(z^{I_0}(t),t) = 0$ are satisfied. See also [3].

Now we give a second characterization of the local stability set $S(t_0)$ which in most cases is more helpful for computational purposes than the first one given in Theorem 1.

Theorem 2: Assume (E1), (V1), (V2), and (V3). Then $S(t_0)$ is the maximally connected subset of

$$\{t \in D(t_0) \mid h_j(x^{I_0}(t),t) \leq 0,\ j = 1,\dots,m;\ u_j^{I_0}(t) \geq 0,\ j \in I_0\}$$

to which t_0 belongs.

Proof: (See [4].)

For our algorithm it is essential to analyze the boundary points of the local stability sets.

Definition 2: A boundary point of $S(t_0)$ is called a critical point of $(P(t), x(t), t_0)$.

Remark 1: Theorem 1 gives an implicit characterization of critical points by help of active index sets. Theorem 2 directly gives a computational device. We restrict our investigation to a finite number of critical points in T, i.e. we assume:

(V4) The number of critical points is finite in T.

Remark 2: Assumption (V4) is fulfilled, for instance, if there is only a finite number of points in T where the strict complementary slackness condition is not satisfied.

Remark 3: Together with (V4) it follows with Lemma 1.3 that $z(t) = (x(t),u(t))$ is Lipschitz continuous in T.

2.2. Convergence of Local Methods on Local Stability Sets

Imbedding allows one to "globalize" any local method of a certain structure. We shall concentrate on superlinear convergent methods. While working with $P(t)$ then, for most of the well known local methods, convergence cannot be guaranteed where the strict complementary slackness condition is violated. For problems like $P^{I_0}(t)$, where no inequality constraints are involved, there does not exist such a problem.

We recall Avila's definition that a continuation process be feasible. For certain reasons, we weaken this definition slightly (Definition 3.2).

Definition 3:

1. Let D be a neighbourhood of $\{(z(t),t) \mid t \in J\}$, $J := [t_A, t_B]$. Assume there exists a mapping $G : D \to \mathbb{R}^n$ with

$$z(t) = G(z(t),t) \qquad t \in J,$$

there exists a partition of J

$$t_A = t_0 < t_1 < \ldots < t_N = t_B$$

and a sequence of integers $\{j_k\}$, $k = 1,\ldots,N-1$ such that the points

$$z_k^{j+1} = G(z_k, t_k^j), \quad j = 0,\ldots,j_k-1; \quad k = 1,\ldots,N-1$$

$$z_{k+1}^0 = z_k^{j_k}, \quad z_1^0 = z_0$$

are well defined and such that

$$z_N^{j+1} = G(z_N^j, t_B), \qquad j = 0,1,\ldots$$

converges to $z(t_B)$ as $j \to \infty$. Then the "continuation" process is called <u>numerically feasible</u>.

2. If some or all integers j_k are allowed to be infinite, then the continuation process is called feasible.

<u>Theorem 3</u>: Assume (E1), (V1), (V2), and (V3). Then for each compact set $K(t_0)$ with $S(t_0) \subset K(t_0) \subset D(t_0)$ the continuation process is numerically feasible for

i) Robinson's procedure from [7].

ii) Wilson's procedure (see e.g. [11]), if additionally differentiability of third order holds for $h_i(x,t)$ with respect to x.

<u>Proof</u>:

i) Avila's Theorem 2.5 [1] has to be combined with the Implicit Function Theorem, see e.g. Schwetlick [8], p. 54.

ii) By direct application of Avila's Theorem.

2.3. Determination of Critical Points

By Theorem 3 we have a local procedure by which we can solve $P(t)$ at least for all $t \in D(t_0)$. In $D(t_0)$ the solution $z^{I_0}(t)$ must satisfy the first order Kuhn-Tucker conditions, i.e. $z^{I_0}(t)$ is the locally unique solution of

$$F(z(t),t) := \begin{bmatrix} \nabla_x h_0(x(t),t) + \sum\limits_{j \in I_0} u_j(t) \nabla_x h_j(x(t),t) \\ h_j(x(t),t), \quad j \in I_0 \end{bmatrix} = 0.$$

Theorem 2 characterizes implicitly a boundary point $\bar{t}$ of $S(t_0)$. In our continuation process we have

$$\bar{t} \in [t_k, t_{k+1}) \Leftrightarrow \{\text{There exists } j_0 \in \{1,\ldots,m\} \setminus I_0 \text{ with}$$

$$h_{j_0}(x^{I_0}(t_{k+1}, t_{k+1}) > 0 \text{ or there exists } i_0 \in I_0 \text{ with } u_{i_0}(t_{k+1}) < 0\}$$

$$\text{and } t_k \in S(t_0).$$

Therefore $\bar{t}$ can be computed for instance by a bisection process. Alternatively, Newton's procedure might be preferable. In this case we search for $\bar{t} \in [t_k, t_{k+1}]$ with

$$h_{j_0}(x^{I_0}(\bar{t}), \bar{t}) = 0 \quad \text{or} \quad u_{i_0}(\bar{t}) = 0.$$

The main task then is the computation of z^{I_0}, $\dot{z}^{I_0}$ by solving linear systems with F_z' as matrix in both cases.

2.4. Determination of the New Active Index Set

After passing a critical point $\bar{t}$ we must determine the index set of active constraints $I(\bar{t}+\varepsilon)$ for $\varepsilon > 0$ sufficiently small and $I(\bar{t})$ known.

Theorem 4: Assume (E1), (V1), (V2), (V3), and (V4). Let $S_0(t_0) = [\underline{t},\bar{t}]$, $\bar{t} < 1$.

i) Then there exists a real number $\varepsilon > 0$ such that $I^+(\bar{t}) \subset I(t) \subset I(\bar{t})$ and $\bar{t} \in S(t_1^0)$ for each $t_1 \in (\bar{t},\bar{t}+\varepsilon]$.

ii) In the special case $I^0(\bar{t}) = \{i_0\}$,

$$I(t) = \begin{cases} I(t_0) \cup \{i_0\}, & I(t_0) = I^+(\bar{t}) \\ \\ I(t_0) \setminus \{i_0\}, & I(t_0) = I(\bar{t}) \end{cases} .$$

Proof: (See [4].)

It is possible to sharpen the inclusion for the new active index set by using the right sided derivative $\dot{z}(t)|_{t=\bar{t}_+}$.

Lemma 2: Assume (E1), (V1), (V2), (V3), and (V4). Let $S(t_0) = [\underline{t},\bar{t}]$, $\bar{t} < 1$. Then:

(i) $\dot{x}(\bar{t}_+)$ is the unique solution of the quadratic optimization problem

$$P(\bar{t}_+) : \min\{\tfrac{1}{2}\, x^T \nabla_{xx} l(x(\bar{t}),u(\bar{t}),\bar{t})x + \nabla_{xt} l(x(\bar{t}),u(\bar{t}),\bar{t})x \mid$$

$$\nabla_x h_j(x(\bar{t}),\bar{t})x + \nabla_t h_j(x(\bar{t}),\bar{t}) = 0, \quad j \in I^+(\bar{t}),$$

$$\nabla_x h_j(x(\bar{t}),\bar{t})x + \nabla_t h_j(x(\bar{t}),\bar{t}) \le 0, \quad j \in I^0(\bar{t})\}.$$

(ii) $\dot{u}(\bar{t}_+)$ is the unique Lagrange multiplier of $P(\bar{t}_+)$ associated with $\dot{x}(\bar{t}_+)$, with zero components for $j \in I(\bar{t})$.

Proof: (See [3].)

Corollary 1: Assume the notations and assumptions of Lemma 2.

1. Then:

$$I^+(\bar{t}) \cup \{j \mid \tfrac{d}{dt} u_j(t)|_{t=\bar{t}_+} > 0\} \subset I^+(t)$$

and

$$I(t) \subset I(\bar{t}) \setminus \{j \mid \tfrac{d}{dt} h_j(x(t),t)|_{t=\bar{t}_+} < 0\}.$$

Assume (V5):

$\frac{d}{dt} u_j(t)\big|_{t=\bar{t}_+} \neq 0$ or $\frac{d}{dt} h_j(x(t),t)\big|_{t=\bar{t}_+} \neq 0$ for each $j \in I^0(\bar{t})$.

2. Then there exists a δ' such that for all $t \in (\bar{t}, \bar{t} + \delta')$

$$I(t) = I^+(\bar{t}) \cup \{j \in I^0(\bar{t}) \mid \frac{d}{dt} h_j(x(t),t)\big|_{t=\bar{t}_+} = 0\}.$$

For numerical purposes, one only has an approximation $\tilde{t}$ of the critical point $\bar{t}$. Therefore some more research will be necessary to support or generalize the results of Theorem 4 and Corollary 1. For some initial results see [4].

3. A Concept of a Globally Convergent Algorithm

The following scheme $A = A(\Delta t_0)$ gives a concept of a feasible continuation method for the solution of $P(t)$, $t \in T$.

Assume (E1), (E2), (E3), (V1), (V2), (V3), (V4), and (V5).

i) Choose a partition of T: $0 = t_0 < t_1 < \ldots < t_N = 1$ with $0 < t_{k+1} - t_k \leq \Delta t_0$, $k = 0,1,\ldots,N-1$. Given x^0, u^0, I_0 (i.e. the solution resp. the associated Lagrange multiplier resp. the active index set for $P(0)$). Set $k = 1$.

ii) Solve $P^{I_{k-1}}(t_k)$ by a local procedure (It) with x^{k-1}, u^{k-1} as a starting point to obtain x^k, u^k.
(It): Robinson's algorithm or Newton's method for $F(z,t_k) = 0$. In the latter case (V1) has to be strengthened as in Theorem 3(ii).

iii) Check, if $h_j(x^k,t_k) \leq 0$, $j \notin I_{k-1}$ and $u_j^k \geq 0$, $j \in I_{k-1}$. If so, set $I_k = I_{k-1}$ and go back to (ii) with $k + 1$ replacing k. If not, then compute a critical point $\bar{t} \in [t_{k-1}, t_k)$ by bisection or Newton's method and determine $x(\bar{t})$, $u(\bar{t})$, $I^+(\bar{t})$, $I^0(\bar{t})$. Solve the quadratic optimization problem $P(\bar{t}_+)$ by Lemke's ([5]) algorithm to obtain $\dot{z}(\bar{t}_+)$. Corollary 1 then gives

$$I_k := I^+(\bar{t}) \cup \{j \in I^0(\bar{t}) \mid \frac{d}{dt} h_j(x(t),t)\big|_{t=\bar{t}_+} = 0\}.$$

Set $x^k = x(\bar{t})$, $u^k = u(\bar{t})$ and go back to (ii) with $k + 1$ replacing k.

For Δt_0 sufficiently small, $A(\Delta t_0)$ is feasible in the sense of Definition 3.2.

4. A Concrete Imbedding for Convex Optimization Problems

Without loss of generality we consider the optimization problem

P_1 $$\min\{x_n \mid f_j(x) \leq 0,\ j = 1,\dots,m\}$$

under the following assumptions:

(A1) $f_j : \mathbb{R}^n \to \mathbb{R}$ $(j = 1,\dots,m)$ is convex.

(A2) $M := \{x \in \mathbb{R}^n \mid f_j(x) \leq 0,\ j = 1,\dots,m\} \neq \emptyset$.

We choose the following imbedding for $P(t)$:

$$h_0(x,t) := tx_n + (1-t)\|x\|^2$$

$$h_j(x,t) := f_j(x) + (t-1)|f_j(0)|, \quad j = 1,\dots,m.$$

Let

$$M(t) := \{x \in \mathbb{R}^n \mid h_j(x,t) \leq 0,\ j = 1,\dots,m\}$$

be the feasible set of $P(t)$ and

$$\psi(t) := \{x(t) \in M(t) \mid h_0(x(t),t) \leq h_0(x,t) \text{ for all } x \in M(t)\}.$$

We have the following theorem.

Theorem 5:

a) If (A2) holds, then the parametric optimization problem $P(t)$ has the following properties:

i) $P(1) = P_1$;

ii) $\psi(t) \neq \emptyset$ for all $t \in [0,1)$ if the $f_j(x)$ $(j = 1,\dots,m)$ are continuous on $\mathbb{R}^n$;

iii) $0 \in \psi(0)$.

b) Let (A1) and (A3) be fulfilled, where

(A3): $\psi(1) \neq \emptyset$ and compact.

Then:

i) $\psi|_T$ is upper semicontinuous in the sense of Berge on T;

ii) $\psi(t) = \{x(t)\}$ for all $t \in [0,1)$ and $x(t)$ is continuous on $[0,1)$;

iii) $\psi(0) = \{0\}$.

Proof: (See [4].)

Remark: Part a) of Theorem 5 gives (E2) and (E3) even without convexity. Part b) together with (V3) gives $\psi(1) = \{x^1\}$. In case (E1) holds, the proposed imbedding can be applicable to more general optimization problems.

REFERENCES

[1] AVILA, J. W.: The Feasibility of Continuation Methods for Nonlinear Equations. SIAM J. Numer. Anal. 11 (1974), 102 - 121.

[2] BANK, B, J. GUDDAT, B. KUMMER, D. KLATTE, AND K. TAMMER: Nonlinear Parametric Optimization. Berlin:Akademie-Verlag Berlin,to app. 1982. A German version as Seminarbericht Nr. 31 der Sektion Mathematik der Humboldt-Universität zu Berlin.

[3] GFRERER, H., J. GUDDAT, Hj. WACKER, AND W. ZULEHNER: A Globally Convergent Algorithm Based on Imbedding and Parametric Optimization. Institutsbericht Nr. 215, Univ. Linz, Mathematisches Institut, 1982.

[4] GUDDAT, J., Hj. WACKER, AND W. ZULEHNER: On Imbedding and Parametric Optimization - A Concept of a Globally Convergent Algorithm for Nonlinear Optimization. Inst. Bericht Nr. 200, Univ. Linz, Mathematisches Institut (to appear in Math. Progr. Stud.), 1981.

[5] LEMKE, C. E.: On Complementary Pivot Theory in Mathematics of the Decision Sciences, Part 1, eds. Dantzig, G. B. and A. F. Veinott. Lectures in Applied Math. 11 (1968), 95 - 114.

[6] RITTER, K.: Ein Verfahren zur Lösung parameterabhängiger nichtlinearer Maximumprobleme. Unternehmensforschung 6 (1962), 149 - 196.

[7] ROBINSON, S. M.: A Quadratically-Convergent Algorithm for General Nonlinear Programming Problems. Mathematical Programming 3 (1972), 145 - 156.

[8] SCHWETLICK, H.: Numerische Lösung nichtlinearer Gleichungen. Berlin: VEB Deutscher Verlag der Wissenschaften, 1979.

[9] TAMMER, K.: Die Abhängigkeit eines quadratischen Optimierungsproblems von einem Parameter in der Zielfunktion. Mathem. Operationsforsch. Statistik 5 (1974), 573 - 590.

[10] WACKER, Hj.: (editor) Continuation Methods. New York-San Francisco-London: Academic Press, 1978.

[11] WILSON, R. B.: A Simplical Method for Convex Programming. Ph.D. Dissertation, Harvard University, 1963.

A THREE-PHASE ALGORITHM FOR SEMI-INFINITE PROGRAMS

Sven-Åke Gustafson

Abstract. In this paper we define general classes of nonlinear semi-infinite programs and developea unified computational scheme for their numerical treatment. This scheme is based on the fact that necessary optimality conditions may be expressed in the form of a nonlinear system of equations with finitely many equations and unknowns. The computational treatment proceeds in three phases: i) A discretized version of the given task is solved, giving an approximate solution;ii) A nonlinear system defining optimality conditions is derived;iii) This system is solved numerically. In general, the *structure* of the nonlinear system is not known before completion of Phase i). Several applications are indicated.

1. Introduction.

A general computational scheme for linear semi-infinite programs was first given in Gustafson (1968), (1970) and further developed in Gustafson-Kortanek (1973) and Glashoff-Gustafson (1978), (1982). The purpose of this paper is to extend this scheme to nonlinear semi-infinite programs

In Section 2 and 3 we define general classes of semi-infinite programs which may be treated by means of the scheme to be introduced in this paper. We illustrate by examples that these problems are encountered in computational practice.

In Section 4 we derive necessary conditions in the form of a nonlinear system of equations with finitely many equations and unknowns.

In Section 5 we show that all semi-infinite programs of the classes discussed here are numerically equivalent to optimization problems with finitely many equations and unknowns.

In the concluding Section 6 we reach the goal of this paper and formulate a general three-phase algorithm combining the ideas put forward in earlier Sections. Thus in Phase i) we solve a discretized version of the problem at hand. The results hereby obtained are used for constructing the nonlinear system of equations and determining an approximate solution to this system, Phase ii). Then in Phase iii) the system is solved numerically, generally by means of some iterative method. It is important to realize that the form of the nonlinear system, even the number of unknowns, is not determined until after the completion of Phase i).

2. Semi-infinite programs of P-type.

In this Section we introduce a class of problems obtained by generalizing the primal problem appearing in a dual pair of linear semi-infinite programs.

Program(P). Let S be a compact subset of R^k, the linear space of k-tuples. Let also f be a continuously differentiable function on R^n. Further, let u(y,s) define a function, which is twice continuously differentiable for all $y \in R^n$ and all $s \in S$. Then Program (P) is

(2.1a) $\quad$ Minimize f(y)

over all $y \in R^n$ subject to the constraints

(2.1b) $\quad$ $u(y,s) \leq 0, \ s \in S.$ ||

Remark. S is often called an *index-set.* If S has a finite number of elements, then (2.1) defines a minimization problem with finitely many constraints. In this case the function u is said to be continuous and differentiable with respect to s. (We introduce here the convention that (2.1) refers to both (2.1a) and (2.1b). Analogous rules will hold for other lettered formulas in this paper.). We shall require S to be a subset of a finite-dimensional space R^k, since during the course of the calculations we need to determine elements $s_i \in S$ such that

$$u(y,s_i)= 0.$$

Hence we must require s_i to have finitely many coordinates only.

The numerical treatment is meaningful only if there is a y meeting the constraints (2.1b). This may be determined by calculating

$$\min_y \max_{s \in S} u(y,s).$$

This task may be written

(2.2a) $\quad$ Minimize y_0

over all real y_0 and all $y \in R^n$ subject to the constraints

(2.2b) $\quad$ $u(y,s)- y_0 \leq 0, \ s \in S.$

Formally, (2.2) is a special case of (2.1) and (2.2b) is always consistent. Select namely $\overline{y} \in R^n$ arbitrarily and put

$$y_0 = \max u(\overline{y},s) \ .$$

Then $y_0, \overline{y}$ satisfy (2.2b). Hence we may investigate whether (2.1) is consistent by solving a feasible problem of the same structure, namely (2.2). This is a direct analog of the two-phase algorithm for linear programs.
We mention some further instances of (2.1).

Example 1: Linear semi-infinite programming. Let $b:S \to R$ be a real-valued and $a:S \to R^n$ a vector-valued function which are defined on S. Let further $c \in R^n$ be a fixed vector. Consider the problem

$$\text{(2.3a)} \qquad \text{Minimize } c^T y$$

over all $y \in R^n$ subject to the constraints

$$\text{(2.3b)} \qquad b(s) - a(s)^T y \leq 0, \ s \in S.$$

Many examples of (2.3) may be found in Glashoff-Gustafson (1978). Computer codes are given in Fahlander (1973). ||

Example 2. Approximation in the maximum norm. Let b again be a real-valued function on S and let u be as in Program (P). Consider the problem

$$\text{(2.4a)} \qquad \text{Minimize } y_0$$

over all real y_0 and all $y \in R^n$ subject to the constraints

$$\text{(2.4b)} \qquad |u(y,s) - b(s)| \leq y_0, \ s \in S.$$

The constraints (2.4b) are equivalent to

$$u(y,s) - b(s) - y_0 \leq 0, \ s \in S$$

$$- u(y,s) + b(s) - y_0 \leq 0, \ s \in S.$$

Hence (2.4) may be recast into the form of (2.1), and (2.4) always defines a consistent problem. This fact is proved in the same way as for (2.2). The numerical treatment is discussed, e.g. in Hettich (1974), (1976), (1979), who considers the nonlinear case. The linear case, when

$$u(y,s) = a(s)^T y$$

is considered, e.g. in Glashoff-Gustafson (1978), (1982).

3. Semi-infinite programs of D-type.

We now define a class of problems obtained by generalizing the dual program appearing in a dual pair of semi-infinite programs. In order to introduce semi-infinite programs of D-type we need the concept of "point-functional", which is given by:

Definition 1. Let S be a compact subset of R^k, the space of k-tuples. Denote by C(S) the linear space of functions, continuous over S. The linear functional P on C(S) is called a *point-functional*, if it admits a representation

$$P(f)=\sum_{i=1}^{q} x_i f(s_i),\ q<\infty, \tag{3.1}$$

where $f \in C(S)$, $s_i \in S$, x_i is a real number, $i=1,\dots,q$, and s_i and x_i are independent of f. If also $x_i>0$, $i=1,\dots,q$ then P is termed a *positive point-functional*||.

We now introduce

Program (D). Let S be a compact subset of R^k, $a_1,\dots,a_n$ fixed continuous and real-valued functions on S. Let also F be a real-valued function on R^n. Then Program (D) is defined to be the task

$$\text{Maximize } F(v) \tag{3.2a}$$

over all vectors v subject to the constraints

$$\sum_{i=1}^{q} x_i a(s_i)= v \tag{3.2b}$$

$$x_i \geq 0,\ i=1,\dots q \tag{3.2c}$$

$$\sum_{i=1}^{q} x_i a_r(s_i)= c_r,\ r=1\dots p. \tag{3.2d}$$

If p=0, then the constraint (3.2d) is considered absent.

Program (D) is a very general problem and we shall present some special instances:

Example 3. Set p=n-1 in (3.2d) and let $b \in C(S)$ be a fixed function.

Put

$$F(v)= v_n,$$

where v_n is the last component of the vector v. Then Program (D) becomes

$$\text{maximize } \sum_{i=1}^{q} x_i a_n(s_i) \tag{3.3a}$$

subject to the constraints

$$\sum_{i=1}^{q} x_i a_r(s_i)= c_r,\ r=1,\dots,n-1, \tag{3.3b}$$

(3.3c) $x_i \geq 0, \quad i=1,\ldots,q.$

Appealing to the theory in Glashoff-Gustafson (1978) we find that (3.3) is the dual of the following semi-infinite program of P-type,

(3.4a) $$\text{minimize} \sum_{r=1}^{n-1} c_r y_r$$

over all $y \in R^{n-1}$ subject to the constraints

(3.4b) $$\sum_{r=1}^{n-1} y_r a_r(s) \geq a_n(s), \quad s \in S.$$

Thus (3.3) and (3.4) are a dual pair of semi-infinite programs and general problems of P-type and D-type may be looked upon as straight-forward generalizations of these problems.

Example 4. Put p=0 in (3.2d) and let $d \in R^n$ be a fixed vector. Further, let g be a continuous function of two arguments s,t where s varies over S and t assumes non-negative values. Last, let $t_1,\ldots,t_n$ be t-values satisfying $0=t_1 < t_2 < \ldots < t_n$. Put $a_r(s) = g(s,t_r)$ and set

$$F(v) = -\,||d-v||,$$

where we have introduced a suitable norm on R^n. Then Program (D) becomes the problem

(3.5a) $$\text{maximize} -||d-v||,$$

subject to the constraints

(3.5b) $$\sum_{i=1}^{q} x_i g(s_i,t_r) = v_r, \quad r=1,\ldots,n$$

(3.5c) $$x_i \geq 0, \quad i=1,\ldots,q.$$

Thus (3.5) may also be interpreted as the nonlinear estimation problem to fit the expression

(3.6) $$\sum_{i=1}^{q} x_i g(s_i,t)$$

to the data pairs t_r, d_r, r=1,...,n. We seek not only the coefficients x_i and the parameters s_i, which appear nonlinearly in the sum (3.6), but also q, the number of terms in this sum. Gustafson (1981) gives a computational scheme for exponential fitting based on these ideas.||

Example 5. Design of regression experiments. Here p=1 and $c_1=1$. Further F is a convex function defined for the set of vectors admitting a representation (3.2b), (3.2c). Numerical schemes for this class of problems are given e.g. in Böhning (1980), Gribik-Kortanek (1977) and Gustafson-Kortanek (1976). We finish this section by showing that if (3.2) has an optimal solution v, then v has a representation (3.2b), (3.2c) with $q \le n$. For this purpose we need

Lemma 1. Let z and $z_1,\dots,z_q$ be vectors in R^n. Assume that z has a representation

$$\sum_{i=1}^{q} x_i z_i = z \text{ where } x_i \ge 0 . \tag{3.7}$$

Then z can be written as a linear combination with positive coefficients of a linearly independent subset of $z_1,\dots,z_q$.
We next show

Theorem 1. If Program (D) has an optimal solution, then Program (D) is equivalent to a constrained maximization problem with p equality constraints and the variables $x_1,\dots,x_q$, $s_1,\dots s_q$ where $q \le n$.

Proof. Using Lemma 1 we conclude that all permissible vectors v have a representation (3.2b), (3.2c), where the column vectors $a(s),\dots,a(s_q)$ are linearly independent and $x_1>0,\dots,x_q>0$. Thus $q \le n$. We may then enter (3.2b) into (3.2a) and obtain

$$F(v)= F(\sum_{i=1}^{q} x_i a(s_i)) .$$

4. Necessary condition for optimality.

In this Section we derive necessary conditions for optimality in the form of non-linear systems of equations. We consider first Program (P) as defined by (2.1) and want to derive the desired result by means of Theorem 1 on p 249 in Luenberger (1969).

We note that if L is a continuous linear functional on C(S) when this space is equipped with the maximum norm, then L admits a representation

$$L(f)= \int_S f(s)d\alpha(s)$$

where $d\alpha$ is a bounded measure. In particular, if L is a positive linear functional, i.e. if $f(s) \ge 0$, $s \in S$ implies $L(f) \ge 0$, then $d\alpha$ is a non-negative measure. A special case is the point-functional introduced in Section 3. A direct application of the result in Luenberger mentioned above now gives

Lemma 2. Let Program (P) have an optimal solution y_0 and assume also that there is a vector h in R^n such that

$$u(y,s)+ h^T u_y(y,s)<0, \; s \in S \text{ for } y = y_o .$$

Then there is a bounded non-negative measure $d\alpha^*$ such that

(4.1a) $$f_y(y)+\int_S u_y(y,s)d\alpha^*(s)=0, \text{ for } y=y_0$$

and

(4.1b) $$\int_S u(y,s)d\alpha^*(s)=0, \text{ for } y=y_0.$$

Here f_y, u_y, etc. denote the gradients with respect to the vector y. Our next step is to show

Lemma 3. Use the same notation as in Lemma 2. Then $d\alpha^*$ in (4.1) may be selected as a point-functional of the form of (3.1) with $q\leq n+1$.

Proof. Set

$$\gamma = \int_S d\alpha^*(s).$$

Then $\gamma>0$. Next put

$$\eta_r = -\frac{1}{\gamma}\frac{\partial f}{\partial y_r} \quad w_r(s)=\frac{\partial u(y,s)}{\partial y_r}, \quad r=1,\dots,n,$$

and

$$d\beta(s)=\gamma^{-1}d\alpha^*(s).$$

Then (4.1a) gives

(4.2a) $$\int_S w_r(s)d\beta(s)=\eta_r, \quad r=1,\dots,n,$$

(4.2b) $$\int_S d\beta(s)=1,$$

(4.2c) $$d\beta(s)\geq 0, \quad s\in S.$$

We next want to show that the relations (4.2) may be satisfied by a point-functional. Consider the set

$$A = \{w(s)|s\in S\}.$$

Since S is compact and w is continuous, A is a compact subset of R^n. Its convex hull h(A) is therefore compact, also. See e.g. Cheney (1966), p 18..We may now approximate the integrals (4.2a) and (4.2b) arbitrarily well with Riemann sums of the form

$$R_N=\sum_{j=1}^{N}\lambda_j w(s_j)$$

where $\lambda_j>0$, $j=1,\dots,N$ and

$$\sum_{j=1}^{N}\lambda_j=1.$$

These sums are obtained by replacing w by piecewise constant functions. Hence R_N is in h(A) and, due to the compactness of this set, $\eta\in h(A)$, also.

Using Caratheodory's theorem (See Cheney (1966) p 17) we conclude that η allows the representation

$$\eta = \sum_{i=1}^{q} \rho_i w(s_i)$$

with

$$\sum_{i=1}^{q} \rho_i = 1, \ \rho_i > 0, \ i=1,\dots,q$$

and $q \leq n+1$. Hence the desired result follows. ||

We are now ready to derive the optimality conditions sought:

Theorem 2. Let the assumptions of Lemma 2 hold. If y is an optimal solution to Program (P), then there are positive numbers x_i and elements $s_i \in S$ such that

(4.3a) $$f_y(y) + \sum_{i=1}^{q} x_i u_y(y,s_i) = 0$$

(4.3b) $$u(y,s_i) = 0, \ i=1,\dots,q,$$

where the vectors $u_y(y,s_i)$, $i=1,\dots,q$ are linearly independent.

(4.3c) The function Δ given by

$$\Delta(s) = u(y,s)$$

has a local maximum at s_i, $i=1,\dots,q$.

Proof. (4.3a) is a consequence of the fact that (4.1a) is satisfied by a point-functional. But then (4.1b) becomes

$$\sum_{i=1}^{q} x_i u(y,s_i) = 0.$$

Since $x_i > 0$ and $u(y,s) \leq 0$, $s \in S$ (4.1b) entails (4.3b). However, $u(y,s) \leq 0$ and $u(y,s_i) = 0$ mean that $\Delta(s) \leq 0$ and $\Delta(s_i) = 0$. Thus Δ has a maximum at s_i. Finally, we use Lemma 1 to conclude that x_i and s_i may be chosen such that the vectors $u_y(y,s_i)$, $i=1,\dots,q$ are linearly independent. ||

We may now prove

Lemma 4. Let F and $a_1,\dots,a_n$ of Program (D) be continuously differentiable. Assume that Program (D) has an optimal solution defined by $x_1,\dots,x_q$ and $s_1,\dots,s_q$ and that the Jacobian of the mapping

$$x_1,\dots,x_q, \ s_1,\dots,s_q \rightarrow (c_1,\dots,c_p)$$

has the rank p. Then there exist reals $y_1,\dots,y_p$ such that the function

(4.4) $$H(x,s,y) = F(v) - \sum_{r=1}^{p} y_r \left(\sum_{i=1}^{q} x_i a_r(s_i) - c_r \right)$$

has a stationary point at $x_1,\dots,x_q$, $s_1,\dots,s_q$.

Proof. The optimal vector v has a representation (3.2b), (3.2c) with $x_i>0$ and $a(s_1),\dots,a(s_q)$ linearly independent, by Theorem 2. If p=0, then $H(x,s,y)=F(v)$ and the statement is obvious. If $p\geq 1$, then $x_1,\dots,x_q$ and $s_1,\dots,s_q$ define a regular point in the sense of p 240 in Luenberger (1969) and the conclusion is a consequence of the Lagrange multiplier theorem on p 243 in this book.||

We can now establish the counterpart of (4.3), namely

Theorem 3. Let the notation and assumptions of Lemma 3 hold. Then $x_1,\dots,x_q$, $s_1,\dots,s_q$ and $y_1,\dots,y_p$ meet the conditions

(4.5a) $$F_v^T a(s_i)-\sum_{r=1}^{p} y_r a_r(s_i)=0,\quad i=1,\dots,q$$

(4.5b) $$\sum_{i=1}^{q} x_i a_r(s_i)=c_r,\quad r=1,\dots,p,$$

(4.5c) $H(x,s,y)$ has a stationary point at s_i, $i=1,\dots,q$.

Proof. (4.5b) is the feasibility condition and (3.2d), (4.5a) and (4.5c) are direct consequences of Lemma 4. Since H depends linearly on x_i, the corresponding partial derivative must vanish, giving (4.5a).||

Remark. If s_i is in the interior of S, then the partial derivatives with respect to the k components of s_i must vanish and (4.5c) generates k equations for that particular s_i.

5. Approximation of Programs (P) and (D) with discretized problems.

Definition 2. Let T be a finite subset of $S \in R^k$. If we replace S by T in Programs (P) and (D), the resulting optimization problems are termed the discretized versions of Programs (P) and (D).

Definition 3. Let $S \subset R^k$ be a given set, $T=\{\sigma_1,\dots\sigma_N\}\subset S$ a fixed subset. (T is often called a *grid*). Let $w_1,\dots,w_N$ be real valued functions with the properties

(5.1a) $$w_j(s)\geq 0,\quad s\in S,\ j=1,\dots,N,$$

(5.1b) $$\sum_{j=1}^{N} w_j(s)=1,\quad s\in S,$$

(5.1c) $$w_j(\sigma_i)=\delta_{ij}.$$

With each $s\in S$ we associate a function, not necessarily a real valued mapping $f(s)$.

Put

$$(Lf)(s)= \sum_{j=1}^{N} w_j(s)f(\sigma_j).$$

Then L is called a *non-negative interpolatory operator based on T.*

Remark. L owes its name to the fact that

$$(Lf)(\sigma_j)= f(\sigma_j).$$

The concept of positive interpolatory operator is fairly general.||

Thus if a: $S \to R^n$ is a vector-valued function, we get

$$(5.2) \qquad (La)(s)= \sum_{j=1}^{N} w_j(s)a(\sigma_j),$$

and for the function u of Program (P)

$$(5.3) \qquad (Lu)(y,s)= \sum_{j=1}^{N} w_j(s)u(y,\sigma_j).$$

The connection between discretization and positive interpolatory operators is given by

Lemma 5. Let $S \in R^k$ be a compact set, $T =\{\sigma_1,\dots\sigma_N\}\subset S$ and L an interpolatory operator based on T. Let

$$\tilde{a} = La, \quad \tilde{u}(y,s)= Lu(y,s).$$

Then we may state:

a) $y \in R^n$ satisfies

$$(5.4) \qquad u(y,\sigma_j)\leq 0, \quad j=1,\dots,N,$$

if and only if y also satisfies

$$(5.5) \qquad \tilde{u}(y,s)\leq 0, \quad s \in S.$$

b) There are an integer q, a subset $\{s_i,\dots,s_q\}\subset S$ and reals $x_1,\dots x_q$ such that

$$(5.6) \qquad \sum_{i=1}^{q} x_i\tilde{a}(s_i)= v, \quad x_i\geq 0, \quad i=1,\dots,q,$$

if and only if there are numbers $\rho_1,\dots,\rho_N$ such that

$$(5.7) \qquad \sum_{j=1}^{N} \rho_j a(\sigma_j)= v \quad \rho_j\geq 0, \quad j=1,\dots,N.$$

Proof a). Using (5.4) we find that (5.5) is equivalent to

$$(5.8) \qquad \sum_{j=1}^{N} w_j(s)u(y,\sigma_j)\leq 0, \quad s \leq S.$$

Putting $s = \sigma_j$ in (5.8) we find that (5.5) implies (5.4). On the other hand we may multiply (5.4) by the non-negative number $w_j(s)$ and then sum over j giving (5.7) and hence (5.5). Thus (5.4) and (5.5) are equivalent.

b) Entering (5.2) into (5.6) we obtain

$$\sum_{i=1}^{q} x_i \sum_{j=1}^{N} w_j(s_i)a(\sigma_j)= v$$

or

$$\sum_{j=1}^{N} a(\sigma_j) \sum_{i=1}^{q} x_i w_j(s_i)= v.$$

Hence, if (5.6) is satisfied, we may take

$$\rho_j= \sum_{i=1}^{q} x_i w_j(s_i)$$

in (5.8). If we on the other hand assume that (5.8) is satisfied, we utilize the fac that $a(\sigma_j)= a(\tilde{\sigma}_j)$ and hence we get

$$\sum_{j=1}^{N} \rho_j \tilde{a}(\sigma_j)= v. \tag{5.9}$$

To satisfy (5.6) we only need to remove those terms in (5.9) with $\rho_j= 0$.||

Using Lemma 5 we may now show that Programs (P) and (D) can be arbitrarily well approximated by discretized problems, i.e. optimization problems having finitely many variables and constraints

Lemma 6. Let the notation and assumptions of Programs (P) and (D) hold. Let $\varepsilon>0$ be a given number and Y be a compact subset of R^n. Then there is a finite subset $T = \{\sigma_j,\ldots,\sigma_N\}\subset S$ and a positive interpolatory operator L based on T such that

$$|La_r(s)- a_r(s)| <\varepsilon, \quad s \in S, \tag{5.10}$$

$$|(Lu)(y,s)- u(y,s)| <\varepsilon, \quad s \in S, \ y \in Y, \tag{5.11}$$

where L is defined as in (5.2) and (5.4).

Proof. Since a_r, $r=1,\ldots,n$ are continuous on the compact set S they are also uniformly continuous on S. Introduce a norm on R^k: Then there is a δ such that $||s'- s''||<\delta$ implies

$$||a_r(s')- a_r(s'')||<\varepsilon, \quad r=1,\ldots,n. \tag{5.12}$$

We next determine a partition of S,

$$S = \bigcup_{j=1}^{N} S_j$$

where the subsets S_j are disjoint and such that if $s'\in S_j$ and $s'' \in S_j$ then

$$||s'- s''||<\delta.$$

We then define a functions $w_1,\ldots,w_N$ through

$$w_j(s)= \begin{cases} 1 & s \in S_j \\ 0 & \text{otherwise,} \end{cases}$$

select a point σ_j in each S_j and set

$$La_r(s)=\sum_{j=1}^{N} w_j(s)a_r(\sigma_j).$$

Because of (5.12), this interpolatory operator satisfies (5.10).
To carry out an analogous construction for (5.11) we observe that

$$|u(y,s_1)-u(y,s_2)|\leq\| s_1-s_2\| \cdot\psi(y,s),$$

where ψ is a function which can be expressed in terms of the first order partial derivatives of u. It is easily shown to be uniformly bounded for $s \in S$ and $y \in Y$.
We now establish the convergence result:

Theorem 3. Assume that Program (P) has an optimal solution $\overline{y}$. Let $T_1\subset T_2\subset\ldots\subset S$ be a sequence of finite grids. Put

$$Y_1=\{y\in R^n|u(y,s)\leq 0,\ s\in T_1\}.$$

Let Y_1 be a compact subset of R^n. Denote by y_ℓ an optimal solution vector to the problem

(5.13a) Minimize $f(y)$

over all $y \in R^n$ subject to the constraints

(5.13b) $u(y,s)\leq 0,\ s\in T_\ell, \ell = 1,\ldots$

Assume also that we can construct non-negative interpolatory operators L_ℓ based on T_ℓ such that

$$\max_{s\in S,y\in y,} |L_\ell u(y,s)-u(y,s)|\to 0,\ \ell\to\infty .$$

Then the accumulation points of $\{y_\ell\}$ are optimal solutions to Program (P).

Proof. Since the set of vectors y satisfying (5.13b) form a compact subset of Y for each ℓ, the problems (5.13) have optimal solutions, and hence the sequence $y_1, y_2,\ldots$ is well defined. This sequence is confined to the compact set Y_1 and has hence an accumulation point y^*. We find

$$f(y_1)\leq f(y_2)\leq\ldots\leq f(\overline{y})$$

giving

$$f(y^*)\leq f(\overline{y}).$$

Since

$$u(y_\ell,s_j)\ 0,\ j\in T_\ell,\ \ell = 1,\ldots$$

we conclude

$$u(y^*,s)\leq 0,\ s\in S.$$

Hence y^* is feasible to Program (P) which has an optimal solution $\overline{y}$. Therefore

$$f(y^*)\geq f(\overline{y}).$$

Thus y^* is optimal to Program (P).

Definition 4. Use the same notations as in the definition of Program (P). Put

$$M_n = \{v \in R^n | v = \sum_{i=1}^{q} x_i a(s_i),\ x_i \geq 0,\ s_i \in S\}.$$

Then M_n is called a *moment cone*.||

Remark. It follows immediately from the definitions of "cone" and "convex set" that M_n is a convex cone. We note that those vectors satisfying (3.2d) form a convex subset of M_n.||

We may now establish a convergence result which is a counterpart of Theorem 3.

Theorem 4. Let the assumptions and notation of Program (D) hold and also assume that the optimal value is achieved for a vector $\overline{v}$. Assume also that (3.2d) is satisfied by some points in the interior of M_n. Let $T_1 \subset T_2 \subset \ldots$ be a sequence of grids such that to each grid there is a positive interpolatory operator L_j with the property

(5.14) $$\lim_{j \to \infty} \max_{s \in S} |L_j a_r(s) - a_r(s)| = 0,\ r=1,\ldots,n.$$

Let v_j be an optimal solution to the problem

(5.15a) Maximize $F(v)$

over all $v \in R^n$ subject to the constraints

(5.15b) $$\sum_{i=1}^{q} x_i a(s_i) = v,$$

(5.15c) $$x_i \geq 0,\ i=1,\ldots q,\ s_i \in T_j,$$

(5.15d) $$\sum_{i=1}^{q} x_i a_r(s_i) = c_r,\ r=1,\ldots,p.$$

Assume that there is a constant $C > 0$, such that $||v_j|| < C$, $j=1,\ldots$ Then the accumulation points of $v_1,\ldots$ are optimal solutions to Program (D).

Proof. Since $T_1 \subset T_2 \subset \ldots$ we have

(5.16) $$F(v_1) \leq F(v_2) \leq \ldots \leq F(\overline{v}).$$

Let

$$\gamma = \lim_{j \to \infty} F(v_j).$$

By (5.16) we have $\gamma \leq F(\overline{v})$. We want to establish that $\gamma < F(\overline{v})$ is impossible. Let $\varepsilon > 0$ be given. Then there is a $\tilde{v}$ satisfying the constraints of Program (D) and such that

$$F(\overline{v}) \geq F(\tilde{v}) > F(\overline{v}) - \varepsilon.$$

The vector $\tilde{v}$ has a representation

$$\sum_{i=1}^{q} x_i a(s_i) = \tilde{v}.$$

Due to (5.14) we may approximate $\tilde{v}$ arbitrarily well with a vector that is feasible to (5.15) by selecting j sufficiently large. Thus

$$F(\tilde{v}) \leq \gamma .$$

Since ε was arbitrary we conclude that $F(\overline{v}) = \gamma$, establishing the desired result.||

Corollary 1. Let the assumptions and notation of Theorem 4 hold. Assume also that $a_1,\dots,a_n$ are such that there is a vector $d \in R^n$ and a positive number δ such that

$$d^T a(s) \geq \delta > 0, \quad s \in S. \tag{5.17}$$

Consider now the sequence $v_1,\dots$ of optimal solutions to (5.15). Let v_j have a representation

$$\sum_{i=1}^{q(j)} x_{ij} a(s_{ij}) = v_j, \quad j=1,\dots \tag{5.18}$$

where $q(j) \leq n$. Then we may select a subsequence of v_j, $j=1,\dots$ such that the vectors in this subsequence have the properties: $q(j) = \overline{q}$, a fixed number, x_{ij} and s_{ij} converge to numbers $\overline{x}_i$ and $\overline{s}_i$ and the vector $\overline{v}$ given by

$$\sum_{i=1}^{\overline{q}} \overline{x}_i a(\overline{s}_i) = \overline{v} \tag{5.19}$$

is an optimal solution to Program (D). Further, by using the reduction process of the proof of Lemma 1 on (5.19) we may construct a representation of the same form, namely

$$\sum_{i=1}^{q} x_i a(s_i) = \overline{v}, \tag{5.20}$$

where $x_i > 0$, and $a(s_1),\dots,a(s_q)$ are linearly independent.

Remark. The relation (5.17) is often called Krein's condition.

Proof. Consider first the sequence $q(1)$, $q(2),\dots$ of integers. Put

$$\overline{q} = \liminf q(j).$$

We consider in the sequel only the subsequence that satisfies $q(j) = \overline{q}$. Multiplying (5.18) by d^T we find

$$\sum_{i=1}^{q} x_{ij} d^T a(s_{ij}) = d^T v_j,$$

giving

$$x_{ij} \leq \delta^{-1} |d^T v_j| .$$

Since $\lim_{j\to\infty} v_j = \overline{v}$, there is a $B > 0$, such that

$$\sum_{i=1}^{q} x_{ij} \leq B.$$

Thus the coefficients x_{ij} are restricted to a bounded set. Further, s_{ij} must remain in the compact set S. Hence we may select a subsequence of v_j, j=1,... with the properties

$$q(j) = \bar{q}$$

$$x_{ij} \text{ converges to } x_i,\ i=1,\dots,\bar{q},$$

$$s_{ij} \text{ converges to } s_i,\ i=1,\dots,\bar{q}.$$

Therefore $\bar{v}$ has a representation (5.19). If now some $x_i = 0$, the corresponding terms are removed. If two s_i, say s_1 and s_2 coincide, the corresponding terms are combined. The reduction process of Lemma 1 is then applied to the resulting representation to obtain (5.20).

6. A general three-phase algorithm.

The results of Section 5 indicate that under certain general conditions it is reasonable to approximate Programs (P) and (D) by the discretized versions. This idea has been successfully applied to practical problems. For examples we refer to the papers in the reference list, in particular those associated with the names Gonzaga, Polak, Trahan, Gorelick, Remson, Cottle, Streit and Nuttall. Other workers have based their treatment on the optimality conditions of Section 4. We refer here to the papers by Hettich. A third approach has been to combine these two strategies as suggested in papers by Gustafson and Kortanek and described in the books by Glashoff and Gustafson. Computer codes implementing this latter idea are given in Fahlander (1973).

The general philosophy is contained in the so-called three-phase algorithm which may be outlined in the case of Program (P) as follows:

Phase 1. A discretized version of Program (P) is solved, giving an approximation to an optimal solution of the originally posed problem.

Phase 2. Optimality conditions in the form of a nonlinear system of equations are derived from (4.3). The results from Phase 1 are used to determine this system.

Phase 3. The nonlinear system is solved numerically, often by means of an iterative scheme based on linearizations, e.g. Newton-Raphson's method.

An analogous scheme may be formulated for Program (D).

By the implementation of this scheme one utilizes the special character of the class of problems one wants to solve. Phase 3 may fail if the initial approximation is too poor for the iterative scheme to converge or if the "wrong" system has been constructed in Phase 2. In both situations it is recommended to return to Phase 1 with a refined grid. A convergence proof for the entire scheme may be based on Theorems 3 or 4.

We now discuss the general implementation of Phase 1 for Program (P). Assume that we replace S with the grid $T = \{\sigma_1,\dots,\sigma_N\}$. Thus we approximate Program (P) by the problem

(6.1a) Minimize $f(y)$

for all $y \in R^n$ subject to the constraints

(6.1b) $u(y,\sigma_j)\leq 0,\ j=1,\ldots,N.$

If the assumptions of Lemma 2 are valid, then we may establish the following conditions for optimality by arguing,as in the proof of Lemma 2.

(6.2a) $f_y(y)+\sum_{j=1}^{N} \lambda_j u_y(y,\sigma_i)= 0,$

(6.2b) $\lambda_j u(y,\sigma_j)= 0,\ j=1,\ldots,N.$

(6.2c) The function $\tilde{\Delta}$, which is defined on T and given by

$$\tilde{\Delta}(s)= u(y,s),$$

has a local minimum at σ_j if $\lambda_j>0$.

Applying a reduction process as in the proof of Lemma 1 to the vector equation (6.2a) we conclude that

i) $\lambda \in R^N$ has at most $\ell\leq N$ positive components $j_1,\ldots,j_\ell$, and

ii) $u_y(y,\sigma_j)$, $i=1,\ldots,\ell$ are linearly independent.

However, if two elements, say σ_{j1} and σ_{j2} are close, it may be reasonable to assume that they approximate the same elements appearing in (4.3) when this system is formed from an optimal solution. Compare the proof of Corollary 1. In this situation one applies the clustering procedure described,e.g. in Fahlander (1973), Gustafson-Glashoff (1978), (1982), or Gustafson-Kortanek (1973).

A tolerance $\delta>0$ is selected and if there are σ_i and σ_k such that $||\sigma_i-\sigma_k||<\delta$ and $\lambda_j>0,\lambda_k>0$, then those two terms are combined in (6.2). Thus we put

$$\bar{\lambda} = \lambda_i+\lambda_k \qquad \bar{\sigma} =(\sigma_i\lambda_i+\sigma_k\lambda_k)/\bar{\lambda} .$$

Next we replace

$$\lambda_i u_y(y,\sigma_i)+\lambda_k u_y(y,\sigma_k)$$

by

$$\bar{\lambda}u_y(y,\bar{\sigma})$$

in (6.2a). In (6.2b) the conditions

$$\lambda_i u(y,\sigma_i)\leq 0,\ \lambda_k u(y,\sigma_k)\leq 0$$

are replaced by

$$\bar{\lambda}u(y,\bar{\sigma})\leq 0.$$

In (6.2c) the function $\tilde{\Delta}$ is considered to have a maximum at $\bar{\sigma}$ instead of at σ_i and σ_k.

This procedure is repeated until all remaining points are separated by distances greater than δ. It is of course essential that the tolerance δ is not chosen so large that clustering occurs, if the (unknown) optimal solution to Program (P) appears as a solution to (6.1). If f and u are nonlinear in y, (6.1) is a difficult problem, but it is still easier than Program (P), since one may ascertain that a given vector y meets the constraints (6.1b) by means of finitely many comparisons. The same statement does not hold for (2.1b).

We next discuss Program (D): Upon discretizing we arrive at the problem

(6.3a) $\quad$ Minimize $F(v)$

over all vectors $v \in R^n$ admitting a representation

(6.3b) $$\sum_{j=1}^{N} \lambda_j a(\sigma_j) = v,$$

and subject to the constraints

(6.3c) $$\lambda_j \geq 0, \quad j=1,\ldots,N,$$

(6.3d) $$\sum_{j=1}^{N} \lambda_j a_r(\sigma_j) = c_r, \quad r=1,\ldots,p.$$

This problem is easier than Program (D), since (6.3) is a linearly constrained optimization problem.

After solving (6.3), clustering and construction of a nonlinear system (this time based on (4.5)) are carried out in the same way as described for Program (P).

An alternative to Phase 3 is described in the papers by Hettich and Watson. The principal idea is to replace Program (P) by the problem of minimizing f subject to (4.3b) and (4.3c). Watson suggests adapting a scheme developed by Han (1977) and Powell (1979). This scheme calls for the solution of a sequence of quadratic programs. Several numerical examples are given in Watson (Sept. 1981). However, this method requires that the form of the conditions generated by (4.3b), (4.3c) be known. It could be obtained by first solving a discretized version of Program (P). Then we would return to the general three-phase strategy.

REFERENCES.

(1) BÖHNING, D.: Numerische Methoden in der Versuchsplanung, PhD-Thesis, Dept. of Mathematics, Freie Universität, Berlin, 1980.

(2) CHENEY, E.W.: Introduction to Approximation Theory, Mc Graw-Hill, New York. 1966.

(3) FAHLANDER, K.: Computer programs for semi-infinite optimization TRITA-NA-7312, Department of Numerical Analysis and Computing Science, Royal Institute of Technology, S-100 44 Stockholm 70, Sweden, 1973.

(4) GLASHOFF, K. and GUSTAFSON, S-Å.: Einfuehrung in die lineare Optimierung, Wissenschaftliche Buchgesellschaft, Darmstadt, 1978.

(5) GLASHOFF, K. and GUSTAFSON, S-Å.: Linear Optimization and Approximation, Springer, to appear (1982).

(6) GLASHOFF, K. and ROLEFF, K.: A new method for Chebyshev approximation of complex-valued functions, Math Comp 36 (1981), 233-239.

(7) GONZAGA, C.and POLAK, E.: On constraint dropping schems and optimality functions for a class of outer approximations algorithms, SIAM J Contr. Opt. 17 (1979), 477-493.

(8) GONZAGA, C., POLAK, E. and TRAHAN, R.: An improved algorithm for optimization problems with functional inequality constraints, IEEE Trans. Autom. Contr. 25 (1980), 40-54.

(9) GORELICK, S.M. and REMSON, I.: Optimal dynamic management model of ground-water pollutant sources, Water Resources Research, to appear.

(10) GORELICK, S.M., REMSON, I. and COTTLE, R.W.: Management model of a groundwater system whith a transient pollutant source, Water Resources Research 15 (1979), 1243-1249.

(11) GRIBIK, P.R. and KORTANEK, K.O.: Equivalence theorems and cutting plane algorithms for a class of experimental design problems, SIAM J. Appl. Math 32 (1977), 232-259.

(12) GUSTAFSON, S-Å.: A numerical solution of a generalized moment problem, TNN-81, Computation Center, University of Texas at Austin, July, 1968.

(13) GUSTAFSON, S-Å.: On the computational solution of a class of generalized moment problems, SIAM J on Numer. Anal. 7 (1970), 343-357.

(14) GUSTAFSON, S-Å.: Lectures on semi-infinite programming, SFB 72, Inst. f. Angew. Mathematik der Univ. Bonn, 1979.

(15) GUSTAFSON, S-Å.: A computational scheme for exponential approximation, ZAMM 61 (1981), T284-T287.

(16) GUSTAFSON, S-Å: A general three-phase algorithm for nonlinear semi-infinite programming problems, In: J.P. Brans (Ed) Operations Research '81, North-Holland, Amsterdam, 1981, p 495-508.

(17) GUSTAFSON, S-Å. and KORTANEK, K.O.: Numerical treatment of a class of semi-infinite programming problems, NRLQ 20 (1973), 477-504.

(18) GUSTAFSON, S-Å. and KORTANEK, K.O.: Computation of optimal design for air quality surveillance, In: P.J. Jansen, O. Moeschlin, O. Rentz (Eds), Quantitative Modelle fuer ökonomisch-ökologische analysen, Schriften zur wirtschafts-wissenschaftlichen Forschung, Band 108, Verlag Anton Hain 8 (1976) p. 43-60.

(19) GUSTAFSON, S-Å. and KORTANEK, K.O.: A comprehensive approach to air quality planning: abatement, monitoring networks, real time interpolation, in Mathematical Models for Planning and Controlling Air Quality, Proceedings of an IIASA Workshop. ed. Fronza, G. and P. Melli. Oxford: Pergamon Press, 1982.

(20) HAN, S.P.: A globally convergent method for nonlinear programming, JOTA 22 (1977), 297-309.

(21) HETTICH, R.: Kriterien zweiter Ordnung fuer lokal beste Approximation, Numer. Math 22 (1974), 409-417.

(22) HETTICH, R.: A Newton-method for nonlinear Chebyshev approximation, Approx. Theory, Proc. Int. Colloqu. Bonn, Lecture Notes Math 556, Springer-Verlag, Berlin Heidelberg, New York (1976), 222-236.

(23) HETTICH, R.: (Ed), Semi-infinite programming, Lecture Notes in Control and Information, No 15, Springer-Verlag, Berlin, Heidelberg, New York, 1979.

(24) LUENBERGER, D.G.: Optimization by Vector Space Methods, John Wiley & Sons, New York, London, Sydney, Toronto (1969).

(25) OPFER, G.: New extremal properties for constructing conformal mappings Numer. Math. 32 (1979), 423-429.

(26) OPFER, G.: Conformal mappings onto prescribed regions via optimization techniques, Numer. Math. 35 (1980), 189-200.

(27) POWELL, M.J.D.: A fast algorithm for nonlinearly constrained optimization calculations: In G.A. Watson (Ed), Numerical Analysis, Lecture Notes in Mathematics No 630, Springer-Verlag, Berlin, Heidelberg, New York, 1979.

(28) STREIT, R.L. and NUTTALL, A.H.: Linear Chebyshev complex function approximation, Naval Underwater Systems Center, Newport, Rhode Island, USA. (Febr.1981).

(29) WATSON, G.A.: The calculation of best one-sided Lp-approximations, Math. Comp 27 (1973), 607-620.

(30) WATSON, G.A.: Globally convergent methods for semi-infinite programming, Dep. of Math.,Univ of Dundee (Jan. 1981).

(31) WATSON, G.A.: Numerical experiments with globally convergent methods for semi-infinite programming problems, Dep. of Math.,Univ of Dundee (Sept.1981).

A REVIEW OF NUMERICAL METHODS FOR SEMI-INFINITE OPTIMIZATION

Rainer Hettich

Abstract. The aim of this paper is to sketch briefly the main ideas that are fundamental in the different types of methods for solving semi-infinite problems and to discuss several difficulties that are inherent in some of them. At the same time, this gives the possibility to compare several methods and to decide in which situation they profitably can be applied. It appears that a partition of the methods in two classes is appropriate: On the one side, methods suitable to improve a "good" approximation to the solution efficiently and, on the other side, those being appropriate to compute those good approximations to the solution. This suggests two phase-methods for solving semi-infinite problems. A number of examples are given to illustrate the complexity of the problems and the performance and efficiency of the methods.

1. Introduction

The subject of this contribution is the numerical treatment of general semi-infinite problems

SIP(B) Minimize $F(z)$ subject to $g(z,x) \leq 0$ for all $x \in B$.

F and g usually will be assumed to be once or twice continuously differentiable functions: $F : Z_o \to \mathbb{R}$, $g : Z_o \times B \to \mathbb{R}^\kappa$ with $Z_o \subset \mathbb{R}^n$ an open and $B \subset \mathbb{R}^m$ a compact set. The inequality $g(z,x) \leq 0$ is to be interpreted as applying to each of the κ components of the vector $g(z,x) \in \mathbb{R}^\kappa$. Usually, for simplicity, we take $\kappa = 1$, the extension to the case $\kappa > 1$ being obvious.

Rather than detailed algorithms the underlying concepts and ideas will be presented to give an insight into advantages and drawbacks of the different approaches. As most of the points become apparent in the linear case already, in the main part of this paper we will confine ourselves to the linear problem.

LSIP(B) Minimize $F(z) = c^T z$ subject to $a^T(x)z - b(x) \leq 0$ for all $x \in B$

with $c \in \mathbb{R}^n$ and once or twice continuously differentiable functions $a : B^o \to \mathbb{R}^n$ and $b : B^o \to \mathbb{R}$, with $B^o \supset B$ and B^o an open set in $\mathbb{R}^m$.

Throughout the paper the following notation is used: A point z for which the constraints hold is called feasible. By Z we denote the set of all feasible points, i.e.

$$Z = \{z \in Z_o \mid g(z,x) \leq 0, \ x \in B\}.$$

With every $z \in Z$ a set $E(z)$ of active points is associated defined by

$$E(z) = \{x \mid x \in B, \ g(z,x) = o\}.$$

The value v(SIP(B)) of the problem SIP(B) is given by

$$v(SIP(B)) = \inf \{F(z) \mid z \in Z\}.$$

By $\bar{z}$ we usually denote a solution of the problem, i.e. $\bar{z} \in Z$ and $F(\bar{z}) = v(SIP(B))$. For short we often write $\bar{E}$ instead of $E(\bar{z})$.

Of course the above notations apply to LSIP(B) as well.

An important subclass of SIP(B) is formed by Chebyshev-approximation problems: Given a function $f \in C[B]$ and a subset $A \subset C[B]$,

$$A = \{a(p,\cdot) \mid p \in P \subset \mathbb{R}^N\},$$

with a,f usually once or twice continuously differentiable functions on $B^o \supset B$ (B^o open) and $P \times B^o$, resp., P an open set of "parameters". Then, $\bar{p} \in P$ is to be determined such that

$$||f - a(\bar{p},\cdot)||_\infty \leq ||f - a(p,\cdot)||_\infty, \ p \in P,$$

with $||\cdot||_\infty$ the maximum norm with respect to B. The equivalent problem of type SIP(B) is given by

(A) Minimize $F(z) = z_n$, $z = \begin{pmatrix} p \\ z_n \end{pmatrix} \subset \mathbb{R}^n$, $n = N+1$, subject to

$$g(z,x) := \begin{pmatrix} f(x) - a(p,x) - z_n \\ -f(x) + a(p,x) - z_n \end{pmatrix} \leq \begin{pmatrix} 0 \\ 0 \end{pmatrix}, \text{ for all } x \in B.$$

In Section 2 we introduce exchange methods (for linear problems), which form the most well-known class of methods, especially for problem (A). To investigate the properties of these methods, it is very instructive to exhibit the relationship to cutting plane methods in convex programming (Section 4). Hereto, in Section 3, we first show that linear semi-infinite programming problems essentially are convex programming problems in a special mathematical description. As a result of the discussion we conclude that exchange methods will have the same drawbacks as cutting plane methods with respect to convergence and numerical stability. The slow convergence is an especially serious difficulty when dealing with LSIP(B) by exchange methods, as in each step a search for local maxima of $g(z,x)$ on B (z fixed) is required, which may be very time-consuming. Good convergence and numerical stability are given only in the case that the solution $\bar{z}$ is strongly unique (Section 5). This, for instance, holds for problems (A) if A is a Haar subspace of $C[a,b]$. In general, discretization methods with appropriate strategies of grid-refinement (cf. Section 6) are superior to exchange methods due to their simplicity and the superfluity of the search for maxima of $g(z,x)$ on B.

Altogether, apart from the strongly unique case, exchange methods as well as discretization are recommendable only for the computation of approximate solutions. If required, in a second step (or "phase"), these can be improved by a method with good local behaviour, which in turn usually may be applied if a good starting point is given. This leads to the concept of two-phase methods, already proposed in the pioneering work of Gustafson [6].

A very powerful means for deriving second-phase methods in the above sense is to reduce the problem locally to a finite convex programming problem (Section 7) which may be treated by some appropriate finite optimization technique. Examples of such methods are given in Section 8. In Section 9 we close with some remarks on the nonlinear case.

2. Exchange methods

Exchange methods certainly are the most common methods in dealing with Chebyshev-approximation problems. Especially in the case that the family A of approximating functions is a Haar subspace of C[a,b], the methods of Remes are well-known and efficient (cf. [17] for instance).

Exchange methods may be described generally as follows:

In step ν a finite subset $B_\nu \subset B$ is given. Then, the substeps (i) - (iii) are performed:

(i) Compute a solution z^ν of the discretized problem SIP(B_ν).

(ii) Compute (some or all) local maxima $x^1, \cdot\cdot, x^r$ of the problem

$$\text{Max } \{\varphi(x) := g(z^\nu, x) \mid x \in B\}.$$

In the sequel we will assume that x^1 is a global maximum, i.e. $\varphi(x^1) \geq \varphi(x)$ for all $x \in B$.

(iii) Choose $B_{\nu+1} \subset B_\nu \cup \{x^1, \cdot\cdot, x^r\}$.

The existing algorithms mainly differ in the choice of $B_{\nu+1}$.

In the linear case LSIP(B_ν) is an ordinary linear programming problem which may be solved by the Simplex-method. Actually the dual problem $\text{LSIP}_D(B_\nu)$ should be treated with regard to the fact that the solution of $\text{LSIP}_D(B_{\nu-1})$ is an appropriate initial vertex for $\text{LSIP}_D(B_\nu)$. By the Simplex-method a set of n points, a so-called reference $R_\nu = \{x_1^\nu, .., x_n^\nu\} \subset B_\nu$, is determined such that z^ν is a solution of LSIP(R_ν), too, and such that the constraints $g(z, x_i^\nu) \leq 0$ are active for $z = z^\nu$. It is actually this reference R_ν of n points in B which has to be adapted (or exchanged) in each step.

In consideration of these remarks we may roughly distinguish the following types of methods:

- Implicit exchange methods, where simply some or all of the points $x^1, \cdot\cdot, x^r$ are added to $B_{\nu-1}$, i.e. $B_{\nu-1} \subset B_\nu$, and where the exchange of points in the references is performed implicitly by the simplex-method.

- Explicit exchange methods, where points are added and others are deleted a priori according to given exchange rules. Famous examples are the Remes-methods in Chebyshev approximation under Haar's condition, where the exchange is performed on the basis of information on the error function generated by the solution $z^{\nu-1}$ of LSIP($B_{\nu-1}$). Stiefel [25,26] has shown that the first algorithm of Remes (one-point exchange, cf. below) selects the same reference as the simplex algorithm does when being applied to the problem LSIP($B_\nu \cup \{x^1\}$). This makes it possible to work with sets B_ν of n points in each step.

- One-point exchange methods are characterized by the property that only x^1 is included in $B_{\nu+1}$ contrary to

- Multiple exchange methods where in general more than one of the points $x^1,\ldots,x^r$ are included in each step.

Implicit methods ([1],[28]) have the advantage that convergence may be proven under rather weak conditions. The following theorem was essentially given in[1] for the implicit one-point exchange method (i.e. $B_\nu = B_{\nu-1} \cup \{x^1\}$):

Theorem 1 (cf. [12]) Let the feasible region Z of LSIP(B) be nonempty and let $B_0 \subset B$ be such that $-c \in \text{int}\, K(\{a(x) \mid x \in B_0\})$, where K(M) denotes the cone generated by a set $M \subset \mathbb{R}^n$. Then LSIP(B_ν), B_ν formed by any implicit (one-point or multiple) exchange method, has a solution z^ν for each $\nu = 0,1,2,\ldots$. Either the algorithm stops after a finite number of steps with a solution of LSIP(B) or we have

(i) $F(z^{\nu+1}) \geq F(z^\nu)$, $\nu = 0,1,..$; $\lim_{\nu\to\infty} F(z^\nu) = v(\text{LSIP}(B))$.

(ii) $\{z^\nu\}$ has at least one point of accumulation and each such point solves LSIP(B).

An obvious disadvantage of implicit methods is the growth in the number of constraints during the iterations. Therefore, numerous proposals for explicit methods have been made. For general semi-infinite problems a reduction to sets B_ν of n points is much more complicated than in the special case of Chebyshev-approximation with Haar subspaces (or more general for problems with a strongly unique solution, cf. Section 5). Rather sophisticated exchange-rules [13] and projection techniques [27], [24] are used to be able to prove convergence. Mostly, one-point exchange is considered. An explicit multiple exchange method - without proof of convergence - is given by Roleff [23].

For a comparison of one-point and multiple exchange methods the following rules - suggested by numerical evidence - are helpful:

- The amount of computational work for solving LSIP(B_ν) in the course of a multiple exchange method (n points exchanged each step) is approximately n times that required by a one-point exchange method.

- The gain in accuracy per step of a multiple exchange method again is approximately n times that of a one-point method.

- A very time-consuming substep is the computation of the $x^1,..,x^r$. As the computation of a global maximum usually requires the computation of all local maxima, one multiple exchange step is comparable to one one-point exchange step.

Altogether, this shows the superiority of multiple against one-point exchange. The following examples may give an impression of the difficulties connected with the computation of the points $x^1,..,x^r$.

Consider problem (A) when approximating $f(x) = x_1^{x_2}$ in $B = [1,2]x[1,2]$ by polynomials in two variables of total degree d, i.e.

$$P_d(p;x) = \sum_{i=o}^{d} \sum_{j=o}^{i} p_{ij} x_1^j x_2^{i-j}.$$

For d = 2 the error function for the best approximation is represented in Fig. 1 by some contour lines. The maximum, denoted by ⊠, is situated close to the boundary on a rather flat ridge. During the iteration it may move to the boundary and back to the interior so that a very careful analysis is required in each step. Even close to the best approximation, it will not in general be sufficient to improve the maximum points of the foregoing step, for instance by applying just one step of Newton's method. Matters are even worse in the case d = 4, as is shown in Fig. 2. Now, there are several maxima on a flat ridge separated by saddle-points on nearly the same level.

3. Linear semi-infinite and differentiable convex programming

Let K be a convex region in $\mathbb{R}^n$ and $F : K \to \mathbb{R}$ a convex function.

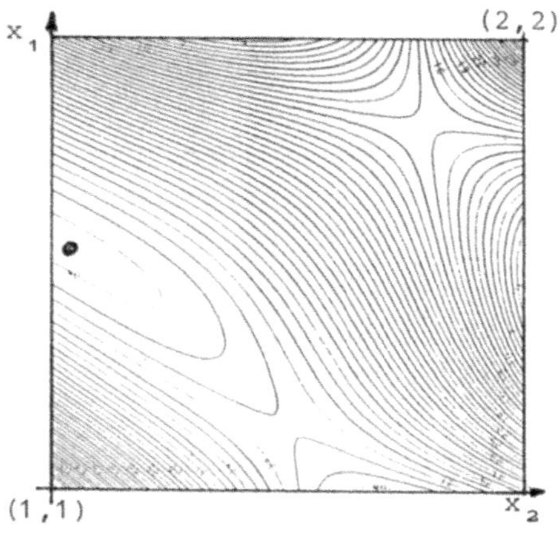

Fig. 1

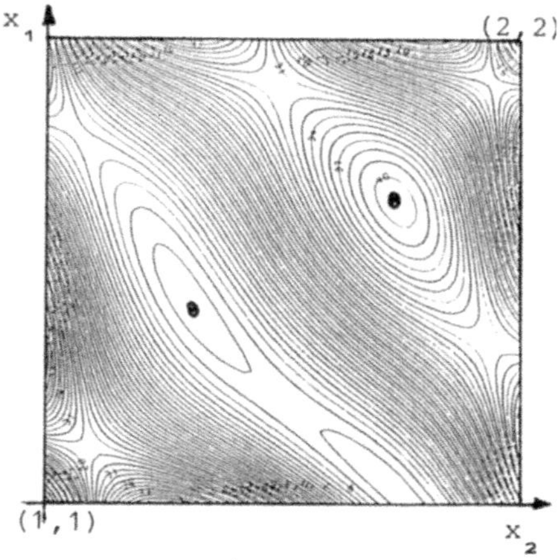

Fig. 2

Consider the convex programming problem

$$\text{Min}\ \{F(z)\ |\ z \in K\}.$$

It is no restriction to assume, that F is a linear function $F(z) = c^Tz$ as every convex problem may be reduced to this case in an obvious way.

Of course, the region Z of any LSIP(B) is convex. Therefore, semi-infinite programming may be considered as a special case of convex programming. Conversely, closed convex sets K may be represented as the intersection of all closed halfspaces containing K (cf.[22]). Obviously this is a description of K by means of an infinite set of linear inequalities. In general it will be difficult or even impossible to find smooth functions $a(x), b(x)$ such that $K = \{a^T(x)z - b(x) \le 0\ |\ x \in B\}$. Yet, if K is a bounded region given by means of a finite number of smooth convex functions $f^i : \mathbb{R}^n \to \mathbb{R}$,

$$K = \{z\ |\ f^i(z) \le 0,\ i = 1,..,k\}$$

a problem of type LSIP(B) is easily obtained with k inequalities $a^T(x)z - b(x) \le 0$ instead of only one.

We will confine ourselves to the discussion of a simple example with $k = 1$.

<u>Example.</u> Minimize $F(z) = c^Tz = z_1 + 2z_2$ with respect to $z \in K$, K the unit disk in $\mathbb{R}^2$:

$$\text{Min } \{z_1 + 2z_2 \mid f(z) := z_1^2 + z_2^2 - 1 \le 0\}.$$

To obtain an equivalent linear semi-infinite problem let $B = [-2,2]\times[-2,2]$ (or some other compact set with $K \subset B$). Then

$$K = \{z \mid g(x,z) := f(x) + (z-x)^T f_z(x) \le 0, x \in B\}.$$

I.e. the inequality $f(z) \le 0$ is replaced by the requirement that the tangent-plane to the graph of $f(z)$ in every point x of B remains below the z-plane in $\begin{bmatrix} z \\ z_{n+1} \end{bmatrix}$ -space. For a function $f : \mathbb{R} \to \mathbb{R}$ this is illustrated by Fig. 3. Fig. 4 shows an approximation to K, when B is reduced to a finite subset of 6 points.

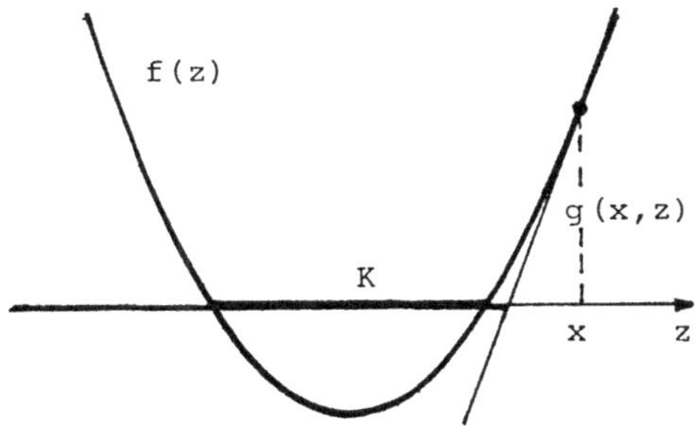

Fig. 3

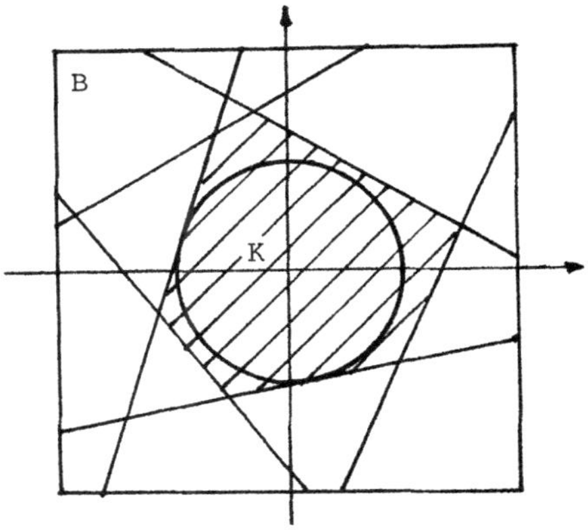

Fig. 4

Using $f(x) + (z-x)^T f_z(x) = 2x_1 z_1 + 2x_2 z_2 - (x_1^2 + x_2^2 + 1)$ we get the linear problem

$$\text{Minimize } c^T z \text{ subject to } a^T(x) z - b(x) \le 0, \; x \in B$$

with $a(x) = 2\begin{bmatrix} x_1 \\ x_2 \end{bmatrix}$ and $b(x) = x_1^2 + x_2^2 + 1$.

4. The relation of exchange methods to cutting plane methods

Let us consider the convex programming problem

$$\text{Min } \{F(z) = c^T z \mid f(z) \le 0\}, \qquad (1$$

with $f : \mathbb{R}^n \to \mathbb{R}$ a convex, twice continuously differentiable function. (The following considerations may be easily extended to problems with more than one constraint). An equivalent semi-infinite problem is

$$\text{Min } \{F(z) = c^T z \mid g(z,x) = f(x) + (z-x)^T f_z(x) \le 0, x \in B\} \tag{2}$$

with $B \supset K = \{z \mid f(z) \le 0\}$ a compact polyhedron.

Then Kelley's [15] cutting plane method applied to (1) (see also [1]) proceeds as follows:

<u>Start</u>: Let $P_o = B$.

<u>Step ν ($\nu \ge 0$)</u>: Given a polyhedron P_ν. Compute a solution z^ν of the linear programming problem Min $\{c^T z \mid z \in P_\nu\}$. Let

$$P_{\nu+1} = P_\nu \cap \{z \mid g(z,z^\nu) = f(z^\nu) + (z-z^\nu)^T f_z(z^\nu) \le 0\}.$$

That means the restrictions of the semi-infinite description (2) of the problem are included, one at a time.

Given z^ν, the implicit one-point exchange method would add the constraint $g(z\ ,x^1) \le 0$, where x^1 is a global maximum of $g(z^\nu,x)$ on B. Assuming $f_{xx}(x)$ positive definite for all x (i.e. f is strictly convex) from

$$g_x(z^\nu,x) = (z^\nu - x)^T f_{xx}(x)$$

one concludes easily that $x^1 = z^\nu$. Therefore, applying the cutting plane method to (1) in this case is equivalent to the application of the implicit one-point exchange method to (2).

In our example

$$\text{Min } \{z_1 + 2z_2 \mid z_1^2 + z_2^2 - 1 \le 0\},$$

all exchange methods yield the same iterates as the cutting plane method. Fig. 5 shows the first iterates, demonstrating the well-known drawbacks of cutting plane methods:

- Zigzagging and, as a consequence, slow convergence.

- Numerical instability due to the fact that the hyperplanes defining the z^ν by intersection become more and more parallel.

- All of the z^ν are infeasible.

- Due to the need for determining a global maximum of $g(z^\nu, x)$ on B, a large amount of computing effort per step.

To avoid the last disadvantage, there are two possibilities:

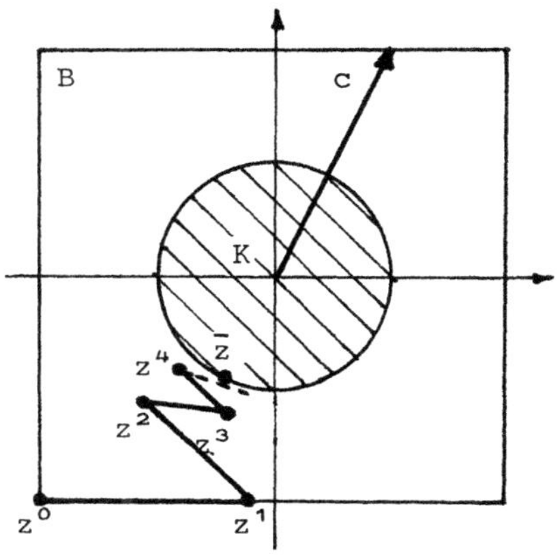

Fig. 5

- Use of a so-called central cutting plane method (cf. [3], [5])

- Application of discretization with grid refinement (Section 6).

The other drawbacks are inevitably attached to exchange methods and apply analoguously to discretization methods as well. An exception is the strongly unique case, which will be discussed in the next section.

5. The case of a strongly unique solution

As we have seen, exchange methods in general exhibit a number of difficulties. Nevertheless, in special cases, they behave very well, as for instance the methods of Remes in the case of Chebyshev approximation problems (A), if Haar's condition holds (cf. [17]). These cases may be characterized generally by the property that the solution $\bar{z}$ of the problem in question is strongly unique (in Chebyshev approximation this is guaranteed by Haar's condition) in the following sense:

Definition. $\bar{z}$ is a strongly unique solution of the problem

$$\operatorname{Min} \{F(z) \mid z \in K\}$$

if there is a $\gamma > 0$ such that

$$F(z) - F(\bar{z}) \geq \gamma \, ||z-\bar{z}|| \text{ for all } z \in K.$$

Fig. 6 illustrates two typical situations by means of some contour lines of F(z) (F is assumed convex). In case a) $\bar{z}$ clearly is not strongly unique, whereas it is in b).

a) b)

Fig. 6

For convex problems

$$\text{Min } \{F(z) \mid f^i(z) \leq 0,\ i=1,..,k\}$$

if Slater's condition holds (i.e. there exists a $\tilde{z}$ such that $f^i(\tilde{z}) < 0$, $i=1,..,k$), strong unicity of $\bar{z}$ implies that at least n constraints are active in $\bar{z}$ (cf.[12]).

In the example of Section 4, as there is only one constraint, a solution is never strongly unique. Therefore we add a second constraint, cutting off half of the disk:

$$\text{Min } \{z_1 + 2z_2 \mid z_1^2 + z_2^2 - 1 \leq 0,\ z_1 - z_2 \leq 0\}.$$

Taking for B the triangle with vertices $\begin{bmatrix}2\\2\end{bmatrix}$, $\begin{bmatrix}-2\\2\end{bmatrix}$, $\begin{bmatrix}-2\\-2\end{bmatrix}$, a simple calculation shows that the cutting plane method is equivalent to solving the system

$$z_1^2 + z_2^2 - 1 = 0$$

$$z_1 - z_2 = 0$$

(with $\bar{z}$ as a locally unique solution) with Newton's method, and therefore we have quadratic convergence in this case. Fig. 7 illustrates the situation.

This applies analogously to much more general situations. In [11] it is shown that (even for nonlinear problems) strong uniqueness together with some regularity conditions implies superlinear convergence of an appropriately defined very general multiple exchange method. Similar to the example above the proof is carried out by showing the equivalence of the method to Newton's method applied to the system $f^i(z) = 0, i \in \{j \mid f^j(\bar{z}) = 0\}$. The result generalizes earlier work of Wetterling [30] who has proved second order convergence for the Remes simultaneous exchange method applied to problem (A), in the case that there are exactly n extrema of the error-function.

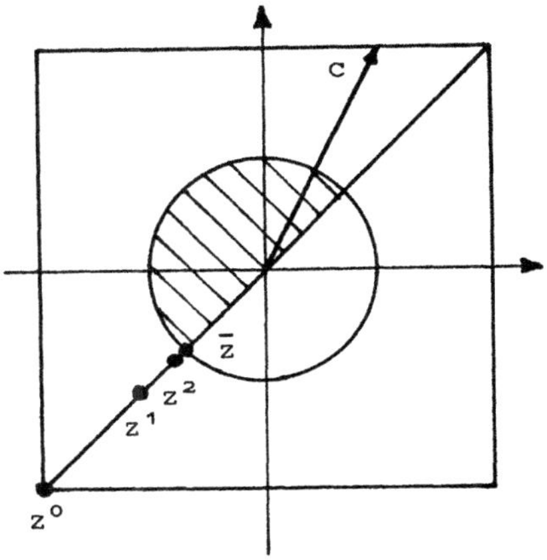

Fig. 7

6. A discretization method.

In this section, we briefly present a discretization method with grid-refinement which has been successfully applied to many problems. As mentioned above, the advantage (in comparison with exchange methods) is that no solution of the problem Max $\{g(z^\nu, x) \mid x \in B\}$ is required, or, more exactly, the problem is reduced to the simple problem of a maximization on a finite subset of B. An important feature of the method below is that instead of the whole grid, with eventually thousands of points in each step, a rather small subset must be considered. The algorithm is as follows:

Start: Choose a (for instance regular) grid $B_o \subset B$. Let $\tilde{B}_o = B_o$.

Step ν ($\nu \geq 0$): Given a grid B_ν and a subset $\tilde{B}_\nu$, perform the following substeps (i), (ii), (iii):

(i) Compute a solution z^ν of the ordinary linear programming problem LSIP($\tilde{B}_\nu$).

(ii) Determine a refined grid $B_{\nu+1} \supset B_\nu$.

(iii) Determine a new subset

$$\tilde{B}_{\nu+1} = \{x \in B_{\nu+1} \mid g(z^\nu, x) \geq -\varepsilon_\nu\}$$

where ε_ν is some given nonnegative number. The choice

$$-\varepsilon_\nu = \tau \cdot \min_{x \in \tilde{B}_\nu} g(z^\nu, x)$$

with $\tau \approx 10^{-2}$ proved to be satisfactory in practice.

Fig. 8 illustrates substep (iii). In substep (i), $LSIP_D(\tilde{B}_\nu)$ is solved starting from the dual feasible vertex given by $z^{\nu-1}$.

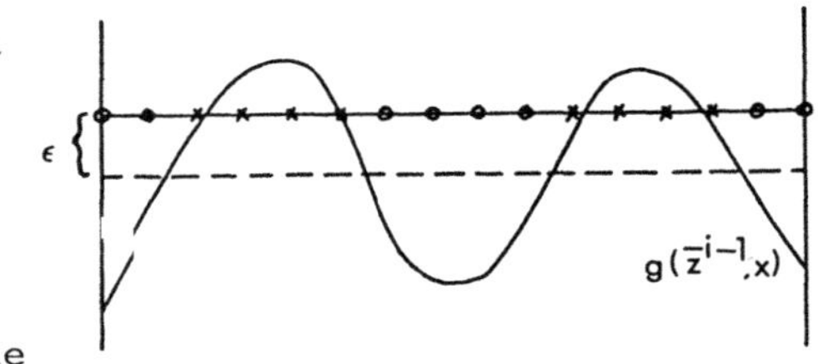

$x : \tilde{B}_i$; $o : B_i \setminus \tilde{B}_i$

Fig. 8

The following example illustrates the power of the method, due to the striking reduction of the number of points in $\tilde{B}_\nu$, compared with that of those in B_ν.

Example. An algorithm based on the above method with $\tau = 10^{-2}$ was applied to the problem of approximating (in the sense of Chebyshev) the function $f(x) = x_1^{x_2}$ in the square $B = [1,2]x[1,2] \subset \mathbb{R}^2$ by polynomials in two variables of total degree 4 (cf. Section 2). Note that in this case n = 16. The following table was obtained:

ν	$N(B_\nu)$	$N(\tilde{B}_\nu)$	‡ Simplex	error
0	36 (= 6^2)	36	33	0.98.... 10^{-4}
1	121 (=11^2)	32	27	1.05.... 10^{-3}
2	1.681 (=41^2)	95	38	1.0756.. 10^{-3}
3	14.641 (=121^2)	73	35	1.0766.. 10^{-3}

The following abbreviations are used:

$N(B_\nu)$: Number of points in the full grid B_ν.

$N(\tilde{B}_\nu)$: Number of points in the reduced grid $\tilde{B}_\nu$.

$\neq$ Simplex: Number of Simplex-steps required for the solution of $LSIP_D(\tilde{B}_\nu)$.

error: The approximation error on the full grid B_ν. Underlined figures are correct.

The number of error extrema in this example is 12 (cf.Fig.2) and so we have a solution which is not strictly unique. Therefore exchange methods perform very badly in this case.

7. Local reduction to a finite convex problem

The discussion in Section 4 has demonstrated the desirability of methods with good local convergence to be used as phase 2 methods in a two-phase concept. A suitable way of deriving such methods is to reduce the problem locally to a finite differentiable convex one and to apply an appropriate method from convex programming.

In Section 3 we have shown that a differentiable convex programming problem may be easily described as a linear semi-infinite problem. Now we will study the converse problem of finding finitely many convex differentiable functions f^i such that

$$Z = \{z \mid g(z,x) \le 0,\ x \in B\} = \{z \mid f^i(z) \le 0,\ i=1,..k\}. \tag{3}$$

Of course, defining the convex function

$$\varphi(z) = \max_{x \in B} g(z,x)$$

we have $Z = \{z \mid \varphi(z) \le 0\}$, but, φ being not differentiable and very expensive to evaluate, this is not a description of practical value. In general it is not possible in practice to find f^i such that (3) holds. Yet, in the sequel, we will give a method for finding f^i such that for some neighbourhood $U(\bar{z})$ of the optimal point $\bar{z}$ we have

$$U(\bar{z}) \cap Z = U(\bar{z}) \cap \{z \mid f^i(z) \le 0,\ i=1,..,k\}. \tag{3'}$$

The main idea for achieving this aim is to consider the local maxima of

$g(z,x)$ with respect to $x \in B$ as functions $x^i(z)$ of z and to replace the constraint $g(z,x) \le 0$ by requiring $g(z,x^i(z)) \le 0$ for all these local maxima. The following Fig. 9 illustrates this.

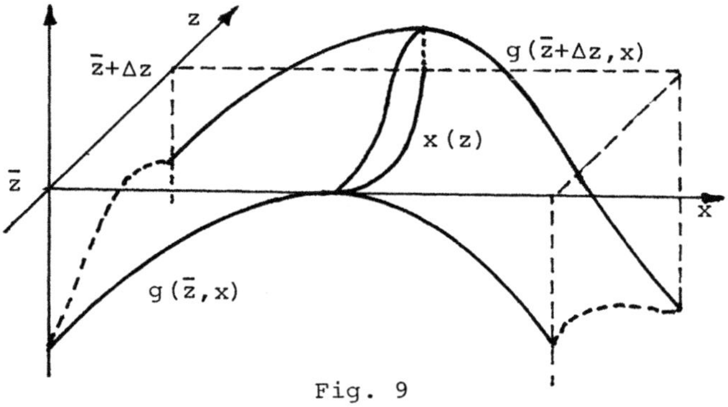

Fig. 9

The existence of the differentiable functions $x^i(z)$ is not given generally. We require:

Assumption (V). Let $\bar{z}$ be optimal for LSIP(B). Then $\bar{E}$ contains only a finite number of points, i.e.

$$\bar{E} = \{x \mid g(\bar{z},x) = 0\} = \{\bar{x}^1,..,\bar{x}^k\}.$$

Moreover, there are neighbourhoods $U(\bar{z})$, $U(\bar{x}^i)$ of $\bar{z}$, $\bar{x}^i$ resp. and continuously differentiable functions $x^i\colon U(\bar{z}) \to U(\bar{x}^i)$, $i=1,..,k$, such that

(i) $\bar{x}^i = x^i(\bar{z})$, $i=1,..,k$.

(ii) For $z \in U(\bar{z})$, $x^i(z)$ is the only local maximum of $g(z,\cdot)$ in $B \cap U(\bar{x}^i)$.

Then, defining

$$f^i(z) = g(z,x^i(z)) \;, \quad f^i : U(\bar{z}) \to \mathbb{R} \tag{4}$$

we have [10], [9], [12]):

Theorem 2: Assume (V) holds. Then the f_i given by (4) are convex, continuously differentiable functions such that for $z \in U(\bar{z})$ LSIP(B) may be replaced (in the sense of (3')) by the convex problem

$$\text{Min } \{c^T z \mid f^i(z) \le 0, \; i=1,..,k\}.$$

Applying the Implicit Function Theorem it is easily seen that in the case B = [0,1] a sufficient condition for (V) to hold is that $g_{xx}(\bar{z},\bar{x}^i) \neq 0$ for $x^i \in (0,1)$ and $g_x(\bar{z},\bar{x}^i) \neq 0$ for $\bar{x}^i \in \{0,1\}$. If this stronger condition holds, then the gradients $f_z^i(z)$ not only exist but may be easily computed for every $z \in U(\bar{z})$. For more general B a similar sufficient condition can be given using second order sufficient optimality conditions for $\bar{x}^i$ to be a maximum of $g(\bar{z},\cdot)$ on B, and again f_z^i may be computed explicitly, if this condition holds (cf.[10]).

Note that the evaluation of $f^i(z)$ requires again the solution of

$$\text{Max } \{g(z,x) \mid x \in B\}.$$

This makes methods with fast convergence especially desirable.

8. Some examples of methods for solving the reduced problem.

In this section we will briefly report on some methods used in solving the reduced problem derived in Section 7.

Newton's method. Consider the locally reduced problem

$$\text{Min } \{F(z) \mid f^i(z) \leq 0,\ i=1,..,k\} \tag{5}$$

with

$$f^i(z) = g(z,x^i(z)) \ ,\ i=1,..,k,\ z \in U(\bar{z}),$$

as in Section 7. Then, making use of the definition of $x^i(z)$ (cf. Assumption (V)) we have

$$f_z^i(\bar{z}) = g_z(\bar{z},\bar{x}^i) \ ,\ i=1,..,k.$$

Therefore, assuming Slater's condition for LSIP(B) holds, a necessary and sufficient condition for $\bar{z}$ to be optimal is that there are $\bar{u}^i \geq 0$ such that

$$F_z(\bar{z}) + \sum_{i=1}^{k} \bar{u}^i f_z^i(\bar{z}) = F_z(\bar{z}) + \sum_{i=1}^{k} \bar{u}^i g_z(\bar{z},\bar{x}^i) = 0. \tag{6}$$

Equation (6) together with

$$f^i(\bar{z}) = g(\bar{z},x^i(\bar{z})) = 0,\ i=1,..,k \tag{7}$$

is a system of n + k nonlinear equations in the n + k unknowns $\bar{z}$, $\bar{u}^i$, i=1,..,k. Then, the method consists in the application of Newton's method for solving the system (6), (7). A disadvantage of the method is that the number k of points $\bar{x}^j$ in the unknown set $\bar{E}$ is required.

Superlinear convergence of this method may be established, assuming some second order sufficient optimality condition holds at $\bar{z}$ (cf. [8], [10]). The same holds for the following two methods (cf. [9], [18]).

Method of quadratic approximation. In [9], [14], [29], [20] the application of methods is investigated which are studied extensively in [21] for the finite case. In each step, a second order approximation of the Lagrangian function is minimized subject to the linearized constraints of the original problem. As an example, we consider Wilson's method ([31]):

Assume that in step ν approximations z^ν to $\bar{z}$ and $u_l^\nu \geq 0$, l=1,..,k, of the optimal Lagrange multipliers $\bar{u}_l$ are given. Let

$$L(z,u) = F(z) + \sum_{l=1}^{k} u_l g(z,x^l(z))$$

be the Lagrangian function of the reduced problem (5). Then $z^{\nu+1}$ and $u_l^{\nu+1}$ are defined as a solution and optimal Lagrange multipliers of the problem

Minimize the quadratic function

$$\tilde{F}(z) = F(z^\nu) + (z-z^\nu)^T F_z(z^\nu) + \frac{1}{2}(z-z^\nu)^T L_{zz}(z^\nu,u^\nu)(z-z^\nu)$$

subject to the linear constraints

$$\tilde{g}^l(z) = g(z^\nu,x^l(z^\nu))+(z-z^\nu)^T g_z(z^\nu,x^l(z^\nu)) \leq 0, l=1,..,k.$$

This method may be globalized - i.e., a start with any approximation to $\bar{z}$ is possible - in different ways (cf. [14], [29]).

Method of augmented Lagrangian. Without giving details, we note that in [18] methods of augmented Lagrangians of finite programming have been applied successfully to semi-infinite problems, also. It is shown that the $x^1(z)$ have to be computed very accurately in each step to ensure superlinear convergence. Again, an algorithm is given which may be started at any point z^o.

9. Some remarks on the nonlinear case.

Apart from the solution of the discretized problems, which becomes much more complicated, the foregoing considerations apply analogously to nonlinear problems SIP(B).

Again, a two-phase concept is recommended:

In phase 1, starting from an arbitrary point, a rough estimate of the solution is computed which is improved in phase 2 by a superlinearly convergent method. To this end, again the problem may be locally reduced to a finite programming problem which, of course, is no longer convex in general. The same methods as in Section 8 may be applied to this reduced problem (cf. [12]).

In phase 1, it is desirable to deal with a discretized problem SIP($\tilde{B}$), $\tilde{B} \subset B$, a finite set. Again, grid-refinement techniques may be applied, similarly to the linear case. To solve SIP($\tilde{B}$), any technique from finite (nonlinear) optimization may be used. In addition to the methods of Section 8 in phase 1, robust methods of descent become especially important. We mention:

- Linearization methods with an appropriate step-length adaption. Methods of this type have been applied, especially to Chebyshev-approximation problems (cf. [19], [2], [4], [16]).

- Steepest descent methods (cf. [32] and, for Chebyshev-approximation, [7]).

Acknowledgement. The author is indebted to the referee for his close reading of the paper and his suggestions for improving the presentation.

References

(1) CHENEY, E.W., and GOLDSTEIN, A.A.: Newton's method for convex programming and Tchebycheff approximation: Numer.Math. 1 (1959), 253-268

(2) CROMME, L: Eine Klasse von Verfahren zur Ermittlung bester nicht-linearer Tschebyscheff-Approximation: Numer. Math. 25(1976), 447-459

(3) ELZINGA, J., and MOORE, TH.G.: A central cutting plane algorithm for the convex programming problem: Math. Programming 8 (1975), 134-145

(4) GEIGER, C.: Zur Konvergenz eines Abstiegsverfahrens für nicht-lineare gleichmäßige Approximationsaufgaben: Univ. Hamburg, preprint 77/14, 1977

(5) GRIBIK, P.R.: A central cutting plane algorithm for semi-infinite programming problems, in: Hettich (ed): Semi-infinite programming, Springer, Berlin-Heidelberg-New-York, 1979, 66-82

(6) GUSTAFSON, S.A.: On the computational solution of a class of generalized moment problems: SIAM J. Numer. Anal. 7 (1970), 343-357

(7) GUTKNECHT, M.: Ein Abstiegsverfahren für nicht-diskrete Tschebyscheff-Approximationsprobleme, in: Collatz et al. (eds.): Numer. Meth. der Approximationstheorie 4: Birkhäuser, Basel-Stuttgart, ISNM 42 (1978), 154-171

(8) HETTICH, R.: A Newton method for nonlinear Chebyshev approximation, in: Schaback; Scherer (eds.): Approximation Theory, Springer, Berlin-Heidelberg-New-York 1976, 222-236

(9) HETTICH, R., and VAN HONSTEDE, W.: On quadratically convergent methods for semi-infinite programming , in: Hettich (ed.): Semi-infinite programming, Springer, Berlin-Heidelberg-New-York, 1979, 97-111

(10) HETTICH, R., and JONGEN, H.TH.: Semi-infinite programming: conditions of optimality and applications, in: Stoer (ed.): Optimization Techniques 2, Springer, Berlin-Heidelberg-New-York, 1978, 1-11

(11) HETTICH, R., and ZENCKE, P.: Superlinear konvergente Verfahren für semi-infinite Optimierungsprobleme im stark eindeutigen Fall, in: Collatz-Meinardus-Wetterling (eds.): Konstruktive Methoden der finiten nichtlinearen Optimierung, Birkhäuser, Basel-Bosten-Stuttgart, ISNM 55 (1980), 103-120

(12) HETTICH, R., and ZENCKE, P.: Numerische Methoden der Approximation und semi-infiniten Optimierung, Teubner, Stuttgart, 1982

(13) HOFFMANN, K.H., and KLOSTERMAIER, A.: A semi-infinite programming procedure, in: Lorentz et al. (eds.): Approximation Theory II, Academic Press, New-York-San Francisco-London 1976, 379 - 389

(14) VAN HONSTEDE, W.: An approximation method for semi-infinite problems, in: Hettich (ed.): Semi-infinite programming, Springer, Berlin-Heidelberg-New-York, 1979, 126-136

(15) KELLEY, J.E.Jr.: The cutting plane method for solving convex programs, J.Soc.Indust.Appl.Math. 8 (1960), 703-712

(16) MADSEN, K.: An algorithm for minimax solution of overdetermined systems of non-linear equations, J. Inst. Maths.Applics. 16 (1975), 321-328

(17) MEINARDUS, G.: Approximation von Funktionen und ihre numerische Behandlung, Springer, Berlin-Göttingen-Heidelberg-New-York 1964

(18) OETTERSHAGEN,K.: Ein superlinear konvergenter Algorithmus zur Lösung semi-infiniter Optimierungsprobleme, Univ. Bonn, Dissertation 1982

(19) OSBORNE, M.R., and WATSON, G.A.: An algorithm for minimax approximation in the nonlinear case, Computer J. 12 (1969), 63-68

(20) POLAK, E., and TITS, A.L.: A recursive quadratic programming algorithm for semi-infinite optimization problems, paper presented at: International Symp. on Semi-infinite Progr.Appl., Austin, 1981

(21) ROBINSON, S.M.: Perturbed Kuhn-Tucker points and rates of convergence for a class of nonlinear programming problems; Math. Programming 7 (1974), 1-16

(22) ROCKAFELLAR, R.T.: Convex Analysis: Princeton University Press, Princeton, 1970

(23) ROLEFF, K.: A stable multiple exchange algorithm for linear SIP, in: Hettich (ed.): Semi-infinite programming, Springer, Berlin-Heidelberg-New-York 1979, 83-96

(24) SCHÄFER, E.: Ein Konstruktionsverfahren bei allgemeiner linearer Approximation, Numer. Math. 18 (1971), 113-126

(25) STIEFEL, E.: Über diskrete und lineare Tschebyscheff-Approximationen, Numer.Math. 1 (1959), 1 - 28

(26) STIEFEL, E.: Note on Jordan elimination, linear programming and Tschebyscheff-approximation: Numer. Math. 2 (1960), 1-17

(27) TÖPFER, H.J.: Tschebyscheff-Approximation bei nicht erfüllter Haarscher Bedingung: Birkhäuser, Basel-Stuttgart, ISNM 7 (1967), 71-89

(28) WATSON, G.A.: A multiple exchange algorithm for multivariate Chebyshev approximation, SIAM J. Num.Anal. 12 (1975), 46-52

(29) WATSON, G.A.: Numerical experiments with globally convergent methods for semi-infinite programming problems: Univ. of Dundee, Rep. NA/49, 1981

(30) WETTERLING, W.: Anwendung des Newtonschen Iterationsverfahrens bei der Tschebyscheff-Approximation, insbesondere mit nichtlinear auftretenden Parametern, MTW Teil I: 61-63, Teil II: 112-115, 1963

(31) WILSON, R.B.: A simplicial algorithm for concave programming, Diss., Harvard Univ., Cambridge (Mass.) 1963

(32) ZOUTENDIJK, G.: Mathematical programming methods: North-Holland, Amsterdam-New-York-Oxford 1976

AN ALGORITHM FOR MINIMIZING POLYHEDRAL CONVEX FUNCTIONS

M.R. Osborne

Abstract. A finite descent algorithm is derived based on an explicit parametrization of the subdifferential of the polyhedral convex function by using continuation applied to its proximal transform. A method for resolving degeneracy is sketched as are certain points relating to implementation. Applications have been made to linear programming, both directly and by the use of penalty methods, to ℓ_1 and ℓ_∞ fitting problems, and to the interesting and challenging rank regression problem.

1. Introduction.

The problem considered in this paper is that of minimising the polyhedral convex function (PCF) $F: X \subseteq R^p \to R$ defined by

$$F(\underset{\sim}{x}) = \max_{1 \le i \le n} \{\underset{\sim}{f}_i^T \underset{\sim}{x} - \alpha_i\} + \delta(\underset{\sim}{x}|X) \tag{1.1}$$

where

$$X = \text{dom } F = \{\underset{\sim}{x};\ \underset{\sim}{c}_i^T \underset{\sim}{x} \ge \beta_i, \quad i = 1,2,\ldots,M\}\ , \tag{1.2}$$

$\delta(t)$ is the one dimensional indicator function

$$\delta(t) = 0\ ,\ t \le 0\ ,\ = +\infty\ ,\ t > 0\ , \tag{1.3}$$

and $\delta(\underset{\sim}{x}|X)$ is the indicator function for X defined by

$$\delta(\underset{\sim}{x}|X) = \sum_{i=1}^{M} \delta(\beta_i - \underset{\sim}{c}_i^T \underset{\sim}{x})\ . \tag{1.4}$$

Such problems occur in many situations, including an important application to semi-infinite programming. This is the cutting plane algorithm for minimizing the convex function $g(\underset{\sim}{x})$. For simplicity assume that $\text{dom } g = R^p$. Then the algorithm is as follows.

Let $g(\underset{\sim}{x}) \geq F_i(\underset{\sim}{x})$ pointwise where F_i is a PCF,

$F_i(x) = \max_{j \in \mu_i} \{\underset{\sim}{f}_j^T \underset{\sim}{x} - \alpha_j\}$, and μ_i is an index set pointing to the affine functions defining F_i .

(i) Compute $\underset{\sim}{x}_i = \arg\min_{\underset{\sim}{x}} F_i(\underset{\sim}{x})$.

(ii) Let ν_i be an index set such that

$$\underset{\sim}{f}_{\nu_i(k)} = \underset{\sim}{v}_k \ , \ k = 1, \ldots, |\nu_i|$$

where

$$\mathrm{conv}(\underset{\sim}{v}_k, k=1,2,\ldots,|\nu_i|) = \partial g(\underset{\sim}{x}_i) \ ,$$ the subdifferential of g at $\underset{\sim}{x}_i$,

and

$$\alpha_{\nu_i(k)} = -g(\underset{\sim}{x}_i) + \underset{\sim}{f}^T_{\nu_i(k)} \underset{\sim}{x}_i \ .$$

(iii) Set

$$\mu_{i+1} = \mu_i \cup \nu_i$$

$$F_{i+1} = \max_{i \in \mu_{i+1}} \{\underset{\sim}{f}_i^T \underset{\sim}{x} - \alpha_i\}$$

$$i = i + 1 \ .$$

(iv) Repeat (i) .

The problem of minimizing a PCF has the equivalent formulation as the linear programming problem

$$\min_{\begin{bmatrix} \underset{\sim}{x} \\ x_{p+1} \end{bmatrix} \in X} x_{p+1} \ : \ X = \{\begin{bmatrix} \underset{\sim}{x} \\ x_{p+1} \end{bmatrix} ; \ \underset{\sim}{f}_i^T \underset{\sim}{x} - \alpha_i \leq x_{p+1}, \ i = 1,2,\ldots,N, \ C\underset{\sim}{x} - \underset{\sim}{\beta} \geq 0\} \qquad (1.5)$$

but in many important examples this does not lead to a practical algorithm. The reason for this can be seen by considering the number of elements in $\partial F(\underset{\sim}{x})$. These determine the $\underset{\sim}{f}_i$ according to the rule

$$\partial F(\underset{\sim}{x}) = \operatorname{conv}(\underset{\sim}{f}_i^T, \quad i \in \sigma) \tag{1.6}$$

where σ is an index set defined by

$$\sigma = \{i;\ \underset{\sim}{f}_i^T \underset{\sim}{x} - \alpha_i = F(\underset{\sim}{x})\} \quad , \tag{1.7}$$

and a suitable spanning set of the $\underset{\sim}{f}_i$ can be very large indeed. This is illustrated in the examples that follow.

For this reason we seek an alternative parametrization of $\partial F(\underset{\sim}{x})$ in terms of a more economical basis. This will have the form

$$\underset{\sim}{u}^T \in F(x) \Leftrightarrow \exists\, \underset{\sim}{\lambda} \in \Lambda \ni \underset{\sim}{u} = \underset{\sim}{g} + V\underset{\sim}{\lambda} \tag{1.8}$$

where $\underset{\sim}{g}, V$ are determined for each fixed $\underset{\sim}{x}$, and Λ is a set specifying the allowable values of $\underset{\sim}{\lambda}$. If

$$\text{column dim } V = \text{rank } (V) \leq p \tag{1.9}$$

we will call the representation achieved in (1.8) nondegenerate.

<u>Example</u> (i) The linear programming problem: Here

$$F(\underset{\sim}{x}) = \underset{\sim}{f}^T \underset{\sim}{x} + \delta(\underset{\sim}{x}|X) \ ,$$

$$\partial F(\underset{\sim}{x}) = \underset{\sim}{f}^T - \sum_{i=1}^{M} \partial\delta(\beta_i - \underset{\sim}{c}_i^T \underset{\sim}{x})\underset{\sim}{c}_i^T$$

where

$$\partial\delta(t) = 0,\ t < 0;\ = [0,\infty),\ t=0;\ = \emptyset\ ,\ t > 0.$$

Let the index set ν point to the constraints (1.2) active at $\underset{\sim}{x}$. Then we have

$$\underset{\sim}{g} = \underset{\sim}{f}\ ,\ \kappa_i(V) = \underset{\sim}{c}_{\nu(i)},\ i=1,2,\ldots,|\nu|,\quad \lambda_i \geq 0$$

where $\kappa_i(\cdot)$ is the operation of selecting the ith column. The corresponding row operator is $\rho_i(\cdot)$.

(ii) Composite problems: Here we assume that $X = R^p$, and we consider the typical situation in which the convex objective function is being used to force a condition that the components of the vector $\underset{\sim}{r}$,

$$\underset{\sim}{r} = A\underset{\sim}{x} - \underset{\sim}{b} \tag{1.10}$$

where $A: R^p \to R^n$, are to be small in order to determine $\underset{\sim}{x}$. Let

$$F(\underset{\sim}{x}) = G(\underset{\sim}{r}) \tag{1.11}$$

where $G(\underset{\sim}{r})$ is the PCF defined by

$$G(\underset{\sim}{r}) = \max_{1 \le i \le N} \rho_i(D)\underset{\sim}{r} \tag{1.12}$$

where $D: R^n \to R^N$. Then

$$\partial F(\underset{\sim}{x}) = \partial G(\underset{\sim}{r})A = \operatorname{conv}(\rho_i(D);\ i \in \sigma)A \tag{1.13}$$

where

$$\sigma = \{i;\ \rho_i(D)\underset{\sim}{r} = G(\underset{\sim}{r})\} .$$

In this case, as a consequence of (1.13), (1.9) becomes

$$\text{column dim } V = \operatorname{rank}(V) \le \operatorname{rank}(A) = K \le p . \tag{1.14}$$

(ii) (a) Let

$$D = \begin{bmatrix} I \\ -I \end{bmatrix} ,$$

then

$$G = \max_i |r_i| , \quad i = 1,2,\ldots,n ,$$

and $N = 2n$. To compute $\partial F(\underset{\sim}{x})$ we have (setting $\underset{\sim}{a}_i = \rho_i(A)^T$, $\theta_i = \operatorname{sgn}(r_i)$, and defining σ as the index set pointing to the components of $\underset{\sim}{r}$ of maximum modulus)

$$\underset{\sim}{g} = \theta_{\sigma(1)}\ \underset{\sim}{a}_{\sigma(1)} \tag{1.15}$$

$$\kappa_i(V) = \theta_{\sigma(i+1)} \underset{\sim}{a}_{\sigma(i+1)} - \theta_{\sigma(1)} \underset{\sim}{a}_{\sigma(1)} ,$$

$$i = 1,2,\ldots,|\sigma|-1 , \qquad (1.16)$$

and

$$0 \leq \lambda_i, \ i = 1,2,\ldots,|\sigma|-1, \ \sum_{i=1}^{|\sigma|-1} \lambda_i \leq 1 . \qquad (1.17)$$

(ii) (b) Let the rows of D be all combinations such that the i'th component in each row is $(u_i \mid -\ell_i)$, $i = 1,2,\ldots,n$. Then $N = 2^n$ and the linear programming formulation (1.5) is impractical. However, the PCF possesses an alternative representation. We introduce the functions

$$\psi(t,u,\ell) = u|t|, \ t > 0, \ \ell|t|, \ t < 0 \qquad (1.18)$$

and consider the PCF

$$F = \mu \underset{\sim}{f}^T \underset{\sim}{x} + \sum_{i=1}^{n} \psi(r_i,u_i,\ell_i) . \qquad (1.19)$$

Two important special cases correspond to :

(i) $\mu = 0$, $u_i = 1$, $\ell_i = 1$ giving $F = \sum_{i=1}^{n} |r_i|$, and

(ii) $\mu > 0$, $u_i = 0$, $\ell_i = 1$. In this second case F can be interpreted as a penalty function method for a particular linear programming problem.

To calculate $\partial F(\underset{\sim}{x})$ note that

$$\partial\psi(t,u,\ell) = -\ell, \ t < 0; \ = [-\ell,u], \ t = 0; \ = u, \ t > 0. \qquad (1.20)$$

Let the index set ν point to the zero residuals. Then we obtain

$$\underset{\sim}{g} = \mu \underset{\sim}{f} + \sum_{\nu^c} \frac{\psi(\theta_k,u_k,\ell_k)}{\theta_k} \underset{\sim}{a}_k , \qquad (1.21)$$

$$\kappa_i(V) = \underset{\sim}{a}_{\nu(i)} , \ i = 1,2,\ldots,|\nu| , \qquad (1.22)$$

and

$$-\ell_k \leq \lambda_k \leq u_k , \quad i = 1,2,\ldots,|\nu| . \qquad (1.23)$$

(ii) (c) We introduce 'scores' d_i , $i = 1,2,\ldots,n$ satisfying

(i) $d_i \le d_2 \le \ldots \le d_n$,

(ii) $d_i = -d_{n-i+1}$, $i = 1,2,\ldots, n$ and

(iii) $d_1 < d_n$,

and define D to be the matrix whose rows consist of all distinct permutations of the d_i . If the d_i are distinct then $N = n!$. Let μ be the ranking set pointing to the components of $\underset{\sim}{r}$ sorted in increasing order. Then we define

$$F = \max_{1\le i\le N} \rho_i(D)\underset{\sim}{r} = \sum_{i=1}^{n} d_i r_{\mu(i)} . \tag{1.24}$$

The problem of minimizing F is called the rank regression problem, and F is the dispersion of $\underset{\sim}{r}$. To calculate $\partial F(\underset{\sim}{x})$ note that a complicating feature is provided by the tied residuals. We put

$$\nu = \nu_1 \cup \nu_2 \cup \ldots \cup \nu_q \tag{1.25}$$

where ν_i points to the i'th group of tied residuals, $i = 1,2,\ldots,q$. It is convenient to set

$$|\nu_i| = m_i + 1,\ i = 1,2,\ldots,q\ ,\ \sum_{i=1}^{q} m_i = m \tag{1.26}$$

and to refer to $\underset{\sim}{a}_{\nu_i(1)}$ as the group origin for the i'th group, $i = 1,2,\ldots,q$. Then $\partial F(\underset{\sim}{x})$ is specified by

$$\underset{\sim}{g} = \sum_{i\in\nu^c} d_{\pi(i)}\underset{\sim}{a}_i + \sum_{i=1}^{q}\{\sum_{j=1}^{m_i+1} d_{\pi(\nu_i(j))}\}\underset{\sim}{a}_{\nu_i(1)} \tag{1.27}$$

where π is the index set which associates with r_j the score $d_{\pi(j)}$, and where we assume that within each group

$d_{\pi(\nu_i(j))} \ge d_{\pi(\nu_i(k))}$, $j \ge k$,

$$V = [V_1|V_2|\ldots V_q] \tag{1.28}$$

where

$$\kappa_j(V_i) = \underset{\sim}{a}_{\nu_i(j+1)} - \underset{\sim}{a}_{\nu_i(1)} \;, \quad j = 1,2,\ldots,m_i \;, \tag{1.29}$$

and

$$\underset{\sim}{\lambda} = \underset{\sim}{\lambda}^{(1)} \oplus \underset{\sim}{\lambda}^{(2)} \ldots \oplus \lambda^{(q)} \tag{1.30}$$

where

$$\sum_{j=1}^{k} d_{\pi(\nu_i(j))} \leq \sum_{j=1}^{k} \lambda^{(i)}_{\omega(j)} \leq \sum_{j=1}^{k} d_{\pi(\nu_i(m_i-j+2))} \;, \tag{1.31}$$

$k = 1,2,\ldots,m_i$, ω is any permutation of $1,2,\ldots,m_i$, and $i = 1,2,\ldots,q$.

This last example shows that determining a representation of ∂F in the form (1.8) can be a nontrivial exercise. A derivation is given in [2] .

2. A Continuation Procedure.

Let $F(\underset{\sim}{x})$ be a PCF. We introduce the strictly convex function of $\underset{\sim}{x}$

$$P(\underset{\sim}{x},\underset{\sim}{x}_0,\gamma) = \frac{1}{2}\|\underset{\sim}{x} - \underset{\sim}{x}_0\|^2 + \gamma F(\underset{\sim}{x}) \ . \tag{2.1}$$

As the minimum of (2.1) is unique for fixed $\underset{\sim}{x}_0$ and finite γ we can define unambiguously

$$\underset{\sim}{x}(\gamma) = \arg\min_{\underset{\sim}{x}} P \tag{2.2}$$

and varying γ gives a well defined trajectory. The connection between this trajectory and the problem of minimizing F is contained in the following theorem ([2], [5]).

<u>Theorem 2.1</u>. Let F be a PCF. Then there exists for each fixed $\underset{\sim}{x}_0$ a finite γ_0 such that $\underset{\sim}{x}(\gamma)$ minimizes F for all $\gamma \geq \gamma_0$.

This result suggests the use of continuation for minimizing F. We next show that if ∂F possesses a representation of the form (1.8) then the continuation trajectory can be computed easily. Note that if $\underset{\sim}{x}(\gamma)$ minimizes P then (1.8) gives a λ such that

$$0 = \underset{\sim}{x} - \underset{\sim}{x}_0 + \gamma\{\underset{\sim}{g} + V\underset{\sim}{\lambda}\} \ . \tag{2.3}$$

Differentiating this equation gives

$$0 = \frac{d\underset{\sim}{x}}{d\gamma} + \underset{\sim}{g} + V\underset{\sim}{\xi} \tag{2.4}$$

where

$$\underset{\sim}{\xi} = \frac{d}{d\gamma}(\gamma\underset{\sim}{\lambda}) \ . \tag{2.5}$$

Requiring that the local structure does not change in the variation implied by the differentiation process implies (compare the examples in section 1)

$$V^T \frac{d\underset{\sim}{x}}{d\gamma} = 0 \ , \tag{2.6}$$

and (2.4), (2.6) determines $\frac{d\underset{\sim}{x}}{d\gamma}$, $\underset{\sim}{\xi}$ uniquely provided the problem is non-degenerate. Note that this does not require A to have full rank. Further $\frac{d\underset{\sim}{x}}{d\gamma}$, $\underset{\sim}{\xi}$ are independent of γ so that they need be revised only at points at which $\underset{\sim}{g}$, V need to be revised. Thus they are piecewise constant on the continuation path. It is not difficult to extend this observation to show the finiteness of the continuation process.

However, equations (2.4), (2.6) are suggestive of the basic equations of a projected gradient algorithm [3] . To support this we note

(i) $\frac{d\underset{\sim}{x}}{d\gamma}$ is downhill for minimizing F . This follows because, by (1.8), (2.6) ,

$$\underset{\sim}{u}^T \frac{d\underset{\sim}{x}}{d\gamma} = \underset{\sim}{g}^T \frac{d\underset{\sim}{x}}{d\gamma} , \forall \underset{\sim}{u} \in \partial F(\underset{\sim}{x})$$

$$= - \left\|\frac{d\underset{\sim}{x}}{d\gamma}\right\|^2 < 0$$

using (2.4) . Also

(ii) $\underset{\sim}{g} \in \mathrm{span}(\kappa_i(V) , \; i = 1,2,\ldots,|\nu|)$, and $\underset{\sim}{\xi} \in \Lambda \Rightarrow 0 \in \partial F(\underset{\sim}{x})$ so that $\underset{\sim}{x}$ is optimal.

This suggests an algorithm in which $\frac{d\underset{\sim}{x}}{d\gamma}$ is generated and used to define a direction for minimizing F until it is necessary to update $(\underset{\sim}{g},V)$. This procedure is continued until $g \in \mathrm{span}(\kappa_i(V), \; i = 1,2,\ldots,|\nu|)$ when $\frac{d\underset{\sim}{x}}{d\gamma} = 0$. Further progress can only be made if $\underset{\sim}{\xi} \notin \Lambda$, and in this case we make changes to $(\underset{\sim}{g},V)$ using information about the infeasible components of $\underset{\sim}{\xi}$ in order to generate a nontrivial $\frac{d\underset{\sim}{x}}{d\gamma}$. The details are worked out for Examples (ii) (a) - (c) in [2] . The projected gradient form of the algorithm has the advantage that it uses only local information so it avoids any problem that could occur by the continuation process remembering about bad choices of $\underset{\sim}{x}_0$.

3. Treatment of Degeneracy.

If degeneracy occurs then V has more columns than expected and the computation of $\frac{d\underset{\sim}{x}}{d\gamma}$, $\underset{\sim}{\xi}$ is no longer straightforward when $\underset{\sim}{g} \in \text{span}(\kappa_i(V), i = 1,2,\ldots,|\nu|)$. In this case we seek $\underset{\sim}{t}$ such that

$$\chi(\underset{\sim}{t}) = \max_{i\in\nu} \underset{\sim}{f}_i^T \underset{\sim}{t} < 0 \tag{3.1}$$

as any such $\underset{\sim}{t}$ is downhill for minimizing F. If such a $\underset{\sim}{t}$ exists then

$$\min_{\underset{\sim}{t}} \chi(\underset{\sim}{t}) = -\infty \tag{3.2}$$

and we call the direction determined by $\underset{\sim}{t}$ a direction of recession for χ. The resolution of degeneracy comes down to computing a direction of recession for χ. One way of proceeding without departing from the general computational scheme is to partition $\nu = \nu_1 \cup \nu_2$ where ν_1 would determine on its own a nondegenerate representation for $\partial F(\underset{\sim}{x})$, and ν_2 contains the additional terms which complicate the situation. We now define

$$\chi_\varepsilon = \max\{\max_{\nu_1}(\underset{\sim}{f}_i^T \underset{\sim}{t}),\ \max_{\nu_2}(\underset{\sim}{f}_i^T \underset{\sim}{t} - \varepsilon_i)\} \tag{3.3}$$

and consider the problem of minimizing χ_ε. We note that the problem is locally just like minimizing F, and the key result is that for any finite $\varepsilon_i > 0$, $i \in \nu_2$,

(a) the problem of minimizing χ_ε is nondegenerate at 0,

(b) $\partial\chi_\varepsilon(0)$ is the representation of $\partial F(\underset{\sim}{x})$ restricted to ν_1, and

(c) $\underset{\sim}{t}$ is a direction of recession for χ if and only if it is a direction of recession for χ_ε.

Thus the basic algorithm applies to minimize χ_ε. Of course the problem might turn out subsequently to be degenerate but fewer $\underset{\sim}{f}_i$ are involved (to obtain a nontrivial $\frac{d\underset{\sim}{x}}{d\gamma}$ it is necessary to delete a column of V so the corresponding constraint in (2.6) must actually be relaxed) so the process can be applied recursively and terminates in a finite number of steps.

Example   For example (ii) (b)

$$\chi(\underset{\sim}{t}) = \underset{\sim}{g}^T\underset{\sim}{t} + \Sigma_\nu \psi(\underset{\sim}{a}_i^T\underset{\sim}{t}, u_i, \ell_i)$$

and

$$\chi_\varepsilon(\underset{\sim}{t}) = \underset{\sim}{g}^T\underset{\sim}{t} + \sum_{i\in\nu_1} \psi(\underset{\sim}{a}_i^T\underset{\sim}{t}, u_i, \ell_i) + \sum_{i\in\nu_2} \psi(a_i^T t + \varepsilon_i, u_i, \ell_i)$$

where $\varepsilon_i \neq 0$, $i \in \nu_2$. This shows clearly that the new minimization problem is considering very familiar quantities.

Remark.

This resolution of degeneracy is of very general applicability. For example, it applies to reduced gradient as well as projected gradient forms of these algorithms. An analogous procedure appropriate for the simplex algorithm of linear programming has been given recently by Perold [4] . Using explicit perturbations to find the direction of recession in the manner suggested above recovers the procedure suggested by Wolfe [6] .

4. Points Relating to Computation.

If we set

$$V = [Q_1 | Q_2] \begin{bmatrix} U \\ 0 \end{bmatrix} \tag{4.1}$$

where Q is orthogonal and U upper triangular, then

$$\frac{d\underset{\sim}{x}}{d\gamma} = -Q_2 Q_2^T \underset{\sim}{g}, \quad \underset{\sim}{\xi} = -U^{-1} Q_1^T \underset{\sim}{g} . \tag{4.2}$$

The computation is conveniently organized by starting with

$$M = [A^T | I_p | \underset{\sim}{g}_0] , \tag{4.3}$$

and

$$\underset{\sim}{w}^T = [\underset{\sim}{r}_0^T | \underset{\sim}{x}_0^T] , \tag{4.4}$$

where zero subscripts indicate initial values, and transforming so that at the current step we have

$$\hat{M} = \hat{Q}^T [A^T | I_p | \hat{\underset{\sim}{g}}] , \quad \hat{\underset{\sim}{w}}^T = [\hat{\underset{\sim}{r}}^T | \hat{\underset{\sim}{x}}^T] . \tag{4.5}$$

As V is a linear function of the columns of M it follows that $\hat{U}$ can be obtained as the same function of the columns of $\hat{M}$. In particular, if

$$\hat{Q}^T \hat{\underset{\sim}{g}} = \begin{bmatrix} \underset{\sim}{c}_1 \\ \underset{\sim}{c}_2 \end{bmatrix}$$

then

$$\underset{\sim}{\xi} = -U^{-1} \underset{\sim}{c}_1 , \quad \hat{Q}_2^T \frac{d\underset{\sim}{x}}{d\gamma} = -\underset{\sim}{c}_2 . \tag{4.6}$$

Let the rate of change of r_i be dr_i , $i = 1,2,\ldots,n$, and that of x_i be dx_i, $i = 1,2,\ldots,p$, then

$$dr_i = \underset{\sim}{a}_i^T \frac{d\underset{\sim}{x}}{d\gamma} = -\underset{\sim}{a}_i^T \hat{Q}_2 \underset{\sim}{c}_2 = -[0 | \underset{\sim}{c}_2^T] \kappa_i(\hat{M}) , \quad i = 1,2,\ldots,n \tag{4.7}$$

and

$$dx_i = -\rho_i(\hat{Q}_2) \underset{\sim}{c}_2 = -\rho_i(\hat{Q}) \begin{bmatrix} 0 \\ \underset{\sim}{c}_2 \end{bmatrix} = -[0 \mid \underset{\sim}{c}_2^T] \kappa_{n+i}(\hat{M}) , \quad i = 1,2,\ldots,p \tag{4.8}$$

so that if

$$\underset{\sim}{x}: = \underset{\sim}{x} + \varepsilon \frac{d\underset{\sim}{x}}{d\gamma} \tag{4.9}$$

then

$$\hat{\underset{\sim}{w}}^T: = \hat{\underset{\sim}{w}}^T + \varepsilon[d\underset{\sim}{r}^T|d\underset{\sim}{x}^T] \quad ,$$

$$= \hat{\underset{\sim}{w}}^T - \varepsilon[0|\underset{\sim}{c}_2^T]\hat{M} \quad . \tag{4.10}$$

It follows that there is no need to hold the matrix transformations at each step explicitly, and the modifications when columns are added to or deleted from V are applied directly to $\hat{M}$.

A final point is that the method used to implement the step in the direction defined by $\frac{d\underset{\sim}{x}}{d\gamma}$ needs to be considered carefully as it can crucially affect the overall efficiency of the algorithm. In many cases it is possible to avoid updating $\hat{M}$ if the update in V leads to a $\underset{\sim}{\xi}$ violating the constraints on Λ as the update can be reversed and further progress made (not necessarily in the same direction). In the case of example (ii) (b) this permits a very efficient line search procedure to be implemented. The importance of this point is stressed in [1] .

REFERENCES

[1] BLOOMFIELD, P. AND STEIGER, W.: Least absolute deviation curve fitting, SIAM J. Sci. Stat. Comp., 1, 290-301, (1981).

[2] CLARK, D.I. AND OSBORNE, M.R.: A descent algorithm for minimizing pölyhedral convex functions, to be published.

[3] GILL, P.E. AND MURRAY, W.: Linearly contained problems including linear and quadratic programming, in The State of the Art in Numerical Analysis (D. Jacobs, ed.), 313-363, Academic Press, (1977).

[4] PEROLD, A.F.: A degeneracy exploiting LU factorization for the simplex method, Math. Prog., 19, 239-254, (1980).

[5] ROCKAFELLAR, R.T.: Monotone operators and the proximal point algorithms, SIAM J.Control and Optimization, 14, 877-898, (1976).

[6] WOLFE, P.S.: A technique for resolving degeneracy in linear programming, SIAM J. Appl. Math., 11, 205-211, (1963).

NUMERICAL EXPERIMENTS WITH GLOBALLY CONVERGENT METHODS FOR SEMI-INFINITE PROGRAMMING PROBLEMS

G. A. Watson

Abstract. To date, the main emphasis in the development of numerical methods for solving semi-infinite programming problems has been on producing good locally convergent methods, and it seems that little attention has been given to the provision of globally convergent algorithms, except in some special cases. For many finite programming problems, good globally convergent methods based on the use of exact penalty functions are now available and it is the purpose of this paper to show that precisely analogous methods may be successfully used for a general class of semi-infinite programming problems.

1. Introduction

There are now available many good locally convergent methods for solving semi-infinite programming problems. An important class of such methods may be interpreted as being analogous to the well-known SOLVER method for the solution of finite programming problems, in which a quadratic programming problem is required to be solved at each iteration (see, for example, [4]) : this idea has been used in the semi-infinite case by, for example, Hettich and van Honstede [9] and van Honstede [10]. A well-established technique for the globalization of methods for finite problems involves using such quadratic subproblems to generate descent directions for an exact penalty function (for example [7], [12]), and it is the purpose of this paper to present details of some numerical experiments with an analogous approach for the semi-infinite case; the intention is to complement some previous theoretical work presented in [14]. We begin by introducing the problem to be solved, and some notation.

Let $X \subset R^N$ be a Cartesian product of closed intervals, and let $g : X \times R^n \to R$, with g twice continuously differentiable as a function of x for all $x \in X$. Let $f : R^n \to R$, and let both f and g be continuously differentiable functions of a, for any $a \in R^n$. (In practice, these assumptions may be weakened.)

Then the problem considered here may be stated as

$$(1.1)\qquad \begin{array}{l}\text{find } a \in R^n \text{ to minimise } f(a)\\ \text{subject to } g(x,a) \le 0 \text{ , } x \in X \text{ .}\end{array}$$

As is usual, we will in fact replace this rather difficult problem by the simpler one of finding a stationary point. Let $\phi_j(a)$ and $\psi_j(x,a)$ respectively denote the partial derivatives of f and g with respect to a_j, $j = 1,2,\ldots,n$.

Definition Let $a^* \in R^n$ be feasible in (1.1) and let there exist points x_i^* with $g(x_i^*,a^*) = 0$, $i = 1,2,\ldots,t$ and non-negative numbers λ_i^* , $i = 1,2,\ldots,t$, such that

$$(1.2)\qquad \phi_j(a^*) + \sum_{i=1}^{t} \lambda_i^* \psi_j(x_i^*,a^*) = 0 \text{ , } j = 1,2,\ldots,n \text{ .}$$

Then a^* is a stationary point of (1.1) .

The Fritz John first order necessary conditions for a^* to solve (1.1) correspond to (1.2) with $\phi_j(a^*)$ replaced by $\lambda_0^*\phi_j(a^*)$, where $\lambda_0^* \ge 0$ (for example, Clarke [1]). Any assumption implying that $\lambda_0^* \ne 0$ represents a constraint qualification which makes the condition (1.2) a necessary one for a^* to solve (1.1). Examples of problems in which this is violated are easy to construct; in case another example is of interest, here is one.

Example 1

$$X = [0,2]$$

$$f = \frac{1}{3} a_1^2 + \frac{1}{2} a_1 + a_2^2 - a_2$$

$$g = a_1^2 + 2a_1a_2x^2 - \sin x$$

For feasibility at $x = 0$, we must have $a_1 = 0$, so that $g = -\sin x$, with zero attained at $x = 0$. Clearly the unique solution is $(0,0.5)^T$, $f = -0.25$, and the Fritz John conditions are

$$\lambda_0^* \binom{0.5}{0} + \lambda_1^* \binom{0}{0} = \binom{0}{0}$$

showing that $\lambda_0^* = 0$.

2. A model algorithm

For given $a \in R^n$, let $E(a)$ denote the set of local maxima of $g(x,a)$ in X which have $g(x,a) \ge -\eta$, where $\eta > 0$ is a prescribed constant. Then we can define, at a , the following problem

$$(2.1)\qquad \begin{array}{l}\text{find } d \in R^n \text{ to minimize } d^T\phi(a) + \frac{1}{2}d^T H d\\ \text{subject to } g(x,a) + d^T\psi(x,a) \le 0 \text{ , } x \in E(a) \text{ ,}\end{array}$$

where ϕ and ψ are vectors in R^n with j^{th} component ϕ_j and ψ_j respectively, and H is a given symmetric $n \times n$ matrix. This problem may be interpreted as arising from (1.1) by making a suitable quadratic approximation to f, and by making linear approximations to g at the points of $E(a)$. Provided that $E(a)$ contains a finite number of points, (2.1) is a standard quadratic programming problem, which will be recognized as analogous to the subproblem which arises in traditional SOLVER - like methods for finite problems. In the basic method, H is the Hessian matrix of an appropriate Lagrangian function, and successive subproblems are generated by replacing a by $a + d$, where d solves (2.1). However, there is no guarantee that this procedure will converge, and we modify the method by exploiting the fact that a solution of (2.1) with H positive definite can be a descent direction for an exact penalty function. We will now define such a function, and begin by making precise its domain of definition.

Given $a \in R^n$, let $x \in X$ with components in positions $\sigma_1, \sigma_2, \ldots, \sigma_\ell$ (and in no others) taking values on the boundary of X. Let $\nabla_1 g$ denote the vector in R^ℓ whose elements are the partial derivatives of g with respect to the components of x in those positions (evaluated at x,a), let $\nabla_2 g$ denote the vector in $R^{N-\ell}$ whose elements are the partial derivatives of g with respect to the components of x in the remaining positions, and let $\nabla_2^2 g$ denote the corresponding $(N-\ell) \times (N-\ell)$ matrix of second partial derivatives of g. Then we introduce $B \subset R^n$ as the set of points a such that

(1) there is a finite number of points $x \in X$ such that $\nabla_2 g = 0$, $g \geq -\eta$,

(2) at each point of (1), $\nabla_2^2 g$ is nonsingular, and each component of $\nabla_1 g$ is non-zero.

Given $a \in B$, let $E(a) = \{x_1, x_2, \ldots, x_p\}$ (where $p = p(a)$). Then for any $\theta > 0$, we may define a function $P : B \to R$ by

$$P(a,\theta) = f(a) + \theta \sum_{i=1}^{p} [h_i(a)]_+ , \tag{2.2}$$

where

$$\begin{aligned} &\nabla_2 g(x_i, a) = 0 , \quad i = 1,2,\ldots,p , \\ &h_i(a) = g(x_i(a),a) , \quad i = 1,2,\ldots,p . \end{aligned} \tag{2.3}$$

The assumptions on B mean that the implicit function theorem may be applied to (2.3) to give the appropriate components of the points x_i, $i = 1.2,\ldots,p$, as differentiable functions of a; this ensures that P is a regular locally Lipschitz function. In addition, P fulfils the role of an exact penalty function for (1.1) : for large enough θ, any point which satisfies first order necessary conditions for a minimum of P is a stationary point of (1.1) [14]. The relationship of the subproblem (2.1) with P is given in the following theorem.

Theorem 2.1 [14] Let $a \in B$, and let d solve (2.1) with H positive definite. Then $d \neq 0$ is a descent direction for P at a provided that there is a

Lagrange multiplier vector λ associated with (2.1) which has no component larger than θ. On the other hand, if $d = 0$ solves (2.1), then a is a stationary point of (1.1).

There are many ways in which a suitable step length γ in the direction d may be determined. In the numerical results quoted later, γ is chosen as the largest of the sequence $\{1, \frac{1}{2}, \frac{1}{4}, \ldots\}$ satisfying

$$T(\gamma,a,\theta) \geq \sigma \ , \tag{2.4}$$

where

$$T(\gamma,a,\theta) = \frac{P(a+\gamma d,\theta) - P(a,\theta)}{\gamma[d^T\phi(a) + \theta \sum\limits_{\substack{x\in E(a)\\ g(x,a)=0}} [d^T\psi(x,a)]_+ + \theta \sum\limits_{\substack{x\in E(a)\\ g(x,a)>0}} d^T\psi(x,a)]} \tag{2.5}$$

and σ is a constant (independent of a) satisfying $0 < \sigma < 1$. The term multiplying γ in the denominator of T is just the directional derivative of P at a in the direction d, and the test (2.4) is a familiar one in optimization algorithms. A basic convergence result is the following.

Theorem 2.2 [14] Let $\{a^k\} \in B$ be a sequence of points generated by applying (2.1) (with $H = H^k$) and (2.4). Then, provided that

(i) there exists a solution d^k to (2.1) at each iteration having a Lagrange multiplier vector with no component larger than θ,

(ii) $\{a^k\}$ remains in a bounded region of B in which f and g have bounded second derivatives,

(iii) the sequence $\{d^k\}$ is bounded, and there exist positive numbers δ_1,δ_2 such that $\delta_1 \leq s^T H^k s \leq \delta_2$ for all $s \in R^n$, $\| s \| = 1$,

the limit points of $\{a^k\}$ are stationary points.

3. An implementation of the algorithm

Of great importance is the choice of H at each iteration, and in common with analogous algorithms for finite problems we look for H to be related to the Hessian matrix of an appropriate Lagrangian function, in this case

$$\mathcal{L}(a,\lambda) = f(a) + \sum_{i=1}^{p} \lambda_i h_i(a) \ ,$$

which may be defined for any $a \in B$. The Hessian matrix, if it exists, is then

$$G(a) = \nabla^2 f(a) + \sum_{i=1}^{p} \lambda_i \nabla^2 h_i(a) \tag{3.1}$$

and for the choice $H = G$, with $\lambda_i, i = 1,2,\ldots,p$, appropriate Lagrange multiplier estimates, it is possible to establish a precise connection between the method of the previous section and Newton's method applied to (1.2) ([14]; see also [9], [10]). We will therefore formally make the assumption (foreshadowed in the statement of

Theorem 2.2) that both f and g are twice-continuously differentiable functions of a, so that the matrix G can be calculated. Use of finite differences, or of quasi-Newton approximations are other possibilities, of course, although we will not consider these further. Values of $\lambda_i, i = 1,2,\ldots,p$, may be obtained from the current Lagrange multiplier vector for (2.1); however, successive values of p may differ far from a stationary point, and in the results quoted, λ was chosen at each iteration to minimize the least squares norm of the vector

$$\nabla \mathcal{L}(a,\lambda) = \phi(a) + \sum_{i=1}^{p} \lambda_i \psi(x_i,a) , \tag{3.2}$$

with any negative components replaced by zeros. The solution of this least squares problem gives a first order estimate of λ^*, and is a choice which does not inhibit the convergence rate of the method. (Non-uniqueness of λ was never encountered, although extra degrees of freedom can obviously be removed in standard ways.)

It is not necessarily appropriate to set H exactly equal to the matrix G given by (3.1) with this choice of λ. In the first place, G may not be positive definite. Secondly, far from a stationary point, the direction d generated by taking $H = G$, even if G is positive definite, may not be a particularly good one. In the program used here, some flexibility was incorporated into the choice of H by allowing a positive multiple μ of the unit matrix to be added to G. This can have the effect of giving some control over the size of d (provided d is not entirely defined by the constraints), as well as providing a possibly better direction of progress. A final check on the positive definiteness of H was made by using the procedure suggested by Gill and Murray in [5], which in the event that H is not positive definite, effectively adjusts H to have this property by the addition of sufficiently large numbers to the diagonal elements.

Different strategies for updating μ from iteration to iteration were tried. They were all somewhat arbitrary, except that they had the common aim of increasing μ if a smaller than unit step was taken in the previous iteration, and decreasing μ if a 'good' unit step was taken. The following set of rules may be regarded as typical; they resulted in satisfactory performance over the range of problems tested, and were the ones used to obtain the numerical results of the next section. Let $\gamma > 0.01$ and T be the values obtained after an iteration of the method with a particular value of μ, and let r denote the maximum modulus difference between corresponding components of the estimated Lagrange multiplier vector found using (3.2), and the Lagrange multiplier vector at the solution to (2.1) (both assumed unique). Then the rules were as follows:

if $\gamma < 0.125$ set $\mu = \mu * 64$
if $\gamma = 0.125$ or $\gamma = 0.25$ set $\mu = \mu * 16$
if $\gamma = 0.5$ set $\mu = \mu * 4$ (where * means multiplication)
if $\gamma = 1$ and $T > 0.9$ set $\mu = \mu/4$
if $\gamma = 1$ and $r < 0.1$ set $\mu = \mu/4$.

The resulting value of μ was bounded by requiring that

if $\mu < 1$ set $\mu = 1$

if $\mu > 256$ set $\mu = 256$.

In the event that no $\gamma > 0.01$ satisfied (2.4), it was assumed that the particular direction d was a bad one, and the iteration was abandoned. If the current value of μ was < 256, then μ was set to 256 and the iteration repeated; otherwise a step with no modification of G was tried. This escape route was found to be required only very rarely, and never resulted in failure of the method under normal circumstances.

The imposition of a lower bound of 1 on μ needs some clarification. The most useful values of μ appeared to be the larger ones, and it was convenient to facilitate rapid expansion when this became necessary. Small values of μ had little effect on d, and the simple choice $\mu = 0$ seemed generally more appropriate. Therefore the choice of H which was input to the procedure in [5] previously mentioned was as follows:

(3.3)
$$H = G \text{ , if } \mu = 1 \text{ ,}$$
$$H = G + \mu I \text{ , otherwise .}$$

Occasionally, it was found that the matrix H used in (2.1) was near enough to singularity to cause an 'unbounded' solution : in this event, the unit matrix was added to H. The initial value of μ was $\mu = 1$.

Finally, we give the rules used for the adjustment of the penalty parameter θ (again these rules are somewhat arbitrary, but typical). Note that the theory given in [14] assumes a fixed value; however, in common with analogous methods for finite problems, there are numerical advantages in allowing some flexibility (indeed this is essential if too small a fixed value is chosen). It is possible to recover rigorous convergence results by making appropriate restrictions to the way in which θ is allowed to change, for example by requiring that it be increased only a finite number of times.

The strategy used here was as follows. The initial value of θ was 1, with θ reset to the maximum value of the Lagrange multipliers at the solution to (2.1) on the first iteration. A larger maximum value occurring on a subsequent iteration resulted in an increase in θ to that value. On the other hand, if the current value of θ exceeded 4 times the current maximum Lagrange multiplier, then θ was reduced by a factor of 4 : the aim here was to ensure that too big a value of θ was not retained from a poor initial approximation, thereby slowing down convergence unreasonably.

4. Numerical results

The algorithm was coded in ALGOL, and run on the DEC-10 computer of the University of Dundee, which gives about 8 decimal places for single precision. The normal stopping criterion was a directional derivative (see (2.5)) greater than -0.0001 , and the parameter values used were

$$\sigma = 0.00001\ ,\ \eta = 0.5\ .$$

The maxima at each step were first determined approximately by a grid search, and then obtained accurately by Newton's method.

We begin by listing the problems on which the algorithm was tested. In all the examples quoted, the point a^* is the point reached by the algorithm when terminated, and f^* is the corresponding function value, except in Examples 7 and 9, when the appropriate stationary points and function values are known exactly.

Example 2

$$X = [0,1]$$

$$f = \frac{1}{3} a_1^2 + a_2^2 + \frac{1}{2} a_1$$

$$g = (1 - a_1^2 x^2)^2 - a_1 x^2 - a_2^2 + a_2$$

Starting point $(1,2)^T$; $a^* = (-0.750000\ ,\ -0.618034)^T$, $f^* = 0.194466$.

Example 3

$$X = [0,1]$$

$$f = a_1^2 + a_2^2 + a_3^2$$

$$g = a_1 + a_2\, e^{a_3 x} + e^{2x} - 2 \sin (4x)\ .$$

Starting point $(1,1,1)^T$; $a^* = (-0.213259\ ,\ -1.36212\ ,\ 1.85306)^T$, $f^* = 5.33469$.

Example 4

$$X = [0,1]$$

$$f = \sum_{i=1}^{n} a_i/i$$

$$g = \tan x - \sum_{i=1}^{n} a_i x^{i-1}$$

$n = 3$ Starting point $(0,0,0)^T$; $a^* = (0.089096\ ,\ 0.423052\ ,\ 1.045259)^T$, $f^* = 0.649042$.

$n = 6$ Starting point $(0,0,0,0,0,0)^T$; $a^* = (0.002084\ ,\ 0.963374\ ,\ 0.203505\ ,\ -0.026589\ ,\ 0.082262\ ,\ 0.332771)^T$, $f^* = 0.616876$.

n = 8 Starting point : a^* for n = 6 , to 3 decimal places, with zeros in the last 2 components; $a^* = (0.003024 , 0.953891 , 0.224076 , -0.018661 , 0.061488 , 0.305691 , -0.006903 , 0.034801)^T$, $f^* = 0.616607$.

This problem arises from the one sided L_1 approximation of tan x by a polynomial (see [13]) .

Example 5

$$X = [0,1]$$

$$f = \sum_{i=1}^{3} e^{a_i}$$

$$g = \frac{1}{1 + x^2} - a_1 - a_2 x - a_3 x^2$$

Starting point $(1,0.5,0)^T$; $a^* = (1.006593 , -0.126881 , -0.379712)^T$, $f^* = 4.301191$.

(See [2].)

Example 6

$$X = [0,1]$$

$$f = (a_1 - 2a_2 + 5a_2^2 - a_2^3 - 13)^2 + (a_1 - 14a_2 + a_2^2 + a_2^3 - 29)^2$$

$$g = a_1^2 + 2a_2 x^2 + e^{a_1+a_2} - e^x$$

Starting point $(1,2)^T$; $a^* = (0.719962 , -1.450488)^T$, $f^* = 97.1589$.

Example 7

$$X = [0,1] \times [0,1]$$

$$f = a_1^2 + a_2^2 + a_3^2$$

$$g = a_1(x + y^2 + 1) + a_2(xy - y^2) + a_3(xy + y^2 + y) + 1$$

Starting point $(2,-1,1)^T$; $a^* = (-1,0,0)^T$, $f^* = 1$.

Example 8

$$X = [0,1] \times [0,1]$$

$$f = a_1 + \frac{1}{2}a_2 + \frac{1}{2}a_3 + \frac{1}{2}a_4 + \frac{1}{4}a_5 + \frac{1}{3}a_6$$

$$g = e^{x^2+y^2} - (a_1 + a_2 x + a_3 y + a_4 x^2 + a_5 xy + a_6 y^2)$$

Starting point $(0,0,0,0,0,0)^T$; $a^* = (2.580159 , -4.109280 , -4.109281 , 4.247403 , 4.532651 , 4.247404)^T$, $f^* = 2.435644$.

(See [2])

Example 9

$$X = [-1,1] \times [-1,1]$$

$$f = -4a_1 - \frac{2}{3}(a_4 + a_6)$$

$$g = a_1 + a_2 x + a_3 y + a_4 x^2 + a_5 xy + a_6 y^2 - 3 - (x - y)^2 (x + y)^2$$

Starting point $(5,1,1,1,1,1)^T$; $a^* = (3,0,0,0,0,0)^T$, $f^* = -12$.
This example has an infinite number of points in $E(a^*)$, corresponding to the line segments of $y = \pm x$ within X (see [6]) .

Example 10 See Example 1 on page 132 of [10]. Note that this example has bounds $0 \le a_i \le 1$, $i = 1,2,3,$ on the parameters, which were dealt with by adding the constraints

$$- a_i \le d_i \le 1 - a_i \ , \ i = 1,2,3,$$

to the problem (2.1) at each iteration.
Starting point $(0,0,0)^T$; $a^* = (0,0,0.275266)^T$, $f^* = 0.275266$.

Example 11 As Example 10 above, but with no parameter bounds.
Starting point $(0,0,0)^T$; $a^* = (1.543011 , -2.101658 , 0.934532)^T$, $f^* = -4.386073$.

Example 12 See Example 2 on page 134 of [10].
Starting point $(0,0,0)^T$; $a^* = (0, 0.355317 , 0.111927)^T$, $f^* = 1.951089$.

Example 13 As Example 12 above, but with no parameter bounds.
Starting point $(0,0,0)^T$; $a^* = (-0.063763 , 0.388230 , 0.111354)^T$, $f^* = 1.950168$.

Table 1 summarises the performance of the algorithm on these test problems (including Example 1, for which the starting point $(1,2)^T$ was used). The column headed k gives the number of iterations, that headed P' gives the final value of the directional derivative, and t gives the final number of active points. The irregularities present in Examples 1 and 9 meant that numerical difficulties forced stopping before the proper criterion was satisfied; however in both cases good approximations were in fact obtained. In Example 4 with $n = 6$ and 8 , the stopping criterion was satisfied before the correct number of maxima (4 and 5 respectively) was established, although further reduction of f is only possible to 0.6161 and 0.6156 respectively.

A more detailed illustration of the progress of the algorithm is given in Table 2, where an iteration by iteration check on its performance on Example 2 is given. The column headed p gives the number of points in $E(a)$, t is the number of active constraints in (2.1), and λ_{max} is the maximum Lagrange multiplier.

Example #	n	k	t	P'	Comments
1	2	16	1	-1.1 -5	$\lambda_1^* = 2730$ ($\to \infty$) $f^* = -0.25001$
2	2	7	1	-3.4 -7	
3	3	14	1	-6.7 -6	
4	3	5	2	-5.3 -8	G^* singular
4	6	25	3	-5.9 -6	G^* singular
4	8	14	3	-9.6 -6	G^* singular
5	3	5	2	-7.5 -6	
6	2	8	1	-5.3 -6	
7	3	3	1	0.0	
8	6	19	4	-7.5 -7	
9	6	9	1	-3.5 -3	$\gamma \to 0$; calculated approximation is correct to 8 decimal places except for $a_4^* = a_6^* = -0.000028$; $f^* = -11.99996$.
10	3	3	1	-3.9 -9	
11	3	22	2	-2.9 -6	$\mu^* = 4$
12	3	4	1	-2.2 -10	
13	3	5	1	-6.9 -7	

Table 1

Summary for all problems

k	p	μ	t	λ_{max}	θ	P'	γ	P
1	0	0	0	-	1	-10.04	1	1.7539
2	2	0	1	2	2	- 4.00	1	0.8125
3	0	0	0	-	2	- 2.00	0.25	0.375
4	2	16	1	0	0.5	- 0.134	1	0.2490
5	2	4	1	0.48	0.5	- 0.055	1	0.1954
6	2	0	1	0.553	0.553	- 0.00097	1	0.194466
7	2	0	1	0.553	0.553	- 0.0000003		

Table 2

Details for Example 2

5. A modified subproblem

Recently, Fletcher [3] [4] has proposed for finite problems a modification of the usual quadratic programming subproblem. For our purposes (2.1) is modified to become

$$\text{(5.1)} \quad \text{find} \quad d \in R^n \text{ to minimise } d^\tau \phi(a) + \tfrac{1}{2} d^\tau H d + \theta \sum_{i=1}^{p} [g(x_i,a) + d^\tau \psi(x_i,a)]_+$$

$$\text{subject to} \quad ||d|| \leq \delta$$

where H is again positive definite, δ is a positive number, and the norm is (usually) the L_∞ norm. The motivation for this modification is basically twofold: firstly it eliminates the possibility that the method using (2.1) will break down because no feasible d exists, and secondly it forces boundedness of d . The idea of restricting d to a 'trust region' in which the approximations to the objective function and constraints are satisfactory is again a familiar one in optimization algorithms. A basic convergence result is possible for a method combining (5.1) with (2.4) (for details, see [14]) ; however unless θ is big enough, it is possible for limit points of the iteration to be infeasible.

When the plus terms in (5.1) are zero, and the constraint is inactive, then the method based on (5.1) becomes identical with that using (2.1). We would expect this to be the case close to a stationary point, and indeed would seek to work towards this so that the fast rate of convergence associated with the use of (2.1) can be achieved if possible. Real differences between the two methods are thus to be expected only in the rate of progress far from stationary points. Judicious choice of θ , and the strategy for adjusting δ , can lead to improvement on some of the results of Table 1 : for example, with (fixed) $\theta = 50$, Example 11 was solved in 18 iterations. However, difficulty was experienced in constructing general rules for adjusting θ and δ which resulted in satisfactory performance over the range of problems. The potentially most serious disadvantage in using (2.1) (no feasible solution) was never encountered in the examples tested, and so to a great extent the extra flexibility in using (5.1) over (2.1) gave no real advantage. It is possible that this is a shortcoming of the implementations which have so far been tried, and further experimentation may exploit more fully the potential of the subproblem (5.1).

6. Concluding remarks

The purpose of this paper is to demonstrate how the good global convergence properties of methods based on the use of an exact penalty function can carry over from finite constrained optimization problems to the semi-infinite case. In the numerical examples no attempt has therefore been made to choose particularly good starting points, although in practice such points would, if available, be used. In particular, for a linear problem (1.1), a good initial approximation can be obtained through the solution of a discretization of (1.1) (for example by linear programming); this may be more efficient than using the methods described here from a poor starting point. When G^* is positive definite, fast ultimate convergence is also a feature of the methods, although, as in the finite case, G^* may well have zero or negative eigenvalues. Thus it would seem that there is a choice in such cases between a guarantee of descent and a superlinear convergence rate. However, Powell [12] shows that in the finite case this is not so, if a suitable choice of positive definite approximation to G is eventually made. It may be that a similar result could be of use here, although this has not been investigated.

References

[1] CLARKE, F H: A new approach to Lagrange multipliers, Mathematics of Operations Research 1, 165-174 (1976).

[2] FAHLANDER, K: Computer programs for semi-infinite optimization, TRITA-NA-7312 (Royal Institute of Technology, Sweden), (1973).

[3] FLETCHER, R: Numerical experiments with an exact L_1 penalty function method, Nonlinear Programming 4, Proceedings of Madison Conference, 1980, eds. O L Mangasarian, R R Meyer, and S M Robinson (to appear).

[4] FLETCHER, R: Practical Methods of Optimization, Vol. II Constrained Optimization, John Wiley and Sons, Chichester (1981).

[5] GILL, P E AND W MURRAY: Newton-type methods for unconstrained and linearly constrained optimization, Math. Prog. 7, 311-350 (1974).

[6] GUSTAFSON, S-A AND K O KORTANEK: Numerical treatment of a class of semi-infinite programming problems, Nav. Res. Log. Quart. 20, 477-504 (1973).

[7] HAN, S P: A globally convergent method for nonlinear programming, J. of Opt. Th. and Appl. 22, 297-309 (1977).

[8] HETTICH, R: Ed. Semi-infinite Programming, Proceedings of a Workshop, Springer-Verlag, Berlin (1979).

[9] HETTICH, R AND W VAN HONSTEDE: On quadratically convergent methods for semi-infinite programming, in [8], 97-111 (1979).

[10] HONSTEDE, W VAN: An approximation method for semi-infinite problems, in [8], 126-136 (1979).

[11] POWELL, M J D: The convergence of variable metric methods for non-linearly constrained optimization calculations, in Nonlinear Programming 3, eds. O L Mangasarian, R R Meyer and S M Robinson, Academic Press, New York (1978).

[12] POWELL, M J D: A fast algorithm for nonlinearly constrained optimization calculations, in Numerical Analysis, Dundee 1977, ed. G A Watson, Springer-Verlag, Berlin (1978).

[13] ROLEFF, K: A stable multiple exchange algorithm for linear semi-infinite programming, in [8], 83-96 (1979).

[14] WATSON, G A: Globally convergent methods for semi-infinite programming, BIT 21, 362-373 (1981).

PART III

PROBLEM ANALYSIS AND MODELING

ON THE PARTIAL CONSTRUCTION OF THE SEMI-INFINITE BANZHAF POLYHEDRON

L. Papayanopoulos

The Banzhaf value (like the Shapley index) is a combinatorial vector function $c(w)$ of a vector w. The difficulty of finding optimal w^* satisfying the Court's one-man one-vote mandate is mitigated by the observation that $wc(w)\leq 1$ defines a bounded "semi-infinite" polyhedron. We describe some pertinent properties of $c(w)$ relative to the polyhedron and an algorithm of successive LP's which constructs a cone with vertex w^* containing the polyhedron.

1. Introduction

Reapportionment became a prominent subject in 1962 when the U.S. Supreme Court, in Baker vs Carr, enunciated the one-man one-vote principle. In essence, this decision mandated that equal numbers of people be given equal influence in their government. When applied to Congressional elections, for example, one-man one-vote requires that Smith's vote in Oregon be as effective as Brown's vote in New York at least in a theoretical sense. Since Baker vs Carr, one obvious way to implement this egalitarian notion has been through "districting." The partitioning of the polity into equipopulous geographic units produced a "symmetrical" situation whereby, in principle, every individual had the same opportunity to select a representative of his liking. In the 1964 decision of Reynolds vs Sims, the one-man one-vote concept was extended to state legislatures.

Political scientists recognize that the equal population approach to districting is a brute force solution for a sensitive problem. To require that maps be districted only according to numbers of people undermines other subtle and perhaps more vital criteria. Intentionally or not, the gerrymanderer may perform political miracles --legally, as long as he produces equal population districts.

In the light of the court decisions, attempts have been made to circumvent the districting process by a less simplistic interpretation of "one man,one vote." The most successful alternative to districting may well be weighted voting.

Under weighted voting district lines need not be redrawn. Given n existing political units as, for example, the towns of a county or the wards of a city, a representative is elected in each unit. Each constituency may be of different size but is represented by a single delegate. The term "weighted voting" derives from the fact that under this system some delegates have more votes than others. The influence of each representative on legislative decisions is a function of his voting weight. Factors such as eloquence experience, and reputation must necessarily be neglected in an a priori analysis of this kind.

The notion of weighted voting is older than Baker vs Carr. Until recent years, it had been employed in a straightforward manner. Without regard to voting power (defined later) a decision-making body would reapportion by assigning voting weights in proportion to the size of the constituencies. For example, each legislator might receive 1 vote for every 100 people in his constituency. In a 3-member legislature with constituencies of 106, 282, and 490 persons the respective votes would be 1, 3, 5. Under this approach, a legislator's voting weight was equated -- or, perhaps, confused -- with his ability to affect decisions.

Banzhaf (1965) differentiated between voting weight and voting power. In the example, 1, 3 and 5 votes do not result in proportional voting power. Under simple majority rule, the third member is, in fact, a dictator.

The court established that weighted voting satisfies "one man--one vote" if the voting power of each of the n legislators is proportional to the population that he represents. Because perfect proportionality may not always be attainable, in Dobish vs Board of Supervisors the court indicated that voting power and population must be in as close proportion as possible. We call this the Basic Principle and adopt it axiomatically. The New York State Supreme Court has ruled that the Basic Principle renders equal population districting and weighted voting equivalent in terms of one man-one vote. This paper outlines a method which apportions votes to satisfy the Basic Principle.

The problem presents a challenge of combinatorial formulation and solution. In a two-member legislature there are three possible "power" distributions: (.5,.5), (1,0), (0,1). Either both members have equal votes and equal power or one member has more votes than the other and holds all the power.

The 3-member case is more complex but simple enough to permit enumeration of all possible ways in which power can be distributed. It can be shown that ten possibilities exist: (1/3,1/3,1/3), (1,0,0), (0,1,0), (0,0,1), (.5,.5,0), (.5,0,.5), (0,.5,.5), (.6,.2,.2), (.2,.6,.2), (.2,.2,.6). Given a constituency vector, say, p=(.27,.27,.46) we need some criterion for deciding how close it is to each of the above power vectors. Although the final choice will depend on the criterion, clearly for all convex distance functions the underlined choices will dominate all others. These three vectors are neighbors; they are outernormals of a polyhedron in the neighborhood of a vertex in Euclidean n-space.

The number of possible power distributions grows very rapidly as the size of the legislature increases so that their complete enumeration becomes impossible. But by taking advantage of the problem's functional convexity the proposed algorithm leads to the neighborhood of the solution in a reasonable number of steps.

2. The Semi-Infinite Problem

The weighted voting problem is characterized by a set of n voters. The voting procedure is similar to that of stockholders whose Yeas and Nays are weighted according to their holdings. Let $w \in R^n_+$ be the vector of voting weights and X be a binary decision vector. When a voting outcome $Z = wX$ exceeds a given quota $\hat{z}$, the decision X is a winning combination -- else it is losing.

In a legislative setting, where representation is that of people, a combinatorial vector function $v = v(\hat{z},w)$ is defined to assess the voting power of the legislators. By its very nature, $v \in R^n_+$ is non-linear in w, thus giving rise to a question with political, legal, and mathematical ramifications.

Supposing that $p \in R^n_+$ is the vector of populations represented by the respective legislators, let $w^0 = ap$ be an assignment of votes for some proportionality constant $a>0$. If v and p are normalized s.t. their elements add up to unity, $v(\hat{z}^0,w^0)$ will generally not equal p. Judicially, this is a violation of the one man-one vote mandate. The established remedy, at least insofar as a large number of court cases involving New York State county legislatures is concerned, involves an optimization whereby w^* is found such that $v^* = v(\hat{z}^*,w^*) \simeq p$ "as closely as practicable".

In this paper we examine the problem structure underlying the Banzhaf (1965) definition of voting power which has prevailed in the New York cases [another well known power index is the Shapley value; see Shapley and Shubik (1954), Dubey and Shapley (1979)]. In this case $v = c(\hat{z};w)/\beta$ where c_i is the number of decision combinations (out of 2^n possible) in which the ith member is pivotal, i.e., essential in a marginally winning coalition, and $\beta = \Sigma c_i$ is a normalization factor. Table 1 shows the computation of c(8; 5, 3, 3, 2, 1). Winning coalitions are identified with boxed total vote in the right-hand-side column. 2^5 voting combinations are shown with Y's for Yea and spaces for Nays. Asterisks indicate "pivotal" votes. The number of asterisks in column i is c_i. Presently, $c=(11, 5, 5, 3, 1)$, $\beta=25$, and $v=(.44, .20, .20, .12, .04)$.

In practice, c may be computed through frequency functions [8]. The latter are defined as:

i	1	2	3	4	5		
w_i	5	3	3	2	1	$\hat{z}=7$	
						0	Total
					Y	1	Yea
				Y		2	Votes
				Y	Y	3	↓
			Y			3	
			Y		Y	4	
			Y	Y		5	
			Y	Y	Y	6	
		Y				3	
		Y			Y	4	
		Y		Y		5	
		Y		Y	Y	6	
		Y	Y			6	
		Y	Y		Y	7	
		Y*	Y*	Y*		8	
		Y*	Y*	Y*	Y	9	
	Y					5	
	Y				Y	6	Winning
	Y			Y		7	Combinations
	Y*			Y*	Y*	8	
	Y*		Y*			8	
	Y*		Y*		Y	9	
	Y*		Y*	Y		10	
	Y*		Y	Y	Y	11	
	Y*	Y*				8	
	Y*	Y*			Y	9	
	Y*	Y*		Y		10	
	Y*	Y		Y	Y	11	
	Y*	Y	Y			11	
	Y*	Y	Y		Y	12	
	Y	Y	Y	Y		13	
	Y	Y	Y	Y	Y	14	
c_i	11	5	5	3	1	$\beta=25$	
v_i	.44	.20	.20	.12	.04		

Table 1.

Computation of Banzhaf Combinations and
Voting Power for a Five-Member Weighted Voting Body

$$f_Z(\zeta)_i = |\{X|\ Z = wX = \zeta,\ X \text{ binary},\ X_i = 0\}|$$

in which case,

$$c_i = S\, f_Z(\zeta)_i = |\ \{X|\hat{z}-w_i < Z \leq \hat{z},\ \ X_i = 0\}|$$

where S is an operator summing a mass function over an interval (as implied by the above expression).

The components of c become quite large as n increases. In addition, the set of all such vectors is, for all practical purposes, nearly infinite, even for n not so large. By systematically varying w through an arbitrary set of a quarter of a million integer values, about 500 distinct c-vectors were obtained for the six-member problem. This was a near-complete search for c-vectors which were near-ordered. Taking permutations into account, the full set may well contain over 10,000 vectors. The growth of this set as a function of n is explosive.

3. Properties of the Semi-Infinite Polyhedron

It can be shown that the inner product g(w)=cw generates a polyhedral cone G. This fact has implications regarding c(w) which are of interest in the search for w*. For example, there is a single c-vector associated with the hyperplane of each "face" of the cone. It can also be said that faces, as well as edges of the cone are themselves convex cones. Faces are open sets whose boundaries constitute edges of the cone G and that unique c-vectors are associated with the edges of G. Even more significant, the c-vector of an edge is an average of the c-vectors of all adjoining faces.

Clearly, faces and edges are sets that can be defined in terms of linear functions $g_i(w)$. If g(w) is linear over some subdomain D_i, then it necessarily follows that c will be constant in that subdomain. The cone G has a finite number of edges and faces. Let m be the total number of them, and let them be numbered arbitrarily 1,2,...,m. If w_1 and w_2 are both in the subdomain of a face or edge i, then $c(w_1) = c(w_2)$, and conversely. Therefore, there must be a finite number of distinct c-vectors. We label them $c^1, c^2, \ldots, c^m$, associating c^i with face (or edge) i. We let $C = (c^1, \ldots, c^m)$ and use C to designate the set of these vectors as well as the m by n matrix which they form.

<u>Definition</u>: (a) Let $D_i = [w|\ c(w) = c^i]$, c^i in C, be the subset of E^n over which c(w) is constant and equal to c^i for i=1,...,m.

(b) Let $H_i = [(w,y)|y = wc^i,\ w \text{ in } D_i]$ be a face or edge of G.

(c) Let $H_i^E = [(w,y) | y = wc^i,\ w \text{ in } E^n]$ be the infinite extension of H_i.

(d) Let $D = (D_1,\dots,D_m)$ be the set of subdomains and $H = (H_1,\dots,H_m)$ and $H^E = (H_1^E,\dots,H_m^E)$ be the corresponding sets of faces and edges, and their infinite extensions.

D is a complete and exclusive partition of E_+^n, the domain of g. All faces and edges H_i of the cone are convex cones. All their subdomains D_i are also convex cones.

Definition: (i) The vector c^i is a primary c-vector if H_i is a face of G; otherwise it is secondary.

(ii) Assuming w is in D_i, let $R(\varepsilon)$ be the number of primary subdomains other than D_i that intersect an ε-neighborhood of w. Any two or more subdomains that intersect an ε-neighborhood of w are said to be adjacent. Then $\mathrm{Adj}(w) = \lim_{\varepsilon \to 0} R(\varepsilon)$ is called the degree of adjacency at w.

(iii) The dimension of a set A in E^n, denoted Dim(A), is the maximum number of linearly independent vectors in A.

If D_i is the subdomain of H_i, then $\mathrm{Dim}(D_i) = \mathrm{Dim}(H_i)$ because (a) H_i and D_i are not orthogonal and (b) every point w in D_i maps uniquely into a point (w,y) in H_i. H_i is a face of G if and only if $\mathrm{Dim}(H_i)=n$. H_i is an edge if $\mathrm{Dim}(H_i)<n$. For w^0 in $\mathrm{Int}(D_i)$, H_i^E is a unique supporting hyperplane of G at $(w^0,g(w^0))$ iff H_i is a face. Clearly, points on the boundaries of H_i can be supported by an infinite number of hyperplanes.

Definition: Let $x(k)$ in E^n, $k=0,1,\dots,2^n$, denote a vector whose components form the binary number k. Then $x(2^n-1-2^{j-1}-k)$ is the j-companion of x(k). x(k)is critical to member j (for some given w) if $z(k) = wx(k)$ is in j's critical zone $I_j(w) = (\hat{z}-w_j,\hat{z}]$ and $x_j(k)=0$. $O_j(w)$ is the set of all k such that z(k) is in $I_j(w)$.

The status of k with respect to j is defined by the following: k is internal if z(k) is in $(\hat{z}-w_j,\hat{z})$; left extremal if $\hat{z}(k) = \hat{z}-w_j$; right extremal, if $z(k)=\hat{z}$. We let the function Stat(k,j,w) denote the status of k with respect to j at point w.

Since w may vary, the notation z(k;w) and h(k;w) is used to show the dependence of these quantities on w. If c^1 and c^2 are adjacent, primary c-vectors, and w^0 is a point in the edge subdomain D_0 between D_1 and D_2, the next theorem establishes that $c(w^0)$ is the average of c^1 and c^2.

Let w^1 and w^2 be interior points of D_1 and D_2, respectively, connected by the line segment $w=w^1+b(w^2-w^1)$, where $0<b<1$. The linearity of the faces guarantees that only a single point on the line be in D_0 at some $b=b_0$.

Lemma 1: If $w^0 \varepsilon \mathrm{Int}(D)$, where D is the subdomain of a face H, then all critical decisions in the set $Q_i(w^0)$ are internal with respect to i, for every i.

Proof: Suppose that $z(k;w^0)$ is extremal for some k. Then $z(k;w)=\hat{z}$ defines an (n-1) - dimensional hyperplane. Since c(w) is distinct on either side of this hyperplane, there is no ε-neighborhood of w^0 in which a c-vector would be constant. Hence, a contradiction.

Lemma 2: Faces are open sets.

Lemma 3: The components of primary c-vectors are even numbers.

Proof: Let w be in the subdomain of a face. From Lemma 1 for every i, Q_i contains only decisions which are internal with respect to i. If k_1 is internal with respect to i, then so is its companion k_2. Since companion indexes are unique pairs,then $Q_i(w)$ must contain only even numbers of elements for every i=1,...,n and w in a face.

c(w) is never zero, except in the trivial case of w=0 or n=0. Given one or more members, at least one of whom has a positive voting weight, there will exist critical combinations for some of the members.

Theorem 1: Let w^1 and w^2 be points in D_1 and D_2 of adjacent faces with respective c-vectors c^1 and c^2. Also let w^0 be on the edge where only D_1 and D_2 intersect such that $w^0 = w^1 + b_0(w^2-w^1)$, for some $0<b_0<1$, and $c^0 = c(w^0)$. Then $c^0 = (1/2)(c^1+c^2)$.

Proof: It suffices to show that $c_i^0 = (c_i^1 + c_i^2)/2$ for an arbitarily chosen member i. If $D_1 \neq D_2$ then $c^1 \neq c^2$ and, hence, $Q_i(w^1) \neq Q_i(w^2)$. Let $Q_i(w^1) = A_i \cup B_i(w^1)$ and $Q_i(w^2) = A_i \cup B_i(w^2)$ where A_i is the intersection of the sets $Q_i(w^1)$ and $Q_i(w^2)$, $B_i(w^1)$ is the set of indexes in $Q_i(w^1)$ but not in $Q_i(w^2)$, and $B_i(w^2)$ those in the latter but not in the former.

Note that inclusion in the above sets is a linear function of w and that, by Lemma 1, all of the above sets must contain strictly internal elements. Thus if $k \varepsilon A_i$ is internal to Q_i at both w^1 and w^2 it must also be internal to it at every point between.

On the other hand, if k in $B_i(w^1)$ is internal to $Q_i(w^1)$ then $z(w^1)$ must be in the open interval $(\hat{z}(w^1)-w_i^1, \hat{z}(w^1))$. If it is external to $Q_i(w^2)$ then it cannot be in the closed interval $[\hat{z}(w^2)-w_i^2, \hat{z}(w^2)]$. Therefore, k must be right (or left) extremal while its companion k^1 must be left (right) extremal at w^0. Hence, although both k and k^1 are in $B_i(w^1)$ only one of these will be in $Q_i(w^0)$ and only half of the indexes in $B_i(w^1)$ will be in $Q_i(w^0)$. Similarly, only one half of the indexes in $B_i(w^2)$ will be in $Q_i(w^0)$. Thus we can write

$$c_i^0 = |Q_i(w^0)| = |A_i| + (1/2)|B_i(w^1)| + (1/2)|B_i(w^2)|$$

which proves the theorem, since

$$c_i^1 + c_i^2 = |Q_i(w^1)| + |Q_i(w^2)| = |A_i| + |B_i(w^1)| + |A_i| + |B_i(w^2)|.$$

Since primary c-vectors are distinct, non-zero, and contain even integer components (Lemma 3), the secondary c-vectors are also distinct and non-zero though not necessarily with even components. It can be shown that a given secondary c-vector contains either all odd or all even components, but not a mixture of odd and even, [Dubey and Shapley (1979), Papayanopoulos (1981)].

Let w^1 be a point in a subdomain D_j. We can express the subdomain as $D_j = \{w|\text{Stat}(k,i,w) = \text{Stat}(k,i,w^1) \text{ for every k and i}\}$. In other words, each member's critical combinations are the same for every point in D_j. The boundaries of D_j are determined by those combinations which are internal on the interior of D_j but extremal on its boundaries. The boundaries, of course, are subdomains of edges, the boundaries of which are similarly determined.

<u>Lemma 4</u>: Let (w,c(w)) be in an edge. Then Adj(w) is a power of 2.

<u>Proof</u>: An edge is characterized by extremal combinations. That is to say, if D_j is an edge then there exist $k_1,\dots k_t$, such that $z(k_i;w) = \hat{z}(w)$ for all w in D_j and $i=1,\dots,t$. The subdomain D_j is defined by the intersection of these hyperplanes and the adjacency, by the half-spaces which they create.

<u>Theorem 2</u>: Let (w^0,c^0) be in the edge occurring at the intersection of distinct faces $H_1,\dots, H_r$ with respective vectors $c^1,\dots, c^r$. If $\text{Adj}(w^0) = r$ then

$$c^0 = (c^1 + c^2 + \dots + c^r)/r.$$

<u>Proof</u>: By the last lemma, r must be a power of 2. If D_i is the subdomain of H_i then for each $i=1,\dots,r$ there exists $j\neq i$, $j=1,\dots,r$ that permits the pairing of points w^i and w^j in D_i and D_j such that the line segment between these points contains w^0. By Theorem 1, $c(w^0) = (c^i+c^j)/2$.

There can be found r/2 distinct pairs in this manner. Summing over all of these proves the theorem.

4. Optimization

Let C denote the matrix with rows of all the distinct c-vectors. If k is any positive constant and e is a vector of ones, $Cw \leq ke$ represents a truncation of the cone G. It defines a polyhedron G(k). Importantly, if w' is a point on G(k), and its Banzhaf vector is $c' = c(\hat{z},w')$ then $c'w'=k$. This implies that the problem size n and the relative quota q, where $\hat{z} = qwe$, determine the polyhedron G uniquely. We ignore the multiplicity produced by k because the resulting polyhedra differ in scale only. Since k is arbitrary we select k=1. Since G(k) is a section of G, the results of Section 3 remain in effect throughout.

The primary difficulty in finding w^* lies in the extremely large vertical dimension of C. Were C fully known, then $c^* = c(\hat{z}^*; w^*) \simeq p\beta^*$ would be one of its rows, found by inspection. Also, it would be in the optimal dual basis of the LP:(Max $pw|Cw \leq e$). Since C is not known, the latter property provides an iterative solution method. Interestingly, the procedure solves an LP with specific but unknown constraints. The constraints are added, one at a time, at each successive step.

The algorithm is a consequence of the polyhedral form and of the behavior of the Banzhaf vector on the polyhedron G. It relies on the LP

$$\text{Max } pw \mid C^i w \leq e,\ w \geq 0$$

where C^i is the constraint matrix in iteration i composed of the c-vectors obtained so far. C^i is a submatrix of the semi-infinite C and, consequently $C^i w \leq e$ defines a superset of G(1).

The simplicity of the algorithm is remarkable in view of the other complexities of this problem. The steps consist of the following:

(1) Let i=0. Obtain any starting submatrix C^0 with a bounded solution for the linear program. Clearly the choice of C^0 will have some effect on the ultimate number of iterations but even $C^0 = c(e)$ would suffice to initiate the algorithm.

(2) Solve the LP and let i=i+1. Denoting the primal solution by w^i, obtain the corresponding Banzhaf vector $c^i = c(w^i)$.

(3) If $c^i w^i = 1$ stop. Else, add c^i to C^{i-1} obtaining C^i and go to (2).

The ending value of $i=i^*$ is the number of iterations and w^* is the final primal solution representing an "optimal" vertex of G(1). This procedure constructs a portion of G(1) where the "objective" hyperplane $pw = pw^*$ supports the polyhedron. The distinct outernormals c associated with the polyhedral facets/edges/vertices in an ε-neighborhood of w^* are those most colinear with p, thus satisfying the one-man one-vote principle.

The algorithm was implemented in an interactive program. It works well for smaller ($7 \leq n \leq 11$) problems which are most troublesome and which require perfect optimality. The larger ones can usually be solved with $O(n)$ heuristics which produce adequate, near-optimal solutions.

In closing, we show an example of the algorithm. Suppose that $n=7$ and $p=(24, 24, 20, 20, 16, 16, 16)$. We choose a known c-vector (for p) in this test in order to have no doubt about the optimal solution. The algorithm must converge to a vertex w^* which adjoins the face with the known outernormal. The starting constraint matrix C^0, obtained by trial and error, is:

26	22	22	18	18	14	14
24	24	24	24	12	12	12
30	20	16	24	12	18	10
24	24	24	12	12	24	12
32	24	12	16	8	16	20
30	30	14	14	14	14	14
0	32	0	32	0	0	32
20	28	20	20	4	0	28

The initial LP produces $w^1 = (0, 0, 0, 12.76, 13.35, 19.36, 18.48)$ which in turn yields $c^1 = (0, 0, 0, 16, 16, 48, 16)$ and the solution is superoptimal, $c^1w^1 = 1.64319$. Iterating with a progressively expanding constraint matrix the algorithm reaches $w^{21} = (9.77, 8.83, 7.70, 6.76, 5.82, 5.26, 5.82)$ whose c-vector is $c^{21}=p$. The subsequent iteration ends the procedure ($c^{22}w^{22}=1$) having reached w^*.

Itera-tion	Non-integer vector w produced by linear program (rounded)							c-vector							cw
1	0	0	0	12.76	13.35	19.36	18.48	0	0	0	16	16	48	16	1.64319
2	2.37	11.20	2.50	11.33	8.43	11.33	8.70	0	24	0	24	24	24	24	1.22468
3	5.47	.66	9.64	10.75	3.42	10.75	16.07	12	0	20	20	12	20	36	1.30844
4	5.42	8.95	6.87	8.10	5.04	8.10	11.46	12	24	16	20	12	20	28	1.09566
⋮				⋮								⋮			
18	7.38	11.20	7.53	7.20	5.76	5.12	5.76	22	26	22	22	14	14	14	1.01148
19	11.53	7.05	5.76	8.97	5.76	5.12	5.76	30	14	14	30	14	14	14	1.028
20	10.75	8.33	6.25	8.49	5.76	5.12	5.76	23	21	19	23	17	17	17	1.00833
21	9.77	8.83	7.70	6.76	5.82	5.26	5.82	24	24	20	20	16	16	16	1.00677
22	9.80	9.80	4.90	9.80	4.90	4.90	4.90	26	26	12	26	12	12	12	1

Table 2. A 7-member problem solved in 22 LP iterations

Some initial and final iterations for this problem are shown in Table 2. A half-dozen diverse problems in the range $n \leq 11$ have behaved similarly. In no case did the number of iterations exceed 130 for the larger problems or 87 for the smaller ones. Because the amount of computation depends on the initial constraints and the algorithm remains to be put to the real reapportionment test, complexity can only be estimated empirically and tentatively as $O(n^2)$. Clearly, the complexity of the simplex computation (per iteration) is of no great concern as the dual problem is of rank $n \leq 11$. Noting that a legislature is normally reapportioned once every ten years, $O(n^2)$ is also relatively insignificant.

References

(1) BANZHAF, J.F., III: Weighted Voting Doesn't Work: A Mathematical Analysis. Rutgers Law Review 19, (1965).

(2) BAKER VS. CARR: 369 U.S. 186 (1962).

(3) DOBISH VS. BOARD OF SUPERVISORS OF WAYNE COUNTY: 279 NYS 2d 565 (1967).

(4) DUBEY, P. AND L.S. SHAPLEY: Mathematical Properties of the Banzhaf Power Index. Math. of Operations Research 4 (1979), 99-131.

(5) IANNUCCI VS. BOARD OF SUPERVISORS OF WASHINGTON COUNTY: 20 N.Y. 2d 244 (1967).

(6) IMRIE, R.W.: The Impact of the Weighted Vote on Representation in Municipal Governing Bodies of New York State. Annals of the N.Y. Academy of Sciences 219 (1973), 192-199.

(7) PAPAYANOPOULOS, L.: Computerized Weighted Voting Reapportionment AFIPS Proceedings 50 (1981), 623-629.

(8) PAPAYANOPOULOS, L.: Power Indices and Combinatorial Frequency Functions. Rutgers Graduate School of Management Report, 1981.

(9) PAPAYANOPOULOS, L.: Quantitative Principles Underlying Apportionment Methods. Annals of the N.Y. Academy of Sciences 219 (1973), 181-191.

(10) REYNOLDS VS. SIMS 377 U.S. 533 (1964).

(11) SHAPLEY, L.S. AND M. SHUBIK: A Method of Evaluating the Distribution of Power in a Committee System. Annals of Political Sciences Review 48, (1954), 787.

SEMI-INFINITE AND FUZZY SET PROGRAMMING

M. L. Parks, Jr.

A. L. Soyster

Abstract:

This paper is about a special class of semi-infinite linear programs and its relationship with fuzzy set programming. In particular, a certain type of convex fuzzy set program is shown to belong to a class of semi-infinite programs characterized by the fact that only one point exists where the constraint inequality is binding at a non-zero optimum. Solution strategies and examples are given both for the semi-infinite program and the fuzzy set program.

(1) Introduction

This paper is about a special class of semi-infinite linear programs and its relationship with fuzzy set programming. The semi-infinite program is specified as follows:

(P) $\sup c \cdot y$

subject to

$$\sum_{r=1}^{n} u_r(x) y_r \leq u_{n+1}(x) \qquad \text{for all } x \in S$$

$$y \geq 0$$

where S is a compact, convex set in Euclidean m space and u_i: $S \to R$ for $i=1,2,\ldots,n+1$.

The corresponding dual problem to problem (P) is:

(D) Determine the integer q, the subset $\{s_1, s_2, \ldots, s_q\} \in S$, and the real numbers $\{t_1, t_2, \ldots, t_q\}$ which solve

$$\inf \sum_{i=1}^{q} t_i \, u_{n+1}(s_i)$$

subject to

$$\sum_{i=1}^{q} t_i\, u_r\,(s_i) \geq c_r \qquad r=1,2,\ldots,n$$

$$t_i > 0$$

Let v(P) and v(D) be the optimal values of problem (P) and problem (D), respectively. It is well known that v(P) ≤ v(D). When v(P) < v(D), a duality gap is said to exist. Charnes, Cooper, and Kortanek (CCK) [2,3] proved one of the first duality theorems that established conditions ensuring that v(D) = v(P) in semi-infinite programming.

Gustafson [6] shows that if q, $(s_1, s_2, \ldots, s_q)$, and $(t_1, t_2, \ldots, t_q)$ is an optimal solution to problem (D) and y* is an optimal solution to problem (P), then the following complementary slackness condition holds,

$$\text{(CS)} \qquad t_i \left[\sum_{r=1}^{n} u_r\,(s_i) y_r^* - u_{n+1}\,(s_i) \right] = 0 \qquad i=1,2,\ldots,q$$

In this paper, we assume that $u_r(x)$, r=1,...,n are concave and $u_{n+1}(x)$ is convex, with at least one of the sets of functions being strictly concave or strictly convex. This class of programs is termed Concave/Convex (C/C) semi-infinite programs.

This class of semi-infinite programs is interesting for at least two reasons. In the first place, solving a C/C program is usually much easier than solving an arbitrary semi-infinite program. This is because, as shown in the sequel, there exists at most one point where the constraint inequality is binding for a non-zero optimal solution to (P). Secondly, an important class ot convex fuzzy set programs can be written precisely in the form ot a C/C semi-infinite program. Hence, the analysis is carried out through semi-infinite programming procedures.

In the next section, some important characteristics of the C/C semi-infinite programs are developed. These characteristics suggest some alternative solution techniques, which are described in the Appendix. A brief review of fuzzy set programming is then given and, in the last section, the relationship between convex fuzzy set programs and C/C semi-infinite programs is discussed.

(2) C/C Semi-Infinite Linear Programs

For mathematical programming problems which belong to the class of C/C semi-infinite linear programming problems, several theorems give rise to efficient solution techniques.

Theorem 1: If $u_1(x)$, $u_2(x),\ldots,$ $u_n(x)$ are strictly concave functions and u_{n+1} (x) is convex, then there exists at most one point $x^* \varepsilon S$ such that the constraint inequality is binding in a non-zero optimal solution to problem (P).

Proof: Suppose y^* is a non-zero optimal solution and assume there are two points, x_1 and x_2, where the constraints are binding. It then follows for $\lambda \varepsilon (0,1)$ that

$$(1) \quad \sum_{r=1}^{n} \lambda u_r(x_1)y_r^* + \sum_{r=1}^{n} (1-\lambda)u_r(x_2)y_r^* = u_{n+1}(x_1)+(1-\lambda)u_{n+1}(x_2).$$

Since each $u_r(x)$ is strictly concave for $x\varepsilon S$, then

$$(2) \quad \sum_{r=1}^{n} u_r\,[\lambda x_1 + (1-\lambda)x_2]\,y_r^* > \lambda \sum_{r=1}^{n} u_r(x_1)y_r^* + (1-\lambda)\sum_{r=1}^{n} u_r(x_2)y_r^*.$$

Furthermore, since $u_{n+1}(x)$ is convex, equations (1) and (2) imply

$$(3) \quad \sum_{r=1}^{n} u_r[\lambda x_1 + (1-\lambda)x_2]\,y_r^* > u_{n+1}\,[\lambda x_1 + (1-\lambda)x_2],$$

which is a contradiction to the feasibility of y^*. Q.E.D.

Let $T= x_0,x_1,\ldots,x_m$ be a discretization of the set S and denote by conv(T) the convex hull of T. A finite approximation to (P), subject to the grid T, is defined as the solution to the following linear program.

(PT) $\quad \max\ c\cdot y$

subject to

$$\sum_{r=1}^{n} u_r(x_j)y_r \le u_{n+1}(x_j) \qquad j=0,1,2,\ldots,m$$

$$y \geq 0$$

Theorem 2: Let $\hat{T} \subseteq T$ be the grid points for which the corresponding constraints are binding at some non-zero optimal solution y^* to problem (PT). Assume that $u_1(x)$, $u_2(x),\ldots,$ $u_n(x)$ are strictly concave functions and $u_{n+1}(x)$ is convex. Then $\bar{x}\ \varepsilon\ T-\hat{T}$ implies $\bar{x} \notin \mathrm{conv}(\hat{T})$.

Proof: Let $\bar{x}\ \varepsilon\ T-\hat{T}$ but suppose $\bar{x}\ \varepsilon\ \mathrm{conv}(\hat{T})$. Then there exist non-negative scalers λ_t such that

$$\bar{x} = \sum_{x_t \varepsilon \hat{T}} \lambda_t\, x_t$$

$$\sum_t \lambda_t = 1$$

Since the function $g(x,y')$ defined by

$$g(x,y') = \sum_{r=1}^{n} u_r(x)y_r' - u_{n+1}(x)$$

is concave in x for a fixed $y' \geq 0$, it follows that

$$g(\bar{x},y^*) \geq \sum_{x_t \epsilon \hat{T}} \lambda_t \; g(x_t, y^*) = 0$$

for all points $\bar{x} \in \text{conv}(\hat{T})$. However, since y^* is a feasible solution to (PT) and $\bar{x} \epsilon T-\hat{T}$, it follows that $g(\bar{x}, y^*) < 0$. Hence, a contradiction is obtained and $\bar{x} \notin \text{conv}(\hat{T})$. Q.E.D.

Theorem 2 implies that if y^* is a non-zero optimal solution to problem (PT), then for all $\bar{x}$ in the interior of the convex hull of $\hat{T}$ one has

$$(4) \qquad \sum_{r=1}^{n} u_r(\bar{x})y_r^* - u_{n+1}(\bar{x}) > 0$$

since $g(x,y^*)$ is strictly concave in x if at least one $y_r^* > 0$, $r=1,\ldots, n$. This implies that in order to obtain a better approximation to the optimal solution of problem (P), a new grid T' should be chosen which includes points from the interior of the convex hull of $\hat{T}$.

Several interesting results may be derived as corollaries to the above theorems if S is a subset of the real line.

<u>Corollary 1</u>. Let $S \subseteq R$, T a discretization of S, and assume that $u_1(x),\ldots,u_n(x)$ are strictly concave functions and $u_{n+1}(x)$ is convex. Then at most two constraints are binding in a non-zero optimal solution to problem (PT).

<u>Proof</u>. By Theorem 2, no grid points of T are in $\text{conv}(\hat{T})$ except those where the constraints are binding. If more than two points are in $\hat{T}$, then since $\text{conv}(\hat{T})$ is a subset of R, there exists a point $\bar{x} \in \hat{T}$ such that $\bar{x}$ is in the interior of $\text{conv}(\hat{T})$. For such an $\bar{x}$, equation (4) holds, which contradicts the fact that $\bar{x} \in \hat{T}$. Q.E.D.

If S is a subset of the real line and $x^* \epsilon S$ is the unique point where the constraint inequality is binding in a non-zero optimal solution to problem (P), another useful corollary results from Theorem 1, Theorem 2, and Corollary 1.

<u>Corollary 2</u>. Let $S \subseteq R$ and assume that $u_1(x),\ldots,u_n(x)$ are strictly concave functions and $u_{n+1}(x)$ is convex. Let $x^* \epsilon S$ be the point where the constraint inequality is binding for a non-zero optimal solution y^* to problem (P). If x^* is in the convex hull of the grid T and $x_1 \leq x_2$ are the two points where the constraints are binding in the finite approximation to (P) subject to T, then $x_1 \leq x^* \leq x_2$.

<u>Proof</u>. Follows immediately from the fact that the function $g(x,y^*)$ defined in the proof of Theorem 2 is concave with $g(x_1, y^*) = g(x_2, y^*)=0$

and $g(x^*, y^*) \geq 0$. Q.E.D.

If the conditions of Theorem 1 hold for problem (P), then there exists at most one point in which the corresponding constraint is binding. Assuming the appropriate regulatory conditions of the CCK Duality Theorem and the complementary slackness condition (CS), it then follows that problem (D) may be simplified to

(D1) $\inf \; t \, u_{n+1}(x)$

subject to

$t \, u_r(x) \geq c_r \qquad r=1,\ldots,n$

$x \in S, \; t \geq 0.$

As one may surmise, formulation (D1) is considerably simpler than (D). In the Appendix, this simplification of the dual for C/C semi-infinite programs is used as a basis for a specialized solution technique for problem (P).

(3) Fuzzy Set Programming

In 1965 Zadeh [16] introduced the concept of a fuzzy set. A fuzzy set is a class of objects which has a function that assigns a grade of membership to each object. If X is a set, then a fuzzy set A in X is a set of ordered pairs $(x, u_A(x))$ where x is in X and $u_A(x)$ is a membership function from X to a membership space M. Usually M consists of the unit interval [0, 1], but a more general definition is where M is a partially ordered set or a lattice (Kaufmann [8]). Some of the basic definitions involving fuzzy sets are straightforward extensions of the corresponding definitions with ordinary sets (see Zadeh [16]). For example,

(a) a fuzzy set is empty if and only if its membership function is identically zero,

(b) two fuzzy sets A and B are equal if and only if $u_A(x) = u_B(x)$ for all $x \in X$,

(c) a fuzzy set A is contained in a fuzzy set B, written $A \subseteq B$, if and only if $u_A(x) \leq u_B(x)$ for all $x \in X$.

Other basic definitions, e.g., union and intersection, are given in [7]. However, to define what is meant by a fuzzy set mathematical program in the context of this paper, we refer to Negoita [11], [12], [13], for two additional definitions.

Definition 1. Let A be a fuzzy set with membership function $u_A(z)$ in which A is a subset of Euclidean n space. Let s be a scalar. Then the fuzzy set sA is defined as the set $sA = \{sa \mid a \in A\}$ with the membership function u_{sA} being defined as

$$u_{sA}(z) = \begin{cases} u_A(y) & y = s^{-1}z \quad s \neq 0 \\ 0 & s = 0 \quad z \neq 0 \\ \sup_x u_A(x) & s = 0 \quad z = 0 \end{cases}$$

Definition 2. If A and B are fuzzy sets with membership functions $u_A(z)$ and $u_B(z)$ respectively, then the fuzzy set A+B is defined as the set $A+B = \{a + b \mid a \varepsilon A,\ b \varepsilon B\}$ with the membership function u_{A+B} defined as

$$u_{A+B}(z) = \sup_{a+b=x} [\min(u_A(a),\ u_B(b)]$$

The fuzzy programming problem of Negoita and Sularia [11] is defined as:

(F) $\sup c \cdot y$

subject to

$$y_1\underset{\sim}{K}_1 + y_2\underset{\sim}{K}_2 + \dots + y_n\underset{\sim}{K}_n \subseteq \underset{\sim}{K}$$

$$y_i \geq 0$$

where $\underset{\sim}{K}_i$ and $\underset{\sim}{K}$ are fuzzy sets with membership functions $u_{\underset{\sim}{K}_i}$ and $u_{\underset{\sim}{K}}$, respectively.

A geometric illustration of a fuzzy set program is illustrated in Figure 1. Consider program (F) and, for the sake of clarity, suppose that the fuzzy sets $\underset{\sim}{K}_i$ and $\underset{\sim}{K}$ are subsets of R. Typical membership functions are shown in Figure 1. To determine whether some vector $y = (y_1, \dots, y_n) \varepsilon R^n$ is feasible for program (F) requires that a certain membership function, say $v_y(z)$, satisfy the requirement that

$$v_y(z) \leq u_{\underset{\sim}{K}}(z) \qquad \text{for all } z \varepsilon R.$$

The membership function $v_y(\cdot)$ is the one, using Definitions 1 and 2, corresponding to the fuzzy set

$$y_1\underset{\sim}{K}_1 + y_2\underset{\sim}{K}_2 + \dots + y_n\underset{\sim}{K}_n.$$

However, the actual construction of $v_z(\cdot)$ is not a simple operation since it involves the convolution of the n membership functions $u_{\underset{\sim}{K}_i}(\cdot)$. Hence, the determination of whether some vector y is even a feasible solution is quite complicated. As such, the specification of an optimal solution to program (F) is a most difficult problem.

The inherent complexity of a general fuzzy set program (presumably) lead Negoita [12] to specify a class of fuzzy set programs with a more well-defined structure. This is the class of convex, fuzzy set programs.

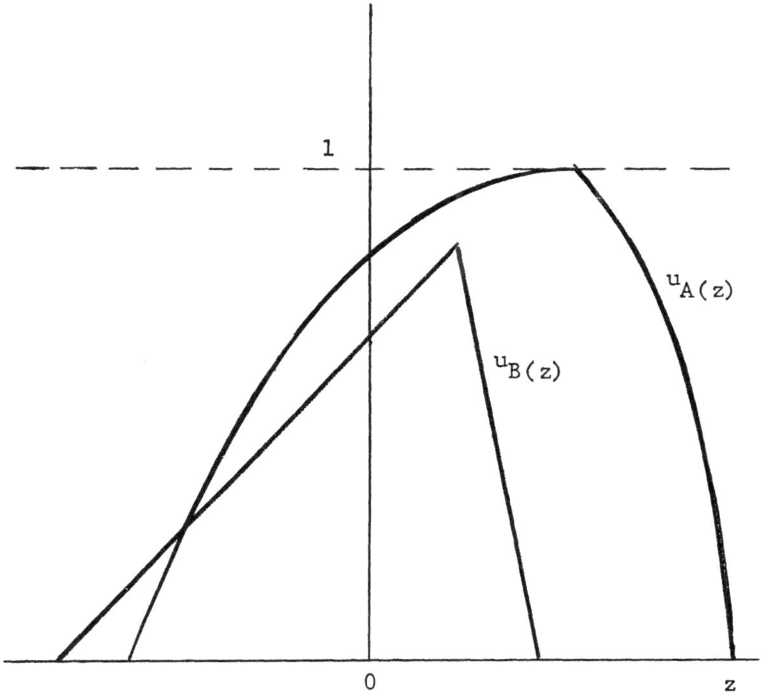

Fuzzy Sets Defined on R

Figure 1

To define what is meant by a convex fuzzy set, consider the following definition:

Definition 3. Let A be a fuzzy set. The alpha level set of A, denoted $S_\alpha(A)$, is

$$S_\alpha(A) = \{x \varepsilon X \mid u_A(x) \geq \alpha\}$$

Following Zadeh [16], a fuzzy set $A \subseteq X$ is convex if and only if its alpha level sets are convex for all $\alpha \varepsilon [0,1]$. Zadeh [16] also shows that a fuzzy set $A \subseteq X$ is convex if for $x_1 \varepsilon X$, $x_2 \varepsilon X$, and $\lambda \varepsilon (0,1)$, then

$$u_A [\lambda x_1 + (1 - \lambda) x_2] \geq \min [u_A(x_1), u_A(x_2)].$$

This means that the membership function for a convex fuzzy set is quasi-concave.

A convex, fuzzy set program is simply a fuzzy program in which the fuzzy sets are convex. However, using the properties of level sets, Negoita et. al. [12] show that a convex fuzzy set programming problem can be written in the form

(E) sup $c \cdot y$

subject to

$$y_1 S_\alpha(\underset{\sim}{K}_1) + y_2 S_\alpha(\underset{\sim}{K}_2) + \ldots + y_n S_\alpha(\underset{\sim}{K}_n) \subseteq S_\alpha(\underset{\sim}{K}) \text{ for all } \alpha \epsilon [0,1]$$

$$y_r \geq 0$$

where the inclusion $\subseteq$ refers to ordinary set inclusion.

The interesting and useful observation about program (E) is its identification with so-called set-inclusive programs. A set-inclusive program [15] is defined in the following manner;

(S) sup $c \cdot y$

subject to

$$y_1 K_1 + y_2 K_2 + \ldots + y_n K_n \subseteq K$$

$$y_r \geq 0$$

where K_r, r=1,..., n are compact convex sets in Euclidean m space. The binary operator + in problem (S) refers to the ordinary addition of sets. A vector $\bar{y} = (\bar{y}_1, \bar{y}_2, \ldots, \bar{y}_n)$ is feasible for (S) if and only if each component of $\bar{y}$ is non-negative and

$$y_1 a_1 + y_2 a_2 + \ldots + y_n a_n \epsilon K$$

for all a_r in K_r, r=1,2,...,n.

It is shown in [14] that the feasible region X, defined by

$$X = \{y \text{ in } R_+^n \mid y_1 K_1 + y_2 K_2 + \ldots + y_n K_n \subseteq K\}$$

is a convex set. Hence, problem (S) can be classified as a convex programming problem. Furthermore, it is shown in [14] that program (S) can be solved by way of a specially constructed linear program. Hence, solving programs of the type (S) is quite easy.

Now observe that for each fixed α, program (E) is a set-inclusive program. In fact, program (E) might well be designated as a semi-infinite, set-inclusive program. However, there is some ambiguity in the case in which some of the alpha (α) level sets are null. But, if one adopts the convention that addition of the null set to any ordinary set yields the null set, the constraints in program (E) are well defined for all $\alpha \epsilon$ [0,1].

In summary, a convex, fuzzy set program is a fuzzy set program of the form (F) in which all the fuzzy sets are themselves convex. If the convex fuzzy set program is expressed in terms of level sets, then one obtains the semi-infinite, set-inclusive program (E), a program in which each level set is an ordinary convex set. In this case, then, for each $\alpha \varepsilon [0,1]$, one obtains an ordinary set-inclusive program which, as indicated earlier, can be solved quite easily. Hence, one straightforward way, as suggested by Negoita et. al. [12], to obtain an approximate solution to program (E), is to select some grid of points $\{\alpha_1, \alpha_2, \ldots, \alpha_m\}$ on the interval [0,1] and solve the "finite", set-inclusive program, i.e., program (E) for $\alpha \in \{\alpha_1,\ldots,\alpha_m\}$, rather than $\alpha \in [0,1]$.

(4) Relationship With C/C Semi-Infinite Programs

In this section, we show that an important special class of convex, fuzzy set programs are equivalent to C/C semi-finite programs. Hence, the study and analysis of C/C semi-infinite programs have direct application to convex, fuzzy set programs. This special case of convex fuzzy sets is one in which the fuzzy sets are defined on R. Further, referring to program (E), assume for each i=1,..., n that the following condition, say C(I), applies to each of the n membership functions:

C(I) a) $u_{\tilde{K}_i}(z)$ is continuous on R

b) $u_{\tilde{K}_i}(z) = 0$ for $z \varepsilon (-\infty, a_i] \cup [b_i, \infty)$

c) $u_{\tilde{K}_i}(z)$ is strictly concave on $[a_i, b_i]$

Also, referring to the fuzzy set $\tilde{K}$ of program (E), assume that $u_{\tilde{K}}(z)$ satisfies either C(II) or C(III) below:

C(II) a) $u_{\tilde{K}}(z)$ is a continuous function

b) $u_{\tilde{K}}(z) = 1$ for $z \in (-\infty, a]$

c) $u_{\tilde{K}}(z) = 0$ for $z \in [c,\infty)$

d) $u_{\tilde{K}}(z)$ is convex for $z \in [a, c]$

C(III) a) $u_{\tilde{K}}(z)$ is a continuous function

b) $u_{\tilde{K}}(a) = 0$ for $z \in (-\infty, a] \cup [c,\infty)$

c) $u_{\tilde{K}}(z)$ is convex and increasing for $a \le z \le b$

d) $u_{\tilde{K}}(z)$ is convex and decreasing for $b \le z \le c$

Typical membership functions which satisfy C(I), C(II) and C(III) are illustrated in Figure 2. Note that any fuzzy set which satisfies C(I),

C(II) or C(III) will be convex since each alpha level set is convex. Also, since each membership function is continuous, it follows that each alpha level set is closed.

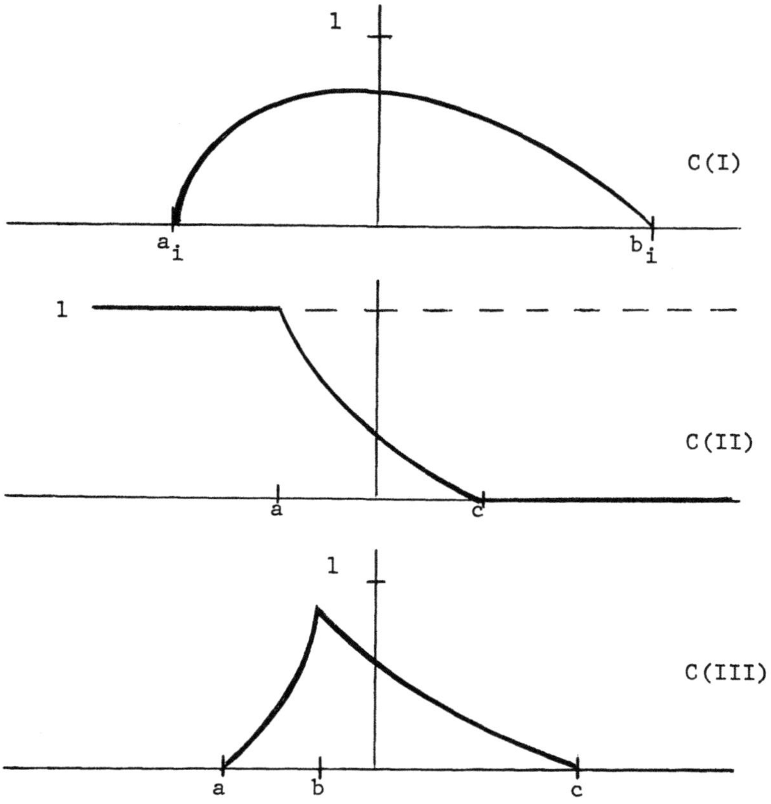

Figure 2

Three Classes of Fuzzy Sets on R

Next, for each $\alpha \in (0,1]$, define the extended 2n real-valued functions

$$U_r^R(\alpha) = \sup \{z \mid z \in S_\alpha(\underset{\sim}{K}_r)\}$$

$$U_r^L(\alpha) = \inf \{z \mid z \in S_\alpha(\underset{\sim}{K}_r)\}$$

where the superscripts R, L are to indicate the right (R) and left (L) points of the alpha level set. If for some $\alpha \in (0,1]$ the alpha level set is empty, then assign sup $= -\infty$ and inf $= \infty$. For $\alpha=0$ assign the values

$$U_r^L(0) = a_r \text{ and } U_r^R(0) = b_r.$$

Similarly, for $\alpha \in (0,1]$ define

$$U^R(\alpha) = \sup \{z \mid z \in S_\alpha(\underset{\sim}{K})\}$$

$$U^L(\alpha) = \inf \{z \mid z \in S_\alpha(\underset{\sim}{K})\}$$

At $\alpha = 0$, define $u^R(\cdot)$ and $u^L(\cdot)$ according to conditions C(II) and C(III) as follows:

$$C(II) : \quad U^L(0) = a \quad U^R(0) = c$$

$$C(III) : \quad U^L(0) = -\infty \; U^R(0) = c .$$

(Note under condition C(III), that $U^L(\alpha) = -\infty$ for all $\alpha \in [0,1]$).

Next, consider the semi-infinite program (U) below:

(U) $\quad \sup c \cdot y$

subject to

$$\sum_{r=1}^{n} U_r{}^R(\alpha) y_r \le U^R(\alpha) \qquad \text{for all } \alpha \in [0,1]$$

$$-\sum_{r=1}^{n} U_r{}^L(\alpha) y_r \le -U^L(\alpha)$$

$$y_r \ge 0.$$

The following theorem establishes an equivalence between the semi-infinite program (U) and the convex fuzzy set program (E).

Theorem 3: Assume the fuzzy sets, $\underset{\sim}{K}_r$, $r=1,2,\ldots,n$ and $\underset{\sim}{K}$ of program (E), satisfy C(I) and C(II) or C(III). Then, a vector $\bar{y}$ is feasible for program (U) if and only if it is feasible for program (E).

Proof: Follows directly from the fact that for each α,

$$\sum_{r=1}^{n} U_r{}^R(\alpha) \bar{y}_r \le U^R(\alpha)$$

$$-\sum_{r=1}^{n} U_r{}^L(\alpha) \bar{y}_r \le -U^L(\alpha)$$

is equivalent to

$$\bar{y}_1 S_{\underset{\sim}{K}_1}(\alpha) + \ldots + \bar{y}_r S_{\underset{\sim}{K}_n}(\alpha) \subseteq S_{\underset{\sim}{K}}(\alpha)$$

since each $S_{\underset{\sim}{K}_i}(\alpha)$ and $S_{\underset{\sim}{K}}(\alpha)$ is a closed interval. Q.E.D.

We now turn to the specific structure of program (U). What we show is that program (U) is a C/C semi-infinite program, i.e., C/C semi-infinite programs are equivalent to a special class of convex, fuzzy set programs.

Theorem 4: Assume the fuzzy sets $\tilde{K}_r$, r=1,2,...,n and $\tilde{K}$ of program (E) satisfy C(I) and C(II) or C(III). Then,

a) $U_r^R(\alpha)$ is strictly concave on $\alpha \in [0,1]$

b) $U_r^L(\alpha)$ is strictly convex on $\alpha \in [0,1]$

c) $U^R(\alpha)$ is convex on $\alpha \in [0,1]$

d) $U^L(\alpha)$ is concave on $\alpha \in [0,1]$

Proof: Follows from the fact that if some function f(x) is a convex strictly increasing function defined on a convex subset A of R, then the inverse is strictly concave. Conversely, if f(x) is a concave, strictly increasing function, then the inverse is strictly convex. See [14] for example.

Consider the following example of a convex, fuzzy set program:

$$\max y_1 + y_2$$

subject to

$$y_1 K_1 + y_2 K_2 \subseteq K$$

$$y_1 \geq 0, \; y_2 \geq 0$$

where K_1, K_2, and K are fuzzy sets whose membership functions are defined as follows,

$$U_{K_1}(x) = \begin{cases} -x^2 + 1/4 & -1/2 \leq x \leq 1/2 \\ 0 & \text{otherwise} \end{cases}$$

$$U_{K_2}(x) = \begin{cases} -x^2 + 1 & -1 \leq x \leq 1 \\ 0 & \text{otherwise} \\ 1 & x \leq 0 \end{cases}$$

$$U_K(x) = \begin{cases} -x + 1 & 0 \leq x \leq 1 \\ 0 & x \geq 1 \end{cases}$$

The alpha level sets of the fuzzy set K are of the form $(-\infty, t]$, where t is a number between zero and one (when $\alpha = 0$, then the alpha level set is equal to the real line for each fuzzy set K_1, K_2, and K). This implies that the function $u^L(\alpha)$ equals negative infinity for all $\alpha \in [0,1]$, and since each function $u_r^L(\alpha)$ is finite for all $\alpha \in [0,1]$, the second constraint inequality in problem (U) is always satisfied. Hence, the equivalent C/C semi-infinite linear programming problem is:

$$\max y_1 + y_2$$

subject to

$$U_1^R(\alpha) y_1 + U_2^R(\alpha) y_2 \leq U^R(\alpha) \quad \text{for all } \alpha \in [0,1]$$

$$y_1 \geq 0, \; y_2 \geq 0$$

where

$$U_1^R(\alpha) = \begin{cases} (1/4 - \alpha)^2 & 0 \leq \alpha \leq 1/4 \\ -\infty & 1/4 < \alpha \leq 1 \end{cases}$$

$$U_2^R(\alpha) = (1-\alpha)^{1/2} \qquad 0 \leq \alpha \leq 1$$

$$U^R(\alpha) = (1-\alpha) \qquad 0 \leq \alpha \leq 1$$

Note that $U_1^R(\alpha)$ and $U_2^R(\alpha)$ are strictly concave functions and $U^R(\alpha)$ is convex. Hence, the example problem belongs to the class of C/C semi-infinite linear programming problems. Using the strategy developed in the Appendix, the optimal solution to the example is $y_1^* = 2$ and $y_2^* = 0$.

APPENDIX

Two techniques for solving C/C semi-infinite linear programming problems are now given. The first algorithm uses the special properties of the C/C semi-infinite linear program when S is a subset of the real line. The second algorithm is more general and is applicable to higher dimensional sets S. Both solution techniques seek the point x^* in the set S at which the constraint inequality is binding for a non-zero optimal solution to problem (P). Once the point x^* is located, a grid T $T \subseteq S$, which contains x^*, may be assumed and problem (PT) solved.

It is assumed that problem (P) has finite value and no duality gaps exist. Such conditions hold if the assumptions of the CCK Duality Theorem are true. Other conditions ensuring that no duality gap exists may be found in Hettich [7].

First, consider the case in which the compact, convex set S of problem (P) is a subset of the real line. By Corollary 1, at most two constraints are binding in any non-zero optimal solution to problem (PT) determined by some discretization $T \subseteq S$. Furthermore, if x^* is the point in S where the constraint inequality is binding for a non-zero optimal solution y^* for (P), then Corollary 2 implies that x^* lies between the two points at which the constraints are binding. These two results suggest a modification to the Alternating Algorithm described in [6]. The Alternating Algorithm is based upon adding a point to a previous grid: the point added is the point corresponding to the most violated constraint.

The determination of this constraint typically requires the explicit solution of a convex sub-problem. However, for x values between the two binding constraints in (PT), the function $g(x, y') > 0$. Hence, the constraint associated with any grid point strictly between these two x values is violated by the current solution. In particular, the midpoint between the two x values is a logical choice for determining the next constraint to append to problem (PT). Hence, for the case in which S is one dimensional, one can determine a sequence of grid points by a simple interval bisection.

For the case in which S has dimension higher than one, the preceding strategy is not applicable. In this more general case, we proceed by first obtaining an optimal solution (t^*, x^*) to the dual problem (D1). Then, an appropriate grid T is selected in which $x^* \varepsilon T$ and all other points $x \varepsilon T$ are close to x^*. The point x^* specifies the unique binding constraint for a non-zero optimal solution to problem (P).

Of particular interest is the situation where the set S is defined by ordinary level sets, i.e., $\{S= x|g_i(x) \geq 0,\ i=1,\ldots,q\}$, with $g_i(x)$, $i=1,\ldots,q$ being real valued, concave functions. Suppose that in this case problem (D1) has an optimal solution with $t > 0$. Then, defining $s=1/t$, problem (D1) may be rewritten as

(D2) $\inf (1/s) u_{n+1}(x)$

subject to

$u_r(x) \geq sc_r \qquad r=1,\ldots,n$

$g_i(x) \geq 0 \qquad i=1,\ldots,q$

$s \geq 0$

Now, suppose that the variable s is considered as some fixed parameter. In particular, let w(s) denote the optimal value of problem (D2) for fixed $s > 0$. Clearly, if (s^*, x^*) is an optimal solution to (D2), then s^* is a global min of $w(\cdot)$ subject to $s > 0$. Furthermore, to characterize the nature of the function $w(\cdot)$, consider a closely related problem to (D2), namely,

(D3) $v(s)=\inf u_{n+1}(x)$

subject to

$u_r(x) \geq sc_r \qquad r=1,\ldots,n$

$g_i(x) \geq 0 \qquad i=1,\ldots,q$

It is well known that v(s) is a convex function. Furthermore, the ratio of a convex function divided by a positive linear function is quasi-convex (see [1]). Since $w(s) = v(s)/s$, it follows that w(s) is quasi-convex.

The foregoing remarks suggest a straightforward approach for solving the dual problem (D1). Since w(s) is quasi-convex, one simply performs a line search to find a minimizing $x^* > 0$. The minimizing t^* in problem (D1) is $t^*=1/s^*$. Then, as before, one selects an appropriate grid T in which $x^* \varepsilon T$ and all other points $x \varepsilon T$ are nearby x^*. Using this grid, one solves the approximating linear program (PT).

References

[1] AVRIEL, MORDECAI: Nonlinear Programming: Analysis and Methods. New Jersey: Prentice-Hall, 1976.

[2] CHARNES, A., W. W. COPPER, AND K. O. KORTANEK: Duality in Semi-Infinite Programs and Some Works of Haar and Caratheodory. Management Sci. 9 (1963), 209 - 228.

[3] CHARNES, A., W. W. COOPER, AND K. O. KORTANEK: On Representations of Semi-Infinite Programs Which Have No Duality Gaps. Management Sci. 12 (1965), 113 - 121.

[4] DUBOIS, D., AND H. PRADE: Fuzzy Sets and Systems: Theory and Applications. New York: Academic Press, 1980.

[5] GAINES, B. R., AND L. J. KOHOUT: The Fuzzy Decade: A Bibliography of Fuzzy Systems and Closely Related Topics. Int. J. Man-Machine Studies 9 (1977), 1 - 68.

[6] GUSTAFSON, S.-Å., AND K. O. KORTANEK: Numerical Treatment of a Class of Semi-Infinite Programming Problems. Naval Research Logistics Quarterly 20 (1973), 477 - 504.

[7] HETTICH, R. (ED.): Semi-Infinite Programming. Lecture Notes in Control and Information Sciences No. 15. Berlin-Heidelberg-New York: Springer-Verlag, 1979.

[8] KAUFMANN, A.: Introduction to the Theory of Fuzzy Subsets, Vol. I. New York: Academic Press, 1975.

[9] KICKERT, WALTER J. M.: Fuzzy Theories on Decision Making. Lieden: Martinus Nijhoff, 1978.

[10] NEGOITA, C. V., AND D. A. RALESCU: Applications of Fuzzy Sets to Systems Analysis. New York: John Wiley & Sons, 1975.

[11] NEGOITA, C. V. AND M. SULARIA: On Fuzzy Mathematical Programming and Tolerances in Planning. Institute of Management and Informatics - Bucharest: Economic Computation and Economic Cybernetics Studies and Research, 1976.

[12] NEGOITA, C. V., P. FLONDOR, AND M. SULARIA: On Fuzzy Environment in Optimization Problems. In: Proceedings of the Third International Congress of Cybernetics and Systems, Bucharest. London: Abacus Press, 1976.

[13] NEGOITA, C. V., S. MINOIU, AND E. STAN: On Considering Imprecision in Dynamic Linear Programming. Institute of Management and Informatics - Bucharest: Economic Computation and Economic Cybernetics Studies and Research, 1976.

[14] PARKS, M. L., JR.: Characterizations, Solution Techniques, and Some Applications of a Class of Semi-Infinite and Fuzzy Set Programming Problems. Ph.D. dissertation. Blacksburg: Virginia Polytechnic Institute and State University, 1981.

[15] SOYSTER, A. L.: Convex Programming with Set Inclusive Constraints and Applications to Inexact Linear Programming. Operations Research 21 (1973), 1154 - 1157.

[16] ZADEH, LOTFI A.: Fuzzy Sets. Information and Control 8 (1965), 338 - 353.

SEMI-INFINITE OPTIMIZATION IN ENGINEERING DESIGN

by

E. Polak

ABSTRACT.

It is shown that a large class of engineering design problems are expressible as nonlinear semi-infinite programming problems. Methods for the solution of these SIP problems are surveyed.

1. INTRODUCTION.

Many industries are facing rapid growth in the cost of raw materials and energy. More and more frequently, competitive product design is becoming an ever more time-consuming and difficult task because design complexity is increasing more rapidly than the number of design variables. All these factors contribute to increasing costs of design and manufacture. Computing power is the only important industrial resource which is declining in cost. Not surprisingly, the engineer is turning more and more frequently to the computer as a way of coping with his tasks.

The growing importance of computer-based tools for the analysis and design of devices, structures, machines and systems has resulted in the evolution of a relatively new interdisciplinary engineering specialty which is commonly referred to as computer-aided design (CAD). Evolution of the more sophisticated forms of CAD capability requires a team effort involving engineering design specialists, computer scientists, optimization experts, and numerical analysts. CAD techniques developed in one area of engineering are often of substantial relevance to other areas.

Both combinatorial and parametric optimization are used in CAD. The most commonly occuring parametric optimization problems in engineering design are usually expressed either as differentiable or as non-differentiable semi-infinite programming (SIP) problems. In this paper we shall illustrate by example how typical SIP problems arise in engineering design and survey some of the more promising methods for their solution.

2. FORMULATION OF ENGINEERING DESIGN PROBLEMS IN SIP FORM.

In this section we shall give four examples of engineering design problems which can be solved in SIP form: one in structural design, one in single-input single-output control system design, one in multi-input multi-output control system design, and one in electronic circuit design.

2.1. Seismic Resistant Design of Structures.

One of the conceptually simplest examples of SIP in engineering design is found in the design of braced frame buildings which are expected to withstand small earthquakes with no damage and large ones with repairable damage. A simple braced frame is shown in Fig. 1a, where the components of the vector design parameter x are the stiffnesses of the members indicated. The horizontal floors are assumed to be rigid and to concentrate the mass of the structure. The displacements of the three floors and "roof" form the components of the displacement vector y. This lumped parameter model Fig. 1b obeys a vector second order differential equation of the form:

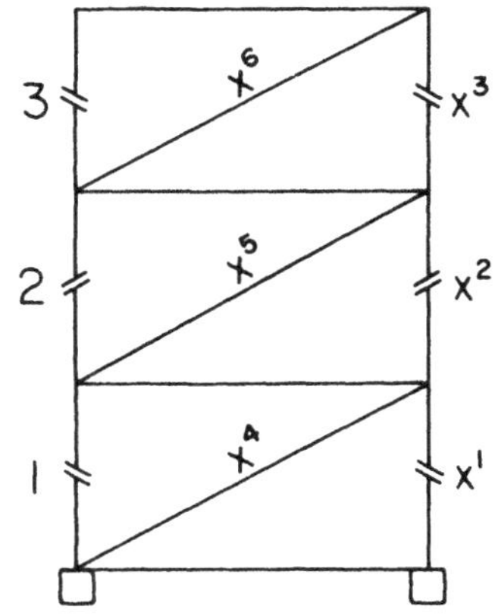

Fig. 1(a) BRACED FRAME

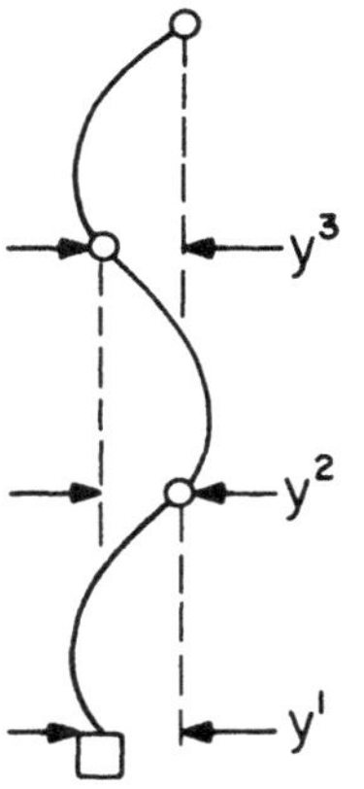

Fig. 1(b) LUMPED MODEL

$$M\ddot{y}(t,x)+D(\dot{y},y,x)\dot{y}(t,x)+K(\dot{y},y,x)y(t,x) = F(t) \tag{2.1}$$

where F(t) represents the seismic forces. For reasonable values of x, when F is small, i.e., it represents a small earthquake, (2.1) is a linear differential equation, but when F is large, the bending of steel introduces gross nonlinearities due to its hysteretic behavior. It is common to consider a whole family of excitatons $\{F_k\}$, both large and small in carrying out a design. A simple cost to minimize is the cross section of the frame members, while the constraints are introduced to limit the relative floor displacements over the entire duration of a sample earthquake. Thus, we obtain a SIP of the form

$$\min\{f(x) \mid |y^j(t,x,F)-y^{j-1}(t,x,F)| \le d^j(F), \tag{2.2}$$
$$j = 1,2,3,\ \forall F \in \{F_k\};\ x \ge L\}$$

In choosing a SIP algorithm for solving structural problems, one must bear in mind that the differential equations are highly nonlinear and quite difficult to integrate. For example, a simple four story frame may require several minutes of cpu time using a VAX 11/780 computer to simulate, while a quadratic programming search direction finding subprocedure requires only fractions of a second. Also, since simulation has to be carried out using standard computer codes, one finds that derivatives must be computed by finite differences, making it difficult to use second order algorithms. The algorithm in (33) was developed with these problems in mind. For further reading, see (3, 4, 21).

2.2 Design of SISO Control Systems.

Single-input single output (SISO) control systems are particularly easy to design by SIP techniques. Consider the block diagram of Fig. 2, which shows a plant, with transfer function P(s), and a compensator, with transfer function C(x,s), where x is a three components vector of design parameters to be chosen. We assume that this system satisfies the following set of equations:

$$\dddot{y}(t,x)+5\ddot{y}(t,x)+8\dot{y}(t,y)+6y(t,x) = u(t,x) \tag{2.3}$$

$$\dot{u}(t,x)+30u(t,x) = x^1\ddot{e}(t,x)+x^2\dot{e}(t,x)+x^3e(t,x) \tag{2.4}$$

$$e(t,x) = r(t)-y(t,x) \tag{2.5}$$

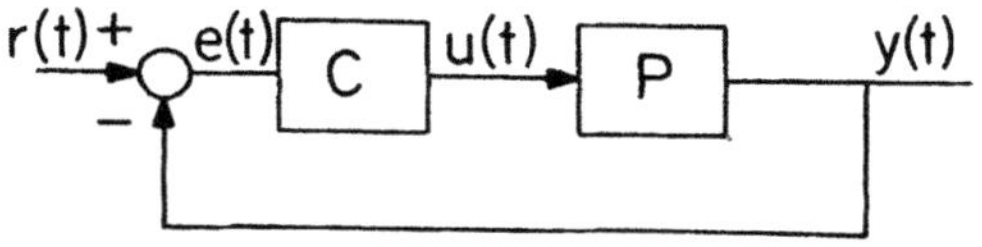

Fig. 2 SISO CONTROL SYSTEM

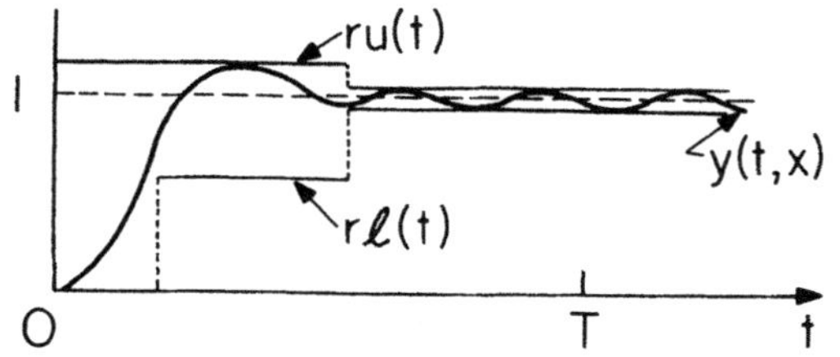

Fig. 3 STEP RESPONSE CONSTRAINTS

and hence that

$$P(s) = \frac{1}{(s^3+5s^2+8s+6)} \tag{2.6}$$

$$C(x,s) = \frac{x^1 s^2 + x^2 s + x^3}{s(s+30)} \tag{2.7}$$

In the simplest case, there are three sets of constraints on the design. First, there are positivity and boundedness constraints on x:

$$0 \le x \le b \tag{2.8}$$

Next, there is a time domain constraint on the step response of the closed loop system (i.e., on the response y resulting from r(t) = 1 for $t \ge 0$ and r(t) = 0 for $t<0$), as shown in Fig. 3. It has the form

$$rl(t) \le y(t,x) \le ru(t) \text{ for } all\ t \in [0,T] \tag{2.9}$$

where rl(t) and ru(t) are piece-wise constant functions.

Finally, see Fig. 4a, it may be required that the poles (eigenvalues) of the closed loop system lie in a parabolic region in the complex plane defined by $g(s) \le 0$, where

$$g(s) = z + aw^2 + c \tag{2.10}$$

with $s = z + iw$, and $a,c \ge 0$. This may be achieved by making use of a modified Nyquist stability criterion, as follows. We may write $P(s) = 1/d(s)$ and $C(x,s) = n(x,s)/m(s)$, where d, n and m are polynomials in s. Then the characteristic polynomial of the closed loop system is

$$X(x,s) = n(x,s) + d(s)m(s) \tag{2.11}$$

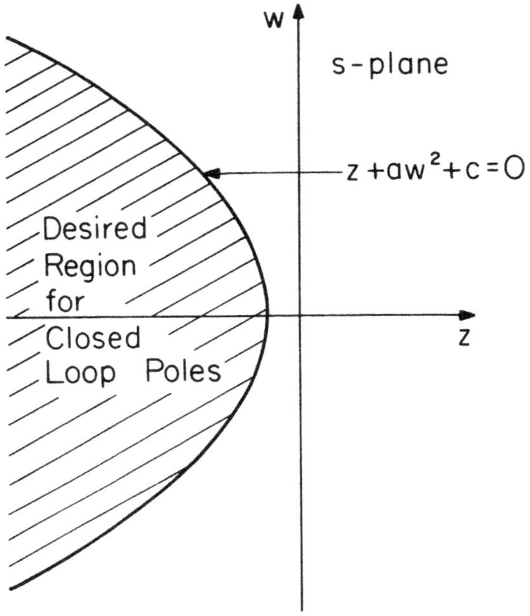

Fig. 4(a) EIGENVALUE CONSTRAINT IN s-PLANE

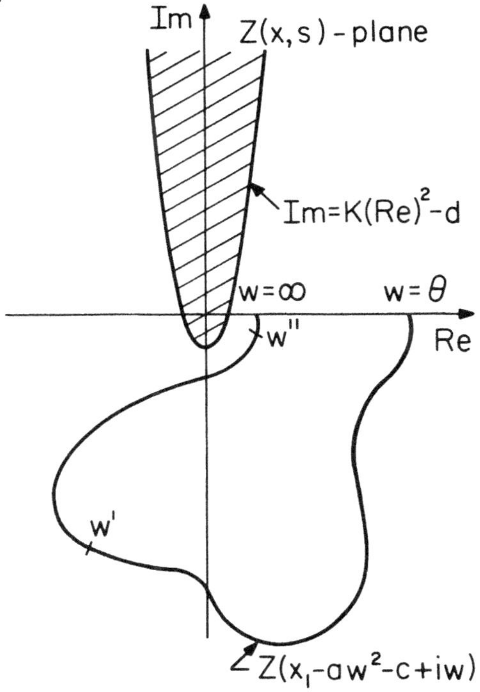

Fig. 4(b) CONSTRAINT IN Z(x,s) PLANE

and its zeros are the same as those of the normalized rational function

$$Z(x,s) = X(x,s)/(s+50)^5 \tag{2.12}$$

It follows from arguments as for the Nyquist stability criterion, that a sufficient condition for the zeros s* of Z(x,s) to satisfy $z^* + aw^{*2} + c \leq 0$ is that the following semi-infinite inequality hold (see Fig.4b):

$$d - K\mathrm{Re}(Z(x,-aw^2-c+iw))^2 + \mathrm{Im}(Z(x,-aw^2-c+iw)) \leq 0 \text{ for all } w \in [w',w''] \tag{2.13}$$

where d,K > 0, Re and Im denote the real and imaginary parts, respectively, of Z, and w', w" define a critical range of values in the complex plane. It is seen (see Fig. 4b) that (2.13) ensures that the image under $Z(x,)$ of the modified Nyquist locus given by (2.10) does not encircle the origin.

Finally, as a performance criterion, one could use

$$f(x) = \int_0^T u(t,x)^2 dt \tag{2.14}$$

for r(t) a unit step.

Problems such as these led to the development of the algorithms (5, 10, 22). For other examples of SISO control design via optimization, see (12, 15, 17, 34, 35).

2.3. Design of MIMO Control Systems.

We shall now consider an elementary example from the design of multiple-input multiple-output (MIMO) control systems in the Laplace transform domain, i.e., via a technique which replaces all the differential equations by their Laplace transforms. Referring to the block diagram in Laplace transform relations given in Fig. 5, the closed loop system is made up of blocks whose inputs and outputs are all m dimensional vector functions. The vector r(s) denotes the Laplace transform of the *closed loop system input* r(t), the m vector y(s) denotes the Laplace transform of the *closed loop system output* y(t), and the m vector u(s) denotes the Laplace transform of the *plant input* u(t). Finally, the m vector d(s) denotes the Laplace transform of the *output disturbance* d(t). The plant transfer function P(s) is an m x m matrix whose elements are proper rational functions in the complex variable s and one is required to design the m x m *compensator* transfer function matrix C(x,s) whose elements are proper rational functions in the complex variable s, with coefficients which depend on the n dimensional *design vector* x. Among other things, the closed loop system is required to be stable and to remain stable under plant perturbations and to be insensitive to the disturbance d(s). Both of these requirements lead to similar, nondifferentiable, semi-infinite inequality constraints and hence we will describe only the latter.

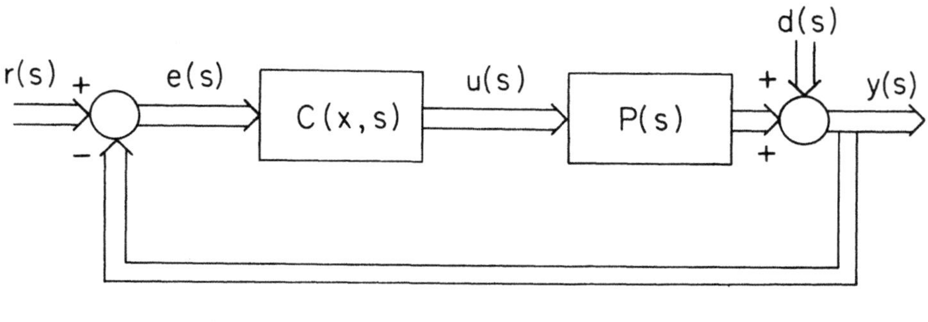

Fig. 5 MIMO CONTROL SYSTEM

For the purpose of expressing insensitivity to the disturbance d(s), we set r(s) ≡ 0, which leads to the equation

$$y(s) = [I+P(s)C(x,s)]d(s) = Q(x,s)d(s) \tag{2.15}$$

$$u(s) = -C(x,s)Q(x,s)d(s) = R(x,s)d(s) \tag{2.16}$$

Let q(x,w) denote the largest singular value of Q(x,iw) and s(x,w) denote the largest singular value of R(x,iw), with w real. The variable w denotes frequency; the matrix Q(x,iw) is complex valued. Since the largest singular values are matrix norms, to make the response y of the system small for a large class of disturbances, without unduly saturating the system as a result of u becoming too large, control system designers strive to keep both q and r small over appropriate frequency ranges. This leads to the following partial formulation of the MIMO control system design problem in SIP form

$$minimize\ f(x) = \{\max q(x,w) \mid w \in [w',w'']\} \tag{2.17}$$

subject to:

$$s(x,w) \le b(w) \text{ for } all\ w \in [w',w''] \tag{2.18}$$

$$c \le x \le d \tag{2.19}$$

where b(w) is a continuous function of the frequency w.

In addition, there are constraints expressing *decoupling* i.e., the requirement that when only a single component of the input vector is a nonzero function, only the corresponding component of the output vector is nonzero, as well as other constraints on time domain responses, all of which are semi-infinite in form. We note that the singular values q and s are non-differentiable and hence that the SIP problem corresponding to MIMO control system design is considerably more difficult than the SISO problem. For algorithms which solve problems of the for (2.17) -(2.19), see (9,27). For other examples and a discussion of the use of singular values in control system design, see (8, 13, 26, 32).

2.4. Electronic Circuit Design.

A well known SIP problem in electronic circuit design is the so called *design centering, tolerancing and tuning* problem. Its formulation is developed in three stages, as follows. First, the responses (see Fig. 6) of the circuit to given inputs must satisfy semi-infinite constraints of the form

$$a(t) \le y(t,x) \le b(t) \text{ for } all\ t \in [t',t''] \tag{2.20}$$

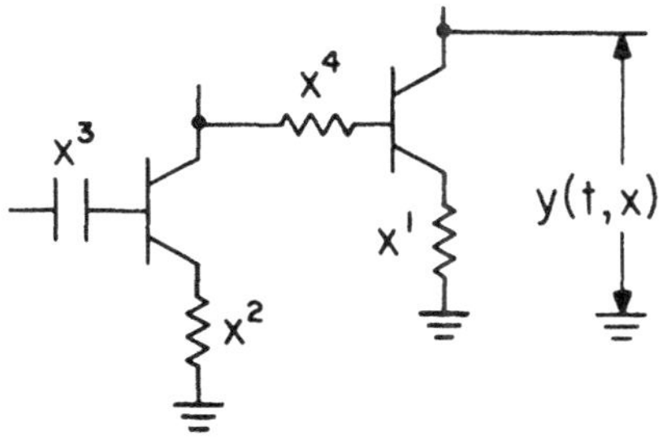

Fig. 6

where x is an n dimensional design vector. Next, due to production errors, when the circuit is built, the actual value of the design parameter will not be the *nominal value* x, but x + g(e), where e is a *production error parameter*, usually of much smaller dimension than x. To obtain 100% yield, the design engineer must therefore require that

$$a(t) \leq y(t,x+g(e)) \leq b(t) \text{ for } all\ t \in [t',t''] \quad \text{for } all\ e \in E \tag{2.21}$$

where E is the production engineer's *tolerance* set. Now, it is not uncommon for the inequalities of the form of (2.21) to define an extremely small, or even empty feasible set and hence engineers have to resort to post manufacture *tuning*, i.e., post manufacture correction of the product. This leads to the introduction of a repair (tuning) parameter r into the picture, so that (2.21) becomes replaced by

$$a(t) \leq y(t,x+g(e)+h(r)) \leq b(t) \text{for } all\ t \in [t',t''] \quad \text{for } all\ e \in E, \text{ for } some\ r \in R \tag{2.22}$$

where R defines the allowable range of the repair parameter. Clearly, (2.22) is an extremely intractable kind of semi-infinite inequality, particularly, since a realistic formulation must replace the single y in (2.22) with the max over all such functions of interest. A certain amount of simplification can be obtained by replacing (2.22) by the following, slightly stricter inequality:

$$a(t) \leq \max_{e \in E} \min_{r \in R} \max_{k \in K} y^k(t,x+g(e)+h(r)) \leq b(t) \quad \text{for } all\ t \in [t',t''] \tag{2.23}$$

where $K = \{1,2,...,k'\}$ is a finite set of integers.

Of course, in addition, to the constraint of the form (2.23), the electronic circuit design problem will also involve a number of others that are much more benign. Thus, the electronic circuit designer sees his problem as that of choosing a design center x so that the set x + g(E), resulting from tolerances which must be allowed in production, is as much as possible in the feasible set specified for x, and of making sure that any part of x + g(E), which is outside of the feasible set, can be brought back into it by post-manufacture tuning.

For further reading, see (6, 7, 16, 22, 29).

3. SIP ALGORITHMS FOR ENGINEERING DESIGN.

As we have seen in the previous section, SIP problems in engineering design are of the form

$$\min\{f(x) \mid g^i(x) \leq 0\ \forall i \in I;\ h^j(x,p) \leq 0\ \forall j \in J,\ \forall p \in P; \quad \max_{e \in E} \min_{r \in R} \max_{t \in T} \max_{k \in K} y^k(x,e,r,t) \leq 0\} \tag{3.1}$$

where f, g^i, h^j, and y^k are, usually, real valued, continuously differentiable functions; P, E, R are compact multidimensional sets, T is a compact interval, and K is a finite set of indices. When the functions in (3.1) are not continuously differentiable, they are usually semi-smooth (18) or, at least, locally Lipschitz.

We shall now describe two algorithms which we have found to be very reliable in engineering design. The first is due to Gonzaga, Mayne, Polak and Trahan (9,10) and it solves problems of the form (3.1) without the max min max max term, when all functions are continuously differentiable, i.e., it solves problems of the form:

$$\min\{f(x) \mid g^i(x) \leq 0 \ \forall i \in I; \quad h^j(x,p_j) \leq 0 \ \forall p_j \in P_j, \ \forall j \in J\} \tag{3.2}$$

The algorithm in (10) is a refinement of the algorithm in (9). In turn, it underwent some refinement, as described in (5), the most significant of which is the introduction of weights w which can be used to improve the conditioning of the problem. For simplicity of exposition, we may as well consider the case of (3.2), where the "simple" inequalities specified by the g^i are not present and there is only one semi-infinite inequality, i.e., J = {1}, so that the index j can be dropped. For this case, we define, with $e \geq 0$, $t \geq 0$, $w \geq 0$,

$$M(x) = \max\{h(x,p) \mid p \in P\} \tag{3.3}$$

$$M(x)_+ = \max\{M(x), 0\} \tag{3.4}$$

$$P_e(x) = \{p \in P \mid h(x,P) \geq M(x)_+ - e, \text{ and } p \textit{ is a local maximizer of } h(x,\cdot) \textit{ in } P\} \tag{3.5}$$

$$W_e(x) = \min\{tu^f M(x)_+ + (1/2)\| u^f \nabla f(x) + \sum_{p \in P_e(x)} u^p \nabla h(x,p) \|^2 \mid w^f u^f + \sum_{p \in P_e(x)} w^p u^p = 1, u^p \geq 0\} \tag{3.6}$$

and

$$d_e(x) = -[u^f \nabla f(x) + \sum_{p \in P_e(x)} u^p \nabla h(x,p)] \tag{3.7}$$

where u^f, u^p solve (3.6). Finally, with 0 < c < 1, and q > 0, we define

$$E = \{0, 1, c, c^2, c^3, \ldots\} \tag{3.8}$$

and

$$e(x) = \max\{e \in E \mid W_e(x) \geq eq\} \tag{3.9}$$

We note that the parameter e in (3.5) controls the number of local maximizers that will be used in the computation of the search direction $d_e(x)$. The parameters w^f, w^p in (3.6) are used to control the angle between the search direction $d_e(x)$ and the corresponding gradients: when w^p is increased, the angle between $-d_e(x)$ and $\nabla h(x,p)$ is decreased. The parameter t controls the phase I - phase II aspect of the algorithm: when t is large, the algorithm places greater emphasis on achieving feasibility than when t is small. Finally, the parameter q is used to control the value of the parameter e that will be used in the computation of the search direction $d_e(x)$: the smaller q, the larger will be e(x). In practice, this rather large number of parameters turns out to be rather easy to adjust, provided the computations are carried out in an interactive environment.

Finally, introducing two parameter $a, b \in (0,1)$ for the Armijo step size rule, we are ready to state the algorithm which will be recognized as a phase I - phase II method of feasible directions, see (29).

Algorithm 1:

Parameters: a,b,c $\in$ (0,1), q > 0, K > 0.

Data: x_0.

Step 0: Set i = 0.

Step 1: Compute $d_{e(x_i)}(x_i)$.

Step 2: If $M(x_i)>0$, compute the largest $s \in \{K, bK, b^2K, ...\}$ such that

$$M(x_i + sd_{e(x_i)}(x_i)) - M(x_i)) \le -sa W_{e(x_i)}(x_i). \tag{3.10}$$

Else, compute the largest $s \in \{K, bK, b^2K, ...\}$ such that

$$M(x_i + sd_{e(x_i)}(x_i)) \le 0 \tag{3.11}$$

and

$$f(x_i + sd_{e(x_i)}(x_i)) - f(x_i) \le -sa W_{e(x_i)}(x_i). \tag{3.12}$$

Step 3: Set

$$x_{i+1} = x_i + sd_{e(x_i)}(x_i) \tag{3.13}$$

set i = i + 1, and go to Step 1.

It can be shown (see (10)) that every accumulation point of Algorithm 1 is feasible and satisfies a standard F. John type condition of optimality.

Algorithm 1 has been used as is and also as a vehicle for stabilizing local superlinearly converging algorithms such as sequential quadratic programming (27). The stabilization is accomplished as follows. A simple comparison test is used to determine whether the local version is in its region of convergence. If the local algorithm is in its region of convergence, it is allowed to proceed, otherwise Algorithm 1 is used to drive the iterates into the region of convergence of the local method. The result is an algorithm with mathematically demonstrable global convergence properties (see (27)).

For non-differentiable problems of the form (2.17) -(2.19), a modification of Algorithm 1 has been proposed in (28). The algorithm in (28) substitutes e-approximations to the generalized gradients for the gradients used in Algorithm 1, and uses the outer decompositions algorithm (10), to be described below, to replace the intervals $[w', w'']$ with finite sets of points.

Finally, for differentiable problems for which derivative computations have not been incorporated into simulation codes, we find a derivative free version of Algorithm 1 in (33).

An important tool for dealing with problems of the form (3.1), either totally or partially, is the family of outer approximations algorithms, see, e.g (9,14,16). Probably the most elaborate use of this tool can be found in (21), where it is used to "unwind" (3.1) into sequences of differentiable, finitely constrained optimization problems. We shall describe an example of these methods in terms of the simplified problem

$$\min\{f(x) \mid h(x,p) \le 0, \forall p \in P\} \tag{3.14}$$

where f and h are real, at least, locally Lipschitz continuous functions defined on R^n . The idea is to decompose (3.14) into a sequence of problems in which P is replaced by finite sets P , which, hopefully, remain of small cardinality.

Algorithm 2:

Parameters: t $\in (0,1)$ and a double subscripted sequence $\{s_{jk}\}$ satisfying

(i) $s_{kk} = 0$ for all k and $s_{jk} > 0$ for all $k>j$;
(ii) $s_{jk} \to \hat{s}_j$ as $k \to \infty$.
(iii) $\hat{s}_j \to 0$ as $j \to \infty$.

Data: A finite set $P_0 \in P$.

Step 0: Set k = 0.

Step 1: Compute by means of Algorithm 1 an x_k such that

$$h(x_k,p) \leq t^k, \forall p \in P, e(x_k) \leq t^k. \tag{3.14a}$$

Step 2: Computer a

$$p_k \in argmax\{h(x,p) | p \in P\}. \tag{3.15}$$

Step 3: Set

$$P_{k+1} = \{p\} \cup \{p_j \in P_k \,|\, h(x_j,p_j) \geq s_{jk}\}. \tag{3.16}$$

set k = k + 1 and go to Step 1.

We note that the parameter t is used to control the precision with which the kth problem is solved. It is necessary to solve the successive problems with progressively greater precision. In (3.14a) an exponential increase of precision is specified, however, one may increase the precision at a slower rate. The double subscripted sequence s_{jk} is used for determining which of the p_j, that were included in P_k, need not be carried over into P_{k+1}, i.e., they form part of the constraint dropping scheme. When one wishes to keep the sets P_k small, the s_{jk} should decrease to zero very slowly as k increases. There are many possibilities for such a sequence, for example, one may use $s_{jk} = 100/[1/(1+j)^{1/10} - 1/(1+k)^{1/10}]$. When computing in an interactive environment, it is possible to exercise highly intelligent control over the constraint dropping mechanism.

In view of our comments on the effect of parameters, it should be clear that algorithms of the type discussed above are very difficult to use in batch mode in an engineering design where function evaluations consume many minutes of computer time. It has been our experience that the computations can be made much more efficient by parameter adjustment in an interactive computing environment, such as the ones described in (2,19).

4. CONCLUSION.

We hope that this brief survey of SIP problems arrising in engineering and of some of the algorithms that have been used for their solution will stimulate the interest of SIP researchers in the very challenging problems that occur in engineering design.

ACKNOWLEDGEMENT: This research was supported by the National Science Foundation under grants ECS-79-13148 and CEE-81-05790 and the Joint Services Electronics Program under grant F49620-79-C-0178.

REFERENCES.

(1) Becker, R. G., A. J. Heunis, and D. Q. Mayne: "Computer-Aided Design of Control Systems via Optimization", Proc. IEE, vol. 126, no. 6, 1979.

(2) Bhatti, M. A., T.Essebo, W. Nye, K. S. Pister, E. Polak, A. Sangiovanni Vincentelli, and A. Tits: "A Software System University of for Optimization Based Interactive Computer Aided Design", Proc. IEEE I.S.C.A.S. Houston Tx., April 1980.

(3) Bhatti, M.A., K. S. Pister, and E. Polak: "Optimal Design of an Earthquake Isolation System", Proc. IUTAM Symp. on Structural Control, Univ. of Waterloo, Waterloo, Ont., Canada, June, 1979.

(4) Bhatti, M.A., K. S. Pister, and E. Polak: "Optimization-Based, Interactive CAD of Dynamically Loaded structures", to appear in Jour. of Structural Dynamics, of the A.S.C.E.

(5) Bhatti, M. A., K. S. Pister, and E. Polak: "Optdyn - A General Purpose Optimization Program for Problems With or Without Dynamic Constraints", Report No. UCB/EERC - 79/16, Earthquake Engineering Research Center, University of California, Berkeley, July 1979.

(6) Brayton R.K., S.W. Director, and G.D. Hachtel: "Yield Maximization and Worst Case Design with Arbitrary Statistical Distributions", IEEE Trans. on Circuits and Systems, Vol. CAS-27, n. 9, (1980).

(7) Bandler, J. W., P. C. Liu, and H. Tromp: "Nonlinear Programming Approach to Optimal Design Centering Tolerancing and Tuning", IEEE Trans. Vol. CAS-23, (1976).

(8) Davison, E. J., and I. J. Ferguson: "The Design of Controllers for the Multivariable Robust Servomechanism Problem Using Parameter Optimization Methods", Systems Control Report No. 8002, University of Toronto, February 1980.

(9) Gonzaga, C., and E. Polak: "On Constraint Dropping Schemes and Optimality Functions for a Class of Outer Approximations Algorithms", J. SIAM Control and Optimization Vol. 17, (1979).

(10) Gonzaga, C., E. Polak and R. Trahan: "An Improved Algorithm for Optimization Problems with Functional Inequality Constraints", IEEE Trans., Vol. AC-25, No. 1, (1980).

(11) Hettich, R.: "Semi-Infinite Programming", Springer-Verlag Lectlure Notes in Control and Information Sciences, Vol. 15, 1979.

(12) Karmarkar J. S., and D. D. Siljak: "Maximization of Absolute Stability Regions by Mathematical Programming Methods", Regelungtechnik No. 2, (1975).

(13) Laub, A. J.: "An Inequality and Some Computations Related to the Robust Stability of Linear Dynamic Systems", IEEE Trans. on Automatic Control Vol. AC-24, No.2, (1979.

(14) Mayne, D. Q., and E. Polak: "A Quadratically Convergent Algorithm for Solving Infinite-Dimensional Inequalities", Memo No. UCB/ERL M80/11, University of California, Berkeley, 1980.

(15) Mayne, D. Q., E. Polak and R. Trahan: "An Outer Approximations Algorithm for Computer-Aided Design Problems", JOTA, Vol. 28, No. 3, (1979).

(16) Mayne, D. Q., E. Polak, and A. J. Heunis: "Solving Nonlinear Inequalities in a Finite Number of Iterations", JOTA Vol. 33, No. 2, (1981).

(17) Mayne, D. Q., E.Polak, and A. Voreadis: "A Cut Map Algorithm for Design Problems with Tolerances", IEEE Trans. Vol. CAS-29, No. 1, (1982).

(18) Mifflin, R.: "Semismooth and Semiconvex Functions in Constrained Optimization", SIAM J. Control and Optimization, Vol. 15, No. 6, (1977).

(19) Nye, W., E. Polak, A. Sangiovanni Vincentelli and A. Tits: "DELIGHT: an Optimization-Based Computer-Aided-Design System", Proc. IEEE Int. Symp. on Circuits and Systems, Chicago, Ill, April 24-27, 1981.

(20) Polak, E.: "Algorithms for a Class of Computer Aided Design Problems: A Review", Automatica, Vol. 15, (1979).

(21) Polak, E.: "An Implementable Algorithm for the Design Centering, Tolerancing and Tuning Problem", JOTA, Vol. 35, No. 3, (1981).

(22) Polak, E., and D. Q. Mayne: "An Algorithm for Optimization Problems with Functional Inequality Constraints", IEEE Trans., Vol. AC-21, No. 2, (1976).

(23) Polak, E., and D. Q. Mayne: "Algorithms for Computer Aided Design of Control Systems by the Method of Inequalities", Proc. 18th IEEE Conference on Decision and Control, Fort Lauderdale, Florida, Dec. 12-14, 1979.

(24) Polak, E., and D. Q. Mayne: "Design of Nonlinear Feedback Controllers", IEEE AC Trans. on Automatic Control, Vol AC-26, No. 3, (1981).

(25) Polak, E., K. S. Pister, and D. Ray: "Optimal Design of Framed Structures Subjected to Earthquakes", Eng. Optimization, Vol. 12, (1976).

(26) Polak, E., and A. Sangiovanni Vincentelli: "Theoretical and Computational Aspects of the Optimal Design Centering, Tolerancing and Tuning Problem", IEEE Trans. Vol CAS-26, No. 9, (1979).

(27) Polak, E., and A. Tits: "A Recursive Quadratic Programming Algorithm for Semi-Infinite Optimization Problems", University of California, Berkeley, ERL Memo No. UCB/ERL M80/50, 22 September, 1980.

(28) Polak, E., and Y. Y. Wardi: "A Nondifferentiable Optimization Algorithm for the Design of Control Systems Subject to Singular Value Inequalities over a Frequency Range", Proceedings IFAC/81 Congress, Kyoto, Japan, August 24-28, 1981.

(29) Polak, E., R. Trahan, and D. Q. Mayne: "Combined Phase I - Phase II Methods of Feasible Directions", Math. Programming, Vol. 17, No. 1, (1979).

(30) Safonov, M. G., A. J. Laub, and G. L. Hartman: "Feedback Properties of Multivariable Systems: The Role and Use of the Return Difference Matrix", IEEE Trans. on Control Vol. AC-26, (1981).

(31) Sandel, N. R.: "Robust Stability of Systems with Applications to Singular Value Perturbations", Automatica Vol. 15, (1979).

(32) Taiwo, O.: "Design of a Multivariable Controller for a High Order Turbofan Engine Model by Zakian's Method of Inequalities", IEEE Trans. Vol. AC-23, No. 5, (1978).

(33) Trahan, R., and E. Polak: "A Derivative Free Algorithm for a Class of Infinitely Constrained Optimization Problems", IEEE Trans. Vol. AC-25, No. 1, (1979).

(34) Zakian, V., and L. Al-Naib: "Design of Dynamical and Control Systems by the Method of Inequalities", Proc. IEE, 120 (11), (1973).

(35) Zakian, V.: "New Formulation for the Method of Inequalities", Proc. IEE, 126(6), (1979).

A MOMENT INEQUALITY AND MONOTONICITY
OF AN ALGORITHM

Ben Torsney

ABSTRACT

Monotonicity of a proposed algorithm for a class of constrained optimisation problem is investigated. A moment lemma is proved which yields a condition sufficient for monotonicity. This condition is seen to be satisfied in one example. The problem is defined in section 2, while examples are revealed and optimality conditions are outlined in sections 3,4. Algorithms are discussed generally in section 5, with the proposed algorithm appearing in the next section. The moment lemma and sufficient conditions are presented in section 7 and empirical results form a concluding section.

1. Introduction

The topic of this paper, we believe, has relevance to the theme of this conference at least in the following respects. Firstly it is concerned with an algorithm for the problem defined below. Secondly a moment inequality is proved, since it provides a condition sufficient for monotonicity of the proposed algorithm. Lastly, as will be seen, the problem can be transformed to a semi-infinite program, although the algorithm does not exploit this.

2. A Problem

We denote the problem by (P1).

Problem (P1)

"Maximise concave $\phi(p)$ over $\mathcal{P} = \{p = (p_1, p_2, \dots, p_J): p_j \geq 0, \Sigma p_j = 1\}$."

Several examples of this arise in the area of statistics including maximum likelihood estimation problems and design problems. The latter however are particular cases of the following general example which is a problem with added structure.

Problem (P2)

"Maximise concave $\psi(X)$ over the convex hull of the points $G(v_1)$, $G(v_2)$, ..., $G(v_J)$, where $G(\cdot)$ is a given one-to-one function and $\mathcal{V} = \{v_1, v_2, \dots, v_J\}$ is a known set of vector (or matrix) vertices of fixed dimension. That is, solve (P1) for

$$\phi(p) = \psi\{E_p[G(v)]\}, \quad X = E_p[G(v)] = \sum_{j=1}^{J} p_j G(v_j)."$$

We wish to discover a probability distribution p^* on the discrete and finite set $\mathcal{V}$ which maximises $\phi(\cdot)$. Clearly a next level of generality is to seek a probability measure defined on a continuous and possibly unbounded space $\mathcal{V}$ to maximise a function $\phi(\cdot)$ defined as in (P2). However Carathéodory's theorem guarantees that at least one optimising probability measure is discrete and so must assign or approximately assign unit mass to a finite discrete subset of $\mathcal{V}$. Hence we confine attention to (P2) although $\mathcal{V}$ there may be a discretisation of a continuous set or a subset of such a discretisation.

We note that in this latter instance there will usually be many v_i for which $p_i^* = 0$. We will define the support of a probability distribution p on $\mathcal{V}$ to be those vertices v_j with non-zero weighting under p and denote it by Supp(p). Often there will be p* such that Supp(p*) is a strict subset of $\mathcal{V}$. It is not ambiguous to say that the solution of (P2) for $\mathcal{V}$ is given by the solution of (P2) when $\mathcal{V}$ is replaced by Supp(p*).

3. Examples

Several examples of (P2) can be quoted. We are primarily interested in a class of examples arising in approximate optimal linear regression design theory, a subject advanced extensively by the late Jack Kiefer. The conference paper by Dankmar Bohning, "An Exchange Algorithm for Optimal Design Problems" is devoted to this topic, while Charnes, Gustafson and Kortanek addressed themselves to it in their plenary review paper. It is an instance of (P2) in which

(i) v_j is a vector of order k×1,

(ii) $G(v) = vv'$ and so,

(iii) $E_p[G(v)] = \sum_{j=1}^{J} p_j v_j v_j' = M(p)$, a matrix of order k×k,

(iv) a variety of functions $\psi(\cdot)$ have been considered, most of which are special cases of $\psi(M) = \psi_t(M|A) = -\mathrm{tr}\{AM^+A'\}^t$,

where $t > 0$, A is of order s×k, $s < k$, rank (A) = s, M^+ is the Moore Penrose generalised inverse of M, and there is a constraint that the null space of M be contained in that of A. The trace of a square matrix is denoted by "tr".

Usually $\mathcal{V}$ is the image under a vector of known regressor function $\underline{f}$ of a discretisation of a bounded practical design space $\mathcal{U}$.

We will be particularly concerned with the function $\psi_1(M|A)$ later and also with $\psi(M) = \det(M)$ or equivalently $\psi(M) = \ln\{\det(M)\} = -\ln\{\det(M^{-1})\}$. This is a limiting case of $\psi_t(M|A)$ since

$$\{(1/s)\psi_t(M|A)\}^{1/t} \to \{-\ln\{\det(AM^+A')\}\} \quad \text{as } t \to 0.$$

We briefly mention other examples of (P2).

A most recently revealed one is contained in White and Welch (14). They consider an experimental situation where each of t treatments is to be applied to r experimental units, there being $n = rt$ homogeneous units available. There are $J = n!/(r!)^t$ distinct allocations or layouts. A layout is to be chosen according to a "valid restricted randomisation scheme", not simply at random. The authors show that the probabilities with which layouts are selected under this scheme are given by those which solve (P2) when

(i) v_j is a matrix of order $n \times n$, whose $(i,i')^{th}$ entry is 1 if units i and i' receive the same treatment in layout j, and is zero otherwise.

(ii) $G(v) = v$.

(iii) $\psi(X) = \det(X)$.

Another instance of (P2) arises when estimating the compounding distribution, given data from a compound Poisson process, an instance in which $\mathcal{V}$ is unbounded. See Simar (11). Yet another can be the apparently innocent generalisation of (P1) which replaces the single linear equality constraint $\Sigma p_j = 1$ by several linear constraints. Finally Silverman and Titterington (8), when concerned with minimum covering ellipses, consider a problem which is more readily seen to be an example of a more flexible formulation of (P2). Its advantage lies in decomposing the argument X of $\psi(\cdot)$ into components each of which can be vectors or matrices.

4. Sufficient Conditions for Optimality - Two Alternative Forms

We now state necessary and sufficient conditions for optimality in (P2) and in fact we state two alternative forms.

The first set are simpler in form but require differentiability. We rely on them implicitly in later sections. However we quote the alternative form as they point to a transformation of (P2) to a semi-infinite program.

Both sets of conditions are expressed in terms of the "point to point directional derivative" of $\psi(\cdot)$ at X in the direction of (Y-X), a concept conceived by Whittle (15, 16). The derivative is

$$F_\psi(X,Y) = \lim_{\varepsilon \downarrow 0} \left\{ \frac{\{\psi[(1-\varepsilon)X+\varepsilon Y] - \psi(X)\}}{\varepsilon} \right\}$$

In respect of (P2) we will call $F_\psi\{X, G(v_j)\}$, for $j = 1, \ldots, J$, the vertex directional derivatives of $\psi(\cdot)$ at X. We will denote them by $F_j(X)$ or simply F_j.

If $\psi(\cdot)$ is differentiable at $X = E_p[G(v)]$ and $\phi(p) = \psi\{E_p[G(v)]\}$, then $F_j = d_j - \underline{p}'\underline{d}$, $\underline{d} = (d_1, \ldots, d_J)'$, $d_j = \partial\phi/\partial p_j$.

<u>Vertex Direction Optimality Theorem</u>

If $\psi(\cdot)$ is differentiable at $X^* = E_{p^*}[G(v)]$, then necessary and sufficient conditions for X* to solve (P2) and for p* to solve the corresponding (P1) is that

$$F_j^* = F_j(X^*) \begin{cases} = 0 & \text{if } p_j^* > 0 \\ \leqslant 0 & \text{if } p_j^* = 0 \end{cases} .$$

A proof is elementary. See Whittle (16).

There is an unmistakable flavour of stationarity in these conditions. We might call X* a constrained stationary value of $\psi(\cdot)$. Corollaries are the class of general equivalence theorems in the design context, the first of these being that of Kiefer and Wolfowitz (7).

A simple motivation for the theorem, and for a less simple analogue when $\psi(\cdot)$ is not differentiable at X*, is that we must be "looking down" (non-differentiability) or "not looking up" (differentiability) in the directions from X* towards all other Y in the convex feasible region. The alternative set of conditions has the converse motivation that we should be "looking up" in directions from all such Y towards X*, assuming concavity of $\psi(\cdot)$.

<u>Alternative Optimality Theorem</u>

The optimum of problem (P2), for strictly concave $\psi(\cdot)$, occurs at $X^* = E_{p^*}[G(v)]$ if and only if

$$F_\psi(Y,X^*) \geq 0$$

for all Y in the convex feasible region of that problem.

A proof of this result parallels that of Gribek and Kortanek (6). They prove the theorem in the design context. Of relevance to this conference is that it suggests the following semi-infinite program transformation of (P2).

<u>Semi-Infinite Program</u>

Maximise $\psi(X)$ over $\mathfrak{F}$ subject to $F_\psi(Y,X) \geq 0$ for all $Y \in \mathfrak{F}$, where $\mathfrak{F}$ is the convex feasible region of problem (P2).

The program has linear constraints if $\psi(\cdot)$ is differentiable in $\mathfrak{F}$ for then $F_\psi(Y,X)$ is a linear transformation of X, the coefficients depending on Y.

5. <u>Algorithms</u>

Several types of algorithm have been formulated for (P2), invariably in the design context. With the exception of Gribek and Kortanek (6) who advocate cutting plane algorithms for their semi-infinite program, the proposers of these techniques were mathematical statisticians, including Atwood, Fedorov, Silvey, Titterington, Torsney, Wu, Wynn. It is however consoling that their proposed methods appear to be particular cases or in the spirit of general techniques advocated at this conference, in particular by Hettich in his plenary talk, which appears in this Volume.

Hettich advocates two-phase methods, a first phase in which a good approximation is computed, a second phase method in which this is improved. In fact Torsney (13) advocates a three-phase method for (P2), allowing for an intermediate phase to those of Hettich. When $\mathcal{V}$ in (P2) is a discretisation of a continuous space many p_j^* will be zero. Vertex direction algorithms which take a step towards or away from a vertex can quickly identify most of the vertices which are not in Supp(p*), and so are attractive first phase methods. For example consider the following evidence.

A D-optimal design ($\psi(\cdot) = \det(M)$) problem, considered by Wynn (18), has a discretised design space which is the image under the vector function $\underline{f} = (1, x, \sin 2\pi x, \cos 2\pi x)'$ of the set $\mathfrak{X} = \{0, .01, .02, \ldots, .99, 1\}$, that is $\mathcal{V} = \underline{f}(\mathfrak{X})$, and the solution is such that $\mathrm{Supp}(p^*) = \underline{f}(\{.08, .09, .38, .73, .74, 1\})$.

A vertex direction algorithm which takes a step towards the vertex with the largest vertex directional derivative, the steplength being that advocated by Wynn (18), was started from 112 different initial designs $p^{(o)}$. As general theoretical results implied that Supp(p*) must contain at least four vertices, this was the size of each Supp($p^{(o)}$), with $p^{(o)}$ always assigning weight 1/4 to the four relevant vertices. For each application the index z was recorded, of the iteration from which the algorithm selected only vertices in the set $\underline{f}$({.07, .08, .09, .10, .37, .38, .39, .72, .73, .74, .75, .99, 1}). This consists of clusters of vertices, namely the elements of Supp(p*) and their "immediate" neighbours in $\mathcal{V}$. The frequencies f(·) of the values achieved by z are

z	1	3	4	5	6	7	8	9	10	11	12	14
f(z)	1	5	1	20	11	26	9	12	15	10	1	1

On average z = 7.4. The two largest values would have been smaller were it not for, in each case, a step towards an immediate neighbour,but one of members of Supp(p*). A natural choice of $p^{(o)}$ has Supp($p^{(o)}$) = $\underline{f}$({0, .33, .67, 1}). For this z = 5. Similar results were observed in polynomial regression models.

Vertex direction algorithms were originally proposed by Fedorov (5), Wynn (18, 19). As well as being suitable first phase methods, they can be useful terminally as outlined in the next section.

The algorithms proposed by Wu (17), Atwood (1, 2) are the most powerful, being either constrained steepest ascent or Newton type iterations. They are most suited to examples of (P2) in which $\mathcal{V}$ = Supp(p*) and hence are possible final phase methods.

The notion of an intermediate phase method was conceived for problem (P2) as a sequel to vertex direction methods that could weed out any further unidentified non-support vertices of p*, in the belief that these would be few in number. Of course such a method would be suitable for a $\mathcal{V}$ which from the outset might contain only a few such points or none at all, as is likely to be the case if $\mathcal{V}$ is not a large set. Torsney (13) considers various ideas for such methods and primarily the algorithm discussed below.

We close this discussion by recording that one particular type of method considered by Hettich seemed to suggest the following recursive approach to solution of (P2). Namely, solve (P2) for an initial subset $\mathcal{V}_{(1)}$ of $\mathcal{V}$ and if necessary modify $\mathcal{V}_{(1)}$ to a second subset $\mathcal{V}_{(2)}$ and repeat, $\mathcal{V}_{(2)}$ being derived from $\mathcal{V}_{(1)}$ by including and possibly excluding vertices that were respectively excluded and included in $\mathcal{V}_{(1)}$. This defines an exchange process. Silvey and Titterington (9) advocated precisely this sort of method in the design context. Vertex direction methods can suggest a good initial $\mathcal{V}_{(1)}$.

6. A First or Intermediate Phase Algorithm

The iteration we wish to advocate requires that $\phi(p)$ have nonnegative derivatives as is the case with $\phi(p) = \psi_t\{M(p)|A\}$ and with many statistical examples of (P1). The iterative rule is

$$p_j^{(r+1)} = p_j^{(r)} d_j^{\delta} \Big/ \sum_{i=1}^{J} p_i^{(r)} d_i^{\delta}, \quad d_j = \partial\phi/\partial p_j^{(r)},$$

where δ is positive but otherwise a free parameter.

Clearly a distinctive feature of the iteration is the preservation of the constraints of (P1). Also $\mathrm{Supp}(p^{(r+1)}) \subseteq \mathrm{Supp}(p^{(r)})$ and there are several other interesting aspects. See Silvey, Titterington and Torsney (10).

The parameter δ offers a degree of flexibility which could be exploited as the latter authors attempt to do. However we wish to pursue the following phenomenon, namely that in some instances there appears to be a value of δ, say δ_s, with a special relationship to $\phi(\cdot)$ which is such that iterations are monotonic under δ_s.

Let $\lambda = p^{(r)}$, $\tau^{(\delta)} = p^{(r+1)}$. It is to be noted that $\tau^{(o)} = \lambda$, while it can be shown that either $F_\phi\{\lambda, \tau^{(\delta)}\}$ is strictly positive for all positive δ, or is zero for all δ. See Silvey, Titterington and Torsney (10). The case of positive $F_\phi\{\lambda, \tau^{(\delta)}\}$ does not of course imply that $\phi(\tau^{(\delta)}) > \phi(\lambda)$ for every positive δ, but at least for concavity it does guarantee the existence of a $\bar{\delta} > 0$ such that $\phi(\tau^{(\delta)}) > \phi(\lambda)$ for $0 < \delta < \bar{\delta}$, $\bar{\delta}$ being typically finite. It is envisaged that the δ_s contemplated above is in $(0, \bar{\delta})$.

The case of zero $F_\phi\{\lambda, \tau^{(\delta)}\}$ occurs when the d_j corresponding to nonzero λ_j are all equal. In consequence $\tau^{(\delta)} = \lambda$ and λ solves (P1) unless weight is needed at non-members of $\mathrm{Supp}(\lambda)$. This is unlikely to be the case if $\mathrm{Supp}(p^{(o)}) = \mathcal{V}$ or has been determined sensibly by a first stage algorithm. If however it does occur then, since $\mathrm{Supp}(p^{(r+1)}) \subseteq \mathrm{Supp}(p^{(r)})$, we are faced with what is an impasse both for this and other algorithms. A different form of iteration is needed and a vertex direction step is to be recommended.

The notion of a δ_s with a special relationship stems from the fact that in simple cases there is a value of δ which will attain the optimum in one step provided $p_j > 0$, $j = 1, \ldots, J$. For example $\delta_s = 1$ in the cases of $\phi_i(\cdot)$ for $i = 1, 2, 3$ and $\delta_s = 1/(t+1)$ in the case of $\phi_4(\cdot)$ where,

$$\phi_1(p) = \prod_{j=1}^{J} p_j \quad ; \quad \phi_2(p) = -\left(\prod_{j=1}^{J} p_j\right)^{-1}$$

$$\phi_3(p) = \prod_{j=1}^{J} p_j^{o_j}, \; o_j > 0; \quad \phi_4(p) = -\sum_{j=1}^{J} p_j^{-t}, \; t > 0 .$$

These functions are homogeneous, a function $\phi(p)$ being homogeneous of degree n if $\phi(cp) = c^n\phi(p)$ for c a scalar. This is a common property in many examples of (P1) and is crucial to the rule which we now proceed to postulate for identifying a special δ_s. In the remaining sections we derive conditions sufficient for monotonicity to hold for the values which can be suggested for δ_s by the rule in a particular case.

Suppose that $\phi(p)$ is homogeneous of degree n. Then $d_j = d_j(p) = \partial\phi/\partial p_j$ is homogeneous of degree (n-1). Suppose that $d_j(p) = c(p)f_j(p)$, where c(p) and $f_j(p)$ are homogeneous factors, and let the degree of homogeneity of $f_j(p)$ be h. A consequence is that $p^{(r+1)}$ will not depend on $c(p^{(r)})$, and this is reflected in the following rule which selects, in the above examples, that δ attaining the optimum in one step.

Rule:

$$\delta_s = -1/h .$$

The rule also selects $\delta_s = 1/(t+1)$ in the case of $\phi(p) = \psi_t\{M(p)|A\}$ and will often do likewise in the case of other functions which are homogeneous of degree -t, t > 0. Hence as $t \to 0$ it selects $\delta_s = 1$ for D-optimality, a value which it also suggests in several other examples in which the resultant iteration can be shown to be an EM algorithm. This is known to be monotonic. See Dempster, Laird and Rubin (4) for its definition and properties.

We now derive a condition which suffices for $\delta = 1/(t+1)$, t>0, to yield monotonicity when $\phi(\cdot)$ is homogeneous of degree -t, and we will see it satisfied in the case of $\phi(p) = \psi_1\{M(p)|A\}$. First we need a moment lemma.

7. Moment Lemma and a Sufficient Condition

Lemma

Let X and Y be two positive random variables and let t be any positive real number.

If
$$E(Y^{t+1}) \leqslant E(X)E(Y^t) \tag{7.1}$$
then
$$E(Y^{t+1}) \leqslant E(X^{t+1}) \tag{7.2}$$

We could state a more general result but this suffices for our purposes.

Proof

We prove a more direct consequence of (7.1), namely that $E(X^{t+1}) \geqslant E(X)E(Y^t)$. The proof is in two parts and twice appeals to the result that the function $g(t) = \{E(Z^t)\}^{1/t}$ is nondecreasing in t when Z is a positive random variable. See Bechenback and Bellman (3), p.16.

(a)
$$\{E(Y^{t+1})\}^{1/t+1} \geqslant \{E(Y^t)\}^{1/t} \qquad (g'(t) \geqslant 0)$$
$$\therefore \{E(Y^t)\}^{(t+1)/t} \leqslant E(Y^{t+1})$$
$$\therefore \{E(Y^t)\}^{(t+1)/t} \leqslant E(X)E(Y^t) \qquad \text{by (7.1)}$$
$$\therefore \{E(Y^t)\}^{1/t} \leqslant E(X)$$
$$\therefore E(Y^t) \leqslant \{E(X)\}^t \tag{7.3}$$

(b)
$$\{E(X^{t+1})\}^{1/(t+1)} \geqslant E(X) \qquad (g'(t) \geqslant 0)$$
$$\therefore E(X^{t+1}) \geqslant \{E(X)\}^{t+1}$$

$$= E(X)\{E(X)\}^t$$

$$\geq E(X)E(Y^t) \qquad \text{by (7.3)}$$

$$\geq E(Y^{t+1}) \qquad \text{by (7.1)}$$

The relevance of the lemma to establishing monotonicity of the above iteration, and indeed the possible relevance of a more general result to establishing monotonicity of any iteration for (P1), lies in the fact that the following property, possessed by any homogeneous $\phi(p)$, can be viewed in terms of expectations when p is a probability vector, and moreover a mean of a positive random variable when $\partial\phi/\partial p_i > 0$. The property is that

$$\sum_{i=1}^{J} p_i \partial\phi/\partial p_i = r\phi(p)$$

where r is the degree of homogeneity.

Thus, given two elements τ and λ, and if $r = -t$, $t > 0$, and also $\partial\phi/\partial p_i > 0$, then $\phi(\tau) \geq \phi(\lambda)$ if and only if $E(Y^{t+1}) \leq E(X^{t+1})$, where X and Y are positive random variables with respective probability distributions

$$P(X = \{\partial\phi/\partial\lambda_j\}^{1/(t+1)}) = \lambda_j, \quad P(Y = \{\partial\phi/\partial\tau_j\}^{1/(t+1)}) = \tau_j$$

because $E(X^{t+1}) = -t\phi(\lambda)$, $E(Y^{t+1}) = -t\phi(\tau)$.

We can now show that one sufficient condition for monotonicity of our algorithm, with $\delta = 1/(t+1)$ and when $\phi(\cdot)$ has positive derivatives and is homogeneous of degree $-t$, $t > 0$, is that

$$\Phi(\lambda|\tau) \geq -t\phi(\tau),$$

where

$$\tau_j = \tau_j(\lambda) = \lambda_j\{\partial\phi/\partial\lambda_j\}^{1/(t+1)} \Big/ \sum_{i=1}^{J} \lambda_i\{\partial\phi/\partial\lambda_i\}^{1/(t+1)} ,$$

and

$$\Phi(\lambda|\tau) = \sum_{j=1}^{J} \lambda_j\{\partial\phi/\partial\lambda_j\}^{1/(t+1)}\{\partial\phi/\partial\tau_j\}^{t/(t+1)} .$$

The result follows since for any λ and for arbitrary τ

$$E(X)E(Y^t) = \left[\Sigma\lambda_j\{\partial\phi/\partial\lambda_j\}^{1/(t+1)}\right]\left[\Sigma\tau_i\{\partial\phi/\partial\tau_i\}^{t/(t+1)}\right] .$$

Hence for $\tau_j = \tau_j(\lambda)$,

$$E(X)E(Y^t) = \Phi(\lambda|\tau) .$$

Thus, appealing to the lemma, and taking $\lambda = p^{(r)}$, $\tau = p^{(r+1)}$, the stated sufficiency is established.

We can go further than this however, with problem (P2) in mind. We have τ,λ related as above. As has been noted, a particular consequence of this is that $\mathrm{Supp}(\tau) \subseteq \mathrm{Supp}(\lambda)$, but usually equality holds here. The latter condition would therefore follow if we had the stronger result that for each probability distribution μ on $\mathcal{V}$, $\Phi(\lambda|\mu) \geq -t\phi(\mu)$ for all distributions λ such that $\mathrm{Supp}(\lambda) = \mathrm{Supp}(\mu)$. Now we note that

$$-t\phi(\mu) = \Sigma\mu_i\partial\phi/\partial\mu_i = \Phi(\mu|\mu) .$$

Thus we have, finally, that a second sufficient condition for the monotonicity under discussion is:

Sufficient Condition

"For fixed μ, $\Phi(\lambda|\mu)$ is minimised over all λ such that $\mathrm{Supp}(\lambda) = \mathrm{Supp}(\mu)$ at $\lambda = \mu$".

It is clearly unlikely that this condition would hold for all $\phi(\cdot)$ satisfying the necessary properties and indeed we can only prove it to hold in the case of $\phi(p) = \psi_1\{M(p)|A\}$, as is seen below. However the following general result suggests that the condition might hold fairly often.

Theorem 7.1

The function $\Phi(\lambda|\mu)$ has, for fixed μ, a stationary value at $\lambda = \mu$, assuming differentiability of $\phi(\cdot)$.

Proof

$$\partial\Phi/\partial\lambda_j = \left\{\frac{\partial\phi}{\partial\lambda_j}\right\}^{1/(t+1)} \left\{\frac{\partial\phi}{\partial\mu_j}\right\}^{t/(t+1)} + \frac{1}{(t+1)} \sum_i \lambda_i \frac{\partial^2\phi}{\partial\lambda_i\partial\lambda_j} \left\{\frac{\partial\phi}{\partial\lambda_i}\right\}^{\frac{-t}{t+1}} \left\{\frac{\partial\phi}{\partial\mu_i}\right\}^{\frac{t}{t+1}}$$

$$\partial\Phi/\partial\lambda_j\Big|_{\underline{\lambda}=\underline{\mu}} = \frac{\partial\phi}{\partial\mu_i} + \frac{1}{(t+1)} \sum_i \mu_i \partial^2\phi/\partial\mu_i\partial\mu_j$$

$$= \frac{\partial\phi}{\partial\mu_j} - \frac{\partial\phi}{\partial\mu_j} = 0.$$

The last step appeals to the homogeneity of $\partial\phi/\partial\mu_j$.

We now prove that the sufficient condition holds in the case of $\phi(p) = \psi_1\{M(p)|A\}$.

Theorem 7.2

If $\phi(p) = -\mathrm{tr}\{AM^+(p)A'\}$ (and hence $t = 1$) then $\Phi(\lambda|\mu) \geq \Phi(\mu|\mu)$ when Supp $(\lambda) = \mathrm{Supp}(\mu)$.

Proof

$$\partial\phi/\partial p_j = v_j'M^+(p)A'AM^+(p)v_j \qquad \text{if } p_j > 0$$

$$= [\underline{w}_j(p)]'\underline{w}_j(p) .$$

Hence

$$\Phi(\lambda|\mu) = \Sigma\lambda_j\{[\underline{w}_j(\lambda)]'\underline{w}_j(\lambda)\}^{\frac{1}{2}}\{[\underline{w}_j(\mu)]'\underline{w}_j(\mu)\}^{\frac{1}{2}}$$

$$\geq \Sigma\lambda_j[\underline{w}_j(\lambda)]'w_j(\mu) \qquad \text{(by the Cauchy-Schwarz inequality)}$$

$$= \Sigma\lambda_j v_j'M^+(\lambda)A'AM^+(\mu)v_j$$

$$= \mathrm{trace}\ [AM^+(\mu)(\Sigma\lambda_j v_j v_j')M^+(\lambda)A']$$

$$= \mathrm{trace}[AM^+(\mu)M(\lambda)M^+(\lambda)A']$$

$$= \mathrm{trace}\{AM^+(\mu)A'\} = -\phi(\mu) = \Phi(\mu|\mu),$$

the last step being valid if the null space of $M(\lambda)$ is contained in that of A.

We emphasise that this only proves the monotonicity of our algorithm with $\delta = 1/(t+1)$ in the particular case $\phi(p) = \psi_1\{M(p)|A\}$ of $\phi(p) = \psi_t\{M(p)|A\}$. However there is much empirical evidence supporting monotonicity for all t in the case of this function. As has been noted, letting t tend to zero drives $\psi_t\{M|A\}$, suitably normalised, to a determinantal criteria and of course then $\delta \to 1$. In fact this power has been shown, by a different approach, to yield monotonicity in the case of D-optimality. See Titterington (12). Empirical results now reported relate to this criterion and choice of δ.

8. Empirical Information

Monotonicity of course does not guarantee good convergence and it must be admitted that the above type of iteration in various forms is slow to converge. See Silvey, Titterington and Torsney (10). However we present some evidence that when a value δ_s is employed enjoying a special relationship as discussed above,then the iterations may have good initial convergence and hence be a possible candidate for a first-phase or intermediate-phase algorithm.

The evidence is that in the case of the D-optimal criterion with $\delta = 1$ and $p_j^{(o)} = 1/J$, the algorithm achieves for each $j = 1, \ldots, J$, $F_j \leq 0.1$ in the case of $\mathcal{V} = \mathcal{V}_1$ and $F_j \leq 0.001$ in the cases of $\mathcal{V} = \mathcal{V}_2$ and $\mathcal{V} = \mathcal{V}_3$ in just one iteration, where

$$\mathcal{V}_1 = \{(1, -1, -1)', (1, -1, 1)', (1, 1, -1)' (1, 2, 2)'\}, \quad (J = 4, k = 3)$$
$$\mathcal{V}_2 = \{(1, x, x^2, x^3)': x = \pm .44, \pm .45, \pm 1\}, \quad (J = 6, k = 4)$$
$$\mathcal{V}_3 = \{(1, x, x^2, x^3, x^4)': x = 0, \pm .65, \pm .66, \pm 1\}, \quad (J = 7, k = 5).$$

The space $\mathcal{V}_1$ is the celebrated space of Wynn (18, 19) and in fact is the support of the D-optimum design over a certain quadrilateral. The spaces $\mathcal{V}_2, \mathcal{V}_3$ are the supports of D-optimum designs on the spaces $\mathcal{V}_D = \{(1, x, \ldots, x^{k-1})': x = -1, -.99, \ldots, .99, 1\}$ for $k = 3,4$ respectively. The space $\mathcal{V}_D$ in turn is a discretisation of $\mathcal{V}_C = \{(1, x, \ldots, x^{k-1})': -1 \leq x \leq 1\}$. It is known that the support of the D-optimum design on $\mathcal{V}_C$ consists of k points. In such a case the optimum weights are $1/k$. See Fedorov (5) on both cases. Inevitably however such points are usually excluded from $\mathcal{V}_D$, though those corresponding to $x = \pm 1$ and, when k is odd, to $x = 0$, are exceptions.

A not unsurprising consequence is that such an excluded point is "replaced" by a cluster consisting of its two nearest neighbours in $\mathcal{V}_D$. Experience is that the D-optimum design on $\mathcal{V}_D$ still assigns weight $1/k$ to points which are common to the supports of the D-optimum designs on $\mathcal{V}_C$ and $\mathcal{V}_D$, and also that it assigns a total weight of $1/k$ to clusters. Interestingly,in the case of $\mathcal{V}_2$ and $\mathcal{V}_3$,$p^{(1)}$ assigns approximately weight $(1/2k)$ to each point in a cluster and weight (1/k) otherwise, a design which, given the above knowledge, would have been a more sensible choice for $p^{(0)}$. However, designs achieving optimality conditions more precisely are markedly different in the weights they assign to points in clusters. For example, a design achieving $F_j \leq 10^{-6}$, $j = 1, \ldots, J$, in the case of $\mathcal{V}_2$, allocates weightings of .0191 to ± .44, .2309 to ± .45. Corresponding weights for $\mathcal{V}_3$ are .1153 to ± .65, .0947 to ± .66.

In conclusion, acknowledgement is due to G.H. Golub who has suggested improvements to the above algorithm.

References

(1) ATWOOD, C.L.: Convergent Design Sequences for Sufficiently Regular Optimality Criteria. Ann. Stats. 4 (1976), 1124 - 1138.

(2) ATWOOD, C.L.: Convergent Design Sequences For Sufficiently Regular Optimality Criteria, II: Singular Case. Ann. Stats. 8 (1980), 894 - 912.

(3) BECKENBACK, E.F., AND BELLMAN, R.: Inequalities. Berlin: Springer-Verlag, 1961.

(4) DEMPSTER, A.P., LAIRD, N.M. AND RUBIN, D.B.: Maximum Likelihood From Incomplete Data Via The EM Algorithm (with discussion). Jl. Royal Stat. Soc. B 39 (1977), 1 - 38.

(5) FEDOROV, V.V.: Theory Of Optimal Experiments. New York: Academic Press, 1972.

(6) GRIBIK, P.R., AND KORTANEK, K.O.: Equivalence Theorems And Cutting Plane Algorithms For A Class Of Experimental Design Problems. SIAM J. Appl. Math. 32 (1977), 232 - 259.

(7) KIEFER, J., AND WOLFOWITZ, J.: The Equivalence Of Two Extremum Problems. Canad. J. Math. 12 (1960), 363 - 366.

(8) SILVERMAN, B.W., AND TITTERINGTON, D.M.: Minimum Covering Ellipses. SIAM J. Sci. Stat. Comput. 1 (1980), 401 - 409.

(9) SILVEY, S.D., AND TITTERINGTON, D.M.: A Geometric Approach To Optimal Design Theory. Biometrika 60 (1973), 21 - 32.

(10) SILVEY, S.D., TITTERINGTON, D.M. AND TORSNEY, B.: An Algorithm For Optimal Designs On A Finite Design Space. Commun. Stats. A 7 (1978), 1379 - 1389.

(11) SIMAR, L.: Maximum Likelihood Estimation Of A Compound Poisson Process. Ann. Stat. 4 (1976), 1200 - 1209.

(12) TITTERINGTON, D.M.: Algorithms For Computing D-Optimal Designs On A Finite Design Space. Proc. 1976 Conf. On Information Sciences And Systems, Dept. Elect. Eng., Johns Hopkins Univ., Baltimore, MD (1976), 213 - 216.

(13) TORSNEY, B.: Algorithms for a Constrained Optimization Problem with Applications in Statistics and Optimum Design. Ph.D. Thesis. University of Glasgow, 1981.

(14) WHITE, L. V. AND WELCH, W. J.: A Method of Constructing Valid Restricted Randomization Schemes Using the Theory of D-Optimal Design of Experiments. Jl. Royal Stat. Soc. B 43 (1981), 167 - 172.

(15) WHITTLE, P.: Contribution to discussion of a paper by H. P. Wynn. Jl. Royal Stat. Soc. B 34 (1972), 172 - 174.

(16) WHITTLE, P.: Some General Points in the Theory of Optimal Experimental Design. Jl. Royal Stat. Soc. B 35 (1973), 123 - 130.

(17) WU, C.-F.: Some Iterative Procedures for Generating Nonsingular Optimal Designs. Commun. Stats. A 7 (1978), 1399 - 1412.

(18) WYNN, H. P.: The Sequential Generation of D-Optimal Experimental Designs. Ann. Math. Stats. 41 (1970), 1655 - 1664.

(19) WYNN, H. P.: Results in the Theory and Construction of D-Optimal Experimental Designs (with discussion). Jl. Royal Stat. Soc. B 34 (1972), 133 - 147, 170 - 186.

PART IV

OPTIMALITY CONDITIONS AND VARIATIONAL PRINCIPLES

SECOND ORDER CONDITIONS IN NONLINEAR NONSMOOTH PROBLEMS OF SEMI-INFINITE PROGRAMMING

A. D. Ioffe

1. Introduction

The problem we shall consider is stated as follows:

$$\text{(SIP)} \qquad \text{minimize} \quad f(x) = \max_{s \in S} f(s,x)$$
$$\text{subject to} \quad F(x) = 0;$$

x takes values in R^n (the n-dimensional linear space with some fixed, say, Euclidean norm), S is a compact Hausdorff space, $f(s,x)$ is a function on $S \times R^n$ and $F : R^n \to R^m$.

We shall be interested in second order conditions for a <u>local</u> minimum in (SIP). Therefore we fix a point $z \in R^n$ and never leave a neighborhood of z while speaking of assumptions or presenting arguments.

It has to be said at once that, as far as optimality conditions are concerned, this problem is equivalent to a seemingly more general problem:

$$(\text{SIP}_o) \qquad \text{minimize} \quad f_o(x) = \max_{s \in S_o} f_o(s,x)$$
$$\text{subject to} \quad f_i(x) = \max_{s \in S_i} f_i(s,x) \le 0, \quad i = 1,\dots,k,$$
$$F(x) = 0.$$

Indeed, given (SIP_o), we set

$$S = \bigcup_{i=0}^{k} S_i, \qquad f(s,x) = \begin{cases} f_o(s,x) - f_o(x), & \text{if } s \in S_o, \\ f_i(s,x), & \text{if } s \in S_i, \quad i = 1,\dots,k, \end{cases}$$

and consider (SIP) with f and S defined in such a way. It is an easy matter to see that

z *is a local solution to* (SIP) *if it is a local solution to* (SIP_o); z *is an isolated local solution to* (SIP_o) *if it is admissible in* (SIP_o) *and is an isolated local solution to* (SIP).

Second order necessary conditions for (SIP) were studied by Ben-Tal, Teboulle and Zowe [2] and (though implicitly, for a different problem) second order necessary and sufficient conditions were considered by Levitin, Miljutin and Osmolovskii [10, Sec. 14]. In both papers, it is assumed that $f(s,x)$ and $F(x)$ are twice continuously differentiable in x.

Also a simplified version of the problem was considered in both of the papers, without the equality constraint in [2] and under the assumption that $f(s,z) = f(z)$ for all s in [10]. For problems lying in the "intersection," [2] and [10] give formally equivalent necessary conditions though as we shall see in the next section they are presented in [10] in a more perfect and usable form.

Our purpose is also to prove second order necessary and second order sufficient conditions. The work is new in several respects. We try to attack the problem in a most general form, i.e. without any of the above mentioned simplifications, and, moreover, we no longer assume $f(s,x)$ and $F(x)$ twice continuously differentiable in x. Each of the generalizations has a dramatic effect on necessary conditions, breaking a perfect relationship between them and sufficient conditions (the necessary condition of [10] can be converted into the sufficient condition merely by replacing $\geq$ by $>$ (just as in the classical second order conditions for a local unconditional minimum of a function). Another interesting phenomenon (first observed by Levitin, Miljutin and Osmolovskii [9] in a different though, in a sense, more general situation) is that we no longer have a single necessary condition but rather a directed set of necessary conditions getting ever stronger as we are moving along. There is a limit object, but it fails to be a necessary condition (unless the assumptions of [10] or some others are satisfied). The phenomenon is completely due to nonsmoothness: it disappears if $f(s,x)$ and $F(x)$ are twice continuously differentiable or if S is a finite set and also in a weaker version of the principal results.

Another and more obvious result of dropping the twice differentiability assumption is that we no longer have the Hessian of the Lagrangian function which usually enters second order conditions. The object that appears instead can be qualified as a "bisublinear function" depending on the Lagrange multipliers also in a sublinear fashion. An analysis enabling one to work with such and other objects arising from non-smoothness was developed in [7]. Fortunately, we need not use most of them here because, in the finite dimensional setting, generalized gradients of Clarke are often sufficient.

As for the approach to second order conditions, the one we use is "ideologically" close to that of Levitin-Miljutin-Osmolovskii. But technically it is very different. We essentially follow the principles developed in [6]. The core is a reduction theorem which allows us to replace the initial constrained problem by an equivalent, in a sense, unconstrained problem having the same solution. Usually this results in a significant simplification of proofs and clarification of underlying ideas. There is also an essential difference in what kind of (and how) a variational analysis is applied to obtain necessary conditions. Briefly, the three authors first use a fairly rich family of variations (much richer than the family of usual directional variations) and they apply separation techniques, while we first use duality to obtain some dual characterization for unconstrained minima of functions and then apply simple directional variations.

The proof of the sufficient conditions here is, largely, along the same lines as in [6] and, in a broader sense, goes back to [9].

Main results are stated in the next section, along with a discussion in more detail. There are two versions of either conditions, a stronger version and a weaker version, which in particular imply a new and stronger result for the twice differentiable case. The proofs are given in Section 4 and Section 3 contains some auxiliary results.

2. Statements of Main Results

Throughout the paper we assume that:

F and $f(s,\cdot)$ are continuously differentiable (in a neighborhood X of z), the derivatives will be denoted by $f'(s,x)$ and $F'(x)$ (the prime relates to the dependence on x only);

there is $k > 0$ such that $F'(x)$ and $f'(s,x)$ satisfy the Lipschitz condition with constant k;

the function $(s,x) \to f(s,x)$ and the mapping $(s,x) \to f'(s,x)$ are continuous (on the Cartesian product of S and a neighborhood X of z).

The problem can be therefore qualified as "second order nonsmooth". We always assume that z is admissible in (SIP), i.e. that $F(z) = 0$.

Let

$$S_\epsilon(x) = \{s \in S \mid f(s,x) \geq f(x) - \epsilon\}.$$

By q we denote any pair (μ, w^*), where μ is a Radon measure on S and w^* a linear functional on R^n. The function

$$\mathcal{L}(q,x) = \int_S f(s,x)d\mu + \langle w^*, F(x)\rangle$$

(where $\langle\cdot,\cdot\rangle$ is the canonical pairing between a space and its dual) is the Lagrangian of (SIP).

Denote by Q_ϵ the collection of all $q = (\mu, w^*)$ having the following properties:

$$\mu \geq 0, \qquad \int_S d\mu + \|w^*\| = 1,$$

μ is supported on $S_\epsilon(z)$ (i.e. $\mu(S \setminus S_\epsilon(z)) = 0$)

and

$$\|\mathcal{L}'(q,z)\| \le \epsilon$$

(where $\mathcal{L}'$ is, as before, the derivative of $\mathcal{L}$ in x and $\|\mathcal{L}'(q,z)\|$ is the norm of $\mathcal{L}'(q,z)$ as a linear functional on R^n). If $\epsilon = 0$, we write $S(x)$ instead of $S_o(x)$ and Q instead of Q_o.

Since w^* is a finite dimensional vector, every Q_ϵ is a weak* compact set.

We observe that $Q \neq \emptyset$ is the first order necessary condition for z to be a local solution of (SIP).

Let us set

$$s_\epsilon(q,e,h) = \sup_{\substack{\|x-z\|<\epsilon \\ \|x+te-z\|<\epsilon \\ 0<t<\epsilon}} t^{-1}(\mathcal{L}'(q,x+te)h - \mathcal{L}'(q,x)h)$$

$$s(q,e,h) = \lim_{\epsilon \downarrow 0} s_\epsilon(q,e,h)$$
$$= \lim_{\substack{x \to z \\ t \downarrow 0}} \sup t^{-1}(\mathcal{L}'(q,x+te)h - \mathcal{L}'(q,x)h).$$

As a function of e, the latter is the Clarke directional derivative of $\mathcal{L}'(q,\cdot)h$ at z. The functions s_ϵ and s (which, as we shall see, are sublinear in each variable) will play the same role as the Hessian of the Lagrangian function plays in the smooth situation.

There are two more objects to be introduced: the <u>critical cone</u>:

$$K = \{h \in R^n \mid f'(s,z)h \le 0,\ \forall\ s \in S(z),\ F'(z)h = 0\}$$

and the <u>narrow critical cone</u>:

$$K_n = \{h \in R^n \mid \max_{s \in S} (f(s,z) + tf'(s,z)h) \le f(z) \text{ for some } t > 0 \text{ (depending on } h),\ F'(z)h = 0\}.$$

<u>Theorem 1</u> (second order necessary condition). <u>If</u> z <u>is a local solution of</u> (SIP), <u>then</u> $Q \neq \emptyset$ <u>and</u>

$$\sup_{q \in Q_\epsilon} s_\epsilon(q,h,h) \ge 0, \qquad \forall\ h \in K_n, \qquad \forall\ \epsilon > 0.$$

<u>Theorem 2</u> (second order sufficient condition). <u>If</u> $Q \neq \emptyset$ <u>and</u>

$$\min_{q \in Q} s(q,-h,h) < 0, \qquad \forall\ h \in K, \quad h \neq 0,$$

<u>then</u> z <u>is an isolated local solution of</u> (SIP).

In particular $K = \{0\}$ is a sufficient condition (in fact, a first order condition).

There are three important distinctions between the structures of the necessary condition and the sufficient condition:

(a) a narrower critical cone enters the necessary condition,

(b) the necessary condition is stated in terms of ϵ-objects,

(c) sufficiency is defined by way of the minimal value of the s-function with one of the arguments having the opposite sign.

The last two distinctions are due primarily to the absence of second derivatives. They disappear if we assume both $f(s,\cdot)$ and F twice continuously differentiable (see Theorem 4 below) and also under some additional assumptions in presence of nonsmoothness (see Proposition 2 and Theorem 3).

The first distinction however is inherent specifically in problems of semi-infinite programming as is seen from the following

Proposition 1. If either S is a finite set or $S = S(z)$, then

$$K_n = K.$$

Indeed, if $f(s,z) + f'(s,z)h \leq f(z)$ and $s \in S(z)$, then $f'(s,z)h \leq 0$ which shows that $K_n \subset K$. If S is a finite set and $h \in K$, then $f(s,z) + f'(s,z)h \leq f(s,z) = f(z)$ if $s \in S(z)$ and $f(s,z) + f'(s,z)h < f(z)$ for all $s \notin S(z)$ if t is sufficiently small. Therefore $h \in K_n$. Likewise, if $S = S(z)$, then $f'(s,z)h \leq 0$ for all s if $h \in K$ which implies that $f(s,z) + f'(s,z)h \leq f(z)$ for all z.

But in general we cannot replace K_n by K in Theorem 1 and K by K_n in Theorem 2 even if everything is smooth. Consider the following

Example. Let $S = \{s = (\alpha,\beta) \,|\, \alpha^2 + \beta^2 = 1\}$, $n = 1$ (i.e. x is a real number) and

$$f(s,x) = -1 + \alpha(2 \cos x - 1) + 2\beta \sin x.$$

Then

$$f(x) = -1 + \sqrt{5 - 4x}$$

attains a strict local minimum at $z = 0$.

The narrow critical cone K_n contains only the zero element. Indeed

$$\max_{s \in S} (f(s,z) + f'(s,z)h) = -1 + \sqrt{1 + 4h^2}$$

may be less than or equal to $f(z) = 0$ only if $h = 0$.

On the contrary, every h belongs to K because $S(z)$ contains a single point $s_o = (1,0)$ and $f'(s_o,z) = 0$.

By definition, Q_ϵ is contained in the set of all probability measures supported on

$$\{s \in S \mid f(s,z) \geq -\epsilon\} = \{s = (\alpha,\beta) \mid \alpha \geq 1 - \epsilon,\ \alpha^2 + \beta^2 = 1\}.$$

Finally, since $f(s,\cdot)$ is twice continuously differentiable,

$$s(\mu,h,h) = \int_S f''(s,z)h^2 d\mu = -2\alpha h^2.$$

It follows that

$$\sup_{\mu \in Q_\epsilon} s(\mu,h,h) \leq -2(1-\epsilon)h^2, \qquad \forall\ h$$

in spite of the fact that f does attain a local minimum at z. Thus K_n cannot be replaced by K in Theorem 1.

On the other hand, let S and X be the same as before and now

$$f(s,x) = -1 + \frac{\alpha}{2}(\cos x + 1) + \frac{\beta}{2} \sin x.$$

If $z = 0$, then the cones K_n and K are as in the previous case, in particular $K_n = \{0\}$ but $f(x) = -1 + \cos 2x$ does not have a local minimum at z. Thus we cannot replace K by K_n in Theorem 2.

It will be clear from the proof that

$$\sup_{q \in Q_\epsilon} s_\epsilon(q,h,h) > 0$$

is not a sufficient condition and

$$\min_{q \in Q} s(q,-h,h) \leq 0$$

is not a necessary condition. But since s_ϵ is sublinear in each variable, the inequality in Theorem 2 implies that

$$\sup_{q \in Q_\epsilon} s_\epsilon(q,h,h) \geq \sup_{q \in Q} s(q,h,h) > 0, \qquad \forall\ h \in K, \qquad h \neq 0.$$

Finally, in general, we cannot remove ϵ from Theorem 1. However the following result is valid.

<u>Proposition 2</u>. <u>If</u> S <u>is a finite set, then</u> $s_\epsilon(q,e,h)$ <u>converges to</u> $s(q,e,h)$ <u>uniformly on every bounded set of</u> $q - s$ <u>for any</u> e,h. <u>In particular, Theorem</u> 1 <u>remains valid in this case if we replace</u> Q_ϵ <u>by</u> Q <u>and</u> s_ϵ <u>by</u> s.

Indeed, if S is a finite set, then q is a finite dimensional vector and s, being sublinear in q are (norm) continuous in q. On the other hand, $s_\epsilon(q,e,h)$ converges to $s(q,e,h)$ for any q,e,h by definition and it remains to take into account that for finite convex functions pointwise convergence and uniform convergence on compact sets are equivalent and that $\cap\, Q_\epsilon = Q$.

Theorems 1 and 2 have weaker versions which are more symmetric in the sense that ϵ no longer enters the necessary conditions.

Let

$$p(s,x,e,h) = \limsup_{\substack{u \to x \\ t \downarrow 0}} t^{-1}(f'(s,u + te)h - f'(s,u)h),$$

$$p(s,e,h) = p(s,z,e,h),$$

$$P(w^*,e,h) = \limsup_{\substack{x \to z \\ t \downarrow 0}} t^{-1}\langle w^*,F'(x + te)h - F'(x)h\rangle$$

and

$$\tilde{s}(q,e,h) = \int_S p*s,e,h)d\mu + P(w^*,e,h).$$

<u>Theorem 3</u>. <u>Assume that, for any</u> e,h, $p(s,x,e,h)$ <u>is upper semi-continuous in</u> (s,x) <u>at every point</u> (s,z), $s \in S$. <u>Then the condition</u>

$$Q \neq \emptyset, \qquad \sup_{q \in Q} \tilde{s}(q,h,h) \geq 0, \qquad \forall\, h \in K_n$$

<u>is necessary and the condition</u>

$$Q \neq \emptyset, \qquad \min_{q \in Q} \tilde{s}(q,-h,h) < 0, \qquad \forall\, h \in K, \qquad h \neq 0$$

<u>is sufficient for</u> z <u>to be a local solution of</u> (SIP).

Proofs of all three theorems will be given in Section 5. We have called Theorem 3 a weaker version of Theorems 1, 2 because under the assumptions of Theorem 3, $\tilde{s}(q,e,h) \geq s(q,e,h)$ and, moreover, there is $\sigma(\epsilon) > 0$ such that

$$\tilde{s}(q,e,h) + \sigma(\epsilon)\|e\|\|h\|\|q\| \geq s_\epsilon(q,e,h)$$

(see the proof of Theorem 3).

Thus the necessary condition given by Theorem 3 is less selective than Theorem 1 and the sufficient condition is less universal than Theorem 2.

If $f(s,\cdot)$ and F are twice continuously differentiable in x, then

$$p(s,e,h) = f''(s,z)(e,h)$$

$$P(w^*,e,h) = \langle w^*,F''(z)(e,h)\rangle$$

so that

$$\tilde{s}(q,e,h) = \mathcal{L}''(q,z)(e,h),$$

where $f''(s,z)(e,h)$, etc., stand for the second order bilinear forms.

It follows that

$$s(q,h,h) = -s(q,-h,h) = \mathcal{L}''(q,z)(h,h),$$

the Hessian of the Lagrangian function, and Theorem 3 implies

Theorem 4. *Assume that* $f(s,\cdot)$ *and* F *are twice continuously differentiable and* $f''(s,x)$ *is jointly continuous in* (s,x). *Then the condition*

$$Q \neq \emptyset, \qquad \max_{q\in Q} \mathcal{L}''(q,z)(h,h) \geq 0, \qquad \forall\ h \in K_n$$

is necessary and the condition

$$Q \neq \emptyset, \qquad \max_{q\in Q} \mathcal{L}''(q,z)(h,h) > 0, \qquad \forall\ h \in K, \qquad h \neq 0$$

is sufficient for z *to be a local solution of* (SIP).

If $S(z)$ is all of S, then Theorem 4 and Proposition 1 together give the result established in [10].

Let us compare Theorem 4 and the result of Ben-Tal, Teboulle and Zowe [2]. Thus, we drop the constraint $F(x) = 0$ for the present. Then Q is the set of all probability measures supported on $S(z)$ and such that

$$\int_S f'(s,z)d\mu = 0, \tag{1}$$

K_n consists of all $h \in R^n$ satisfying

$$\max_{s\in S} (f(s,z) + tf'(s,z)h) \leq f(z)$$

for some $t > 0$ (depending on h) and the necessary condition of Theorem 4 assumes the form:

$$\max_{\mu\in Q} \int_S f''(s,z)(h,h)d\mu \geq 0, \qquad \forall\ h \in K_n. \tag{2}$$

The theorem of Ben-Tal, Teboulle and Zowe is stated as follows. Let

$$S(z,h) = \{s \in S(z) | f'(s,z)h = f'(z;h)\},$$

where

$$f'(z;h) = \lim_{t\downarrow 0} t^{-1}(f(z + th) - f(z)).$$

Denote by $Q(h)$ the collection of all probability measures μ on S satisfying (1) and supported on finite subsets of $S(z,h)$ each containing at most $n + 1$ points. The necessary condition proved in [2] states that

$$\max_{\mu\in Q(h)} \int_S f''(s,z)(h,h)d\mu \geq 0 \tag{2'}$$

for any h satisfying the condition

$P(h)$: there is a neighborhood N of h and $r > 0$ such that $f'(s,z)h \leq 0$ for all $s \in S(z + te)$ whenever $t \in [0,r]$, $e \in N$.

There is of course an unessential difference, that only discrete measures are considered in [2] while Theorem 4 refers to arbitrary measures. Indeed, since μ enters (1) and (2) in a linear fashion, the relations will hold for a discrete measure with at most $n + 1$ atoms (also belonging to Q) if they are satisfied for some element of Q (thanks to the Caratheodory representation theorem for convex hulls of cones).

On the other hand, it is obvious that any h satisfying $P(h)$ belongs to K_n but not vice versa. Thus even in the absence of equality constraints Theorem 4 gives a stronger result.

Another advantage of Theorem 4 over the theorem of Ben-Tal, Teboulle and Zowe is that, in the latter, the maximum in (2') is taken over different sets depending on h. In particular, it is necessary to calculate $S(z,h)$, which may be difficult.

This procedure is redundant however because the sets $Q(h)$ do not actually depend on h. Indeed, if μ is a discrete measure belonging to Q (i.e. $\mu = \Sigma\mu_i \epsilon(s_i)$, $\epsilon(s)$ being a unit mass at z), then

$$0 = \int_S f'(s,z)d\mu = \Sigma\mu_i f'(s_i,z).$$

On the other hand, $\mu_i f'(s_i,z)h \leq 0$ for any $h \in K_n$ and any i because $s_i \in S(z)$ and $\mu_i \geq 0$. Therefore $\mu_i f'(s_i,z)h = 0$ for any $h \in K_n$.

An important point to be emphasized is that no regularity assumption has been imposed in any of the four theorems stated above, in contrast to classical results such as, say, the theorem of McCormick [5] whose second order regularity assumption excludes most inequality constrained problems. (Of course, if the problem is degenerate, i.e. if $\mu = 0$ whenever $(\mu,w^*) \in Q$, the necessary condition carries little information about the minimum. On the other hand, the sufficient condition is also efficient, in this case.)

This is closely connected with the fact that each one of our necessary conditions uses the whole set of Lagrange multipliers, so that no information carried by first order conditions is lost. Levitin, Miljutin and Osmolovskii [9] were the first who realized this in full generality and also found that sufficient conditions have the same structure. But much earlier Cox [4] showed that, in a necessary condition, different Lagrange multipliers provide nonnegative values of the corresponding quadratic forms for different critical vectors. This principle was later rediscovered by Ben-Tal [1], who was apparently unaware of the work of Levitin, Miljutin and Osmolovskii.

3. An Auxiliary Problem

As was mentioned in the introduction, the proofs of Theorems 1 and 2 follows the same scheme as in [6]. So we start by considering an auxiliary problem of unconstrained minimization of the function

$$\varphi(x) = g(G(x)),$$

where G is a mapping from R^n into a Banach space Y, continuously differentiable near z and g, continuous sublinear function on Y.

To begin with, we shall quote a fundamental result containing a dual characterization of local minima of such a function. For any $\epsilon > 0$ we set

$$\Omega_\epsilon = \{y^* \in Y^* \mid \|G'^*(z)y^*\| \leq \epsilon, \qquad y^* \in \partial_\epsilon g(G(z))\}$$

$$\Psi_\epsilon(x) = \max\{\langle y^*, G(x)\rangle \mid y^* \in \Omega_\epsilon\}.$$

Here

$$\partial_\epsilon g(w) = \{y^* \mid g(y) - g(w) \geq \langle y^*, y - w\rangle - \epsilon, \ \forall\, y\}$$

is the ϵ-subdifferential of g at w, $G'(x)$ is the derivative of G at x, $G'^*(x)$ is the adjoint operator and $\langle \cdot,\cdot \rangle$ is the canonical pairing between Y and Y^*. We shall write Ω instead of Ω_o if $\epsilon = 0$. Thus

$$\Omega = \{y^* \in Y^* \mid G'^*(z)y^* = 0, \ y^* \in \partial g(G(z))\}.$$

Every Ω_ϵ is norm bounded, hence weak* compact, because it is contained in $\partial_\epsilon g(G(z)) \subset \partial g(0)$. (The latter inclusion is due to the fact that g is sublinear.) By definition, Ω is the intersection of all Ω_ϵ. We also observe that $\Omega \neq \emptyset$ is a (first order) necessary condition for φ to have a local minimum at z.

Proposition 3 ([6], p. 268). *The following two statements are equivalent:*

(a) φ *attains a local (strict local) minimum at* z;

(b) $\Omega \neq \emptyset$ *and* Ψ_ϵ *attains a local (strict local) minimum at* z *for any* $\epsilon > 0$.

Note (see [6]) that

$$\varphi(z) = \varphi_\epsilon(z), \qquad \forall\ \epsilon > 0,$$

provided $\Omega \neq \emptyset$.

We shall assume further that $G'(x)$ satisfies the Lipschitz condition (near z) with constant $k > 0$. We set

$$s_\epsilon(y^*,e,h) = \sup_{\substack{\|x-z\|<\epsilon \\ \|x+te-z\|<\epsilon \\ 0<t<\epsilon}} t^{-1}\langle y^*, G'(x + te)h - G'(x)h\rangle,$$

$$s(y^*,e,h) = \lim_{\epsilon\to 0} s_\epsilon(y^*,e,h)$$

$$= \limsup_{\substack{x\to z \\ t\downarrow 0}} t^{-1}\langle y^*, G'(x + te)h - G'(x)h\rangle.$$

As follows from the definitions, $s_\epsilon(y^*,e,h) \geq s(y^*,e,h)$ for any y^*,e,h.

Proposition 4. *The functions* s_ϵ *and* s *are (separately) sublinear in each variable,*

$$s_\epsilon(y^*,e,h) \leq k\|y^*\|\|e\|\|h\|,$$

$$s_\epsilon(y^*,e,h) - s_\epsilon(y^*,\bar{e},\bar{h}) \leq k(\|e - \bar{e}\|\|h\| + \|h - \bar{h}\|\|\bar{e}\|)\|y^*\|$$

and the same inequalities are valid for s. *In particular,* s_ϵ *and* s *are continuous in* (e,h) *uniformly in* y^* *on every bounded subset of* $Y^* \times R^n \times R^n$.

Proof. It follows immediately from the definition that s_ϵ and s are sublinear in y^* and in h. Further, $s(y^*,\cdot,h)$ is the Clarke directional derivative of a Lipschitz function, hence it is also sublinear [3] and it follows from Proposition 8.2 of [7] that s_ϵ is sublinear in e.

The first of the inequalities is a direct consequence of the definition and the Lipschitz property, the second results from the following string of estimates:

$$\begin{aligned} s(y^*,e,h) &- s(y^*,\bar{e},\bar{h}) \\ &= s(y^*,e,h) - s(y^*,\bar{e},h) + s(y^*,\bar{e},h) - s(y^*,\bar{e},\bar{h}) \\ &\leq s(y^*,e - \bar{e},h) + s(y^*,\bar{e},h - \bar{h}) \\ &\leq k\|y^*\|\|e - \bar{e}\|\|h\| + k\|y^*\|\|\bar{e}\|\|h - \bar{h}\|. \end{aligned}$$

Proposition 5.

$$s_{\|h\|}(y^*,h,h) \geq 2\langle y^*, G(z + h) - G(z) - G'(z)h\rangle \geq -s_{\|h\|}(y^*,-h,h).$$

Proof. We have

$$\langle y^*, G(z+h) - G(z) - G'(z)h\rangle$$

$$= \int_0^1 \langle y^*, G'(z+th)h - G'(z)h\rangle dt$$

(setting $u = h/\|h\|$)

$$= \|h\|^{-1} \int_0^{\|h\|} \langle y^*, G'(z+tu)h - G'(z)h\rangle dt$$

$$\leq \|h\|^{-1} \int_0^{\|h\|} s_{\|h\|}(y^*, u, h)\, dt$$

$$= \frac{\|h\|}{2} s_{\|h\|}(y^*, u, h) = \frac{1}{2} s_{\|h\|}(y^*, h, h).$$

On the other hand, setting $v(t) = z + tu$, we have

$$\langle y^*, G(z+h) - G(z) - G'(z)h\rangle$$

$$= -\|h\|^{-1} \int_0^{\|h\|} \langle y^*, G'(v(t) - tu)h - G'(v(t))h\rangle dt$$

$$\geq -\|h\|^{-1} \int_0^{\|h\|} s(y^*, -u, h)\, dt = -\frac{1}{2} s(y^*, -h, h).$$

Denote by K_c the collection of all $h \in R^n$ satisfying

$$g(G(z) + tG'(z)h) \leq g(G(z)) \tag{3}$$

for some $t > 0$ (depending on h). Obviously, K_c is a cone which we shall also call the <u>critical cone</u>. Observe that if (3) holds for some t, it is also valid for all smaller positive t because g is convex and (3) trivially holds for $t = 0$.

<u>Theorem 5</u>. <u>If</u> φ <u>attains a local minimum at</u> z, <u>then</u> $\Omega \neq \emptyset$ <u>and</u>

$$\sup_{y^* \in \Omega_\epsilon} s_\epsilon(y^*, h, h) \geq 0, \qquad \forall\, h \in K_c, \qquad \forall\, \epsilon > 0.$$

<u>Proof</u>. As follows from Proposition 3, $\Omega \neq \emptyset$ and $\Psi_\epsilon(x) \geq \Psi_\epsilon(z) = \varphi(z)$ for all x of a neighborhood of z (depending on ϵ). Fix an $\epsilon > 0$ and an $h \in K_c$. Then (3) holds for all sufficiently small t and

$$\langle y^*, G(z+th) - G(z) - tG'(z)h\rangle \leq \frac{t^2}{2} s_\epsilon(y^*, h, h) \tag{4}$$

whenever $\|th\| < \epsilon$ (Proposition 5).

Thus if t is sufficiently small, then

$$\begin{aligned}\varphi(z) &\leq \Psi_\epsilon(z + th)\\ &= \max\{\langle y^*, G(z + th)\rangle \mid y^* \in \Omega_\epsilon\}\\ &\leq \max\{\langle y^*, G(z) + tG'(z)h\rangle \mid y^* \in \Omega_\epsilon\}\\ &\quad + \max\{\langle y^*, G(z + th) - G(z) - tG'(z)h\rangle \mid y^* \in \Omega_\epsilon\}.\end{aligned}$$

The first maximum in the right side is not greater than $g(G(z) + tG'(z)h)$ because $\Omega_\epsilon \subset \partial g(0)$ and hence then $\varphi(z)$ since $h \in K_c$. But by virtue of (4), the second maximum is majorized by

$$(t^2/2)\ \sup\{s(y^*, h, h) \mid y^* \in \Omega_\epsilon\}. \qquad \text{Q.E.D.}$$

<u>Theorem 6</u>. <u>Assume</u> <u>that</u> $G(z) = 0$. <u>If</u> $\Omega \neq \emptyset$ <u>and</u>

$$\min_{y^* \in \Omega} s(y^*, -h, h) < 0, \qquad \forall\ h \in K_c,$$

<u>then</u> φ <u>attains</u> <u>a</u> <u>strict</u> <u>local</u> <u>minimum</u> <u>at</u> z.

<u>Proof</u>. Since $\varphi(z) = 0$, it suffices to show that

$$a = \liminf_{\substack{h \to 0\\ h \neq 0}} \|h\|^{-2} \varphi(z + h) > 0.$$

If $a = \infty$, there is nothing to prove. So assume that $a < \infty$.

Let $\|h_m\|$ be a sequence of nonzero elements of R^n converging to zero and such that

$$\lim_{m \to \infty} \|h_m\|^{-2} \varphi(z + h_m) = a.$$

We may write $h_m = t_m e_m$, where $\|e_m\| = 1$ and $t_m = \|h_m\|$. Taking, if necessary, a subsequence, we may regard the sequence $\{e_m\}$ as converging to some h, $\|h\| = 1$.

Let $y^* \in \partial g(0)$. Then (since G is continuously differentiable near z and $G(z) = 0$)

$$\begin{aligned}0 = \lim_{m\to\infty} t_m a &= \lim_{m\to\infty} t_m^{-1} \varphi(z + t_m e_m)\\ &\geq \lim_{m\to\infty} t_m^{-1} \langle y^*, G(z + t_m e_m)\rangle\\ &= \lim_{m\to\infty} \langle y^*, G'(z) e_m\rangle = \langle y^*, G'(z)h\rangle.\end{aligned}$$

This is true for any $y^* \in \partial g(0)$. Therefore

$$g(G(z) + G'(z)h) = g(G'(z)h) \leq 0 = \varphi(z)$$

which shows that $h \in K_c$.

By Proposition 5, for any y^*

$$\langle y^*, G(z + t_m e_m) - G(z) - t_m G'(z) e_m\rangle \geq -\frac{t_m^2}{2} s_{t_m}(y^*, -e_m, e_m).$$

Therefore for any $y^* \in \Omega$ (i.e. such that $y^* \in \partial g(0)$ and $G'^*(z)y^* = 0$) we have (using Proposition 2):

$$\begin{aligned} a &= \lim_{m\to\infty} t_m^{-2}\varphi(z + t_m e_m) \\ &\geq \lim_{m\to\infty} t_m^{-2}\langle y^*, G(z + t_m e_m)\rangle \\ &= \lim_{m\to\infty} t_m^{-2}\langle y^*, G(z + t_m e_m) - G(z) - t_m G'(z)e_m\rangle \\ &\geq -\frac{1}{2}\lim_{m\to\infty} s_{t_m}(y^*, -e_m, e_m) = -\frac{1}{2}\, s(y^*, -h, h). \end{aligned}$$

This is true for any $y^* \in \Omega$ so that

$$2a \geq \max_{y^*\in\Omega} (-s(y^*, -h, h)) = -\min_{y^*\in\Omega} s(y^*, -h, h) > 0.$$

Remarks. Theorems 5 and 6 are very close to Theorems 1 and 2 of [6], Part 3 and play the same role in the proofs of the main results. But the assumptions of Theorem 6 do not include any regularity assumption similar to what was imposed in [6] (see condition (4.3) in 6, p. 271). This appeared to be possible because X is finite dimensional and $G(z) = 0$. To emphasize the importance of not using such a regularity assumption we note that, in general, it cannot be valid for problems of semi-infinite programming.

§4. Proofs of Main Theorems

Proofs of Theorems 1 and 2 are very similar. Each time we replace (SIP) by an equivalent (in a appropriate sense) problem of unconstrained minimization of a function having the form $g(G(x))$ and the proofs reduce to calculation of Ω_ϵ, K_c and s_ϵ associated with the function.

1. Proof of Theorem 1. If the range of $F'(z)$ is not all of R^m, then there is a linear functional w^* on R^m with $\|w^*\| = 1$ such that $\langle w^*, F'(z)h\rangle = 0$ for all h. This means that both $q = (0, w^*)$ and $-q = (0, -w^*)$ belong to Q and hence to every Q_ϵ. Since either $s(q,h,h)$ or $s(-q,h,h)$ is nonnegative (because s is sublinear in each variable), the theorem is trivially valid.

We may assume therefore that the range of $F'(z)$ is all of R^m. If so, then we can apply the reduction theorem of [6, Part 1] which says that z is a local minimum of the function

$$\varphi_r(x) = f(x) + r\|F(x)\|,$$

if r is sufficiently large.

To represent φ_r as $g(G(x))$ (in a neighborhood of z), let us take $Y = C(S) \times R^m$, ($C(S)$ being the space of continuous functions on S with the uniform norm), so that elements of Y are pairs $(\omega(\cdot),w)$, $\omega(\cdot) \in C(S)$, $w \in R^m$. Let $G : R^n \to Y$ be defined by

$$G(x) = (f(\cdot,x),F(x)).$$

Finally, let us fix $\epsilon > 0$ and set

$$g_r(y) = \max_{s \in S_\epsilon(z)} \omega(s) + r\|w\|.$$

We claim that $\varphi_r(x) = g_r(G(x))$ if x is sufficiently close to z. Indeed,

$$\max_{s \in S_\epsilon(z)} f(s,x) = f(x)$$

for such x for otherwise we would have sequences $\{s_k\} \subset S$ and $x_k \to z$ such that $s_k \notin S_\epsilon(z)$, i.e. $f(s_k,z) < f(z) - \epsilon$, $f(s_k,x_k) = f(x_k) \to f(z)$. These two relations are contradictory because $f(s_k,x_k) - f(s_k,z) \to 0$ as $k \to \infty$ since S is compact and $f(s,x)$ jointly continuous.

According to the assumptions, G is continuously differentiable near z,

$$G(x) = (f'(\cdot,x),F'(x)),$$

$G'(x)$ is Lipschitz near z and g_r is a continuous sublinear function by definition.

Elements of the dual space Y^* are pairs $y^* = (\mu,w^*)$, where μ is a Radon measure on S and $w^* \in (R^m)^*$. It is a well known fact of convex analysis (see [8] for example) that $\partial g_r(0)$ consists of all pair pairs (μ,w^*) such that μ is a probability measure on $S_\epsilon(z)$ and $\|w^*\| \leq r$.

We have further

$$G'^*(z)y^* = \int_S f'(s,z)d\mu + F'^*(z)w^* = \mathcal{L}'(y^*,z). \tag{5}$$

It follows that $\Omega_\epsilon(r)$ (the Ω_ϵ corresponding to φ_r) belongs to

$$\tilde{\Omega}_\epsilon(r) = \{(\mu,w^*) | \mu \geq 0, \int_S d\mu = 1, \mu(S \backslash S_\epsilon(z)) = 0,$$
$$\|w^*\| \leq r, \|\mathcal{L}''(y^*,z)\| \leq \epsilon\}.$$

Let $K_c(r)$ be the critical cone associated with φ_r. Fix an r_o such that φ_{r_o} attains a local minimum at z. Then $\Omega(r_o) \neq \emptyset$ and (whenever y^* belongs to $\Omega(r_o)$)

$$g_{r_o}(G(z) + G'(z)h) \geq \langle y^*,G(z) + G'(z)h\rangle = \langle y^*,G(z)\rangle = \varphi_{r_o}(z) = f(z) \tag{6}$$

for any h. If $r > r_o$ and $h \in K_c(r)$, then for some $t > 0$

$$g_r(G(z) + tG'(z)h) \leq \varphi_r(z) = f(z).$$

Together with (6), this gives

$$0 \geq g_r(G(z) + tG'(z)h) - g_{r_o}(G(z) + tG'(z)h) = (r - r_o)\|F'(z)h\|$$

which shows that $F'(z)h = 0$ and $K_c(r)$ is defined by the relations

$$\max_{s \in S_\epsilon(z)} (f(s,z) + tf'(s,z)h) \leq f(z), \qquad F'(z)h = 0. \tag{7}$$

Finally, as follows from (5),

$$s_\epsilon(y^*,e,h) = \sup_{\substack{\|x-h\|<\epsilon \\ \|x+te-h\|<\epsilon \\ 0<t<\epsilon}} t^{-1}(\mathcal{L}'(y^*,x + te)h - \mathcal{L}'(y^*,x)h).$$

Let us take some $r > r_o$. By Theorem 5,

$$\sup_{y^* \in \tilde{\Omega}_\epsilon(r)} s_\epsilon(y^*,h,h) \geq 0, \qquad \forall\, h \in K_c(r).$$

But

$$q = (1 + \|w^*\|)^{-1}y^* \in Q_\epsilon$$

whenever $y^* = (\mu,w^*) \in \tilde{\Omega}_\epsilon(r)$, as immediately follows from definitions of Q_ϵ and $\tilde{\Omega}_\epsilon(r)$ and (7) implies that $K_n \subset K_c(r)$. Therefore

$$\sup_{q \in Q_\epsilon} s_\epsilon(q,h,h) \geq 0, \qquad \forall\, h \in K_n. \qquad \text{Q.E.D.}$$

2. Proof of Theorem 2. We take the same Y as above but define G and g in a different manner:

$$G(x) = (f(\cdot,x) - f(\cdot,z), F(x)),$$

$$g(y) = \max\{\max_{s \in S(z)} \omega(s), \|w\|\}.$$

Then

$$\varphi(x) = g(G(x)) = \max\{\max_{s \in S(z)} (f(s,x) - f(s,z)), \|F(x)\|\}.$$

It is an easy matter to see that z is an isolated local solution of (SIP) if φ attains a strict local minimum at z. Indeed, if $\varphi(x) > \varphi(z)$, then either $F(x) \neq 0$ which means that x is not admissible in (SIP) or $F(x) = 0$ and $f(x) \geq f(s,x) > f(s,z) = f(z)$ for some $s \in S(z)$.

Every element $y^* = (\mu,w^*)$ belonging to $\partial g(0)$ can be represented in the form

$$\mu = \alpha\nu, \qquad w^* = (1-\alpha)v^*,$$

where $0 \le \alpha \le 1$, is a probability measure on $S(z)$ and $\|v^*\| \le 1$. Therefore Ω consists of those $y^* = (\mu, w^*)$ which satisfy

$$\begin{gathered}\mu \ge 0, \qquad \int_S d\mu + \|w^*\| \le 1, \qquad \mu(S\setminus S(z)) = 0, \\ \mathcal{L}'(y^*,z) = \int_S f'(s,z)d\mu + F'^*(z)w^* = 0\end{gathered} \quad . \tag{8}$$

The critical cone K_c contains $h \in R^n$ satisfying

$$g(G(z) + G'(z)h) = \max\{\max_{s\in S(z)} f'(s,z)h, \|F'(z)h\|\} \le \varphi(z) = 0,$$

in other words,

$$K_c = \{h|F'(z)h = 0,\ f'(s,z)h \le 0,\ \forall\ s \in S(z)\},$$

i.e. K_c coincides with the critical cone K associated with (SIP).

Finally, the derivative of G obviously coincides with the derivative of the mapping that was used in the preceding proof. Therefore $s(y^*,e,h)$ is the same function as was introduced in Section 2.

We shall show that, under the assumptions of Theorem 2, all of the assumptions of Theorem 6 are fulfilled for φ. Indeed, $Q \subset \Omega$ (the only difference between them is that the normalizing equality in the definition of Q is replaced by the inequality in (8)), so that *a fortiori*

$$\min_{y^*\in\Omega} s(y^*,-h,h) < 0, \qquad \forall\ h \in K.$$

On the other hand, $G(z) = 0$ (because $F(z) = 0$).

By virtue of Theorem 6, φ does attain a local minimum at z and this finishes the proof.

3. *Proof of Theorem 3*. Let us set

$$p_\epsilon(s,e,h) = \sup_{\substack{\|x-z\|<\epsilon \\ \|x+te-z\|<\epsilon \\ 0<t<\epsilon}} t^{-1}(f'(s,x+te)h - f'(s,x)h),$$

$$P_\epsilon(w^*,e,h) = \sup_{\substack{\|x-z\|<\epsilon \\ \|x+te-z\|<\epsilon \\ 0<t<\epsilon}} t^{-1}\langle w^*, F'(x+te)h - F'(x)h\rangle.$$

Then for any $q = (\mu, w^*)$ with positive

$$s_\epsilon(q,e,h) \le \int_S p_\epsilon(s,e,h)d\mu + P_\epsilon(w^*,e,h). \tag{9}$$

It follows from the mean value theorem for generalized gradients of Clarke that

$$t^{-1}(f'(s,x + te)h - f'(s,x)h) \leq \sup_{0\leq\tau\leq t} p(s,x + \tau e,e,h).$$

Therefore

$$p_{\epsilon}(s,e,h) \leq \sup_{\|x-z\|<\epsilon} p(s,x,e,h). \tag{10}$$

Since S is compact and $p(s,x,e,h)$ is upper semicontinuous in (s,x) at every (s,z), $s \in S$, for any given $\delta > 0$, we can find such an $\epsilon > 0$, that

$$p(s,e,h) = p(s,z,e,h) \geq p(s,x,e,h) - \delta/2 \tag{11}$$

whenever $\|x - z\| < \epsilon$.

On the other hand, since w^* is finite dimensional, $P_{\epsilon}(w^*,e,h)$ converges to $P(w^*,e,h)$ for every e,h on every bounded subset of the w^*-space (Proposition 2). Together with (9)-(11), this implies that we can find $\epsilon = \epsilon(\delta)$ such that

$$s_{\epsilon}(q,e,h) \leq \int_S p(s,e,h)d\mu + P(w^*,e,h) - \delta = \tilde{s}(q,e,h) - \delta \tag{12}$$

whenever $\mu \geq 0$, $\int d\mu \leq 1$, $\|w^*\| \leq 1$.

Further, if μ_k weak* converges to μ $(\mu_k \geq 0)$, then

$$\limsup_{k\to\infty} \int_S p(s,e,h)d\mu_k \leq \int_S p(s,e,h)d\mu$$

since $p(\cdot,e,h)$ is upper semicontinuous. It follows in view of (12) that

$$\limsup_{\substack{\epsilon\downarrow 0\\ q\in Q}} s_{\epsilon}(q,e,h) \leq \tilde{s}(q,e,h)$$

which proves the necessity part of Theorem 3.

To prove the sufficiency part, we note that, according to (12), $s(q,e,h) \leq \tilde{s}(q,e,h) - \delta$ for any $\delta > 0$, hence $s(q,e,h) \leq \tilde{s}(q,e,h) < 0$ implies that $s(q,e,h) < 0$.

REFERENCES

[1] BEN-TAL, A.: Second Order Theory of Extremum Problems in Extremal Methods and Systems Analysis: An International Symposium on the Occasion of Professor Abraham Charnes' Sixtieth Birthday (eds. A. V. Fiacco and K. O. Kortanek), in Lecture Notes in Economics and Mathematical Systems, Vol. 174, Berlin-Heidelberg-New York: Springer-Verlag, 1980.

[2] BEN-TAL, A., M. TEBOULLE AND J. ZOWE: Second Order Necessary Optimality Conditions for Semi-Infinite Programming Problems. In Semi-Infinite Programming, Lecture Notes in Control and Information Sciences No. 15. Berlin-Heidelberg-New York: Springer-Verlag, 1979.

[3] CLARKE, F. H.: Generalized Gradients of Lipschitz Functionals. Advances in Math. 40 (1981), 52-67.

[4] COX, M. J.: On Necessary Conditions for Relative Minima. Amer. J. Math. 66 (1944).

[5] FIACCO, A. V. AND G. P. MCCORMICK: Nonlinear Programming. New York: John Wiley and Sons, 1968.

[6] IOFFE, A. D.: Necessary and Sufficient Conditions for a Local Minimum. SIAM J. Control Optimization 17 (1979), 245 - 288.

[7] IOFFE, A. D.: Nonsmooth Analysis: Differential Calculus of Nondifferentiable Mappings. Trans. Amer. Math. Soc. 266 (1981), 1 - 56.

[8] IOFFE, A. D. AND V. M. TIKHOMIROV: Theory of Extremal Problems. North Holland, 1979.

[9] LEVITIN, E. S. A. A. MILJUTIN AND N. P. OSMOLOVSKII: On Conditions for a Local Minimum in a Problem with Constraints. Math. Economics and Functional Analysis. Moscow: "Nauka", 1974.

[10] LEVITIN, E. S. A. A. MILJUTIN AND N. P. OSMOLOVSKII: Higher Order Conditions for a Local Minimum. Uspehi Matem. Nauk 33 (1978), 83 - 148.

ON STOCHASTIC CONTROL PROBLEMS WITH IMPULSE COST VANISHING

José-Luis MENALDI and Edmundo ROFMAN

ABSTRACT

We consider stochastic control problems for diffusion processes with impulse and continuous controls when the cost of each impulse vanishes. Some properties of the optimal cost and the existence of optimal impulse controls are studied using perturbation techniques and quasi-variational inequality methods.

1 - INTRODUCTION

We are interested in stochastic control problems for diffusion processes with impulse and continuous controls when the cost of each impulse vanishes.

After perturbing this problem with a fixed positive cost associated with each impulse we obtain a classical strong non-linear second order quasi-variational inequality.

In the first part of this paper we show, under suitable assumptions, the convergence of the perturbed optimal cost to the expected optimal cost of our problem. Next we give an example where this expected optimal cost is obtained by perturbing dynamics having only continuous type controls.

(This work has been partly supported by D.O.E., Office of Electric Energy Systems, under contract 01 - 80 RA - 50154).

In the second part we study the existence of optimal impulse controls. We show that the classical impulse control derived from the continuation set is optimal. The main hypothesis herein is to assume that, in some direction, all admissible impulses are bounded below by a positive constant.

2 - ASSUMPTIONS AND NOTATIONS

We now give notation and assumptions which will remain valid throughout, unless otherwise noted.

Let V be a convex closed subset of $\mathbb{R}^N$. We call an admissible continuous system a set

$$(\Omega,\ F,\ F^t,\ P,\ W(t),\ v(t),\ y_x^o(t))$$

where :

(Ω, F, P) is a probability space,
F^t is a non decreasing right continuous family of completed sub σ-algebras of F,
$W(t)$ is a standard Wiener process with respect to F^t,
$v(t)$ is a measurable adapted process taking values in some compact subset V_o of V (which may depend on $v(\cdot)$),
$y^o(t) = y_x^o(t)$ is the solution of the following Itô equation in $\mathbb{R}^N$:

$$(2.1)\qquad \begin{cases} dy^o(t) = \sigma(y^o(t),\ v(t))\ dW(t) + g(y^o(t),\ v(t))dt,\ t \geq 0 \\ y^o(0) = x \end{cases}$$

where $\sigma : \mathbb{R}^N \times V \to \mathbb{R}^N \times \mathbb{R}^N$, $g : \mathbb{R}^N \times V \to \mathbb{R}^N$ are continuous bounded functions, uniformly Lipschitz continuous in $\mathbb{R}^N$.

We shall refer to the diffusion $y^o(t)$ as the continuous output process of the system.

Let Λ be a closed subset of $\mathbb{R}^N$. An impulse control ν is a set $\{\theta_1, \xi_1, \ldots, \theta_i, \xi_i, \ldots\}$ where $\{\theta_i\}_{i=1}^{\infty}$ is an increasing unbounded sequence of stopping times with respect to F^t(i.e. $\theta_i \leq \theta_{i+1}$, $\theta_i \to \infty$) and $\{\xi_i\}_{i=1}^{\infty}$ is a sequence of random variables taking values in Λ, adapted with respect to $\{\theta_i\}_{i=1}^{\infty}$ (i.e. $\xi_i : \Omega \to \Lambda$, F^{θ_i}-measurable). We consider the diffusion $y(t) = y_x(t)$ with jumps, which is right-continuous, having left-hand limits, defined by the stochastic equation

(2.2) $$\begin{cases} dy(t) = \sigma(y(t), v(t))dW(t) + g(y(t), v(t))dt + \sum_{i=1}^{\infty} \xi_i \, \delta(t-\theta_i)dt, & t \geq 0 \\ y(0) = x & x \in \mathbb{R}^N. \end{cases}$$

The set $(\Omega, F, F^t, P, W(t), v(t), \nu, y_x(t))$ will be called an <u>admissible system</u> A if the mathematical expectation of the number of impulses is finite, i.e.

(2.3) $$E\left\{\sum_{i=1}^{\infty} e^{-\alpha\theta_i}\right\} < \infty, \quad \text{where } \alpha > 0 \text{ is a discount factor.}$$

We remark that an admissible continuous system is a particular class of admissible systems (where we do not excite any impulse).

Let $f(x,v)$ be a continuous bounded function on $\mathbb{R}^N \times V$, uniformly Lipschitz continuous in $\mathbb{R}^N$, taking values in $\mathbb{R}_0^+$. We define the cost function

(2.4) $$J_x^k(A) = E\left\{\int_0^{\infty} f(y_x(t), v(t))\, e^{-\alpha t}\, dt + k \sum_{i=1}^{\infty} e^{-\alpha\theta_i}\right\},$$

where $k \in \mathbb{R}^+$ is a parameter.

The optimal cost is

(2.5) $$\hat{u}_k(x) = \inf \{J_x^k(A) \;/\; A \text{ is an admissible system}\}.$$

We shall study its behavior when k tends to zero and we shall give some characterization of this limit.

We recall that, under classical hypotheses (e.g., A. Bensoussan and J.L. Lions [1]) the mathematical expectation of the number of impulses is unbounded as k approaches zero, i.e.

(2.6) $$E\left\{\sum_{i=1}^{\infty} e^{-\alpha\theta_i}\right\} \leq \frac{c}{k}$$

with the constant c independent of x and k.

Let us collect our assumptions :

$\sigma = (\sigma_{ij})$, $g = (g_i)$ $i,j = 1, \ldots, N$

If Φ represents σ_{ij}, g_i or f ; $\forall x, x' \in \mathbb{R}^N$, $\forall v, v' \in V$ we have :

$$
(2.7)\quad \begin{cases} |\phi(x,v) - \phi(x', v')| \le C|x-x'| + \rho(|v-v'|) \\ |\phi(x,v)| \le C \\ \alpha > \alpha_o = \sup \{tr [(\sigma(x,v) - \sigma(x',v)) (\sigma(x,v) - \sigma(x',v))^* |x-x'|^{-2} + \\ + 2(x-x')(g(x,v) - g(x',v)) |x-x'|^{-2} \} \\ f(x,v) \ge 0, \end{cases}
$$

where C denotes a constant and ρ is a continuous function from $\mathbb{R}_o^+$ into itself satisfying $\rho(0) = 0$.

REMARK 2.1. It is not so hard to relax assumptions (2.7). For instance, we can take $\alpha = \alpha(x,v) \ge C > 0$, $k = k(x,\xi)$, σ and g unbounded, f uniformly continuous. We can also consider a domain $\mathcal{O}$ instead of $\mathbb{R}^N$.

3 - STOCHASTIC IMPULSE CONTROL PROBLEM

3.1. The general case

We recall that, following the results of P.L. Lions and J.L. Menaldi [5], J.L. Menaldi [6] and classical techniques (e.g. A. Bensoussan and J.L. Lions [1], W.J. Fleming and R. Rishel [3], A. Friedman [4]) it is possible to show under assumptions (2.7) that the optimal cost $\hat{u}_k(x)$ given by (2.5) is the maximum solution of the problem

$$
(3.1)\quad \begin{cases} \text{Find } u_k \in W^{1,\infty}(\mathbb{R}^N) \text{ such that} \\ A_v\, u_k \le f(.,v) \text{ in } \mathcal{D}'(\mathbb{R}^N), \ \forall v \in V, \\ u_k \le M_k\, u_k \text{ in } \mathbb{R}^N, \end{cases}
$$

where $W^{1,\infty}(\mathbb{R}^N)$ and $\mathcal{D}'(\mathbb{R}^N)$ denote the spaces of bounded Lipschitz continuous functions and of distributions, respectively ; the differential second order operator A_v is defined by

$$
(3.2)\quad A_v = -\frac{1}{2}\ tr[\sigma(.,v)\ \sigma^*(.,v)\ \frac{\partial^2}{\partial x^2}] - g(.,v)\ \frac{\partial}{\partial x} + \alpha
$$

and M_k is the mapping

(3.3) $$[M_k u](x) = k + \inf \{u(x+\xi) \,/\, \xi \in \Lambda\}.$$

Now we introduce the case k = 0.

We set

(3.4) $$\hat{u}(x) = \inf \{J_x(A) \,/\, A \text{ admissible system}\},$$

where $J_x(A)$ denotes the cost function (2.4) with the impulse cost k = 0.

Furthermore we consider the problem

(3.5) $$\begin{cases} \text{Find } u \in W^{1,\infty}(\mathbb{R}^N) \text{ such that} \\ A_v u \le f(.,v) \text{ in } \mathcal{D}'(\mathbb{R}^N),\ \forall v \in V \\ u \le Mu \text{ in } \mathbb{R}^N, \end{cases}$$

where M is the mapping

(3.6) $$[Mu](x) = \inf\{u(x+\xi)/\xi \in \Lambda\}.$$

REMARK 3.1. If $0 \in \Lambda$, the inequality $u \le Mu$ and (3.6) imply the equality $u = Mu$. It follows that the argument of maximum solution is essential at this point, since the complementary condition is not meaningful.

Regarding (3.4) and (3.5), we have

THEOREM 3.1

Let assumptions (2.7) hold. Then, the optimal $\hat{u}$ defined by (3.4) is the maximum(*) solution of problem (3.5). Moreover, we have the convergence

(3.7) $$\hat{u}_k \to \hat{u} \text{ in } C_0(\mathbb{R}^N), \text{ as } k \to 0$$

with $\hat{u}_k$ given by (2.5).

Proof

Clearly $\hat{u}_k$ is decreasing with k. So, since the $\hat{u}_k$ are equibounded we can define

(*) Cfr. Remark 3.1.

(3.8) $$u_o(x) = \lim_{k \to 0^+} \hat{u}_k(x), \quad \forall x \in \mathbb{R}^N.$$

As in J.L. Menaldi [6], from Itô's formula we obtain the estimate

(3.9) $$E\{|y_x(t) - y_{x'}(t)|^2 \; e^{-\alpha_o t}\} \leq |x - x'|^2 \; ;$$

hence with (2.4) and (2.5), we obtain

(3.10) $$|\hat{u}_k(x) - \hat{u}_k(x')| \leq (\alpha - \alpha_o)^{-1} \; C_f \; |x - x'| \quad \forall x, \; x' \in \mathbb{R}^N$$

where C_f is the Lipschitz constant of f (cfr. (2.7)).

Then, it is easy to check that the function $u_o(x)$ defined by the decreasing limit (3.8) is a solution of problem (3.5). Moreover, since any solution of problem (3.5) is also a solution of problem (3.1), we deduce that u_o is the maximum solution of the nonlinear quasi-variational inequality (3.5).

At this point we have proved that the maximum solution $\hat{u}_k$ of the Q.V.I. (3.1) converges to the maximum solution u_o of Q.V.I. (3.5), in $C_o(\mathbb{R}^N)$ (and in $W^{1,\infty}(\mathbb{R}^N)$ weakly star), as k tends to zero. It remains only to show that $u_o(x)$ coincides with the optimal cost $\hat{u}(x)$ given by (3.4). We remark that the classical technique of building an ε-optimal impulse control associated with the continuation set cannot be used. The cost for each impulse is zero and the condition $\theta_i \to \infty$ a.s. for that impulse control is not satisfied a priori. Notice that if $\nu_k = \{\theta_1, \xi_1, \ldots, \xi_i, \ldots\}$ is either an optimal or ε-optimal impulse control for (2.5), then we deduce the estimate (2.6) as in [6;7] and clearly, the upper bound is not independent of k at this level.

However a simple argument shows that $\hat{u}_k(x)$ converges to $\hat{u}(x)$, given (3.4). Indeed, let ε be a given positive constant. From the definition of infimum (3.4), there exists an ε-optimal control $A_\varepsilon(x)$, independent of k, such that

(3.11) $$J_x(A_\varepsilon(x)) \leq \hat{u}(x) + \varepsilon.$$

Since A_ε is an admissible control, (2.3) is satisfyied. Thus we can compare A_ε in (2.5) :

(3.12) $$\hat{u}_k(x) \leq J_x^k(A_\varepsilon) = J_x(A_\varepsilon) + k \; E\left\{\sum_{i=1}^{\infty} e^{-\alpha\theta_i}\right\}.$$

From (3.11) and (3.12) we obtain

(3.13) $$\hat{u}_k(x) \leq \hat{u}(x) + \varepsilon + k \ E\left\{ \sum_{i=1}^{\infty} e^{-\alpha\theta_i} \right\} .$$

Hence, letting $k \to 0$, we deduce

(3.14) $$\overline{\lim_{k\to 0^+}} \ \hat{u}_k(x) \leq \hat{u}(x) \quad \forall x \in \mathbb{R}^N$$

and taking into account that $\hat{u}_k \geq \hat{u}$, we conclude our proof. □

<u>REMARK 3.2</u>. On the other hand, the last part of the proof of Theorem 3.1. can be achieved as follows. Since $u_o(x)$ is a solution of problem (3.1), it is easy to deduce (as in J.L. Menaldi [6]) that the optimal cost $\hat{u}(x)$ satisfies $u_o(x) \leq \hat{u}(x)$. Then, because of the convergence of $\hat{u}_k(x)$ to $u_o(x)$ and since $\hat{u}_k(x) \geq \hat{u}(x)$, we prove $u_o(x) = \hat{u}(x)$. However the proof presented in Theorem 3.1 is more elementary, is valid under weaker assumptions and lets us obtain an estimate (cf. Remark 4.3). □

3.2. <u>A particular case</u>

We take

(3.15) $$\Lambda = \{x = (x_1, x_2) \in \mathbb{R}^{N_1} \times \mathbb{R}^{N_2} \ / \ x_1 = 0 \text{ and } x_2 \geq 0\} \cdot$$

Obviously we are able to apply Theorem 3.1. Now our purpose is to characterize the optimal cost $\hat{u}(x)$ defined by (3.4) as an optimal cost of a stochastic control problem without impulse control.

Let $\mathcal{B} = \{\Omega, F, F^t, P, W(t), v(t), \eta(t), \tilde{y}^o_x(t)\}$ be control systems defined in the same way as admissible control systems A but, instead of an impulse control ν and an output $y_x(t)$, we assume a measurable adapted bounded process $\eta(t)$ taking values in $\mathbb{R}_+^{N_2}$ and the output $\tilde{y}^o_x(t) = \tilde{y}_o(t)$ satisfies Itô's equation in $\mathbb{R}^N$:

(3.16) $$\begin{cases} d\tilde{y}^o(t) = \sigma(\tilde{y}^o(t), v(t)) \, dW(t) + g(\tilde{y}^o(t), v(t))dt + (\eta'(t))dt, \ t \geq 0 \\ \tilde{y}^o(0) = x \end{cases}$$

with $\eta'(t)$ the transpose of $(0,\eta(t))$.

We set the cost

(3.17) $$J_x(\mathcal{B}) = \int_0^{\infty} f(\tilde{y}^o(t), v(t)) \, e^{-\alpha t} \, dt$$

and the optimal cost

(3.18) $\hat{u}_*(x) = \inf \{J_x(\mathcal{B}) \ / \ \mathcal{B}$ is a control system$\}$.

After remarking that (3.18) corresponds to a "continuous" stochastic control problem with

(3.19) $\tilde{g}(x, v, \eta) = g(x, v) + \binom{0}{\eta}$

(which is unbounded), we consider the problem :

$$(3.20) \quad \begin{cases} \text{Find } u \in W^{1,\infty}(\mathbb{R}^N) \text{ such that} \\ A_v u \leq f(.,v) \text{ in } \mathcal{D}'(\mathbb{R}^N), \quad \forall v \in V \text{ and} \\ \dfrac{\partial u}{\partial x_2} \geq 0 \quad \text{a.e. in } \mathbb{R}^N. \end{cases}$$

THEOREM 3.2.

Let assumptions (2.7) and (3.15) hold. Then the optimal cost $\hat{u}_*$ defined by (3.18) is the maximum solution of problem (3.20). Moreover, we have

(3.21) $\hat{u}_*(x) = \hat{u}(x) \quad \forall x \in \mathbb{R}^N$

with $\hat{u}(x)$ given by (3.4).

Proof

First notice that under hypothesis (3.15) we have for $u \in W^{1,\infty}(\mathbb{R}^N)$

(3.22) $u \leq Mu$, in $\mathbb{R}^N \iff \dfrac{\partial u}{\partial x_2} \geq 0$, a.e. in $\mathbb{R}^N$.

Now let us introduce the following ε-optimal cost ($\varepsilon > 0$) :

(3.23) $\hat{u}_\varepsilon(x) = \inf \{J_x(\mathcal{B}) \ / \ \mathcal{B}$ is a control system with $0 \leq \eta(t) \leq \frac{1}{\varepsilon}\}$

This stochastic control problem is included in the class of those studied in P. L. Lions and J.L. Menaldi [5]. Then, $\hat{u}_\varepsilon(x)$ is the maximum solution of the problem:

$$(3.24)\quad \begin{cases} \text{Find } u_\varepsilon \in W^{1,\infty}(\mathbb{R}^N) \text{ such that} \\ A_v u_\varepsilon - \eta \dfrac{\partial u_\varepsilon}{\partial x_2} \le f(.,v) \text{ in } \mathcal{D}'(\mathbb{R}^N) \ ; \forall v \in V,\ 0 \le \eta \le \dfrac{1}{\varepsilon} . \end{cases}$$

Since the constant α_o given in (2.7) (and computed with $\tilde{g}$ instead of g) is independent of η, the estimate (3.9) is still valid for $\tilde{y}^o_x(t)$. Thus we deduce

$$(3.25)\qquad |\hat{u}_\varepsilon(x) - \hat{u}_\varepsilon(x')| \le (\alpha - \alpha_o)^{-1} C_f |x-x'| \ , \quad \forall x,x' \in \mathbb{R}^N$$

where C_f is again the Lipschitz constant of f given in (2.7).

Clearly $\hat{u}_\varepsilon(x)$ is decreasing and convergent to $\hat{u}_*(x)$ as ε tends to zero. Since the $\hat{u}_\varepsilon$ are equibounded in $L^\infty(\mathbb{R}^N)$, it is enough to take advantage of the estimate (3.25) to show (after taking $\varepsilon \to 0^+$) that $\hat{u}_*(x)$ is a solution of problem (3.20). Moreover, using the fact that any solution of (3.20) is also a solution of (3.24), we obtain that $\hat{u}_*$ is the maximum solution of problem (3.20).

Finally, Theorem 3.1 and assertion (3.22) let us obtain (3.21) and the proof is concluded. □

REMARK 3.3. Theorems 3.1 and 3.2 can be extended to the case of a domain $\mathcal{O}$ instead of $\mathbb{R}^N$. The results can also be obtained with weaker assumptions than (2.7). □

REMARK 3.4. The condition (2.3) is not necessary. Indeed, any impulse control $\nu = (\theta_1, \xi_1, \ldots, \theta_i, \xi_i, \ldots)$ can be approached by a finite impulse control $\nu_n = \{\theta_1, \xi_1, \ldots, \theta_n, \xi_n \ ; \infty, \xi_{n+1}, \ldots\}$. Clearly $J_x(A_n)$ converges to $J_x(A)$ and then the infimum (3.4) can be taken over all control systems. □

4 - EXISTENCE OF AN OPTIMAL IMPULSE CONTROL

For the sake of simplicity we will only consider in this section a *pure* impulse control problem. Clearly, under suitable assumptions we can extend all the following results to the general stochastic impulse control problem stated in the beginning.

We suppose that the set of continuous controls V is only one point. Thus

$$(4.1)\qquad \sigma(.,v) = \sigma(.) \ ; \ g(.,v) = g(.) \ ; \ f(.,v) = f(.),\ \forall v \in V$$

and the differential operator (3.2) becomes A, independent of $v \in V$.

For obtaining the existence of an optimal admissible impulse control we introduce the following hypothesis ;

(4.2) There exists $r \in \mathbb{R}^N$ such that $(\xi,r) \geq \beta > 0$, $\forall \xi \in \Lambda$ where $(.,.)$ denotes the scalar product in $\mathbb{R}^N$.

Let $\mathcal{O}$ be a bounded domain of $\mathbb{R}^N$. We assume that there exists a Lipschitz subsolution of the Dirichlet problem of A on $\mathcal{O}$, i.e.

(4.3) there exists $\bar{u} \in W_o^{1,\infty}(\mathcal{O})$ such that $A\bar{u} \leq -1$ in $\mathcal{D}'(\mathcal{O})$.

Conditions in order to insure (4.3) can be found in L.C. Evans and J.L. Menaldi [2] ; P.L. Lions and J.L. Menaldi [5] or J.L. Menaldi [6].

An admissible control system $A = (\Omega, F, F^t, P, W(t), \nu, y_x(t))$ is defined similarly as in Section 2. The cost function becomes

(4.4) $$J_x(A) = E\{\int_0^\tau f(y(t))\, e^{-\alpha t}\, dt\}$$

where $\tau = \tau_x$ is the first exit time from $\bar{\mathcal{O}}$ of the process $y(t) = y_x(t)$, i.e.

(4.5) $$\tau = \inf\{t \geq 0 \,/\, y(t) \notin \bar{\mathcal{O}}\}$$

The optimal cost is

(4.6) $$\hat{u}(x) = \inf\{J_x(A) \,/\, A \text{ is an admissible impulse control}\}.$$

Our purpose is to build an admissible control $\hat{A}$ as the "exit time" of the continuation set.

We recall that Λ is a closed subset of $\mathbb{R}^N$ and the operator M is now given by

(4.7) $$[Mu](x) = \inf\{u(x+\xi) \,/\xi \in \Lambda,\ x+\xi \in \bar{\mathcal{O}}\}$$

We remark that Theorems 3.1 and 3.2 apply under hypothesis (4.3).

On the other hand we consider the following Q.V.I :

(4.8) $$\begin{cases} \text{Find } \hat{u} \in W_o^{1,\infty}(\mathcal{O}) \text{ such that} \\ A\hat{u} \leq f \text{ in } \mathcal{D}'(\mathcal{O}),\ \hat{u} \leq M\hat{u} \text{ in } \mathcal{O}, \\ A\hat{u} = f \text{ in } \mathcal{D}'([\hat{u} < M\hat{u}]) \end{cases}$$

where $[\hat{u} < M\hat{u}]$ denotes the set of points $x \in \bar{\mathcal{O}}$ satisfying $\hat{u}(x) < M\hat{u}(x)$.

THEOREM 4.1.

Let assumptions (2.7), (4.1), (4.2), and (4.3) hold. Then the Q.V.I (4.8) has one and only one solution $\hat{u}$ which is given by (4.6). Moreover, there exists an optimal admissible impulse control $\hat{A}$.

Proof

First, using Theorem 3.3 in J.L. Menaldi [6], we know that the optimal cost $\hat{u}_k$ given by (2.5) solves a Q.V.I like (4.8) with M_k instead of M. Thus, the uniform convergence established in Theorem 3.1, allows us to prove that the optimal cost $\hat{u}$ given by (4.6) satisfies (4.8).

Let $(\Omega, F, F^t, P, W(t))$ be any Wiener fixed space. Suppose $\hat{u}$ is a solution of problem (4.8). We will build an admissible impulse control system

$$\hat{A} = (\Omega, F, F^t, P, W(t), \nu, y_x(t)) \text{ with}$$

$$\nu = \{\theta_1, \xi_1, \ldots, \theta_i, \xi_i, \ldots\}$$

associated with $\hat{u}$ as follows.

We define the diffusion $y^o(t) = y_x^o(t)$ by

$$(4.9)\qquad \begin{cases} dy^o(t) = \sigma(y^o(t))\, dW(t) + g(y^o(t))dt, & t \geq 0 \\ y^o(0) = x & x \in \bar{\mathcal{O}} \quad ; \end{cases}$$

and the function $\hat{\xi} = \hat{\xi}(x)$ by

$$(4.10)\qquad \begin{cases} \hat{\xi} : \bar{\mathcal{O}} \to \Lambda \text{ Borel measurable set such that} \\ x + \hat{\xi}(x) \in \bar{\mathcal{O}} \text{ and } \hat{u}(x + \hat{\xi}(x)) = M\hat{u}(x), \ \forall x \in \bar{\mathcal{O}} \cdot \end{cases}$$

Thus, by induction $i = 1, 2, \ldots$, we set $\theta_o = 0$ and

$$(4.11)\qquad \tau^i = \inf \{t \geq 0 \,/\, y^{i-1}(t) \notin \bar{\mathcal{O}}\}$$

$$(4.12)\qquad \theta_i = \inf \{t \in [\theta_{i-1}, \tau^{i-1}[\,/\, y^{i-1}(t) \notin [\hat{u} < M\hat{u}]\}$$

(4.13) $\qquad \xi_i = \hat{\xi}(y^{i-1})(\theta_i))$

(4.14) $$\begin{cases} dy^i(t) = dy^{i-1}(t) & t \geq \theta_i \\ y^i(\theta_i) = y^{i-1}(\theta_i) + \xi^i & \\ y^i(t) = y^{i-1}(t) & t < \theta_i \end{cases}$$

We recall that $\tau^i = \infty$ if $y^{i-1}(t) \in \bar{\mathcal{O}}$, $\forall t \geq 0$ and that $\theta_i = \infty$ if $\tau^{i-1} = \theta_{i-1}$ or $y^{i-1}(t) \in [\hat{u} < M\hat{u}]$ $\forall t \in [\theta_{i-1}, \tau^{i-1}[$. If $\theta_i = \infty$ we set $\xi_i = \xi_*$, some point in Λ.

Then, because of

(4.15) $$\begin{cases} y^n(t)\, e^{-\alpha t} + \alpha \int_0^t y^n(s)\, e^{-\alpha s}\, ds = \sum_{i=1}^n (\xi_i^i\, e^{-\alpha\theta_i})\, I(\theta_i \leq t) + \\ + \int_0^t \sigma(y^n(s))\, e^{-\alpha s}\, dW(s) + \int_0^t g(y^n(s))\, e^{-\alpha s}\, ds, \end{cases}$$

and since $\mathcal{O}$, σ, g are bounded we deduce

(4.16) $$E\left\{ \sum_{i=1}^n (\xi_i, r)\, e^{-\alpha\theta_i} \right\} \leq C, \quad \forall n$$

where C denotes a constant depending only on σ, g, $\mathcal{O}$ and the direction r is given by (4.2).

Now we can define

(4.17) $$y(t) = \lim_{n\to\infty} y^n(t),\ t \geq 0\ ;$$

hence, hypothesis (4.2) and estimate (4.15) insure that the impulse control system A just built is admissible, i.e. (2.3) is satisfied.

Therefore, as in J.L. Menaldi [4], from Markov's property we have

(4.18) $$\hat{u}(x) = E\left\{ \int_0^{\theta_{n+1}} f(y^n(t))\, e^{-\alpha t}\, dt + \hat{u}(y^n(\theta_{n+1}))\, e^{-\alpha\theta_{n+1}} \right\};$$

so, since $\hat{u}$ is bounded and $\theta_n \to \infty$ we deduce

(4.19) $$\hat{u}(x) = J_x(\hat{A})$$

Taking into account that for any solution $\hat{u}$ of (4.8)

$$\hat{u}(x) \leq J_x(A) \quad \forall A\ ,$$

the equality (4.19) shows the uniqueness of the Q.V.I. (4.8) and the existence of an optimal admissible impulse control system. □

REMARK 4.1 Let r and β be the constants appearing in (4.2). We set

$$K = \sup \{(rg(x))^- \ / \ x \in \bar{\mathcal{O}}\} \tag{4.20}$$

and without assuming g, $\mathcal{O}$ bounded we will only suppose $K < \infty$ and $\mathcal{O}$ bounded in the direction r, i.e.

$$\sup \{(x,r) \ / \ x \in \bar{\mathcal{O}}\} < \infty$$

Thus, as in (4.16) we deduce

$$E\left\{\sum_{i=1}^{\infty} e^{-\alpha\theta_i}\right\} \leq K(\alpha \ \beta)^{-1}, \tag{4.21}$$

where θ_i is defined by (4.12). Hence, Theorem 4.1 still applies.

REMARK 4.2 Consider the classical sequence of variational inequalities (cf. A. Bensoussan and J.L. Lions [1]) associated with the variational inequality (4.8):

Let $\hat{u}^o$ be given by

$$\hat{u}^o \in W_o^{1,\infty}(\mathcal{O}), \ A\hat{u}^o = f \text{ in } \mathcal{D}'(\mathcal{O}). \tag{4.22}$$

We define $\hat{u}^n$ by induction as the solution of

$$\begin{cases} \hat{u}^n \in W_o^{1,\infty}(\mathcal{O}), \ \hat{u}^n \leq M\hat{u}^{n-1} \\ A \ \hat{u}^n \leq f \text{ in } \mathcal{D}'(\mathcal{O}), \ A \ \hat{u}^n = f \text{ in } \mathcal{D}'([\hat{u}^n < M\hat{u}^{n-1}]). \end{cases} \tag{4.23}$$

Since k = 0, we cannot deduce that $\hat{u}^n$ converges uniformly to $\hat{u}$ by using a technique similar to that used in [6]. On the other hand, if we assume that the Q.V.I. (4.8) has a maximum solution (the complementary condition is not used herein), an argument of maximum solution shows that $\hat{u}^n$ converge to $\hat{u}$ uniformly on $\mathcal{O}$. However we would like to point out that from (4.21) we obtain

$$\|\hat{u}^n - \hat{u}\|_{L^\infty(\mathcal{O})} \leq C(n+1)^{-1} \tag{4.24}$$

where $C = K(\alpha,\beta)^{-1} \ \|f\|_{L^\infty}$. Then, all essential results contained in J.L. Menaldi [6] can be extended to this case, with impulse cost vanishing.

REMARK 4.3. Using (4.21) we can improve Theorem 3.1. We have the estimate

$$||u_k - u||_{L^\infty(\mathcal{O})} \leq K(\alpha\,\beta)^{-1}k, \ \forall k > 0,$$

where u_k and u are given by (2.5) and (3.4) respectively (but with $\mathcal{O}$ instead of $\mathbb{R}^N$).

REFERENCES

[1] A. BENSOUSSAN - J.L. LIONS — Contrôle Impulsionnel et Inéquations Quasi-Variationnelless, Dunod, Paris, To appear, See also : C.R.A.S. Paris, Tome 276, Série A, 1973, pp. 1189-1192.

[2] L.C. EVANS - J.L. MENALDI — Gradient Bounds for Solutions of Degenerate Variational Inequalities, Applied Math. Optimization, Vol 7, n° 3 (1981), pp. 247-252.

[3] W.H. FLEMING - R. RISHEL — Optimal Deterministic and Stochastic Control, Springer-Verlag, New York, 1975.

[4] A. FRIEDMAN — Stochastic Differential Equations and Applications, Vol I, and Vol II, Academic Press, New York, 1975-76.

[5] P.L. LIONS - J.L. MENALDI — Control of Stochastic Integrals and Equations of Hamilton-Jacobi-Bellman, Part I and II, SIAM Journal on Control and Optimization, Vol. 20, n° 1 (1982) pp. 58-95 . See also C.R.A.S. Paris, Tome 287, Serie A, 1978, pp. 409-502. and Proc. 20 IEEE CDC. Dec.1981, San Diego,California USA pp. 1340-1344.

[6] J.L. MENALDI — On the Optimal Impulse Control Problem for Degenerate Diffusions, SIAM Journal on Control and Optimization, Vol. 18, n° 6, 1980, pp. 722-732. See also C.R.A.S. Paris, Tome 284, Série A, 1977 pp. 1499-1502.

[7] J.L. MENALDI - J.P. QUADRAT E. ROFMAN — On the Role of the Impulse Cost in Stochastic Optimal Control. An Application to the Management of Energy Production, Tenth IFIP Conference on System Modeling and Optimization, New York, September 1981, Lectures Notes in Control and Information Sciences, Vol. 38, 1982, Springer-Verlag.

DUAL VARIATIONAL PRINCIPLES
IN MECHANICS AND PHYSICS

R. Temam

INTRODUCTION.

In this article we present some results concerning variational problems in infinite dimension, which arise in different areas of mechanics and physics. The particularity (and common property) of these problems is that they are coercive on a non reflexive function space of the type L^1. As a consequence of this lack of coercivity, the solutions of these problems, when they exist, lie in generalized spaces. Part of the work presented here consists, for these problems, in the definition of an appropriate generalization of the considered problem, and the proof of existence of solution of the generalized problem.

However this generalization which solves in a satisfactory manner the question of existence of solution, leads to another difficulty connected with duality ; while we can define very naturally the dual $(\mathcal{P}^*)$ of the initial variational problem $(\mathcal{P})$, there is no obvious duality between $(\mathcal{P}^*)$ and the generalization $(\mathcal{G}\mathcal{P})$ of $(\mathcal{P})$. An attempt is made here to extend the duality and to exhibit in some cases the duality between $(\mathcal{P}^*)$ and $(\mathcal{G}\mathcal{P})$. This is the second aspect of the work presented here, and this aspect relies mostly on an article to appear of R. Kohn and the author [4]. We did not intend to present the duality results in an abstract framework and we restricted ourself to specific cases, which are still interesting and typical from our point of view.

Sections 1 and 2 contain the description of the primal problem, its dual and some examples. The material in these Sections and in the beginning of Section 3 (generalized solutions) is related to that of [10], and for some aspects to [7] [8] [9]. Section 3 describes the generalized problem, the existence of solutions to the generalized problem and the extension of duality which is based on [4], as mentioned before.

1. DESCRIPTION OF THE PRIMAL PROBLEM - EXAMPLES.

Let ϕ denote an even convex continuous real function on $\mathbb{R}$ which satisfies

(1.1) $$c_o(|s| - 1) \leqq \phi(s) \leqq c_1(|s| + 1), \quad \forall\, s \in \mathbb{R},$$

where c_1, c_o are two positive constants. We denote by Ω an open bounded set of $\mathbb{R}^n$, with a smooth boundary Γ. We are given also a function f defined on Ω, and two functions u_o and g defined respectively on Γ_o and Γ_1, Γ_o denoting a part of Γ, and Γ_1 its complement in Γ; all the data are supposed to be sufficiently regular.

The problem $(\mathcal{P})$ in which we are interested can now be formulated :

(1.2) To find a real function u defined on Ω which minimizes

$$E(v) = \int_\Omega \phi(|\nabla v|)dx - L(v)$$

among the functions $v = u_o$ on Γ_o,

∇v = grad v, and we have set :

(1.3) $$L(v) = \int_\Omega f\ v\ dx + \int_{\Gamma_1} g\ v\ d\Gamma.$$

Some regularity property must be assumed for the functions v considered in (1.2), so that the functional E(v) makes sense. As we will see, the class of functions we consider here is not too important ; for instance we can consider functions v belonging to the Sobolev space $H^1(\Omega)$:

(1.4) $H^1(\Omega)$ = the space of real functions on Ω which are square integrable together with their first derivatives.

Problem (1.2) appears as an infinite dimensional convex program. Due to the linear growth at infinity of ϕ, the infimum in (1.2) may or may not be finite ($\geqq -\infty$). Sufficient conditions for finiteness will be given through the study of its dual. Duality, and the question of existence of solutions will be treated in the next two sections. Before that, let us describe examples of classical problems in mechanics and physics which are particular cases of (1.2).

EXAMPLES.

Example 1 : Minimal surfaces.

Here $\phi(s) = \sqrt{1+s^2}$, Γ_1 is empty, $\Gamma_o = \Gamma$, $f = 0$. The problem reduces to,

$$\text{(1.5)} \qquad \underset{v=u_o \text{ on } \Gamma}{\text{Inf}} \left\{ \int_\Omega \sqrt{1+|\nabla v|^2}\, dx \right\}$$

which is the classical problem of minimal area surface. The Euler equation of this problem, satisfied by a smooth solution (when it exists) is the minimal surface equation.

The case where $f \neq 0$ (everything else being unchanged) is also classical (in the theory of nonlinear differential equations), the corresponding Euler equation being the mean curvature equation.

Example 2 : Capillarity.

Here again $\phi(s) = \sqrt{1+s^2}$, $f = 0$, but Γ_o is empty, $\Gamma_1 = \Gamma$ and g is a constant of the form $\cos\theta$ (where θ, which is a characteristic of the capillarity phenomena, is the angle between the free surface and the tube $\Gamma \times \mathbb{R}$). The problem is

$$\text{(1.6)} \qquad \underset{v}{\text{Inf}} \left\{ \int_\Omega \sqrt{1+|\nabla v|^2}\, dx - \cos\theta \int_\Gamma v\, d\Gamma \right\}$$

Example 3 : Plasticity (anti-plane shear).

In the anti-plane shear phenomena (cf. G. Strang [6]), we study the plastic deformation of an infinite cylinder of cross section $\Omega \subset \mathbb{R}^2$, and $u = u(x_1, x_2)$ is the displacement parallel to the axis of the cylindar for the points of coordinate $x = (x_1, x_2, x_3)$. In this case a typical function ϕ is the following one :

$$\text{(1.7)} \qquad \phi(s) = \begin{cases} \dfrac{s^2}{2} \text{ if } |s| \leq 1 \\ |s| - \dfrac{1}{2} \text{ if } |s| \geq 1. \end{cases}$$

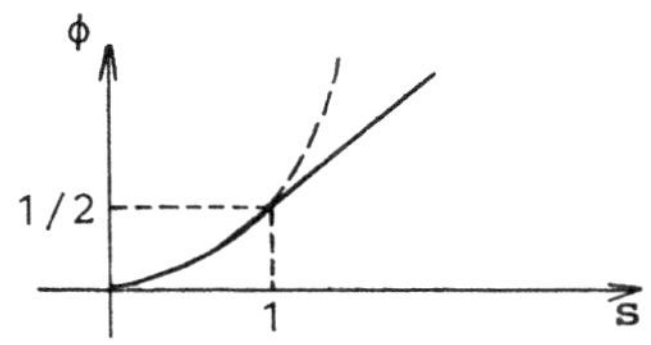

Fig. 1 : Function ϕ

The sets Γ_o, Γ_1, the given functions f, g, are otherwise arbitrary.

2. DUAL PROBLEM.

We now set the general problem (1.2) in a form suitable for duality, and we apply the general duality method of the calculus of variations (cf. Ekeland-Temam [1], also W. Fenchel [2], R.T. Rockafellar [5]).

Let V, V*, and Y, Y* be two paired Hilbert spaces, let Λ be a linear continuous operator from V into Y and let Λ^* be its adjoint, linear continuous from Y* into V*. We are also given a proper convex lower semi-continuous function F (respectively G) on V (respectively Y), with values in $\mathbb{R} \cup \{+\infty\}$. The primal problem is then

(2.1) $$\inf_{v \in V} \{F(v) + G(\Lambda v)\} .$$

We denote by F* and G* the conjugate functions of F and G, defined respectively on V* and Y*,

$$F^*(v^*) = \sup_{v \in V} \{\langle v^*,v\rangle - F(v)\} , \qquad \forall\, v^* \in V^*,$$

$$G^*(p^*) = \sup_{p \in Y} \{\langle p^*,p\rangle - G(p)\} , \qquad \forall\, p^* \in Y^*.$$

The dual problem of (2.1) is then

(2.2) $$\sup_{p^* \in Y^*} \{-F^*(\Lambda^* p^*) - G^*(-p^*)\}.$$

The relations between (2.1) and (2.2) are well known and are described for instance in the above quoted references.

This framework applies to problem (1.2) in the following manner : $V = H^1(\Omega)$, V^* = the dual of $H^1(\Omega)$, $Y = Y^* = L^2(\Omega)^n$, and $\Lambda u = \text{grad } u$. Then

(2.3) $$F(u) = \begin{cases} -L(u) & \text{if } u = u_o \text{ on } \Gamma_o, \\ +\infty & \text{otherwise.} \end{cases}$$

(2.4) $$G(p) = \int_\Omega \phi(|p(x)|)dx.$$

In this manner, problem (2.1) reduces to problem (1.2). In order to determine its dual, we have to determine F* and G*. By Proposition 2.1, Ch. IX of [1],

$$G^*(p) = \int_\Omega \phi^*(|p(x)|)dx,$$

or

$$(2.5) \qquad G^*(p) = \begin{cases} \int_\Omega \phi^*(|p(x)|)dx, & \text{if } \phi^* \circ |p| \in L^1(\Omega) \\ +\infty \text{ otherwise,} \end{cases}$$

where dom $\phi^* = \{s \in \mathbb{R}, \phi^*(s) < +\infty\}$

For the determination of $F^*(\Lambda p)$, $p \in Y^*$, we write

$$F^*(\Lambda p) = \sup_{\substack{v \in V \\ v=u_o \text{ on } \Gamma_o}} r(v)$$

$$r(v) = \int_\Omega (p.\nabla v + fv)dx + \int_{\Gamma_1} g\ v\ d\Gamma$$

Hence, setting $v = u_o + w$,

$$F^*(\Lambda p) = r(u_o) + \sup_{\substack{w \in V \\ w=0 \text{ on } \Gamma_o}} r(w)$$

The last supremum is easy to compute (see for instance [9] or [1]). The supremum is $+\infty$, unless

$$(2.6) \qquad -\operatorname{div} p + f = 0 \text{ in } \Omega, \quad p.\nu + g = 0 \text{ on } \Gamma_1,$$

ν the unit outward normal on $\Gamma = \partial\Omega$. For p satisfying (2.6), it follows from Green's formula that

$$r(u_o) = \int_\Gamma p.\nu\ u_o d\Gamma.$$

Therefore

$$(2.7) \qquad F^*(\Lambda p) = \begin{cases} \int_{\Gamma_o} p.\nu\ u_o d\Gamma & \text{if (2.6) is satisfied,} \\ +\infty \text{ otherwise.} \end{cases}$$

The dual $(\mathcal{P}^*)$ of (1.2) is then

$$(2.8) \qquad \sup_{\substack{p \in L^2(\Omega)^n \\ -\operatorname{div} p+f=0 \text{ in } \Omega \\ p.\nu+g=0 \text{ on } \Gamma_1 \\ \phi^* \circ |p| \in L^1(\Omega)}} \left\{ -\int_{\Gamma_o} p.\nu\ u_o\ d\Gamma - \frac{1}{2}\int_\Omega |p(x)|^2 dx \right\}$$

We denote by $\mathcal{S}$ the set of p's in $L^2(\Omega)^n$ which satisfy (2.6) and by κ the set of p's in $L^2(\Omega)^n$ such that $\phi^* \circ |p| \in L^1(\Omega)$. If $\mathcal{S} \cap \kappa$ is not empty then (2.8) possesses a unique solution $\bar{p}$, and the supremum in (2.8) is equal to the infimum in (1.2) and is finite. If $\mathcal{S} \cap \kappa$ is empty then there is no solution to (2.8), the supremum is $-\infty$, and the infimum for (1.2) is $-\infty$, too.

Finiteness of the infimum.

Let us assume that Φ enjoys the following properties :

(2.9) $B = \text{dom}\,\Phi^* = \{s \in \mathbb{R},\ \Phi^*(s) < +\infty\}$ is a closed bounded interval of $\mathbb{R}$, which contains 0 in its interior.

(2.10) Φ^* is continuous (and thus bounded) on B.

Note that these properties are satisfied in the examples above (where $B = [-1,+1]$ and, on B, $\Phi^*(s) = -\sqrt{1-s^2}$ in Examples 1 and 2, and $= \frac{1}{2}s^2$ in Example 3).

Then we can derive a necessary and sufficient condition for $\mathcal{S} \cap K$ to be non-empty by considering an auxiliary variational problem (P_{LA}) (called limit analysis problem in plasticity) :

Let us define Φ_p by setting

$$\Phi_p(s) = \sup_{t \in B} st \quad , \quad \forall\, s \in \mathbb{R}, \tag{2.11}$$

i.e. Φ_p is the support function of B, and since B is of the form $[-\alpha,+\alpha]$, $\alpha > 0$, we simply have

$$\Phi_p(s) = \alpha|s| \quad , \quad \forall\, s \in \mathbb{R}. \tag{2.12}$$

The problem P_{LA} is then

$$\inf_{\substack{v \in H^1(\Omega) \\ v=0 \text{ on } \Gamma_o \\ L(v)=1}} \left\{\alpha \int_\Omega |\nabla v|\,dx\right\} \tag{2.12}$$

We are going to determine the dual problem of (2.12) and then show its relation with (1.2). This problem can be set in the form (2.1) by letting $V, V^*, Y, Y^*, \Lambda, \Lambda^*$, be as before and by defining now F and G as follows

$$F(v) = \begin{cases} 0 \text{ if } v = 0 \text{ on } \Gamma_o \text{ and } L(v) = 1 \\ +\infty \text{ otherwise} \end{cases} \tag{2.13}$$

$$G(p) = \alpha \int_\Omega |p(x)|\,dx. \tag{2.14}$$

In order to determine the dual of (2.12), we compute F^* and G^*. By [1], for every $p \in L^2(\Omega)^n$,

$$G^*(p) = \begin{cases} 0 \text{ if } |p(x)| \leqq \alpha \text{ a.e.} \\ +\infty \text{ otherwise.} \end{cases}$$

With (2.9) and (2.10) it is equivalent to say that

(2.15) $$G^*(p) = \begin{cases} 0 \text{ if } p \in K, \text{ i.e. } \Phi^* \circ |p| \in L^1(\Omega) \\ +\infty \text{ otherwise.} \end{cases}$$

For F*, we denote by v_o any element of V $(=H^1(\Omega))$, such that $v_o = 0$ on Γ_o and $L(v_o) = 1$, and for any v which is feasible for (2.12), we set $v = v_o + w$, $Lw = 0$, $w = 0$ on Γ_o. Hence, for $p \in Y^*$:

$$F^*(\Lambda p) = \sup_{\substack{v \in V \\ v=0 \text{ on } \Gamma_o \\ Lv=1}} \int_\Omega p\nabla v \, dx$$

$$= \int_\Omega p\nabla v_o + \sup_{\substack{w \in V_o \\ Lw=0}} \int_\Omega p.\nabla w \, dx,$$

where

(2.16) $$V_o = \{v \in V = H^1(\Omega), \ v = 0 \text{ on } \Gamma_o\}.$$

Now, the last supremum involve two linear forms on V_o, L and $\int_\Omega p.\nabla w \, dx$. Therefore this supremum is 0 if the two forms are linearly dependent and $+\infty$ otherwise. Assuming that L is not identically 0 on V_o this means :

There exists $\lambda \in \mathbb{R}$, such that

(2.17) $$\int_\Omega p.\nabla w \, dx = -\lambda L(w), \quad \forall \, w \in V_o,$$

and thus :

(2.18) $$F^*(\Lambda p) = \begin{cases} \int_\Omega p\nabla v_o dx \quad \text{if (2.17) holds} \\ +\infty \text{ otherwise.} \end{cases}$$

It is easy to see that the relation

$$\int_\Omega p.\nabla w \, dx = -\lambda L(w) = -\lambda \int_\Omega fw \, dx - \lambda \int_{\Gamma_1} gw \, d\Gamma, \quad \forall \, w \in V_o,$$

is equivalent to

(2.19) $$-\operatorname{div} p + \lambda f = 0 \text{ in } \Omega, \quad p.\nu + \lambda g = 0 \text{ on } \Gamma_1.$$

Also, by Green's formula, for a function p which satisfies (2.19), and v_o as above :

$$\int_\Omega p\nabla v_o \, dx = - \quad L(v_o) \ = - \lambda$$

and finally, for $p \in Y^*$:

$$(2.20) \qquad F^*(\Lambda p) = \begin{cases} -\lambda \text{ if there exists } \lambda \in \mathbb{R} \text{ such that (2.19) holds} \\ +\infty \text{ otherwise.} \end{cases}$$

We can make explicit the dual problem of (2.12) (of the form (2.2)) :

$$(2.21) \qquad \sup_{\substack{p \in L^2(\Omega)^n \\ -\operatorname{div} p + \lambda f = 0 \text{ in } \Omega \\ p.\nu + \lambda g = 0 \text{ on } \Gamma_1 \\ p \in K}} \{ \lambda \}$$

Setting $p = \lambda q$, this problem becomes

$$(2.22) \qquad \sup_{\substack{q \in L^2(\Omega)^n \\ q \in \mathcal{S} \cap (\lambda^{-1} K)}} \{ \lambda \}$$

which means that we are looking for the largest λ such that $\mathcal{S} \cap (\lambda^{-1}K)$ is not empty. We note that $\mathcal{S} \cap (\lambda^{-1}K)$ is certainly not empty for $\lambda > 0$ sufficiently small, and the supremum in (2.22) is then positive. By the classical primal-dual relation (see for instance [1]), the infimum for (2.12) is equal to the supremum for (2.21)((2.22)). The problem (2.21)((2.22)) gives, on the other hand, the necessary and sufficient condition for $\mathcal{S} \cap K$ to be non empty :

$$(2.23) \qquad \inf (2.12) = \sup (2.22) \leq 1.$$

We conclude therefore that:

(2.24) The infimum of problem (1.2) is finite if and only if

$$\inf_{\substack{v \in H^1(\Omega) \\ v = 0 \text{ on } \Gamma_o \\ \int_\Omega fv \, dx + \int_{\Gamma_1} gv \, d\Gamma = 1}} \alpha \int_\Omega |\nabla v| dx \leq 1$$

One can show also as in [7], that if the inequality in (2.24) is strict (infimum < 1), then

(2.25) Every minimizing sequence of (1.2) is bounded in the Sobolev space $W^{1,1}(\Omega)$, i.e. the integrals

$$\int_\Omega |u_m| dx, \quad \int_\Omega \left| \frac{\partial u_m}{\partial x_i} \right| dx, \quad i = 1,\dots,n,$$

remain bounded as $m \to \infty$.

3. RELAXED PROBLEM AND EXTENSION OF DUALITY.

Orientation.

The problem (1.2) may not possess a solution belonging to the Sobolev space $H^1(\Omega)$ (or to $W^{1,1}(\Omega)$) even if its infimum is finite or (2.25) is satisfied. This is due to some discontinuities which the actual solution may possess and, in order to be able to define a solution, we have to extend the class of admissible solutions by allowing functions even less regular than those in $H^1(\Omega)$. We will do that and obtain the existence of a generalized solution $\bar{u}$. Finally, the problem will be to study the duality between such generalized solutions and the (unique) solution $\bar{p}$ of the dual problem (2.8). This will be done through an extension of the concept of duality which we will then present.

Generalized solution.

We consider the space $BV(\Omega)$, made of functions which are in $L^1(\Omega)$ and have a bounded variation, i.e.

$$\int_\Omega |\nabla u| = \operatorname*{Sup}_h \int_\Omega \operatorname{div} h.u \, dx < \infty, \tag{3.1}$$

where the supremum is for those functions h of the form $h = (h_1,\dots,h_n)$, the h_i's being $\mathscr{C}^\infty$ functions with a compact support in Ω, and $|h(x)|^2 = \sum_{i=1}^n |h_i(x)|^2 \leq 1$.

The functional $E(v)$ makes sense for $v \in BV(\Omega)$, provided we extend properly the definition of the integral $\int_\Omega \phi(|\nabla v|)dx$. This is done in [9] ; the definition is (for $v \in BV(\Omega)$)

$$\operatorname*{Inf}_{v \in BV(\Omega)} \int_\Omega \Phi(|\nabla v|) = \operatorname*{Sup}_h \int_\Omega h \,\nabla v - \int_\Omega \Phi(|h(x)|)dx \tag{3.2}$$

where the supremum is for the h's of the form $(h_1,\dots,h_n)$, the h_i's being $\mathscr{C}^\infty$ functions with a compact support in Ω, and $\Phi^* \circ |h| \in L^1(\Omega)$. It makes then sense to set the problem

$$\operatorname*{Inf}_{v \in BV(\Omega)} \int_\Omega \Phi(|\nabla v|) + \int_{\Gamma_0} \alpha|v-u_0|d\Gamma - L(v). \tag{3.3}$$

Problem (3.3) is an extension of (1.2) since we are minimizing the <u>same functional</u> on a larger set. In some special cases (for instance $\Gamma_1 = \emptyset$, or $\Gamma_1 \neq \emptyset$ and $g = 0$), it is possible to show directly, using the assumption (2.24) (with a strict inequality) and (2.25) that the infimum for (3.3) is the same as for (1.2) and that (3.3) possesses solutions which are (in particular) the cluster points in $L^1(\Omega)$ of the minimizing sequences of (1.2). We can establish a similar result also for the general case ($\Gamma_1 \neq \emptyset$, $g \neq 0$), but before doing that we must define the duality between problems (3.3) and (2.8).

Extension of duality.

If $u \in BV(\Omega)$ and $p \in L^2(\Omega)^n$, the product $p.\nabla u$ of an L^2-function with a bounded measure does not make sense in general, and this is a fundamental difficulty if we want to show that (2.8) and (3.3) are dual problems.

Now, we have more information on the admissible p's for (2.8), and using this information we can (following [4]), formulate a duality between these problems.

The first step lies in the following lemma:

Lemma 3.1.

i) *For every* u *in* $L^{\frac{n}{n-1}}(\Omega)$ *and for every* p *in* $L^n(\Omega)^n$ *with* $\operatorname{div} p \in L^n(\Omega)$ *we can define a distribution on* Ω *denoted* $p.\nabla u$ *through the formula*

$$(3.4) \qquad \langle p.\nabla u, \theta\rangle = -\int_\Omega u \nabla p\, \theta\, dx - \int_\Omega u\, p\, \nabla\theta\, dx,$$

$\forall\, \theta$ *real* $\mathscr{C}^\infty$ *function on* Ω *with a compact support.*

Furthermore the mapping $\{u,p\} \to p.\nabla u$ *is bilinear weakly continuous from* $L^{\frac{n}{n-1}}(\Omega)\times X$ *into the space of distributions on* Ω. *Here*

$$(3.5) \qquad X = \{p \in L^n(\Omega)^n,\ \operatorname{div} p \in L^n(\Omega)\}$$

which is a Banach space for the natural form

$$||p||_X = |p|_{L^n(\Omega)^n} + |\operatorname{div} p|_{L^n(\Omega)}.$$

Lemma 3.2.

Under the assumptions of Lemma 3.1 *and if moreover* $u \in BV(\Omega)$ *and* $p \in L^\infty(\Omega)^n$, *then* $p.\nabla u$ *is a bounded signed measure,*

$$(3.6) \qquad \int_\Omega |p.\nabla u| \leq |p|_{L^\infty(\Omega)} \cdot \int_\Omega |\nabla u|$$

and the following generalized Green formula holds

$$(3.7)\qquad \int_\Omega \theta\ p.\nabla u = \int_\Gamma p.\nu\, u\, \theta\, d\Gamma - \int_\Omega u\ \nabla p\ \theta\ dx - \int_\Omega u\, p\, \nabla\theta\ dx$$

for every θ *continuous in* $\bar{\Omega}$ *with* grad $\theta \in L^n(\Omega)^n$.

Proof of Lemma 3.1.

The right-hand side of (3.4) clearly makes sense for u, p, θ as indicated, and for u and p fixed this depends linearly and continuously on θ for the norm : $||\theta||_{\mathcal{C}^1(\bar{\Omega})}$. Hence $p.\nabla u$ is defined as a distribution (and coincides with the function p(x).u(x) if p and u are smooth enough).

For θ fixed, if $u_m \to u$ in $L^{\frac{n}{n-1}}(\Omega)$ and $p_m \to p$ in X, then the right hand side of (3.4) with p_m and u_m converges to the analogous expression with p and u. This establishes the continuity of the mapping

$$\{u,p\} \longmapsto p.\nabla u.$$

Proof of Lemma 3.2.

First note that $BV(\Omega) \subset L^{\frac{n}{n-1}}(\Omega)$ and $p.\nabla u$ makes sense by Lemma 3.1. For (3.6), let p and u be fixed and let p_m be an approximating sequence for p which is obtained by mollification of the function p extended by 0 outside Ω and restriction (of the mollified functions) to Ω. Then

$$|p_m|_{\mathcal{C}(\bar{\Omega})^n} \leq |p|_{L^\infty(\Omega)^n}$$

$$p_m(x) \to p(x) \quad \text{a.e. in } \Omega,$$

$$\text{div } p_m \to \text{div } p \quad \text{in } L^n_{loc}(\Omega).$$

If $\theta \in \mathcal{C}^\infty_c(\Omega)$, then by (3.4) and these convergence results,

$$\int_\Omega p_m.\nabla u\ \theta\ dx \to \langle p.\nabla u, \theta\rangle, \text{ as } m \to \infty,$$

and, on the other hand,

$$\left|\int_\Omega p_m.\nabla u\ \theta\ dx\right| \leq |p_m|_{\mathcal{C}(\bar{\Omega})^n} |\theta|_{\mathcal{C}(\bar{\Omega})} \int_\Omega |\nabla u|$$

$$\leq |p|_{L^\infty(\Omega)^n} |\theta|_{\mathcal{C}(\bar{\Omega})} \int_\Omega |\nabla u|$$

so that

$$|\langle p.\nabla u,\theta\rangle| \leq |p|_{L^\infty(\Omega)^n} |\theta|_{\mathcal{C}(\bar\Omega)} \int_\Omega |\nabla u|,$$

$\forall\ \theta \in \mathcal{C}_c^\infty(\Omega)$, and (3.6) is proved.

The proof of (3.7) is obtained after another technical approximation similar (but simpler) than one used in the proof of Theorem 3.2 in [4].

Remark 3.1.

We emphasize the important fact that these lemmas allow us to define a pairing between the feasible u's for (3.3) and the feasible p's for (2.8).

Main result.

The final result can now be stated :

Theorem 3.1.

i) *The infimum for relaxed Problem* (3.3) *is the same as the infimum of Problem* (1.2) [(1)] *and is equal to the supremum for Problem* (2.8).

This number is finite if and only if the inequality in (2.24) *is satisfied.*

ii) *If a strict inequality holds in the relation in* (2.24), *then* (2.8) *possesses a unique solution* $\bar p$, (3.3) *possesses at least one solution* $\bar u$ *and the following extremality relations hold between* $\bar p$ *and* $\bar u$:

$$(3.8)\qquad \int_\Omega \bar p\ \nabla\bar u = \int_{\Gamma_o} \bar p.\nu\ u_o\ d\Gamma + \int_{\Gamma_1} g\ \bar u\ d\Gamma + \int_\Omega f\ \bar u\ dx$$

$$(3.9)\qquad \Phi(|\nabla\bar u|) + \Phi^*(|\bar p|) = -\ \bar p.\nabla\bar u = -\ |\bar p|.|\nabla\bar u|$$

Sketch of the proof.

If a strict inequality holds in (2.24) then, the minimizing sequences of Problem (1.2) are bounded in BV(Ω). Since the imbedding of BV(Ω) into $L^1(\Omega)$ is compact we obtain by extraction of a subsequence, a sequence u_m which is bounded in BV(Ω) and converges in $L^1(\Omega)$ to a function u belonging to BV(Ω). The fact that u is a solution of (3.3) is established if we show that:

α) the functional in (3.3) is lower semi-continuous

(1) Minimization for $v \in BV(\Omega)$ and $v \in H^1(\Omega)$ respectively.

$$(3.10)\quad \int_\Omega \Phi(|\nabla u|) + \int_{\Gamma_o} \alpha|u-u_o|\,d\Gamma - L(u) \leq \lim_{m\to\infty}\left\{\int_\Omega \Phi(|\nabla u_m|) + \int_{\Gamma_o}\alpha|u_m-u_o|\,d\Gamma - L(u_m)\right\}$$

β) the infima for Problems (3.3) and (1.2) are the same.

By the definition of $\int_\Omega \Phi(|\nabla u|)$ (cf. [11]),

$$(3.11)\quad \int_\Omega \Phi(|\nabla u|) \geq \int_\Omega p.\nabla u - \int_\Omega \Phi^*(|p|)\,dx$$

for every $p \in \mathscr{C}_o(\Omega)^n$, and by continuity (using Lemmas 3.1, 3.2), this holds for every p in $L^\infty(\Omega)^n$, and in particular for every p admissible for (2.8). Similarly, for every p in $L^2(\Omega)^n$, with div $p \in L^n(\Omega)$ and $|p(x)| \in B$ a.e. :

$$(3.12)\quad \int_{\Gamma_o} \alpha|u-u_o|\,d\Gamma \geq -\int_{\Gamma_o} p.\nu(u-u_o)\,d\Gamma \quad ;$$

(3.12) holds in particular for every p admissible for (2.8) (i.e. $p \in \mathscr{S} \cap K$).

Now we can prove (3.10) : for $p \in \mathscr{S} \cap K$:

$$\int_\Omega \Phi(|\nabla u_m|) + \int_{\Gamma_o} \alpha|u_m-u_o|\,d\Gamma - \int_\Omega f\, u_m\,dx - \int_{\Gamma_1} F\, u_m\,d\Gamma$$

$$= \int_\Omega \Phi(|\nabla u_m|) + \int_{\Gamma_o} \alpha|u_m-u_o|\,d\Gamma - \int_{\Gamma_1} p.\nu\, u_m\,d\Gamma - \int_\Omega f\, u_m\,dx$$

$\geq$ (by (3.11),(3.12) for u_m)

$$\int_\Omega p.\nabla u_m - \int_\Gamma p.\nu\, u_m\,d\Gamma + \int_{\Gamma_o} p.\nu\, u_o\,d\Gamma - \int_\Omega f\, u_m\,dx$$

$\geq$ (by (3.7) with $\theta = 1$)

$$-\int_\Omega u_m \nabla p\,dx + \int_{\Gamma_o} p.\nu\, u_o\,d\Gamma - \int_\Omega f\, u_m\,dx.$$

For $m \to \infty$, we find that the right-hand side of (3.10) is larger than

$$-\int_\Omega u\,\nabla p\,dx + \int_{\Gamma_o} p.\nu\, u_o\,d\Gamma - \int_\Omega f\,u\,dx\ .$$

Using (3.7) again and taking the supremum with respect to p, we obtain (3.10). The proof of point β) is similar. We obtain (3.8),(3.9) by utilization of the extremality properties of the problem (cf. [1])

and the properties of a convex function of a measure [11] [13]. For more details on these last two points, the reader is referred to [4] and [12].

REFERENCES.

[1] EKELAND, I., TEMAM, R., Convex Analysis and Variational Problems, North-Holland, Amsterdam, 1976.

[2] FENCHEL, W., Convex Cones, Sets and Functions. Mimeographed notes, Princeton: Princeton University, 1951.

[3] GIUSTI, E., Minimal Surfaces and Functions of bounded Variation, Lecture Notes on Pure Mathematics, n° 10, Australian National University, Canberra, 1977.

[4] KOHN, R., TEMAM, R., Duality between Spaces of Stresses and Strains for Plasticity and Applications, to appear, and Comptes Rendus Ac. Sc. Paris, Série I, 294, (1982), 205-208.

[5] ROCKAFELLAR, R.T., Convex Analysis. Princeton: Princeton University Press, 1970.

[6] STRANG, G., A Family of Model Problems in Plasticity, in Proc. Symp. Comp. Meth. Appl. Sci. eds. Glowinski, R., and J. L. Lions. Lecture Notes in Computer Sciences 704. Berlin-Heidelberg-New York: Springer-Verlag, 1979.

[7] STRANG, G., TEMAM, R., Duality and Relaxation in the Variational Problems of Plasticity, J. de Mécanique, 19, (1980), 493-527.

[8] STRANG, G., TEMAM, R., A Problem in Capillarity and Plasticity, Mathematical Programming Study, 18, 1982.

[9] TEMAM, R., Solutions généralisées de certaines équations du type hypersurfaces minima, Arch. Rat. Mech. Anal., 44, (1971), 121-156.

[10] TEMAM, R., Mathematical Problems in Plasticity Theory in Variational Inequalities and Complementarity Problems Theory and Applications. eds. Cottle, R. W., F. Giannessi and J.-L. Lions. New York: John Wiley & Sons, 1980.

[11] TEMAM, R., Approximation des fonctions convexes d'une mesure et applications, Bulletin Canadien de Math., 1982.

[12] TEMAM,R., An existence theorem for a variational problem of plasticity, Proceedings of the Journées P. de Fermat, (1979), Atteia Bancel-Gumowski Editors, Pitman, 1981.

[13] DEMENGEL,F., TEMAM,R., Convex functions of a measure and applications, to appear.

AUTHORS, PARTICIPANTS, AND AFFILIATIONS

Dr. Layek L. Abdel-Malek
Department of Industrial Engineering
Rutgers University
P.O. Box 909
Piscataway, NJ 08854

Dr. Christian Agunwamba
Department of Statistics
University of Nigeria
Nsukka, Nigeria
AFRICA

Dr. Walter Alt
Mathematisches Institut
Universität Bayreuth
Postfach 3008, D-8580
Bayreuth
WEST GERMANY

*Dr. E. J. Anderson
University of Cambridge
University Engineering Department
Mill Lane
Cambridge, ENGLAND CB2 1RX

Dr. Leonard Asimow
Department of Mathematics
University of Wyoming
Laramie, WY 82071

Professor A. Auslender
Université de Clermont
Department de Mathematiques
Appliques
Boite Postale 45
63170 Aubere
FRANCE

Dr. Achim Bachem
University of Erlangen
Martensstr. 3
Erlangen D-8520
WEST GERMANY

Dr. E. J. Balder
University of Ubrecht
Budapestlaan 6
Ubrecht
NETHERLANDS

Dr. Jonathan Barzilai
RLM 8.100
University of Texas at Austin
Austin, TX 78712

Dr. Stavros A. Belbas
Department of Electrical Engineering
University of Maryland
College Park, MD 20742

*Dr. Charles E. Blair
University of Illinois
1206 S. Sixth Street, Room 350
Champaign, IL 61820

Dr. Hans-Peter Blatt
Universität Mannheim
A5, D-6800 Mannheim
WEST GERMANY

Dr. Dankmar Böhning
Free University of Berlin
Iltisstrasse 7
1000 Berlin 33
WEST GERMANY

*Dr. Jonathan M. Borwein
Department of Mathematics, Statistics
and Computer Science
Dalhousie University
Halifax, N.S. B3H 4H8
CANADA

Dr. Patrick L. Brockett
Department of Finance
University of Texas at Austin
Austin, TX 78712

Dr. Bruno H. Brosowski
Department of Mathematics
University of Frankfurt
6 Frankfurt A.M.
Robert-Mayer-Strasse 6-10
D-6000 Frankfurt
WEST GERMANY

Dr. Graham F. Carey
Department of Aerospace Engineering
University of Texas at Austin
Austin, TX 78712

Mr. Walter Carrington
System Development Corporation
55 Broadway
Cambridge, MA 02138

*Dr. A. Charnes
BEB 203E
The University of Texas
Austin, TX 78712

---

*Indicates author of a paper in this collection.

Dr. W. W. Cooper
Institute for Constructive Capitalism
The University of Texas
Austin, TX 78712

Dr. Sam Cox
Department of Finance
University of Texas at Austin
Austin, TX 78712

Dr. Bruce D. Craven
University of Melbourne
Mathematics Department
Parkville, Victoria 3052
AUSTRALIA

Dr. George Cybenko
Department of Mathematics
Tufts University
Medford, MA 02155

Dr. George B. Dantzig
Department of Operations Research
Stanford University
Stanford, CA 94305

Dr. Ulrich Dieter
University of Graz
Hamerlinggasse 6
A-8010 Graz
AUSTRIA

Dr. Doug Divine
Center for Cybernetic Studies
The University of Texas at Austin
Austin, TX 78712

*Dr. R. J. Duffin
Department of Mathematics
Carnegie-Mellon University
Pittsburgh, PA 15213

Mr. Salih O. Duffuaa
Center for Cybernetic Studies
University of Texas at Austin
Austin, TX 78712

Dr. Dieter Eschenbach
Hochschule der Bundeswehr München
Werner-Heisenberg-Weg 39
Neubiberg D-8014
WEST GERMANY

Dr. Anthony V. Fiacco
Operations Research Department
The George Washington University
Washington, DC 20052

Dr. Jacob Flachs
NRIMS - CSIR
P.O. Box 395
Pretoria, 0001
SOUTH AFRICA

Dr. Avner Friedman
Department of Mathematics
Lunt Hall
Northwestern University
Evanston, IL 60201

Mr. Juan Simon Gallegos-Malias
Center for Cybernetic Studies
The University of Texas at Austin
Austin, TX 78712

Mr. Gilles Garcia
I.M.S.L.
7500 Bellaire Boulevard
NBC Building, 6th Floor
Houston, TX 77036

*Dr. H. Gfrerer
Institut für Mathematik
Johannes Kepler Universität Linz
A-4040 Linz
AUSTRIA

Dr. Neal Glassman
Office of Naval Research (Code 411-MA)
Mathematics Program
800 N. Quincy Street
Arlington, VA 22217

Dr. Miguel Angel Goberna
Department of Statistics
Universidad de Valencia
Valencia 15
SPAIN

Dr. Gene H. Golub
Department of Computer Science
Stanford University
Stanford, CA 94305

Dr. Ignacio E. Grossmann
Department of Chemical Engineering
Carnegie-Mellon University
Pittsburgh, PA 15213

*Dr. J. Guddat
Humboldt University
Mathematics Section
Unter den Linden 6 PSF 1297
1086 Berlin, DDR

---

*Indicates author of a paper in this collection.

Dr. Sven-Åke Gustafson
Department of Numerical Analysis
and Computing Sciences
Royal Institute of Technology
S-100 44 Stockholm 70
SWEDEN

Dr. J. M. Gutierrez-Diez
Fac. Mathematicas
Universidad de Valencia
Burjasot, Valencia
SPAIN

Dr. Abraham H. Haddad
National Science Foundation
Division of Electrical, Computer
and Systems Engineering
Washington, DC 20550

*Dr. R. Hettich
Fb. IV (Math.)
Universität Trier
Postfach 3825
55 - Trier
WEST GERMANY

Dr. J. B. Hiriart-Urruty
Université Paul Sabatier
(Toulouse III)
U.E.R. Mathematiques, Informatique,
Gestion
118, route de Narbonne
Toulouse 31062
FRANCE

*Dr. A. D. Ioffe
Profsoyusnaya 85-1-203
Moscow 117279
U.S.S.R.

Dr. G. Isac
Collège Militaire Royal
St. Jean, Québec J0J 1R0
CANADA

Dr. Johannes Jahn
Fb. Mathematik der T.H. Darmstadt
Schlossgartenstr. 7
6100 Darmstadt
WEST GERMANY

*Dr. Robert Jeroslow
College of Management
Georgia Institute of Technology
Atlanta, GA 30332

Dr. Les Karlovitz
School of Mathematics
Georgia Institute of Technology
Atlanta, GA 30332

Dr. Dennis F. Karney
College of Management
Georgia Institute of Technology
Atlanta, GA 30332

*Dr. J.H.B. Kemperman
Department of Mathematics
University of Rochester
Rochester, NY 14627

*Dr. Kenneth O. Kortanek
Department of Mathematics
Carnegie-Mellon University
Pittsburgh, PA 15213

Dr. Werner Krabs
Fb. Mathematik der T.H. Darmstadt
Schlossgartenstr. 7
6100 Darmstadt
WEST GERMANY

Dr. Yueh-er Kuo
Department of Mathematics
University of Tennessee
Knoxville, TN 37916

Dr. Marco Antonio Lopez
Universidad de Valencia
Valencia 15
SPAIN

*Ms. Vicki Lovegren
Center for Cybernetic Studies
The University of Texas at Austin
Austin, TX 78712

Dr. Lynn McLinden
Department of Mathematics
1409 W. Green Street
University of Illinois - Urbana
Urbana, IL 61801

Dr. D. H. Martin
NRIMS - CSIR
Box 395
Pretoria 0001
SOUTH AFRICA

*Dr. José Luis Menaldi
Department of Mathematics
Wayne State University
Detroit, MI 48202

---

*Indicates author of a paper in this collection.

Dr. Hans D. Mittlemann
Abt. Mathematik
Universität Dortmund
Postfach 500500
4600 Dortmund
WEST GERMANY

Dr. Tom Morley
School of Mathematics
Georgia Institute of Technology
Atlanta, GA 30332

Dr. M. Zuhair Nashed
Department of Mathematical Sciences
University of Delaware
Newark, DE 19711

Dr. W. Oettli
Universität Mannheim (WH)
Lehrstuhl für Mathematik VII
Schloss
6800 Mannheim
WEST GERMANY

*Dr. M. R. Osborne
Department of Statistics
Australian National University
P.O. Box 4
Canberra, A.C.T. 2600
AUSTRALIA

Dr. Michael Overton
Courant Institute of Mathematical Sciences, New York University
251 Mercer Street
New York, NY 10012

*Dr. Lee Papayanopoulos
Graduate School of Management
92 New Street
Rutgers University
Newark, NJ 07102

*Dr. Melvin Lee Parks, Jr.
E.I. DuPont
I.S.D., Farmer's Bank Building
5th Floor
Wilmington, DE 19898

Dr. Jesus Pastor-Ciurana
University of Valencia
Avda. Burjasot S/U
Valencia
SPAIN

Dr. Andre F. Perold
Harvard Business School
Boston, MA 02163

Dr. Fred Phillips
M.R.C.A.
3001 N. Lamar
Austin, TX 78705

*Mr. A. B. Philpott
University of Cambridge
University Engineering Department
Mill Lane
Cambridge, ENGLAND CB2 1RX

*Dr. Elijah Polak
EECS Department
University of California
Berkeley, CA 94720

Dr. Jean Charles Pomerol
Université Pierre et Marie Curie
Laboratorie d'Économétrie
4 Place Jussieu
75230 Paris, Cedex 05
FRANCE

*Dr. Edmundo Rofman
Institut National de Recherche en Informatique et en Automatique
B.P. 105
Domaine de Voluceau
Rocquencourt
78150 Le Chesnay
FRANCE

Dr. Eckhard Sachs
Technical Universität Berlin
Fb. Mathematik
Str. Des 17. Juni 135
1000 Berlin 12
WEST GERMANY

Dr. Larry Seiford
Department of General Business
University of Texas at Austin
Austin, TX 78712

Dr. Prabha Sharma
Department of Mathematics
Indian Institute of Technology
Kanpur, U.P. 208016
INDIA

*Dr. A. L. Soyster
Dept. Ind. & Mgt. Systems Engr.
Pennsylvania State University
207 Hammond Building
University Park, PA 16802

---

*Indicates author of a paper in this collection.

Dr. Josef Stoer
Institüt für Angewandte und Statistik
University of Würzburg
Am Hubland
D-8700 Würzburg
WEST GERMANY

Ms. Barbara Storbeck
Center for Cybernetic Studies
The University of Texas at Austin
Austin, TX 78712

Dr. Gilbert Strang
Department of Mathematics, Room 2-240
Massachusetts Institute of Technology
Cambridge, MA 02139

Dr. J. J. Strodiot
Department of Mathematics
Facultes Univ. Namur
Rempart de la Vierge
8, Namur B-5000
BELGIUM

*Professor Roger Temam
Analyse Numerique - BAT 425
Université Paris - Sud
Orsay 91405
FRANCE

*Dr. Bernard Torsney
Department of Statistics
University of Glasgow
Glasgow G12
UNITED KINGDOM

Dr. John Sølve Tyssedal
Center for Cybernetic Studies
BEB 203E
The University of Texas at Austin
Austin, TX 78712

Dr. Maria Enriqueta Vercher
Universidad de Valencia
c/o Puerto de Santa Maria, 4-12A
Valencia 15
SPAIN

*Dr. Hj. Wacker
Institut für Mathematik
Johannes Kepler Universität Linz
A-4040 Linz
AUSTRIA

*Dr. G. A. Watson
Department of Mathematics
University of Dundee
Dundee
SCOTLAND

Dr. Reinhard Weber
Fb. Wirtschaftswissenschaften
FG Unternehmensforschung
(Operations Research)
6600 Saarbruecken 11
WEST GERMANY

Professor W. Wetterling
Techn. Hogeschool Twente
Postbus 217
7500 AE Enschede
THE NETHERLANDS

Mr. Chester Wilson
Center for Cybernetic Studies
BEB 203E
The University of Texas at Austin
Austin, TX 78712

Dr. Henry Wolkowicz
Department of Mathematics
The University of Alberta
Alberta T6G 2G1
CANADA

*Dr. Maretsugu Yamasaki
Department of Mathematics
Shimane University
Matsue, Shimane
JAPAN

Mr. Shin-Tai Yao
Center for Cybernetic Studies
The University of Texas at Austin
Austin, TX 78712

Dr. Peter Zencke
Fb. IV (Math)
Universität Trier PF 3825
55 Trier
WEST GERMANY

Dr. Sanjo Zlobec
McGill University
805 Sherbrooke W.
Quebec H3A 2K6
CANADA

Professor Jochem Zowe
Mathematisches Institut
Universität Bayreuth
Bayreuth
WEST GERMANY

*Dr. W. Zulehner
Institut für Mathematik
Johannes Kepler Universität Linz
A-4040 Linz
AUSTRIA

---

* Indicates author of a paper in this collection.

REFEREES

ROBERT F. ANDERSON
CHARLES E. BLAIR
JONATHAN M. BORWEIN
PAUL R. GRIBIK
IGNACIO E. GROSSMANN
S.-Å. GUSTAFSON
DENNIS F. KARNEY
MASAKAZU KOJIMA
K. O. KORTANEK
BRUCE G. LINDSAY
STEVEN E. SHREVE
LARRY SEIFORD
ALLEN L. SOYSTER
GILBERT STRANG
DOUGLAS WARD
HENRY WOLKOWICZ
MARETSUGU YAMASAKI
H.-J. ZIMMERMANN

TABLE OF CONTENTS

of

The Book of Abstracts

Compiled and Edited by

Sanjo Zlobec, Program Chairman

CONTENTS

CAREY, G. F. and M. UTKU

Penalty Finite Elements for Interface and Boundary Constraints

CHARNES, A., S.-Å. GUSTAFSON AND K. O. KORTANEK

Semi-Infinite Programming -- A Look at Some Trends of Development

CHARNES, A., K. O. KORTANEK and V. LOVEGREN

A Saddle Value Characterization of Fan's Equilibrium Points

CHENEY, E. W.

Recent Progress in Infinite-Dimensional Best Approximation -- A Survey

CHARRIER, P.

Variational and Quasi-Variational Inequalities: Stationary and Evolution Problems

CRAVEN, B. D.

Perturbed Minimization, with Constraints Adjoined or Deleted

CYBENKO, George

Affine Minimax Problems and Semi-Infinite Programming

DEFERT, PH.

Best Uniform Multivariate Approximation

DIETER, U.

Roulette as a Ruin Game: Optimal Strategies for Winning

DUFFIN, R. J.

Numerical Estimation of Optima by Use of Duality Inequalities

DUFFIN, R. J., R. G. JEROSLOW and L. A. KARLOVITZ

Uniform Duality in Semi-Infinite Linear Programming

ECKHARDT, Ulrich

Semi-Infinite Quadratic Programming

EVANS, Robin J.

Optimization in Signal Processing

FAN, Ky

Some Covering Properties of Convex Sets Related to Minimax and Variational Inequalities

FLACHS, Jacob

Saddle-Point Theorems for Rational Approximation

FRIEDMAN, A.

Variational Inequalities

GLASHOFF, K.

Numerical Solution of Partial Differential Equations by Semi-Finite Programming

GOBERNA, M. A., M. A. LOPEZ, J. PASTOR and E. VERCHER

An Approach to Semi-Infinite Programming Via Consequence Relations

GROSSMANN, Ignacio E., K. P. HALEMANE and K. O. KORTANEK

Optimal Design of Flexible Chemical Plants

GUDDAT, J.

On Nonlinear Parametric Optimization and Some Applications

GUTIERREZ DIEZ, J. M.

A Necessary and Sufficient Dual Optimality Condition for Convex Semi-Infinite Programming

GUSTAFSON, Sven-Åke

Application of a Three-Phase Algorithm to a Class of Nonlinear Semi-Infinite Programs

HETTICH, R.

A Review of Numerical Methods for Semi-Infinite Optimization

HIRIART-URRUTY, J.-B.

Approximate Solutions in Mathematical Programming

IOFFE, A.

Second Order Conditions in Nonlinear, Nonsmooth Problems of Semi-Infinite Programming

ISAC, G.

Critical Points, Nuclear Cones and the Existence of Pareto Efficient Points

JAHN, J.

Duality in Vector Optimization

JEROSLOW, R. G.

Necessary and Sufficient Constraint Qualifications

KARLOVITZ, L.

The Interplay Between Semi-Infinite Programming and Approximation Theory

KARNEY, Dennis F.

Duality in Semi-Infinite Programs -- A Second Look

KEMPERMAN, J.H.B.

On the Use of Duality in the Theory of Moments

KOHLER, M. T. and ÜNAL, A.

Isoperimetric Inequality for the First Eigenvalue of the Clamped Plate

KORTANEK, K. O. and YAMASAKI, M.

Semi-Infinite Transportation Problems

KRABS, W.

On a Moment Problem in Heat Control

KUO, Yueh-Er

Tensor Products of Linear Programming and Related Systems

LEMPIO, Frank

Quadratic Forms on Hilbert Spaces and Sufficient Optimality Conditions for Optimal Control Problems

LENHART, Suzanne M. and BELBAS, Stavros A.

Certain Implicit Variational Problems Related to the Optimal Switching Control of Diffusion Processes

LOUVEAUX, F. V. and SMEERS, Y.

Stochastic Optimization for the Introduction of a New Energy Technology

MARTIN, D. H. and JACOBSON, D. H.

On Conditionally Definite Quadratic Forms

McLINDEN, L.

Stability and Successive Approximation for Extremum Problems of Convex-Concave Minimax Type

MENALDI, José Luis and ROFMAN, Edmundo

On Stochastic Control Problems with Impulse Cost Vanishing

MITTLEMANN, H. D.

On the Solution of Bifurcation Problems for Variational Inequalities

MORLEY, Tom

A Farkas Lemma for Certain Infinite Programs

NASHED, M. Z.

An Iterative Method for Ill-Posed Problems with Inequalities

OSBORNE, M. R.

A Descent Algorithm for Minimizing Polyhedral Convex Functions

OVERTON, Michael L.

A Quadratically Convergent Method for Minimizing a Sum of Euclidean Norms

PAPAYANOPOULOS, L.

A Linear Programming Approach to the Construction of the Weighted Voting Polyhedron

PARKS, JR. M. L. and SOYSTER, A. L.

Semi-Infinite and Fuzzy Set Programming

PENOT, Jean Paul

Central and Peripheral Results in the Study of Marginal Functions

PEROLD, Andre F.

Optimality Conditions and Strong Duality in Continuous Time Linear Programming

POLAK, E. and TITS, A. L.

A Recursive Quadratic Programming Algorithm for Semi-Infinite Optimization Problems

POMEROL, J.-CH.

Inequality Systems and Minimax Theorems

SCAHS, Ekkehard

Nonlinear Parabolic Control Problems in Semi-Infinite Programming

SCHECHTER, Murray

Some Developments in Homogeneous Programming

SMEERS, Y. and TYTECA, D.

A Geometric Programming Model for the Optimal Design of Wastewater Treatment Plants

STRANG, G.

A Continuous Max Flow -- Min Cut Theorem and Transportation Problem

STRODIOT, J.-J., NGUYEN, V. H. and HEUKEMES, N.

Epsilon-Optimal Solutions in Convex Programming and Some Related Problems

TEMAM, R.

Minimization of Nonsmooth Functionals

THERA, M.

Fenchel's Duality for Convex Mappings with Values in C(T)

TORSNEY, B.

A Moment Inequality and Monotonicity of an Algorithm

ÜNAL, A. and KOHLER, M. T.

Some Bounds for the Classical Plate Problem with Nonconstant Mass Distribution

WAHBA, G.

Smoothing and Inequality Constraints in the Approximate Solution of Ill-Posed Problems with Noisy Data

WARDI, Y., TITS, A. L. and SANGIOVANNI-VINCENTELLI, A. L.

Implementable Nondifferentiable-Optimization Algorithms for Computer-Aided Design

WATSON, G. A.

Numerical Experiments with Globally Convergent Methods for Semi-Infinite Programming Problems

WEBER, R.

Decision Making Under Uncertainty -- A Semi-Infinite Programming Approach

WETTERLING, W.W.E.

Boundary Data of Nonlinear Semi-Infinite Optimization Problems

WOLKOWICZ, H.

The Abstract Convex Program and Semi-Infinite Programming

WONG, W. H.

Algorithms for Interpolating Splines Under Linear Inequality Constraints

WU, C.-H.

Choice of Technique in a Continuous Time Infinite Horizon Optimal Growth Model

YAMASAKI, Maretsugu

Existence Theorems in Semi-Infinite Programs

ZENCKE, P.

Algorithms Related to Newton-Method for Semi-Infinite Programming

ZOWE, Jochem

Necessary and Sufficient Optimality Conditions for the ℓ_1/L_1 - Approximation Problem

Vol. 101: W. M. Wonham, Linear Multivariable Control. A Geometric Approach. X, 344 pages. 1974.

Vol. 102: Analyse Convexe et Ses Applications. Comptes Rendus, Janvier 1974. Edited by J. P. Aubin. IV, 244 pages. 1974.

Vol. 103: D. E. Boyce, A. Farhi, R. Weischedel, Optimal Subset Selection. Multiple Regression, Interdependence and Optimal Network Algorithms. XIII, 187 pages. 1974.

Vol. 104: S. Fujino, A Neo-Keynesian Theory of Inflation and Economic Growth. V, 96 pages. 1974.

Vol. 105: Optimal Control Theory and its Applications. Part I. Proceedings 1973. Edited by B. J. Kirby. VI, 425 pages. 1974.

Vol. 106: Optimal Control Theory and its Applications. Part II. Proceedings 1973. Edited by B. J. Kirby. VI, 403 pages. 1974.

Vol. 107: Control Theory, Numerical Methods and Computer Systems Modeling. International Symposium, Rocquencourt, June 17–21, 1974. Edited by A. Bensoussan and J. L. Lions. VIII, 757 pages. 1975.

Vol. 108: F. Bauer et al., Supercritical Wing Sections II. A Handbook. V, 296 pages. 1975.

Vol. 109: R. von Randow, Introduction to the Theory of Matroids. IX, 102 pages. 1975.

Vol. 110: C. Striebel, Optimal Control of Discrete Time Stochastic Systems. III. 208 pages. 1975.

Vol. 111: Variable Structure Systems with Application to Economics and Biology. Proceedings 1974. Edited by A. Ruberti and R. R. Mohler. VI, 321 pages. 1975.

Vol. 112: J. Wilhelm, Objectives and Multi-Objective Decision Making Under Uncertainty. IV, 111 pages. 1975.

Vol. 113: G. A. Aschinger, Stabilitätsaussagen über Klassen von Matrizen mit verschwindenden Zeilensummen. V, 102 Seiten. 1975.

Vol. 114: G. Uebe, Produktionstheorie. XVII, 301 Seiten. 1976.

Vol. 115: Anderson et al., Foundations of System Theory: Finitary and Infinitary Conditions. VII, 93 pages. 1976

Vol. 116: K. Miyazawa, Input-Output Analysis and the Structure of Income Distribution. IX, 135 pages. 1976.

Vol. 117: Optimization and Operations Research. Proceedings 1975. Edited by W. Oettli and K. Ritter. IV, 316 pages. 1976.

Vol. 118: Traffic Equilibrium Methods, Proceedings 1974. Edited by M. A. Florian. XXIII, 432 pages. 1976.

Vol. 119: Inflation in Small Countries. Proceedings 1974. Edited by H. Frisch. VI, 356 pages. 1976.

Vol. 120: G. Hasenkamp, Specification and Estimation of Multiple-Output Production Functions. VII, 151 pages. 1976.

Vol. 121: J. W. Cohen, On Regenerative Processes in Queueing Theory. IX, 93 pages. 1976.

Vol. 122: M. S. Bazaraa, and C. M. Shetty, Foundations of Optimization VI. 193 pages. 1976

Vol. 123: Multiple Criteria Decision Making. Kyoto 1975. Edited by M. Zeleny. XXVII, 345 pages. 1976.

Vol. 124: M. J. Todd. The Computation of Fixed Points and Applications. VII, 129 pages. 1976.

Vol. 125: Karl C. Mosler. Optimale Transportnetze. Zur Bestimmung ihres kostengünstigsten Standorts bei gegebener Nachfrage. VI, 142 Seiten. 1976.

Vol. 126: Energy, Regional Science and Public Policy. Energy and Environment I. Proceedings 1975. Edited by M. Chatterji and P. Van Rompuy. VIII, 316 pages. 1976.

Vol. 127: Environment, Regional Science and Interregional Modeling. Energy and Environment II. Proceedings 1975. Edited by M. Chatterji and P. Van Rompuy. IX, 211 pages. 1976.

Vol. 128: Integer Programming and Related Areas. A Classified Bibliography. Edited by C. Kastning. XII, 495 pages. 1976.

Vol. 129: H.-J. Lüthi, Komplementaritäts- und Fixpunktalgorithmen in der mathematischen Programmierung. Spieltheorie und Ökonomie. VII, 145 Seiten. 1976.

Vol. 130: Multiple Criteria Decision Making, Jouy-en-Josas, France. Proceedings 1975. Edited by H. Thiriez and S. Zionts. VI, 409 pages. 1976.

Vol. 131: Mathematical Systems Theory. Proceedings 1975. Edited by G. Marchesini and S. K. Mitter. X, 408 pages. 1976.

Vol. 132: U. H. Funke, Mathematical Models in Marketing. A Collection of Abstracts. XX, 514 pages. 1976.

Vol. 133: Warsaw Fall Seminars in Mathematical Economics 1975. Edited by M. W. Loś, J. Loś, and A. Wieczorek. V. 159 pages. 1976.

Vol. 134: Computing Methods in Applied Sciences and Engineering. Proceedings 1975. VIII, 390 pages. 1976.

Vol. 135: H. Haga, A Disequilibrium – Equilibrium Model with Money and Bonds. A Keynesian – Walrasian Synthesis. VI, 119 pages. 1976.

Vol. 136: E. Kofler und G. Menges, Entscheidungen bei unvollständiger Information. XII, 357 Seiten. 1976.

Vol. 137: R. Wets, Grundlagen Konvexer Optimierung. VI, 146 Seiten. 1976.

Vol. 138: K. Okuguchi, Expectations and Stability in Oligopoly Models. VI, 103 pages. 1976.

Vol. 139: Production Theory and Its Applications. Proceedings. Edited by H. Albach and G. Bergendahl. VIII, 193 pages. 1977.

Vol. 140: W. Eichhorn and J. Voeller, Theory of the Price Index. Fisher's Test Approach and Generalizations. VII, 95 pages. 1976.

Vol. 141: Mathematical Economics and Game Theory. Essays in Honor of Oskar Morgenstern. Edited by R. Henn and O. Moeschlin. XIV, 703 pages. 1977.

Vol. 142: J. S. Lane, On Optimal Population Paths. V, 123 pages. 1977.

Vol. 143: B. Näslund, An Analysis of Economic Size Distributions. XV, 100 pages. 1977.

Vol. 144: Convex Analysis and Its Applications. Proceedings 1976. Edited by A. Auslender. VI, 219 pages. 1977.

Vol. 145: J. Rosenmüller, Extreme Games and Their Solutions. IV, 126 pages. 1977.

Vol. 146: In Search of Economic Indicators. Edited by W. H. Strigel. XVI, 198 pages. 1977.

Vol. 147: Resource Allocation and Division of Space. Proceedings. Edited by T. Fujii and R. Sato. VIII, 184 pages. 1977.

Vol. 148: C. E. Mandl, Simulationstechnik und Simulationsmodelle in den Sozial- und Wirtschaftswissenschaften. IX, 173 Seiten. 1977.

Vol. 149: Stationäre und schrumpfende Bevölkerungen: Demographisches Null- und Negativwachstum in Österreich. Herausgegeben von G. Feichtinger. VI, 262 Seiten. 1977.

Vol. 150: Bauer et al., Supercritical Wing Sections III. VI, 179 pages. 1977.

Vol. 151: C. A. Schneeweiß, Inventory-Production Theory. VI, 116 pages. 1977.

Vol. 152: Kirsch et al., Notwendige Optimalitätsbedingungen und ihre Anwendung. VI, 157 Seiten. 1978.

Vol. 153: Kombinatorische Entscheidungsprobleme: Methoden und Anwendungen. Herausgegeben von T. M. Liebling und M. Rössler. VIII, 206 Seiten. 1978.

Vol. 154: Problems and Instruments of Business Cycle Analysis. Proceedings 1977. Edited by W. H. Strigel. VI, 442 pages. 1978.

Vol. 155: Multiple Criteria Problem Solving. Proceedings 1977. Edited by S. Zionts. VIII, 567 pages. 1978.

Vol. 156: B. Näslund and B. Sellstedt, Neo-Ricardian Theory. With Applications to Some Current Economic Problems. VI, 165 pages. 1978.

Vol. 157: Optimization and Operations Research. Proceedings 1977. Edited by R. Henn, B. Korte, and W. Oettli. VI, 270 pages. 1978.

Vol. 158: L. J. Cherene, Set Valued Dynamical Systems and Economic Flow. VIII, 83 pages. 1978.

Vol. 159: Some Aspects of the Foundations of General Equilibrium Theory: The Posthumous Papers of Peter J. Kalman. Edited by J. Green. VI, 167 pages. 1978.

Vol. 160: Integer Programming and Related Areas. A Classified Bibliography. Edited by D. Hausmann. XIV, 314 pages. 1978.

Vol. 161: M. J. Beckmann, Rank in Organizations. VIII, 164 pages. 1978.

Vol. 162: Recent Developments in Variable Structure Systems, Economics and Biology. Proceedings 1977. Edited by R. R. Mohler and A. Ruberti. VI, 326 pages. 1978.

Vol. 163: G. Fandel, Optimale Entscheidungen in Organisationen. VI, 143 Seiten. 1979.

Vol. 164: C. L. Hwang and A. S. M. Masud, Multiple Objective Decision Making – Methods and Applications. A State-of-the-Art Survey. XII, 351 pages. 1979.

Vol. 165: A. Maravall, Identification in Dynamic Shock-Error Models. VIII, 158 pages. 1979.

Vol. 166: R. Cuninghame-Green, Minimax Algebra. XI, 258 pages. 1979.

Vol. 167: M. Faber, Introduction to Modern Austrian Capital Theory. X, 196 pages. 1979.

Vol. 168: Convex Analysis and Mathematical Economics. Proceedings 1978. Edited by J. Kriens. V, 136 pages. 1979.

Vol. 169: A. Rapoport et al., Coalition Formation by Sophisticated Players. VII, 170 pages. 1979.

Vol. 170: A. E. Roth, Axiomatic Models of Bargaining. V, 121 pages. 1979.

Vol. 171: G. F. Newell, Approximate Behavior of Tandem Queues. XI, 410 pages. 1979.

Vol. 172: K. Neumann and U. Steinhardt, GERT Networks and the Time-Oriented Evaluation of Projects. 268 pages. 1979.

Vol. 173: S. Erlander, Optimal Spatial Interaction and the Gravity Model. VII, 107 pages. 1980.

Vol. 174: Extremal Methods and Systems Analysis. Edited by A. V. Fiacco and K. O. Kortanek. XI, 545 pages. 1980.

Vol. 175: S. K. Srinivasan and R. Subramanian, Probabilistic Analysis of Redundant Systems. VII, 356 pages. 1980.

Vol. 176: R. Färe, Laws of Diminishing Returns. VIII, 97 pages. 1980.

Vol. 177: Multiple Criteria Decision Making-Theory and Application. Proceedings, 1979. Edited by G. Fandel and T. Gal. XVI, 570 pages. 1980.

Vol. 178: M. N. Bhattacharyya, Comparison of Box-Jenkins and Bonn Monetary Model Prediction Performance. VII, 146 pages. 1980.

Vol. 179: Recent Results in Stochastic Programming. Proceedings, 1979. Edited by P. Kall and A. Prékopa. IX, 237 pages. 1980.

Vol. 180: J. F. Brotchie, J. W. Dickey and R. Sharpe, TOPAZ – General Planning Technique and its Applications at the Regional, Urban, and Facility Planning Levels. VII, 356 pages. 1980.

Vol. 181: H. D. Sherali and C. M. Shetty, Optimization with Disjunctive Constraints. VIII, 156 pages. 1980.

Vol. 182: J. Wolters, Stochastic Dynamic Properties of Linear Econometric Models. VIII, 154 pages. 1980.

Vol. 183: K. Schittkowski, Nonlinear Programming Codes. VIII, 242 pages. 1980.

Vol. 184: R. E. Burkard and U. Derigs, Assignment and Matching Problems: Solution Methods with FORTRAN-Programs. VIII, 148 pages. 1980.

Vol. 185: C. C. von Weizsäcker, Barriers to Entry. VI, 220 pages. 1980.

Vol. 186: Ch.-L. Hwang and K. Yoon, Multiple Attribute Decision Making – Methods and Applications. A State-of-the-Art-Survey. XI, 259 pages. 1981.

Vol. 187: W. Hock, K. Schittkowski, Test Examples for Nonlinear Programming Codes. V. 178 pages. 1981.

Vol. 188: D. Bös, Economic Theory of Public Enterprise. VII, 142 pages. 1981.

Vol. 189: A. P. Lüthi, Messung wirtschaftlicher Ungleichheit. IX, 287 pages. 1981.

Vol. 190: J. N. Morse, Organizations: Multiple Agents with Multiple Criteria. Proceedings, 1980. VI, 509 pages. 1981.

Vol. 191: H. R. Sneessens, Theory and Estimation of Macroeconomic Rationing Models. VII, 138 pages. 1981.

Vol. 192: H. J. Bierens: Robust Methods and Asymptotic Theory in Nonlinear Econometrics. IX, 198 pages. 1981.

Vol. 193: J. K. Sengupta, Optimal Decisions under Uncertainty. VII, 156 pages. 1981.

Vol. 194: R. W. Shephard, Cost and Production Functions. XI, 104 pages. 1981.

Vol. 195: H. W. Ursprung, Die elementare Katastrophentheorie. Eine Darstellung aus der Sicht der Ökonomie. VII, 332 pages. 1982.

Vol. 196: M. Nermuth, Information Structures in Economics. VIII, 236 pages. 1982.

Vol. 197: Integer Programming and Related Areas. A Classified Bibliography. 1978 – 1981. Edited by R. von Randow. XIV, 338 pages. 1982.

Vol. 198: P. Zweifel, Ein ökonomisches Modell des Arztverhaltens. XIX, 392 Seiten. 1982.

Vol. 199: Evaluating Mathematical Programming Techniques. Proceedings, 1981. Edited by J.M. Mulvey. XI, 379 pages. 1982.

Vol. 201: P. M. C. de Boer, Price Effects in Input-Output-Relations: A Theoretical and Empirical Study for the Netherlands 1949–1967. X, 140 pages. 1982.

Vol. 202: U. Witt, J. Perske, SMS – A Program Package for Simulation and Gaming of Stochastic Market Processes and Learning Behavior. VII, 266 pages. 1982.

Vol. 203: Compilation of Input-Output Tables. Proceedings, 1981. Edited by J. V. Skolka. VII, 307 pages. 1982.

Vol. 204: K.C. Mosler, Entscheidungsregeln bei Risiko: Multivariate stochastische Dominanz. VII, 172 Seiten. 1982.

Vol. 205: R. Ramanathan, Introduction to the Theory of Economic Growth. IX, 347 pages. 1982.

Vol. 206: M.H. Karwan, V. Lotfi, J. Telgen, and S. Zionts, Redundancy in Mathematical Programming. VII, 286 pages. 1983.

Vol. 207: Y. Fujimori, Modern Analysis of Value Theory. X, 165 pages. 1982.

Vol. 208: Econometric Decision Models. Proceedings, 1981. Edited by J. Gruber. VI, 364 pages. 1983.

Vol. 209: Essays and Surveys on Multiple Criteria Decision Making. Proceedings, 1982. Edited by P. Hansen. VII, 441 pages. 1983.

Vol. 210: Technology, Organization and Economic Structure. Edited by R. Sato and M.J. Beckmann. VIII, 195 pages. 1983.

Vol. 211: P. van den Heuvel, The Stability of a Macroeconomic System with Quantity Constraints. VII, 169 pages. 1983.

Vol. 212: R. Sato and T. Nôno, Invariance Principles and the Structure of Technology. V, 94 pages. 1983.

Vol. 213: Aspiration Levels in Bargaining and Economic Decision Making. Proceedings, 1982. Edited by R. Tietz. VIII, 406 pages. 1983.

Vol. 214: M. Faber, H. Niemes und G. Stephan, Entropie, Umweltschutz und Rohstoffverbrauch. IX, 181 Seiten. 1983.

Vol. 215: Semi-Infinite Programming and Applications. Proceedings, 1981. Edited by A. V. Fiacco and K. O. Kortanek. XI, 322 pages. 1983.

Ökonometrie und Unternehmensforschung
Econometrics and Operations Research

Vol. I	Nichtlineare Programmierung. Von H. P. Künzi und W. Krelle unter Mitwirkung von W. Oettli. Vergriffen
Vol. II	Lineare Programmierung und Erweiterungen. Von G. B. Dantzig. Ins Deutsche übertragen und bearbeitet von A. Jaeger. – Mit 103 Abbildungen. XVI, 712 Seiten. 1966. Geb.
Vol. III	Stochastic Processes. By M. Girault. – With 35 figures. XII, 126 pages. 1966. Cloth
Vol. IV	Methoden der Unternehmensforschung im Versicherungswesen. Von K. H. Wolff. – Mit 14 Diagrammen. VIII, 266 Seiten. 1966. Geb.
Vol. V	The Theory of Max-Min and its Application to Weapons Allocation Problems. By John M. Danskin. – With 6 figures. X, 126 pages. 1967. Cloth
Vol. VI	Entscheidungskriterien bei Risiko. Von H. Schneeweiss. – Mit 35 Abbildungen. XII, 215 Seiten. 1967. Geb.
Vol. VII	Boolean Methods in Operations Research and Related Areas. By P. L. Hammer (Ivănescu) and S. Rudeanu. With a preface by R. Bellman. – With 25 figures. XVI, 329 pages. 1968. Cloth
Vol. VIII	Strategy for R & D: Studies in the Microeconomics of Development. By Th. Marschak. Th K. Glennan Jr., and R. Summers. – With 44 figures. XIV, 330 pages. 1967. Cloth
Vol. IX	Dynamic Programming of Economic Decisions. By M. J. Beckmann. – With 9 figures XII, 143 pages. 1968. Cloth
Vol. X	Input-Output-Analyse. Von J. Schumann. – Mit 12 Abbildungen. X, 311 Seiten. 1968. Geb.
Vol. XI	Produktionstheorie. Von W. Wittmann. – Mit 54 Abbildungen. VIII, 177 Seiten. 1968. Geb.
Vol. XII	Sensitivitätsanalysen und parametrische Programmierung. Von W. Dinkelbach. – Mit 20 Abbildungen. XI, 190 Seiten. 1969. Geb.
Vol. XIII	Graphentheoretische Methoden und ihre Anwendungen. Von W. Knödel. – Mit 24 Abbildungen. VIII, 111 Seiten. 1969. Geb.
Vol. XIV	Praktische Studien zur Unternehmensforschung. Von E. Nievergelt, O. Müller, F. E. Schlaepfer und W. H. Landis. – Mit 82 Abbildungen. XII, 240 Seiten. 1970. Geb.
Vol. XV	Optimale Reihenfolgen. Von H. Müller-Merbach. – Mit 45 Abbildungen. IX, 225 Seiten. 1970. Geb.
Vol. XVI	Preispolitik der Mehrproduktenunternehmung in der statischen Theorie. Von R. Selten. – Mit 20 Abbildungen. VIII, 195 Seiten. 1970. Geb.
Vol. XVII	Information Theory for Systems Engineers. By L. P. Hyvärinen. – With 42 figures. VIII, 197 pages. 1970. Cloth
Vol. XVIII	Unternehmensforschung im Bergbau. Von F. L. Wilke. – Mit 29 Abbildungen. VIII, 150 Seiten. 1972. Geb.
Vol. XIX	Anti-Äquilibrium. Von J. Kornai. – Mit 31 Abbildungen. XVI, 382 Seiten. 1975. Geb.
Vol. XX	Mathematische Optimierung. Von E. Blum, W. Oettli. IX, 413 Seiten. (davon 75 Seiten Bibliographie). 1975. Geb.
Vol. XXI	Stochastic Linear Programming. By P. Kall. VI, 95 pages. 1976. Cloth.

GPSR Compliance

The European Union's (EU) General Product Safety Regulation (GPSR) is a set of rules that requires consumer products to be safe and our obligations to ensure this.

If you have any concerns about our products, you can contact us on ProductSafety@springernature.com

In case Publisher is established outside the EU, the EU authorized representative is:

Springer Nature Customer Service Center GmbH
Europaplatz 3
69115 Heidelberg, Germany

Batch number: 10844827

Printed by Printforce, the Netherlands